Creative. Original. Ground-breaking. Excellent. The book is bold in design and convincing in implementation. This book is a superb, critical, dialogue with three quite different thinkers/activists in order to develop a culturally appropriate theological ethic. The initial application is for Christians in Myanmar. But the basic methodology deserves widespread use. Highly recommended.

Ronald J. Sider, PhD
Distinguished Professor Emeritus of Theology, Holistic Ministry and Public Policy,
Palmer Theological Seminary, St Davids, Pennsylvania, USA

Dr Aung Htoo's knowledge of Myanmar and the situation of the Christian community is impressive. The book offers a creative exploration of non-violence and its significance for the local Christian community.

David Tombs, PhD
Howard Paterson Chair of Theology and Public Issues,
University of Otago, Dunedin, New Zealand

Issues of power, oppression, justice, and compassion are at the heart of this challenging and important work that brings together diverse voices from outside the modern West in dialogue with the ethical paradigm of Walter Wink and his "Powers trilogy." This work brings into conversation political theology, practical theology, and moral theology and the result is a penetrating challenge to Christians in Myanmar, and the rest of us, to live with wisdom and courage in an increasingly post-secular society.

Myk Habets, PhD
Head of Theology, Laidlaw College, Auckland, New Zealand
Senior Research Fellow, Australian College of Theology, Sydney, Australia

Engaging Politics in Myanmar

A Study of Aung San Suu Kyi and Martin Luther King Jr
in Light of Walter Wink's Political Theology

Aung Htoo

MONOGRAPHS

© 2020 Aung Htoo

Published 2020 by Langham Monographs
An imprint of Langham Publishing
www.langhampublishing.org

Langham Publishing and its imprints are a ministry of Langham Partnership

Langham Partnership
PO Box 296, Carlisle, Cumbria, CA3 9WZ, UK
www.langham.org

ISBNs:
978-1-78368-781-7 Print
978-1-78368-832-6 ePub
978-1-78368-833-3 Mobi
978-1-78368-834-0 PDF

Aung Htoo has asserted his right under the Copyright, Designs and Patents Act, 1988 to be identified as the Author of this work.

All rights reserved. No part of this publication may be reproduced, stored in a retrieval system or transmitted, in any form or by any means, electronic, mechanical, photocopying, recording or otherwise, without the prior written permission of the publisher or the Copyright Licensing Agency.

Requests to reuse content from Langham Publishing are processed through PLSclear. Please visit www.plsclear.com to complete your request.

Scripture quotations marked ESV are from The Holy Bible, English Standard Version® (ESV®), copyright © 2001 by Crossway, a publishing ministry of Good News Publishers. Used by permission. All rights reserved.

British Library Cataloguing-in-Publication Data
A catalogue record for this book is available from the British Library

ISBN: 978-1-78368-781-7

Cover & Book Design: projectluz.com

Langham Partnership actively supports theological dialogue and an author's right to publish but does not necessarily endorse the views and opinions set forth here or in works referenced within this publication, nor can we guarantee technical and grammatical correctness. Langham Partnership does not accept any responsibility or liability to persons or property as a consequence of the reading, use or interpretation of its published content.

To the Christians of Myanmar who are devoted to witnessing the whole gospel in a holistic way.

Contents

Acknowledgements xi

Abstract xiii

List of Abbreviations xv

Part I

Chapter 1 3
Introduction
    1.1 Context of the Study 3
    1.2 Significance of the Study 5
    1.3 Method of the Study 10
    1.4 Thesis of the Study 12
    1.5 Outline of the Study 15

Chapter 2 19
Two Contrasting Orders: The Domination System and God's Domination-Free Order
    2.1 Exploring Wink's Theology of Nonviolence 20
        2.1.1 An Analytical Summary of Wink's *Powers* Trilogy 20
        2.1.2 Why Wink? 35
    2.2 Wink in Dialogue with Others: Toward a Constructive Frame 37
        2.2.1 The Powers as the Basis of a Christian Social Ethic 37
        2.2.2 The Powers and the Domination System 50
        2.2.3 The Powers and God's Domination-Free Order 58
    2.3 Summary of the Chapter 62

Chapter 3 65
Jesus's Third Way or Nonviolent Engagement: A Critical Construct
    3.1 Engaging the Powers Nonviolently 65
        3.1.1 Jesus's Third Way 66
        3.1.2 Why Nonviolence? 70
        3.1.3 Just War, Pacifism, Christian Realism, Just Peacemaking, and Nonviolence 76
        3.1.4 Violence and the Cross 84
    3.2 An Examination of the "What If" Dilemma 95
    3.3 The Powers, Church and Nonviolence 98

3.4 What's Next When the Powers Fall? Toward a Reconciliation.....104
3.5 Summary of the Chapter..107

Part II

Chapter 4 111
   Martin Luther King Jr on Nonviolence
     4.1 Biographical Exploration: How King Came to Believe in
        Nonviolence..112
        4.1.1 Parental Influences..113
        4.1.2 Intellectual Quest 116
     4.2 Involvement in the Civil Rights Movement 137
     4.3 King's Principles of Nonviolence: A Critical Examination 146
        4.3.1 Nonviolence as a Method of the Strong 146
        4.3.2 Nonviolence as a Path to Reconciliation 148
        4.3.3 Nonviolence as the Weapon against Evil 150
        4.3.4 Nonviolence and Redemptive Suffering 152
        4.3.5 Nonviolence and Inner Strength 153
        4.3.6 Nonviolence and Justice..154
     4.4 What Would You Do?..155
     4.5 Summary of the Chapter...157

Chapter 5 161
   Suu Kyi on Nonviolence
     5.1 Parental Influences..162
     5.2 Intellectual Upbringing...166
     5.3 Entry into the Myanmar Politics...168
     5.4 Political Life of Suu Kyi (1988–the Present): A Survey...............169
        5.4.1. The Military Regime and Suu Kyi...................................170
        5.4.2 Physical Attacks on Suu Kyi...175
     5.5 Principles of Nonviolence: A Critical Examination 177
        5.5.1 Why Not Violence? 177
        5.5.2 Nonviolence as a Buddhist Ethic......................................180
        5.5.3 *Mettā* as the All-Embracing Principle of Nonviolence 184
        5.5.4 Nonviolence as a Revolution of the Spirit 189
     5.6 Dialogue, Forgiveness, and Reconciliation 192
     5.7 Rule of Law and Nonviolence 195
     5.8 A Proponent of Principled or Pragmatic Nonviolence?...............198
     5.9 Suu Kyi after 2010: A Look at Her Current Political Life...........199
     5.10 Summary of the Chapter...207

Part III

Chapter 6 211
King and Suu Kyi in Dialogue with Walter Wink
    6.1 Nonviolence and Leadership: A Correlation 211
    6.2 Religion: Engaging Buddhism with Christianity 221
    6.3 Ethics of Nonviolence: Engaging King and Suu Kyi Via
        Wink's Eyes 229
        6.3.1 Why Not Violence? 229
        6.3.2 Nonviolence and Love: Engaging King's *Agape* and
             Suu Kyi's *Mettā* through Wink's Loving Enemies 232
        6.3.3 Principled or Pragmatic? 234
        6.3.4 Principles of Nonviolence: King and Suu Kyi Via
             Wink's Eyes 237
    6.4 What If . . . or Self-Defence? 253
    6.5 Nonviolence and the Church 255
    6.6 Summary of the Chapter 256

Chapter 7 259
Engaging with the Politics of Myanmar through Wink,
King and Suu Kyi
    7.1 Violence, Power-Struggles, and Buddhism:
        A Historical Review 260
        7.1.1 Monarchical Period 260
        7.1.2 Colonial Period 265
        7.1.3 Postcolonial Period 267
    7.2 Supernaturalism, Politics and Buddhism 269
    7.3 Ethnic Diversity and Religion 272
    7.4 A Quest for the Spirit of Burmese Politics 276
        7.4.1 Understanding Politics in Myanmar 277
        7.4.2 General Ne Win as a Resuscitator of the Spirit of the
             Traditional Myanmar Politics 278
        7.4.3 Suu Kyi as an Agent for Political Transformation 285
        7.4.4 The Failure of the Four Eights Protest 292
        7.4.5 Traditionalism or Transformation? 294
    7.5 Summary of the Chapter 304

Chapter 8 305
Conclusion: Political Implications for Christians in Myanmar
    8.1 Implications of Nonviolence for Christians in Myanmar 305
        8.1.1 Theological Implications 306

  8.1.2 Ethical Implications..310
  8.1.3 Socio-political Implication...315
 8.2 How Should Christians in Myanmar Begin to Engage
  with Politics?..316

Bibliography..321

Acknowledgements

I believe that writing a thesis is not merely an intellectual business. To come to fruition, it needs other support: financial, emotional, spiritual and social. Without these aids, this work would have never been brought out. First and foremost, it is God who has stirred up a passion in me for this research. Let him alone be praised! At the same time, I would especially like to express my gratitude to the following people for their manifold assistances.

My supervisors Stephen Garner, Nicola Hoggard Creegan, and Myk Habets for their tolerance with the tardiness of my work, English writing, and their thoughtful, yet critical advice that has sharpened my arguments.

The Leadev-Langham for funding tirelessly not just for my study, but also for my family during our stay in Auckland, New Zealand.

Laidlaw College for sharing an office to study and being a community of theology where my theological horizon was broadened, and Auckland University of Technology for providing research and book costs.

Merv Coates and his friends who shared their time with me amid their hectic schedules for proofreading.

My parents and parents-in-law for their prayer support and encouragement during my study years.

Auckland Chin Bethel Church where I spoke God's Word on Sundays, and for fellowship over the years of my stay in Auckland.

My wife Esther Van Dawt Kim and our children Teresa, Katherine and Francis for their company and endless patience the whole way through.

Abstract

Myanmar has been under a military dictatorship for fifty-three years. This work examines the spirit of the politics of Myanmar, interacting with the conceptual framework of Martin Luther King Jr, Aung San Suu Kyi and Walter Wink. It begins with a critical exploration of various ethical formulations of nonviolence by Wink and other scholars. After the exploration of Wink's theology of nonviolence, chapters 4 and 5 consider King and Suu Kyi's philosophical and practical applications of nonviolence. King and Suu Kyi masterfully advance their views of nonviolence in their own contexts. A critical interaction between King, Suu Kyi and Wink in the fields of leadership, religion, and ethical principles (chapter 6) constructs a theoretical basis for the main body of this study (chapter 7). This interaction reveals that violence and nonviolence are far greater than a means to achieve the desired end. Both have a spiritual dimension. When this spiritual aspect is saturated in a particular culture, it cannot be easily removed. The true political spirit of Myanmar is revealed by its long history of violence being employed as a means to change the government. This political spirit of Myanmar pervades the areas of leadership, religion, and ethics. Against this backdrop, Suu Kyi rises up to transform the spirit of politics in Myanmar. This work concludes that expounding politics of Myanmar through the eyes of King, Suu Kyi, and Wink enables us to discern its spiritual nature that is deep-rooted throughout the nation's history and to draw some implications for Christians in Myanmar.

List of Abbreviations

BIA	Burmese Independence Army
BSSP	Burmese Socialist Programme Party
DFO	God's domination-free order
DS	domination system
EMHD	English Methodist High School
IQ	intelligence quotient
IR	interpersonal / individual reconciliation
KIA	Kachin Independence Army
MPC	Myanmar Peace Centre
NLD	National League for Democracy
NUR	national unity and reconciliation
SCLC	Southern Christian Leadership Conference
SLORC	State Law and Order Restoration Council
SPDC	State Peace and Development Council
SQ	spiritual quotient
TRC	Truth and Reconciliation Council

Part I

CHAPTER 1

Introduction

1.1 Context of the Study

My passion for the topic of nonviolence is birthed out of personal experience and my knowledge of the fraught history of Myanmar. The military rule was well entrenched before my birth. I was born in July 1972 in the Ne Win era. Under his authoritarian rule, I grew up in a politically naïve and unconcerned way. In 1988, a historic protest broke out, known as "the Four Eights" (08/08/1988).[1] I was a high school student at the time. The countrywide protest opened my eyes to the true nature of the military government. From then on, my concern over the politics of Myanmar began to grow. However, the church where I grew up had a different view of politics. Pastors and Christians with whom I was familiar were unconcerned about politics. The church's interest was solely in the spiritual. The impression I had was that politics has nothing to do with Christianity. This attitude might perhaps have been exacerbated by the government's unofficial policy on non-Buddhist religions. All non-Buddhist religious people did not find favour in the eyes of the political elites. Even worse, the passivity of Christians in Myanmar in times of political upheaval led me to question the relationship between Christianity and politics. This study is part of my quest for the nexus between

---

1. Useful resources covering the Four Eights include, Bertil Lintner's *Outrage: Burma's Struggle for Democracy*; Alan Clements and Leslie Kean's *Burma's Revolution of the Spirit*; and Dr Maung Maung's *The 1988 Uprising in Burma*, which is a personal account of the former president of the Socialist Republic of the Union of Burma.

Christianity and politics in the context of Myanmar. Therefore, it entails a brief survey of the political context of the country.

Myanmar is known as the country under the longest military rule. To be specific, the country had been under two successive military regimes: the first ruled the nation from March 1962 to July 1988; the second from August 1989 to November 2015. The year between 1988 and 1989 was a transitional period. The history of Myanmar – monarchical, colonial, and the post-independence period – is full of bloody, brutal and violent acts in times of political and power struggles. Father Sangermano, who worked as a missionary in Myanmar from 1883 to 1806, once described, "There is not in the whole world a monarch so despotic as the Burmese Emperor."[2] Monarchs of Myanmar viewed themselves as absolute lords of the lives, properties and personal services of their subjects.[3] In the post-independence period (1948–1962), the country became politically democratic; however, the communist and ethnic insurgent groups rose up against the democratic government.

In 1962, General Ne Win staged a coup and ruled the country ruthlessly until he resigned in 1988. During that year, the whole country was in utter chaos, which lasted until August 1989.[4] Those days were rife with violence, and people seemed to be demonized and callous. Out of his own experiences in those days, James Mawdsley reflects:

> I nearly cry every time I think about it. What horrifies me every time is trying to imagine a man who is fit, strong, well-armed and surrounded by colleagues, who is backed up as well by one of the world's largest armies, charging after hapless young girls and clubbing them to death . . . She will not die with one or two blows. He must hit her on the arms and back and chest before getting a few good shots in at her face. They are floundering in the water and he cannot get a good clear swing. But blows to the face will not kill her either. They just smash her into a pulp.

---

2. Sangermano, *Burmese Empire*, 73.

3. The topic of the practice of power among monarchs of Myanmar will be discussed at greater length in chapter 7.

4. The uprising on 8 August 1988 is known as the Four Eights (8/8/88), at the end of which another military regime replaced the old one.

At last he gets one on the back of her skull and suddenly she is still and her face sinks below the water.⁵

In short, the history of the nation and the brutal onslaught of the regime against any political protests has imprinted on the minds of the people of Myanmar that nonviolence seems inappropriate in this context, and is likely to be ineffective.

In the context where Christianity is a minority religion, how should Christians in Myanmar live out their understanding of the gospel? What might the resources from general Christian theology in dialogue with the context of Myanmar offer the Christians to help them understand their everyday world and how to live in it? This study draws on both perspectives in Myanmar and Christian perspectives of nonviolence and nonviolent engagement with society, drawing particularly from Walter Wink, Martin Luther King Jr, and Aung San Suu Kyi, to answer that question and contribute to the well-being of the context of Myanmar.

1.2 Significance of the Study

This thesis and its argument are located in the field of practical theology, which is "first of all an interpretative or hermeneutical task,"⁶ as Terry Veling argues. Gerben Heitink, in tracing the history of practical theology, concludes that modern practical theology has its beginnings in the 1960s. Since then a considerable consensus has emerged regarding the view that practical theology is a theological theory of action.⁷ Practical theologians, by and large, lay an emphasis on experience, the interplay of theory and practice, faith and action, the content of the gospel and the context.⁸ Simply stated, doing practical theology is an exploration of an interface between faith and action. Therefore, it is not a dichotomized understanding of theory versus practice,

---

5. Mawdsley, *Heart Must Break*, 285.
6. Veling, *Practical Theology*, 54.
7. Heitink, *Practical Theology*, 104.
8. Cahalan and Mikoski, "Introduction," from *Opening the Field*, 2–4, 271; Swinton and Mowat, *Practical Theology*, 5–26; Veling, *Practical Theology*, 8–9.

faith versus action, tradition versus context, and so on, rather, it is an attempt to investigate the interplay or interface between them.

Jeanne Stevenson-Moessner figuratively describes that practical theology, unlike a soloist or guest musician, plays with concern for other disciplines or areas in theology.[9] Viewing it in this light, practical theology can have a dialogue both with theological education (biblical, historical, and systematic theological reflection) and non-theological disciplines, like sociology, psychology, anthropology, and so on. In other words, practical theology covers many disciplines, ranging from ethics, leadership, and religion to cultural studies.

Therefore, practical theology entails all human practices in our world, which is why it interacts affirmatively and critically with other disciplines – theological (biblical studies, church history, systematic theology and theological ethics) and non-theological (psychology, sociology, cultural anthropology, and so on). As a dynamic and differentiated field, practical theology involves an interdisciplinary element.[10] This is also one of the reasons why practical theologians use a variety of methods to do practical theology: literature-based, qualitative, and quantitative research methods.[11] Engaging theologically with the socio-political context of Myanmar clearly falls into the domain of practical theology, where the theological implications are lived out daily, and the daily living refines the theological reflection.[12]

---

9. Stevenson-Moessner, *Prelude to Practical Theology*, 1.

10. Cahalan and Mikoski, *Opening the Field*, 1, 4.

11. See Heitink, *Practical Theology*, 220–240. Cartledge, *Practical Theology*, 69–102; Newton Poling, *Rethinking Faith*, 150–153; Swinton and Mowat, *Practical Theology*; and Miller-McLemore, *Companion to Practical Theology*.

12. This study of violence and nonviolence is located in practical theology because "practical theology's focal interest is not directly in the philosophical but in the 'performative speech acts' of faith practice," Cameron, et al., *Talking about God*, 13. There is a number of research on the study of violence and nonviolence in the field of practical theology. David Tombs, "Lived Religion, (In)tolerance and the Dehumanising Violence of the Cross," a lecture given in Centre for the Study of Lived Religion, Free University of Amsterdam; See Tombs, "Lived Religion." In her doctoral dissertation, Julie Marie Todd uses a practical theological approach to evaluate Christian (non)violence by interviewing twelve scholars and activists. She highlights three points that any evaluation of the transformative effect of a Christian theology must: "first, be set within an analysis of historical … context of struggle; second, seek to understand the complex nature of violence in its … cultural forms; and third, remain committed to examining the role and participation of Christian individuals, institutions and theology in violence in all three forms," see Todd, "Evaluating Violence," 295–296. Nicole L.

This study is, by and large, an engagement between Walter Wink, Martin Luther King Jr and Aung San Suu Kyi to synthesize a Christian response to the political environment of Myanmar. It does this to offer theological insight and teaching to the church and Christians in Myanmar that have, in my opinion, been lacking in engaging with their contemporary context. The hope is that this work may awaken and stir up the conscience of Christians in Myanmar, the majority of whom are politically indifferent.

Using Wink, King, and Suu Kyi to speak to the context of Myanmar raises the question, why Wink and King? This will be discussed in detail in the next chapter but introducing them in brief, Walter Wink (21 May 1935 – 10 May 2012) was an American biblical scholar, theologian and activist. He taught at Auburn Theological Seminary in New York City. He was widely known for his *Powers* trilogy, *Naming the Powers* (1984), *Unmasking the Powers* (1986), and *Engaging the Powers* (1992). "The myth of redemptive violence," was the concept he raised in his seminal work on *Powers*. Martin Luther King Jr (15 January 1929 – 4 April 1968) was a black American Baptist pastor, but he is widely known as the most prominent leading activist in the civil rights movement. He was awarded the Nobel Peace Prize for fighting for racial equality in his time through nonviolent resistance. Like King, Aung San Suu Kyi is also best known for her unswerving commitment to nonviolence in resisting one of the most oppressive military regimes in the world. She also received a Nobel Peace Prize in 1991 for her nonviolent resistance.

In this study, Wink's *Powers* trilogy is used as a principal voice to engage the political context of Myanmar where power is arbitrarily practiced. He is employed because he offers a well-developed theory of Christian nonviolence

---

Johnson also examines nonviolence that centred on the teachings and example of Jesus Christ as a path of authentic Christian discipleship within the context of the United Methodist Church, see her dissertation "Practising Discipleship: Lived Theologies of Nonviolence in Conversation with the Doctrine and Teachings of the United Methodist Church." This research, though not having used any particular qualitative research methodology, analyzes a historical context and discusses the complex nature of violence in the political context of the country. Likewise, there are some doctoral dissertations that examine violence and nonviolence from the angle of practical theology without employing qualitative or quantitative research methodology. For example, Myles Werntz argues that a nonviolence that is thoroughly Christian must account for how nonviolence is related to the structures and practices of the church, see Werntz, "Ontology, Ecclesiology, Nonviolence." Likewise, Stephen Thomas Krupa also studies the spirituality of Dorothy Day as a potential resource for contemporary Christian nonviolence, see Krupa, "Dorothy Day." See also Cone, "Martin and Malcolm," 173–183.

that provides a way to describe how power and violence function in a nation, a society and an institution, as well as in an individual within these institutions. Likewise, King and Suu Kyi are also used as dialogue partners with Wink, who practice and promote the concept of nonviolence. As the study aims to provide political implications for Christians in Myanmar where Buddhism is the state religion, King becomes a model to represent Christians of Myanmar, whereas Suu Kyi becomes a representative of the majority Buddhists. Hence, King and Suu Kyi are dialogue partners to engage with Wink in the sociopolitical location of Myanmar.[13]

Since Christianity is a minority religion and theological education in Myanmar has lagged far behind other Asian countries, information and research available in biblical and theological education is sparse. Most doctoral studies done by native Christians in Myanmar are, by and large, concentrated on the fields of Christian missions, Christian-Buddhist dialogue, and moderately historical, pastoral and church growth studies.[14] There is a paucity of study in Myanmar from a theological perspective on politics in Myanmar.[15] Situating the research in the context of Myanmar where many Christians are politically unconcerned, the research also seeks to discuss the relationship between Christianity and politics.

---

13. A detailed discussion of the reasons for using Wink, King and Suu Kyi in the study of the politics of Myanmar will follow in later chapters: Wink, in chapter 3; King, in chapter 4; and Suu Kyi in chapter 5.

14. When searching theses relating to Christianity in Myanmar in the search engines of ProQuest Dissertations and Theses Global, EthOS – British Library's Electronic Theses Online Service, and Open Access Theses and Dissertations, most of the theses found are intercultural, missions, evangelism, pastoral and historical studies of Christianity. If there are theses and dissertations focusing on the politics of Myanmar, they are all secular or non-theological studies.

15. During the two successive military regimes (1962–2015), freedom of press had been strictly restricted. Expressing personal opinion on political matters was not allowed. Writing any critical comments on the regimes was prohibited. To quote George Orwell, "It is a world in which every word and everything is censored . . . Free speech is unthinkable. All other kinds of freedom are permitted. You are free to be a drunkard, an idler, a coward, a backbiter, a fornicator; but you are not free to think for yourself." Orwell, *Burmese Days*, 96. Under such an extremely restricting law on press freedom, it is little wonder that there is a paucity of reliable information on politics of Myanmar. Even if a native scholar of Myanmar completes a critical study of the military regime somewhere outside of the nation, that scholar would never dare to go back to his home country in Myanmar. If they did, the government would arrest and directly imprison them. Truly, that is one of the reasons why sufficient information on politics of Myanmar is hard to find.

This research will also contribute to Christians, both lay and full-time Christian ministers in Myanmar in a significant way. By arguing that Christians are socio-politically responsible for what happens in their society, the study aims to foster Christians of Myanmar, many of whom are politically apathetic, to become a consciousness-raising community. Furthermore, the contribution that the thesis pursues does not localize the context of Myanmar alone, but seeks to contribute to global Christianity as well. As located in the area of practical theology, this study will contribute to its field, especially in engaging with a particular non-Christian context through a theological lens. In this engagement, the study does not employ a single theologian alone, instead it seeks to include other voices – Christian (King) and Buddhist (Suu Kyi).

So, this work is primarily concerned with Wink's contribution as a theorist of nonviolence, and King and Suu Kyi as the practitioners of nonviolence. Hence, through an integrated lens, it refers to an angle which is created from the study of Wink, King and Suu Kyi on nonviolence; therefore, it is not necessarily a view of Wink, King or of Suu Kyi. Instead, it is a view created through a dialogue between a theologian (Wink) and two practitioners (King and Suu Kyi). This will be a lens through which to engage politics of Myanmar. Even though the thesis is located in the theory of nonviolence, it also extends to other fields such as politics, leadership, history, and religion.[16] In doing so, the emphasis is not on politics, leadership, or religion in Myanmar per se. Instead, the discussion is centred on the principles and practices of violence and nonviolence that have predominated over the ways of practicing leadership, religion and politics.

Another significance of the study is that it also extends to the area of interfaith dialogue. The context in which the study is located is Myanmar where Buddhism is a majority, while Christianity is a minority religion. That necessitates the work having an integrated lens that reflects both Christianity and Buddhism respectively. Therefore, Suu Kyi, as an exemplar of nonviolent proponents who define and practice nonviolence from a Buddhist perspective

---

16. Kathleen Cahalan and Gordon Mikoski describe the interdisciplinary nature of practical theology. They state that practical theologians engage fields of knowledge beyond their own, ranging from biblical studies, church history, ethics, and systematic theology to psychology, sociology, cultural anthropology and so on, see Cahalan and Mikoski "Introduction," 4.

in the Buddhist context, is contextually appropriate; at the same time, it is also inter-religiously relevant to bring her into the dialogue. However, the study does not go beyond the scope of nonviolence and its related themes.

The underlying assumption in the whole work is that the notion of nonviolence, when regarded as more than a method but as a way of life, has some implications that can be applied in the fields of leadership and politics as well as in religion. The study also assumes that an integrated analysis of Wink, King and Suu Kyi will provide a penetrating lens by which to scrutinize the root problems of politics in Myanmar, thereby proposing some answers to them.

However, there are some limitations entwined in the study. As mentioned earlier, the primary concern of the thesis is the theory of nonviolence; however, it endeavours to cover a wide range of other disciplines such as leadership, religion, and ethics. The purpose of covering these disciplines is not to discuss each of them at large, but to focus on the issues relating to the view and practice of nonviolence. It is assumed that we can make numerous implications behind the notion of nonviolence. For instance, the question in relation to leadership is, "Can a nonviolent leader be a tyrant or dictator?" For religion, "Does a religion enslave or emancipate people?" In relation to ethics, "Can the means be justified by the end?" Hence the treatment of leadership, religion, and ethics in this study is limited to the issues concerned with the notion and practice of nonviolence.

1.3 Method of the Study

This research is a literature-based study, that seeks to engage the politics of Myanmar through the integrated lens of Walter Wink, Martin Luther King Jr, and Aung San Suu Kyi with the intention of fostering Christians in Myanmar to become a consciousness-raising community. In this work, readers will come across such terms as "spirits," "spiritual," "spirituality," and "principalities and powers." Such terms are quite unusual within the professional vocabulary of the social and empirical scientists. However, this is a study in the field of practical theology, and hence it necessitates the use of the theological and biblical language that comprises its professional vocabulary.

John Swinton and Harriet Mowat define practical theology as "critical, theological reflection on the practices of the Church as they interact with the practices of the world, with a view to ensuring and enabling faithful participation in God's redemptive practices in, to and for the world."[17] According to this definition, the practices of the church are supposed to reflect God's redemptive practices in, to, and for the world. In order to be so, a critical theological reflection on how the church interacts with the world is essential. The thesis adopts this definition to locate it in the field of practical theology.

This definition highlights the what and why of practical theology. That is, practical theology seeks to examine the way in which Christians engage in the world in order for them to faithfully participate in God's redemptive practices. With this definition in mind, we will see the way in which Christians in Myanmar interact with the world. The aim for doing this is to ensure if their engagement faithfully reflects God's redemptive practices. Christians in Myanmar, as a minority religious group, have several challenges in practicing their faith in everyday living. This disadvantage leads many Christians to be silent and passive in public affairs. That is one of the reasons why preaching on social justice has not been heard in many churches.

In order to enable Christian involvement in Myanmar, this research seeks to draw practical implications for Christians by exploring Martin Luther King Jr and Aung San Suu Kyi via Walter Wink's *Powers*. The outcome of the study will challenge, inspire and enable Christians in Myanmar to get involved in the public square so that they might participate holistically in God's redemptive practices. Most of all, the study will give the ground and motivations Christians in Myanmar should have for engaging in nonviolent political action. This is what is original about this research, and a contribution to the field of practical theology in such a way that practical implications for Christians in a particular context can be drawn through having a critical interaction between a theologian and practitioners.

Based on Swinton and Mowat's definition, the study looks at the history of Myanmar in relation to the use of violence in politics through the integrated lens of Wink, King and Suu Kyi, with the aim of drawing political implications for Christians in Myanmar, who view politics as an utterly worldly thing. As practical theology is multidisciplinary, this research covers a number of subjects such as the study of biblical vocabulary, ethics, history, and politics.

---

17. Swinton and Mowat, *Practical Theology*, 6.

But this research, unlike other research in practical theology, does not employ any qualitative research methodology, because its aim is to draw political implications for Christians in Myanmar by looking at the issue of violence and nonviolence in the political context of Myanmar via an integrated lens of Wink, King and Suu Kyi. Therefore, the approach of this thesis is not biblical studies, ethics, or history, but an integration of these subjects, along with politics and sociology, centring on the issue of violence in the political context of Myanmar.

On the basis of this approach, this study seeks to engage first Wink and other voices on nonviolence, King and Suu Kyi second, and third an integration of Wink, King and Suu Kyi. In doing so, all voices will be critically compared with the view of achieving a synthesized or integrated lens. Once an integrated lens of Wink, King and Suu Kyi is established, it will be an interpretive framework to engage with the political context of Myanmar and to draw political implications for Christians in Myanmar. In doing so, this research will enable the church in Myanmar to faithfully participate in God's redemptive practices in, to and for the world.

1.4 Thesis of the Study

As practical theology is multidisciplinary, this study engages fields of knowledge beyond its own – theological and non-theological disciplines such as peace and political studies. This engagement will not create a fuzziness – having no focus on the research aims. Instead, as practical theologians do, this research undertakes a commitment to critically engage multiple sources available to it that can shed light on its purpose.[18] In engaging with other disciplines, the focus is not to get side-tracked but to deepen the research. Therefore, this study explores not only a theologian and two practitioners of nonviolence, but also the socio-political context of Myanmar through surveying its history in order to bring a critical dialogue between them. This critical dialogue will bring out the contextual, practical implications for Christians in Myanmar. As Stephen Bevans argues, theology needs to take into account

---

18. Cahalan and Mikoski, "Introduction," 4.

both the context of the past and that of the present.[19] This study takes a serious exploration of King and Suu Kyi in their own contexts and engages the socio-political context of Myanmar with a view to drawing the implications for Christians in Myanmar. So bringing a late-twentieth-century Christian theologian, a mid-twentieth-century Christian activist and a contemporary Buddhist politician together in dialogue to speak to the Christians who live in the predominantly Buddhist Myanmar, where military despotism had been booming for half a century, will be the uniqueness and originality of this research.

Most contemporary literature on nonviolence focuses on its philosophical, religious, moral or pragmatic reasons. By and large, there are two approaches in practicing nonviolence: pragmatic and principled. The practitioners of pragmatic nonviolence are greatly emphatic about the role of an end or result over the means; whereas, for those of principled nonviolence, the means and ends are intrinsically linked. For the former, what matters most is the desired result, not the methods, techniques or tactics; as the saying goes, the end justifies the means. In contrast, the principled approach suggests that the means to be employed must be consistent with the desired result.

This study argues that approaching nonviolence in either a pragmatic or principled (philosophical) way is too particularistic because it fails to discern the backdrop behind the notion of nonviolence. It is insubstantial to say that we choose nonviolence because it is effective. If so, the questions arise: Is nonviolence effective always? What if it fails to achieve the desired outcome? It is doubtless to say that the method of nonviolence does not guarantee success. Thus, the pragmatic approach to nonviolence is apparently superficial. For instance, King, known as a proponent of the principled approach, will be discussed in chapter 4, and Suu Kyi, described as more pragmatic, will be examined in chapter 5. We will see how sticking to one approach, either principled or pragmatic, raises questions since the context is often more complex than we imagine.

Hence, the consistency of the principled approach regarding the inseparability of means and end seems to underestimate the complexities of socio-cultural situations. If the desired end is peace, the way to achieve it must be

---

19. Bevans, *Models of Contextual Theology*, 10.

through peaceful means. It cannot be through violent means. Logically speaking, the principled approach is more consistent than the pragmatic approach, because the word "nonviolence" might be synonymous with peace, while violence might not. However, practically speaking, the principled approach has some problems. For instance, it would be inapposite and inapplicable for the practitioners of the principled approach in the context of Adolf Hitler's Germany, Mao Zedong's China, and Joseph Stalin's Russia. Simply stated, the world in which we live, the social issues we encounter, and the situations we are in are more complicated, defective, and enigmatic than we can think.

Therefore, sticking to the principled approach in such an imperfect world may not truly make sense, and some compromises must be made. This study seeks to explore the idea of nonviolence not in the way mentioned above, but through looking at the system as a whole. Instead of asking which approach – pragmatic or principled – the research seeks to establish a theological framework through which to investigate the notion of nonviolence. That is why the study looks at Wink's theoretical formulation of nonviolence in the light of other scholars, using King and Suu Kyi as exemplars.

Furthermore, this thesis argues that characteristically, the study of nonviolence entails not only philosophical and practical elements, but also spiritual. Wink discovers the spiritual characteristic of nonviolence through an in-depth analysis of the *Powers* language in the New Testament. In Wink's vocabulary, it is the "myth of redemptive violence,"[20] meaning violence can be overcome by violence. When this myth is deeply rooted in the world, it becomes the spirit, which cannot be superseded by anything else except through nonviolence. Likewise, Suu Kyi and King also acknowledge the importance of the spiritual dimension in nonviolent resistance. Suu Kyi perceives nonviolent resistance as a revolution of the spirit,[21] whereas King sees it as fighting against the forces of evil, not the persons doing the evil, therefore it "is strongly active spiritually."[22] Thus, nonviolent resistance requires enormous spiritual or inner exertion, not merely physical action.

---

20. Wink, *Powers That Be*, 42.
21. Suu Kyi, *Freedom from Fear*.
22. King Jr, *Stride toward Freedom*, 90.

Here King and Suu Kyi have a similar view on the indispensable role of spiritual or inward exertion in the life of a nonviolent activist in the process of nonviolent resistance. Nonviolent resistance is, subjectively speaking, a way of spiritual exercise. However, Wink's special concern for the spiritual dimension of nonviolent resistance is primarily non-subjective. In talking about the spiritual aspect of nonviolence, Wink's emphasis is not upon the individual subjective dimension, but rather, on institutional, and therefore objective. Simply put, what matters for Wink is the spiritual aspect of an institution. To juxtapose King and Suu Kyi with Wink, the former argues that the real problem is not basically "out there" (rule, policy, regulation, administrative structures of an institution, organization and so on), but "in here" (our social and psychological ego constructed by the context in which we are living), whereas the latter (Wink) stresses that the fundamental predicament is not just "in here" (our ego), but also "out there"; that is, the inward, invisible spiritual dimension of an institution, or the process of socialization. This will be discussed in detail in a later chapter containing a critical commentary of Wink's *Powers*.

The thesis will also contribute to the ongoing study of violence and nonviolence by emphasizing the spiritual feature of violence and nonviolence. Conclusions drawn in this research will provide all the practitioners of nonviolence, whether they are using the pragmatic or principled approach in general, with information and insight that would lead them to a deeper understanding of the nature and power of nonviolence. Particularly, findings from this research will also help Christians in Myanmar perceive that the method of nonviolence is not passive; but rather, it is active resistance to evil itself.

Finally, by using the Christian and Buddhist approaches of King and Suu Kyi, this thesis also engages the Buddhist and Christian views on nonviolence. In a sense, this study provides an interfaith dialogue considering both views. As love (*mettā* in Sanskrit, meaning loving-kindness) is at the heart of the idea of nonviolence both in Buddhism and Christianity, the study will in some measure contribute to the area of inter-religious studies.

1.5 Outline of the Study

The thesis question is, "What can reading the political culture of Myanmar through an integrated lens of Walter Wink, Martin Luther King Jr, and Aung

San Suu Kyi contribute to Christians of Myanmar in particular, and non-Christians in general?" In answering this question, this work is divided into three parts with eight chapters in total. The first chapter of part I introduces the thesis by clarifying why the study has been chosen, how it will be organized, and the method for completing the study. Chapters 2 and 3 contain a critical analysis of Wink's theology of the *Powers*. Chapter 2 examines Wink's view of the two orders in conflict, which Wink calls the Domination System and God's domination-free order. In doing so, I will bring in some dialogue partners such as Jacques Ellul, John H. Yoder, Miroslav Volf, Michael Foucault and Gene Sharp to engage with Wink as necessary. The chapter also examines an overview of Wink's theology of nonviolence, as seen primarily in his own writings, to posit the framework of his theology. Among his own writings, the *Powers* trilogy (*Naming the Powers; Unmasking the Powers; and Engaging the Powers*), upon which Wink's whole theological system of nonviolence is constructed, will be critically examined.

Chapter 3 is a critical commentary of Walter Wink's idea of nonviolence or Jesus's third way through the eyes of other nonviolence scholars and theologians. This examination will be done in the light of his critics as well as supporters to articulate the whole structure of the theology of nonviolence. To reach the aim of the chapter, the study constructively appraises Wink's theology from the angles of the aforementioned scholars, as well as others, such as Stanley Hauerwas, Glen Stassen, and Dietrich Bonhoeffer. It then looks at secular work on nonviolence and power, such as that by Michel Foucault and Gene Sharp, as necessary, to show points of similarity and difference, and to strengthen the thesis of the study. Overall, chapters 2 and 3 seek to critically integrate Wink's theology of nonviolence with the views of other scholars and theologians in the field.

Part II is comprised of two chapters (4 and 5) which explore the nonviolent resistance Martin Luther King Jr and Aung San Suu Kyi practiced in their respective contexts. These chapters examine the socio-political contexts and religious influences upon each person in their own historical backgrounds. In addition, the principles of nonviolence that they adhered to as they fought against their respective regimes are examined.

There are three chapters (from 6 to 8) in part III. Chapter 6 is an interactive discussion between King and Suu Kyi through the lens of Wink's theology of nonviolence. In the discussion, similarities and differences between King, Suu Kyi and Wink are identified, followed by an assessment of each person's view in the light of Wink's theology. This chapter aims to create an integrated view of nonviolence for Wink, King and Suu Kyi, so that it could be a lens through which to engage the politics of Myanmar. Chapter 7 is a critical engagement of the politics of Myanmar through the integrated lens of Wink, King and Suu Kyi. The first section of this chapter provides an overview of political and religious situations of the country of Myanmar throughout history. This review highlights how Buddhism has played a crucial role in the politics of Myanmar through the centuries. Additionally, the chapter also observes the general understanding of politics among the people of Myanmar, racial diversities and conflicts, and the role of supernaturalism in politics. It also examines the spirit of politics of Myanmar, which has been dominant in Myanmar since the precolonial period. The chapter establishes that reading the politics of Myanmar via Wink's *Powers* unmasks the fundamental flaws of the politics of Myanmar.

The last chapter is the conclusion of the thesis, looking at the politics of Myanmar through Wink, King and Suu Kyi in the areas of leadership, religion, and ethical roles; thereby drawing political implications for Christians in Myanmar. Engaging the politics of Myanmar via the eyes of Wink, King and Suu Kyi exposes the deep-seated problems of the country, and at the same time it also sheds light on a range of possibilities for transforming the country into the culture of democracy. Therefore, this chapter is the crux of the whole thesis because it examines the spirit of politics of Myanmar in the light of the Buddhist-Christian dialogue, informed by Wink, King and Suu Kyi.

CHAPTER 2

Two Contrasting Orders: The Domination System and God's Domination-Free Order

This study engages the politics of Myanmar by utilizing the works of Walter Wink, Martin Luther King Jr and Aung San Suu Kyi. Wink provides a theological-sociological lens for examination, and King and Suu Kyi act as contextual exemplars. This raises a question: Why are two Americans, Wink and King, used in a study on the politics of Myanmar, when their context is very different from that of Myanmar? Myanmar is a South-East Asian country, religiously Buddhist, and politically under military rule, while the context of King and Wink is mostly secular and practicing a democratic system of government. This chapter and the next provide fundamental reasons why Wink and King are employed as key informants in this research to engage with Burmese politics despite contextual differences.

This chapter examines Wink's construction of two conflicting orders: the domination system (DS) and God's domination-free order (DFO). What are the DS and the DFO? How do they sharply contrast each other? How does each come into existence? What or who birthed them? To achieve this, Wink's theology of nonviolence will be surveyed first, and then a critical interaction between Wink and other scholars will follow. This will establish a rationale for nonviolence. The following chapters will be a critical dialogue between Wink and other scholars on the notion and principles of nonviolence. As noted in the introduction, the method employed in this chapter will be a critical, theological reflection to examine Wink's *Powers* trilogy in the light of other scholars. In question, how can scholars respond to Wink's *Powers* trilogy? At the same time, what can Wink offer back to those scholars? The outcome of this dialogue will be a lens through which to engage the two practitioners of nonviolence, Martin Luther King Jr and Aung San Suu Kyi.

2.1 Exploring Wink's Theology of Nonviolence

Walter Wink (21 May 1938 – 10 May 2012) was a professor of Biblical Interpretation at Auburn Theological Seminary, New York. Upon his retirement, he became an Emeritus Professor. He was a cross-disciplinary theologian who tried to integrate theology and psychology, especially the psychoanalysis of Carl Jung. Best known as a theologian of nonviolence, Wink was not only an academic, but was also actively involved in social activism. His book, *Violence and Nonviolence in South Africa*, is a product of his participation in nonviolent resistance in South Africa.[1] Moreover, Wink was actively involved in the American civil rights movement, the anti-Vietnam War struggle and the campaign for nuclear disarmament. These experiences and active participation in resistance movements show that Wink, though a white American, has a strong sense of what it looks like living under despotic rule.

2.1.1 An Analytical Summary of Wink's *Powers* Trilogy

Before engaging critically with Wink's *Powers* trilogy, it will be helpful to summarize each of those and how they contribute to the development of Wink's thinking on nonviolence. The three volumes are, *Naming the Powers*; *Unmasking the Powers*; and *Engaging the Powers*.

Wink's first volume of the *Powers* is the most extensive investigation of the Powers language in the New Testament. Wink asserts that his work is a "pilgrimage away" from his predecessors who demythologized the Powers language to interpret and apply it to their contemporary settings.[2] The key argument Wink proposes in *Naming the Powers* is,

---

1. Wink, *Violence and Nonviolence*.
2. Wink, *Naming the Powers*, 5.

> ... "principalities and powers" are the inner and outer aspects of any given manifestation of power. As the inner aspect they are the spirituality of institutions, the "within" of corporate structures and systems, the inner essence of outer organization of the power. As the outer aspect they are political systems, appointed officials, the "chair" of an organization, laws – in short, all the tangible manifestations which power takes. Every Power tends to have a visible pole, an outer form – be it a church, a nation, or an economy – and an invisible pole, an inner spirit or driving force that animates, legitimates, and regulates its physical manifestation in the world.[3]

Wink buttresses this argument on the bases of exegetical study, Carl Jung, a process philosopher named Alfred North Whitehead, and a Jesuit priest named Pierre Teihard de Chardin who in some measure influences the process philosophy. As a New Testament scholar, Wink firstly completed a great deal of work examining biblical texts that spoke to both natural and supernatural powers, such as, "principalities and powers" (Eph 6:12). Wink draws six preliminary hypotheses about the powers:

1. The language of power pervades the whole New Testament.
2. The language of power in the New Testament is imprecise, liquid, interchangeable, and unsystematic.
3. Despite all this imprecision and interchangeability, clear patterns of usage emerge.
4. Because these terms are to a certain degree interchangeable, one, a pair, or a series can be made to represent them all.
5. These powers are both heavenly and earthly, divine and human, spiritual and political, invisible and structural.
6. These powers are also both good and evil.[4]

After studying the powers language in the Bible, Wink lays out the last hypothesis, "Unless the context further specifies ... we are to take the terms

---

3. Wink, 5.
4. Wink, 7–11.

for power in their most comprehensive sense, understanding them to mean both heavenly *and* earthly, divine *and* human, spiritual *and* political, invisible *and* structural, good *and* evil."[5] Previous studies on the Powers draw a sharp distinction between spiritual and non-spiritual, heavenly and earthly, and visible and invisible. In contrast, Wink tries to synthesize those distinctions by creating what he calls an "integral worldview."[6] This synthesis runs counter to his predecessors who see spiritual and non-spiritual, heavenly and earthly, and good and evil separately.[7] Against the backdrop of such interpretation, Wink insists that the "Powers are not separate heavenly or ethereal entities, but *the inner aspect of material or tangible manifestations of power*."[8]

As a cross-disciplinarian, Wink's interpretation of the Powers from the perspective of myth relies heavily on a psychoanalyst named Carl Jung. For him, myths are not to be discarded, but instead considered revelatory. For instance, ancient Babylonians believed that the king and royal house were divine, and so shared divine supremacy. However, Wink believes that, "such myths of power are simply fabrications by the ruling classes;" thus, "they are the unconscious distillate of the actual spiritual quality . . . from the value systems and power relations of the existing state."[9] Therefore, myths are to be read as speaking symbolically of the real but invisible spiritual dimension of personal, corporate earthly existence.[10] The Powers, for him, have dual identity – inner and outer.

---

5. Wink, 39. Emphasis in original.

6. Wink, *Engaging the Powers*, 5.

7. For instance, Wesley Carr insists that the NT writers saw the Powers to be altogether good. For Carr, the concept of mighty forces that are hostile to man, from which he sought relief, was not prevalent in the thought world of the first century AD. Carr continues to insist that the Powers language demonstrates that the chief emphasis was upon angels as a means both of interpreting the activity of God among men, and of extolling the Lordship of Yahweh. In fact, evil was increasingly focused in the figure of Satan. See Carr, *Angels and Principalities*, 122, 174. Wink was so dissatisfied with the way in which Carr argued because he saw that Carr's work was largely in error. Reading Carr's work led Wink to re-examine the Powers language in a much deeper and comprehensive way, so that he might be able to formulate Christian social ethics from it, see Wink, *Naming the Powers*, ix–x.

8. Wink, *Naming the Powers*, 104, italic is his.

9. Wink, 134.

10. Wink, 142. Wink's emphasis on the interiority of an institution is also very similar to the Jungian concept of archetype. Archetype, according to Jung, refers to, "the structural components of the collective unconscious which are inherited and have developed through the consistent experiences of previous generations and seek expression in individual lives,

Not only does Wink justify his interpretation of the Powers as the visible and invisible aspects of a material entity by the Jungian approach, he also affirms it through the lens of process philosophy. With the paradigm of process philosophy, Wink redefines heaven not as a transcendent otherworldly place, but as a "home of the possible."[11] For him, heaven is not "out" there, but "within," that is, when a transformative possibility is accomplished, we experience the reality of heaven. In arguing so, Wink does not aim to advance a particular ontological position. Instead, he calls for the spiritual warfare to which the Christian church is called. Hence, he states that the war we are to fight is,

> . . . the unseen clash of values and ideologies, of the spirituality of institutions and the will of God, of demonic factionalism and heavenly possibilities. The unique calling of the church in social change lies in making clear the dual nature of our task. We wrestle on two planes, the earthly and the heavenly – what I have called the outer and inner aspects of reality.[12]

The second volume of the *Powers* trilogy, *Unmasking the Powers*, is a comprehensive exploration of seven words in the language of the Powers: Satan, demons, angels of churches, angels of nations, gods, elements of the universe, and angels of nature. In defining these words, Wink follows in the path of Rudolf Bultmann's demythologized approach, which is an attempt to interpret the *kerygma* (the message of God's decisive act in Christ) for the modern people by divesting the mythical forms to uncover the meaning of the Bible.[13]

---

i.e., archetypes include self, shadow, anima and animus, mandala, hero, god, sage, great mother, acolyte, the sun and moon, mother, father, son, daughter, and various animals," from Matsumoto, *Cambridge Dictionary of Psychology*, 50.

11. Wink, *Naming the Powers*, 129. A process philosopher named Alfred North Whitehead views religion fundamentally as a struggle to internalize over our external living. He says, "Life is an internal fact for its own sake, before it is an external fact relating itself to others . . . *Therefore*, Religion is the art and the theory of the internal life of man, so far as it depends on the man himself and on what is permanent in the nature of things," Whitehead, *Religion in the Making*, 15–16, emphasis added.

12. Wink, *Naming the Powers*, 130.

13. Rudolf Bultmann believed that the world picture of the New Testament is pre-scientific and a mythical world picture. For instance, the Bible's picture of the world as a three-story structure, with earth in the middle, heaven above it, and hell below it is, in fact, a myth. See Bultmann, *New Testament and Mythology*, 1.

As a modern western product, Wink discards the belief in the real existence of personal spirit-beings. Satan, for him, is not a metaphysical entity, but a function in the divine economy. Satan is a dialectical movement in God's purpose that becomes evil only when humanity breaks off the dialectic by refusing creative choice. In short, Satan can be seen to be a chameleon that can be either a servant of God or evil, depending on our choice. In application, Wink suggests that we are not to deny and repress our evil but to strive "to face our own evil . . . to release the energy formerly devoted to restraining it, and use it for the service of life."[14] However, Wink seems to admit to the mystery of evil by saying that there is a residue of evil that we cannot defeat, of which we can trust God alone to transform.[15]

In comprehending Satan, Wink's approach is similar to René Girard, a French cultural anthropologist, whose mimetic theory is the backdrop through which Wink expounds the sacrifice and death of Jesus. Girard also sees that "Satan is the name of the mimetic process seen as a whole; that is why he is the source not merely of rivalry and disorder but of all the forms of lying order inside which humanity lives. That is the reason why he was a homicide from the beginning; Satan's order had no origin other than murder and this murder is a lie."[16]

Regarding demons, Wink separates himself from the liberationist approach, which demonizes the structural evil of the system and overlooks the predicament of the personal psyche. However, he also does not support the view held by many Americans, who symbolize the demonic as individual developmental malfunctions. What is more, the "third wave" or the Pentecostal-Charismatic's view of demons as actual entities also does not satisfy him.[17] The term "third wave" refers to a movement that is similar to both the Pentecostal movement (the first wave) and the charismatic movement (the second wave). It is composed largely of evangelical Christians who, while applauding and supporting the work of the Holy Spirit in the first two waves, have chosen not to be identified with either. The desire of those in

---

14. Wink, *Unmasking the Powers*, 40.
15. Wink, 40.
16. Girard, *Girard Reader*, 161.
17. Wink, *Unmasking the Powers*, 41.

the movement is to experience the power of the Holy Spirit in healing the sick, casting out demons, receiving prophecies, and participating in other charismatic-type manifestations. This movement affirms the actual existence of spirit-beings.[18] For example, C. Peter Wagner, a key leader in the third wave movement, views "principalities and powers" as evil spiritual beings, which can manifest themselves through institutions, natural phenomena, manufactured items, or human beings. These spirit-beings can possess a human person, and when they do so, they can be exorcised only in and by the name of Jesus Christ who defeated all evil spirits and his arch-angel Satan.

To reconcile these approaches, Wink creates three types of demonic manifestations: outer personal possession, collective possession, and the inner personal demonic. If a person has outer personal possession, they are possessed by "something that is alien and extrinsic to the self."[19] For instance, the demon-possessed man in the story of the Gerasenes (Mark 5:1–20) bears the brunt of the collective demonism, thereby personally having "a collective malady afflicting an entire society,"[20] which is beyond personal restraints. Unlike outer personal possession, collective possession is the possession of groups or even nations by a god or demon that overpowers them to do whatever he or she wills.[21] Wink sees the baptism practiced in the early church as a form of exorcism because it "regarded *everyone* prior to baptism as possessed, by virtue of nothing more than belonging to a world in rebellion against God." Simply put, "the very essence of collective demonism is its explicit and avowed idolatry of the leaders,"[22] such as Adolf Hitler. For Wink, this possession is much subtler than others, because those who are possessed seldom know until it is too late. The inner personal possession is the struggle for integrity within ourselves which is not to be exorcised, but "to be owned, embraced,

---

18. Wagner, "Third Wave."
19. Wink, *Unmasking the Powers*, 43.
20. Wink, 50.
21. Wink, 43.
22. Wink, 51. As Wink unmasks the Powers language from the Jungian view, the notion of collective possession is basically adapted from Jung's collective shadow. For Jung, human psyche is not confined to individuals alone, but has a collective nature too. This collective psyche forms the "Zeitgeist" or spirit of the age. Nazi Germany is the best example to describe collective shadow (or possession for Wink). This possession or shadow can be seen in any mass movement, trend or gathering. A crowd at a football match forms a collective ego which casts a shadow or possession – uncontrolled hooliganism. See Hyde and McGuinness, *Jung for Beginners*, 90.

loved, and transformed as part of the struggle for wholeness."[23] By defining demonic possession in three ways, Wink intends that his proposal will help the readers to "identify the demonic as the psychic or spiritual power emanated by societies or institutions or individuals . . . whose energies are bent on overpowering others."[24]

By the angels of the churches, Wink refers to the actual invisible spirituality of a congregation.[25] Similarly, the angels of the nations also mean the real interiority of a social group or state.[26] Gods, in Wink's view, are structures that have mentality and communicability, through which personality and society are formed.[27] By the elements of the universe, Wink refers to basic principles or entities through which the whole is established and sustained. However, the problem arises when a single principle is elevated above the whole, as it invites the rebound of the whole against the part. For example, "when we seek to justify ourselves by performing the tenets of some religious law, we can only feel guilty for failing."[28] Lastly, Wink sees the angels of nature as the archetypal beauty of the physical world and the whole universe.[29] Overall, the entire volume of *Unmasking the Powers* is an exposition of all these powers in the light of the previous volume (*Naming the Powers*), wherein Wink argues that, "the Powers are simultaneously the outer and inner aspects of one and the same indivisible concretion of power."[30] Wink, through the angles of the Jungian psychoanalysis and process philosophy, presents that there is a spirituality of every institution in the world – church, nation, or social groups.[31]

To juxtapose the two volumes (*Naming the Powers* and *Unmasking the Powers*), the former lays a foundational premise for the argument, whereas

---

23. Wink, *Unmasking the Powers*, 52.
24. Wink, 68.
25. Wink, 69–86.
26. Wink, 87–107.
27. Wink, 108–127.
28. Wink, 151.
29. Wink, 153–171.
30. Wink, *Naming the Powers*, 107.
31. Wink used to emphasize this statement, "there is a spirituality of every institution in the world." In his last public interview, he appeared to be convinced of that as he mentioned, "no matter where it goes or how it gets there, there is a spiritual reality," see Holt, "Confronting the Powers," 32.

the latter affirms the substantiation of the premise through examples – using the premise and applying it in interpreting the Powers. If so, the conclusion of the premise would be the third volume, *Engaging the Powers*,[32] where Wink contends that nonviolence is the only means by which to bring the rebellious powers back to the original divine purpose. It is crucial to note that Wink attempted to convey his purpose to formulate a Christian social ethic through the study of the Powers language. Practically speaking, the first volume highlights that any Power can become idolatrous by placing itself above God's purpose for the good of the whole. If that happens, the onus is on the church to unmask this idolatry and bring the Powers back to their original divine purpose in the world.[33] In the second volume, Wink sheds light on the ways in which Powers can become idolatrous, rebellious, and astray from God's humanizing purposes, that is, serving the basic human need to be fulfilled.[34] In the third volume, Wink shows us *how* we can engage the Powers in order that they might be brought back to their original divine plan. We will now take a look at how we can engage the rebellious Powers.

In *Engaging the Powers*, Wink begins by introducing a worldview, which he calls "integral."[35] Wink sees worldviews as the very foundation of the house of our minds. His description is succinct, stating:

> On that foundation we erect the walls and roof, which are myths we live by, the symbolic understandings of our world. The furnishings – the stuff to sit on, lie down on, and eat with – are our

---

32. Wink, *Engaging the Powers*. This third volume of the Powers is the winner of three book-of-the-year awards: Pax Christi Award, 1993; Academy of Parish Clergy Book of the Year, 1993; and Midwest Book Achievement Award – Best Religious book, 1993. Further, Ted Grimsrud wrote "A Tribute to Walter Wink," where he acknowledges *Engaging the Powers* as a classic like Reinhold Niebuhr's *Moral Man and Immoral Society*, Martin Buber's *I and Thou*, and John H. Yoder's *The Politics of Jesus*. See Grimsrud, "Tribute to Walter Wink."

33. Wink, *Naming the Powers*, 5. See also McAlpine, *Facing the Powers*, 22.

34. Wink, *Powers That Be*, 34. According to Wink, this volume is "in large part a digest of the third volume of the trilogy on the Powers, *Engaging the Powers* with elements from the previous two volumes: *Naming the Powers* and *Unmasking the Powers*," Wink, *Powers that Be*, ix. Therefore, I will cite from *Powers That Be* sometimes, depending on the clarity of Wink's presentation, since these two books (*Engaging the Powers* and *The Powers That Be*) are overlapped.

35. Wink, *Engaging the Powers*. Wink, in his autobiographical reflections, describes that he has had great interest in worldview since he was a student at Southern Methodist University, Wink, *Just Jesus*, 52.

> theologies and personal philosophies. People notice the sofa and rugs (our theologies), they comment on the structure (the key myths), but few notice the foundation (our worldview). It is covered, hidden from view.[36]

There are, according to Wink, fundamentally five different worldviews: the ancient worldview, which sees everything earthly and heavenly as counterparts; the spiritualistic worldview, which values spirit over material; the materialistic worldview, which is the opposite of the spiritualistic worldview; the theological worldview, that looks at the spiritual world as noumenal; and lastly, an integral worldview, which sees everything as having an outer and an inner aspect.[37] For Wink, this worldview opens the way for us to perceive the actual spirituality or "withinness" at the centre of the political, economic, and cultural institutions of our time.[38] After introducing an integral worldview, Wink powerfully applies his interpretation of the Powers as inner and outer manifestations of the same indivisible concretion of power and an integral worldview in creating a strong Christian social ethic. By and large, Wink's social ethic can be categorized into three ways: the "domination system" (DS), "God's domination-free order" (DFO), and the "third way of Jesus."

2.1.1.1 *The Domination System*

Wink views the world as operating under the domination system (henceforth DS). For Wink, the DS is a system in which people stay within their own groups; a system where the poor become poorer and the rich, richer, or a vicious circle in which a person is enslaved. Regardless of doing their best with all their might, they are unable to escape from the system. This DS can be characterized as, "unjust economic relations, oppressive political relations, biased race relations, patriarchal gender relations, hierarchical power relations, and the use of violence to maintain them all."[39] How did the DS originate in the human world? Who or what caused it to exist? For Wink,

---

36. Wink, *Just Jesus*, 51.
37. Wink, *Engaging the Powers*, 4–6; *Powers That Be*, 15–20; *Just Jesus*, 87–89.
38. Wink, *Engaging the Powers*, 6. For Carl Jung, the spirituality or "withinness" is the collective unconscious, which means a realm of largely unexplored spiritual reality linking everyone to everything.
39. Wink, *Powers That Be*, 39.

the reason the DS came into existence is the Powers' rebellious derailment from the original divine purpose.

As noted above, God created the Powers for the welfare of humanity. However, they become demonic when they are derailed from their divine purpose. The derailment results in the DS. The "myth of redemptive violence"[40] is the spirit or soul of the DS. Wink contends that the DS has been deeply ingrained in human society throughout history. He unearths ancient Babylonian cosmogony and the myth of human creation, and puts this alongside children's comics and cartoons such as *Teenage Mutant Ninja Turtles, Superman, Superwoman, Captain America, Lone Ranger, Batman,* and so on, with the ideology of national security, which makes a nation what it is.[41]

The ancient Babylonian cosmogony found in a mythic structure of other Ancient Near Eastern cultures, alludes to the fact that humans are inherently and intrinsically evil and violent; hence, it is no wonder why the belief in the myth of redemptive violence overpowers the whole human race. This DS irresistibly besieges all human races, so that no single person or community is exempted from its presence.[42] Unlike the Babylonian myth, the Bible pictures a good God as the author of good creation. Neither evil nor violence is a part of creation, but they enter as the result of the actions of human beings.[43] Wink's attempt to picture the world as the DS helps us perceive the actual reality of the place in which we are living, whether we agree with his view or not. In a sense, Wink exposes the harsh reality of our world. The question before us is, "Should we pretend not to see it so, run away from it, or face its reality as it is?" Nevertheless, Wink shows that God does not leave humanity in a dead end; there is an alternative through which we can transform it into something.

---

40. The phrase "the myth of redemptive violence" is coined by Wink, referring to the belief that violence can be overcome by violence alone. In other words, it is a way of thinking and the belief that we can defeat violence through the use of violence alone.

41. Wink, *Powers That Be*, 43. One of the recent Marvel Comic characters is Captain America, a noble and honest superhero. The character was, in fact, created to help enhance the patriotic spirit of young Americans, thereby embodying the transcendent American ideals of liberty and justice, and becoming a unique symbol of the values underpinning the republic, See Weiner, *Captain America*, 9, 15.

42. Wink, *Engaging the Powers*, 13–31.

43. Wink, 14.

2.1.1.2 God's Domination-Free Order

Despite the fact that the world in which we live is cruel, Wink argues that there is an answer to the DS that Jesus envisioned and implemented. It is God's domination-free order (henceforth DFO), or in biblical vocabulary, the reign or kingdom of God, which is antithetical to the DS. This DFO is characterized by gender equality, power-sharing, economic equity, equality of race, nonviolent confrontation, inclusive God-images, interdependent relationships, and the like.[44] Nonviolence is the spirit or soul of the DFO. Jesus taught this, and demonstrated it in the way he lived.

In Wink's eyes, not only did Jesus envision the reign of God, he also demonstrated how it could be achieved through his willing submission to death. The death of Jesus has broken the spiral of violence. To support this view, Wink relies on a French anthropologist René Girard's theory of the "scapegoat mechanism,"[45] and reads the sacrificial system of the Israelites in the Old Testament in the light of this view. According to Girard, we imitate each other (mimesis) by desiring what others desire. This desire leads to mimetic rivalry when two or more people want the same thing at the same time.[46] The rivalry between two people tends to spread in a mimetic contagion to everyone in contact with it. The mimetic contagion affects each individual, and the unrest between them becomes a spiritual mimetic force. This is the mimetic crisis.[47] Finally, this rivalry causes the breakdown of the order of the social distinctions which Girard calls the "crisis of anti-differential" or "sacrificial crisis."[48] To prevent this breakdown, society has to find a scapegoat upon which all hatred, resentments, and violent impulses are heaped.[49] For Girard, real or symbolic, sacrifice is primarily a collective activity of the entire community, which purifies itself of its own disorder through the unanimous immolation of a victim.[50] When a ritual was done in this manner, a scapegoat practice

---

44. Wink, 46–47.
45. Wink, 145–146.
46. Wink, 145.
47. Johnston, "René Girard's Mimetic Theology," 29.
48. Girard, *Violence and Sacred*, 50, 52.
49. Wink, *Engaging the Powers*, 145–146.
50. Girard, *Girard Reader*, 10. In saying that, Girard does not mean that all rituals have the same implication in the same manner.

took place, "... the strange process through which two or more people are reconciled at the expense of a third party who appears guilty or responsible for whatever ails, disturbs, or frightens the scapegoaters. They feel relieved of their tensions and they coalesce into a more harmonious group."[51] Therefore, Girard sees the function of sacrifice as an action "to quell violence within the community and to prevent conflicts from erupting."[52]

Wink believes that the scapegoat mechanism or sacrificial system is the soul of the DS. But Jesus has exposed that mechanism and broken the spiral of violence through his death on the cross. What made the death of Jesus unique was neither his suffering nor persecution, but his willing submission unto death. Through this submission, Jesus exposed the judgment upon him as a total miscarriage of justice and a crime against God. In rejecting revenge and violence, Jesus broke the spiral of violence. So, in Wink's words, "God was working through violence to expose violence for what it is and to reveal the divine nature as nonviolent."[53] Thus Jesus became the last scapegoat so as to reconcile us, once and for all, to God.[54]

In short, through Jesus, the scapegoat mechanism, the heart of the DS is exposed, and the spiral of violence broken. So, the gospel of Jesus has the power to render the scapegoat mechanism impotent and unmask the behind-the-scenes work of the Powers. The church, as the body of Christ, is called to live out the true meaning of the gospel; namely to unmask the scapegoat mechanism and disarm the Powers.[55] Wink moves a step further than Girard regarding Jesus's sacrifice. That is, Jesus's willing submission to the powers that be, for Wink, is not just a way to expose the scapegoat mechanism of that time, but also a kind of resistance which Wink calls the "third way."[56]

---

51. Girard, 11.

52. Girard, *Violence and Sacred*, 14.

53. Girard, 85–86.

54. If Wink owes his treatment of the scapegoat mechanism to René Girard (a French philosophical anthropologist), he too owes his dealing with the violence of the Old Testament to Raymund Schwager (a Swiss Catholic theologian).

55. Atonement theory is such a crucial theological theme for all Christians – both for conservative evangelicals and those more liberal. Therefore, a comprehensive discussion on Wink's treatment of atonement is needed. Wink's view of atonement will be critically discussed in a later section of this chapter.

56. Wink, *Powers That Be*, 98–111.

2.1.1.3 Nonviolence or Jesus's Third Way: The Way to End the DS

Walter Wink believes that Jesus as the bringer of the kingdom of God or the DFO demonstrated its realistic vision through his teaching and example. He calls it Jesus's third way or nonviolent resistance, which is an exegetical exposition of Jesus's instruction in the Sermon on the Mount.

> You have heard that it was said, "An eye for an eye and a tooth for a tooth." But I say to you, do not resist the one who is evil. But if anyone slaps you on the right cheek, turn to him the other also. And if anyone would sue you and take your tunic, let him have your cloak as well. And if anyone forces you to go one mile, go with him two miles. Give to the one who begs from you, and do not refuse the one who would borrow from you (Matt 5:38–42 ESV).

For Wink, there are two standard responses to violence: flight or passivity and fight or violence. Jesus's way is not the first or the second, but the third way: nonviolent direct action. Violence, for Wink, can only encounter the advocates of a system, not its spirit; thus, it does not tackle the system deeply enough. Instead of violence, through nonviolence we can transform the Powers and bring them back to their divine purpose, which is the welfare of the human race. In other words, Jesus's third way alone can deal with both the outer, physical, visible aspects and the inner, spiritual, invisible dimensions of a particular social system.

Wink's reasons for nonviolence can be highlighted in seven points. First, through nonviolent loving, an enemy can be transformed into a friend. Second, nonviolence affirms that means and ends go hand in hand. Third, nonviolence demonstrates respect for the rule of law. Fourth, through nonviolence, we can overcome our own evil within us. Fifth, nonviolence is not legislation, but a gift and a method of discipleship. Sixth, nonviolence is Jesus's way of dealing with evil – it is the way of the cross. Seventh, nonviolence is not reserved only for Christians; its principles are relevant to other religions.[57] Wink's last point affirms the inclusive nature of nonviolence for

---

57. Wink, *Jesus and Nonviolence*, 57–93.

any religion as this research explores nonviolence from both Christian and Buddhist perspectives.

In listing these principles, Wink is aware of the risk of choosing a nonviolent response to violence. According to Wink, Jesus's third way is much tougher and more demanding than the flight or fight positions because it requires a person to be courageous and to dare to sacrifice even their own life. In addition, Wink affirms that the way to nonviolence is a lifelong journey, preparing oneself to be ready to encounter whatever sacrifice at any time. Thus, Wink redefines the theological term "rebirth," or being "born-again," as dying to what our socialization has spuriously produced in us.

The term "rebirth" or "being born-again" is one of the key theological themes in Christianity, especially among conservative evangelicals. For conservative evangelicals, rebirth is synonymous with regeneration. It is a change in a person's disposition: from the lawless, godless self-seeking that dominates, to a disposition of trust and love, marked by repentance for past rebelliousness and unbelief, and ready compliance with God's law.[58] According to this definition, rebirth is more concerned with a change in the inner attitude in relation to God, than with social conditions. In contrast, Wink's view of rebirth is more about the business of social conditioning, a horizontal relationship, rather than the vertical person-to-God relationship. This also means "abandoning our egocentricity not only as individuals, but as cultures, as nations, even as a species, and voluntarily subordinating our desires to the needs of the total life system."[59] With this radical commitment, Christians are called to live nonviolently. So, nonviolence becomes more than a method: it becomes a lifestyle. Nonviolence or the third way that Jesus taught and exemplified through his life is, therefore, neither a fight nor flight response. It is "a way by which evil can be opposed without being mirrored, the oppressor resisted without being emulated, and the enemy neutralised without being destroyed."[60]

In the last two chapters of *Engaging the Powers*, Wink articulates the way in which both prayers can sustain our inner life during the time of our engagement with the Powers. As traditionally understood, Wink does not see

---

58. Elwell, *Evangelical Dictionary of Theology*, s.v. "Regeneration."
59. Wink, *Powers That Be*, 95, 97.
60. Wink, *Engaging the Powers*, 189.

prayer like sending a letter to Heaven where God dwells; but through prayer, we are engaged in the act of co-creation with God. Having understood prayer in this way, Wink expands the scope of prayer by including the Powers, saying that prayer is not just a two-way transaction. Prayer involves not just God and people, but God and people and the Powers. The fallen Powers always hinder, block and thwart our prayers to God, like they did with Daniel (Dan 10:12).[61] But we are not to be dismayed, because God can raise up the leader like Cyrus who delivered the Jews from Babylon. So, we pray because we trust in God's miracle-working power. For Wink, he prays because he

> ... sees the demonic as arising within the institution itself, as it abandons its divine vocation for a selfish, lesser goal. Therefore I would not attempt to cast out the spirit of a city, for example, but, rather, to call on God to transform it, to recall it to its divine vocation. My spiritual conversation is with God, not the demonic.[62]

Finally, Wink discusses what should come next after the Powers fall as a result of nonviolent engagement.[63] Put differently, Wink sheds light on the necessity of what needs to follow in the process of reconciliation when liberation or revolution succeeds. He addresses the important questions, "How can the perpetrators and the perpetrated be reconciled? What are the essentials in the process of reconciliation?" Wink believes that the key to the process of reconciliation is forgiveness, without which no true reconciliation can come into fruition. However, he clarifies that reconciliation is the goal, whereas forgiveness is the means by which to achieve it. To illustrate, a victim can forgive their perpetrator who may be still alive or already dead. This kind of act is the attempt of a victim alone without the participation of the perpetrator. In contrast, reconciliation requires both parties – a victim and a perpetrator – to forgive and confess to each other and go forward into the common future together.[64] Though forgiveness plays a crucial role in the

---

61. Wink, 309–311; *Powers That Be*, 190.

62. Wink, *Powers That be*, 197.

63. Wink's Powers studies are commonly known as a trilogy. But after the third volume, Wink wrote a follow-up book (*When the Powers Fall: Reconciliation in the Healing of Nations*), so it could be called the fourth volume of the Powers.

64. Wink, *When the Powers Fall*, 13–15.

process of reconciliation, the steps (truth telling, apology and amnesty) to reach reconciliation vary from case to case.[65]

2.1.2 Why Wink?

As mentioned before, Walter Wink was an American scholar and activist, whose socio-political context is fundamentally different from the context in which this thesis is located. The question "Why do I then use Wink as a framework to formulate theological implications for Christians in Myanmar?" can be posed. There are five specific reasons why Wink is chosen among a high number of Christian and non-Christian theorists of nonviolence.

First, Wink's comprehensive framework for interpreting the biblical term kosmos (the world) as the Domination System is convincing and germane to the context of Myanmar, where the domineering attitude is rampantly ingrained in the fraught history of the nation. Hence, this naming of the world as the DS will be a key thought through which to scrutinize the historical root of power-hungry attitudes in the areas of political leadership and administration in Myanmar via the eyes of Wink.

Second, Wink's foremost accentuation of Jesus's teaching (i.e. loving enemies), decisively relates to Myanmar where Buddhism is claimed as the state religion. What is more, his thought-provoking question "how can we find God in our enemies?"[66] is, to the Myanmar context, challenging as well as inspiring to all who struggle to surmount domination without creating new forms of domination. Since love (*mettā*) plays a vital role for all Buddhists, Wink's exposition of love would apply to the Myanmar context where Buddhism is deeply entrenched in various sectors of society. Thus, through the conscientious study of love (for Buddhists, *mettā*), this research will bring out a common ground upon which both Christian and Buddhist activists can stand together to fight for the domination-free order (to borrow Wink's term).

The third reason why Wink is chosen is the way he expounds the nature of the Powers. To put it in order: the Powers are good because God has created them to serve the humanizing purposes of God; the Powers are fallen because they serve their own interests rather than God's; and the Powers will be

---

65. Wink, 21, 33–35.
66. Wink, *Engaging the Powers*, 263.

redeemed because what fell can be redeemed in time.[67] Wink sees this schema as both temporal and simultaneous, in sequence and all at once. It is temporal because it is time-bound. It is simultaneous because the redemption of the Powers cannot be done once and for all due to their fallenness. Wink further explains that God's liberation is for both human beings bound by the Powers and the Powers themselves. Therefore, the undertaking of redemption goes beyond the change in the individual; it reaches the fallen institutions. In other words, liberation is social as well as personal. This theological framework can be a foundation for assessing the socio-cultural structure of Myanmar, in which liberation is mostly considered as personal among Christians and non-Christians alike.

Fourth, Christians in Myanmar, by and large, view the Powers as actual spirit-beings, and regarding them as structural is hardly ever heard in preaching and teaching in churches or Christian gatherings. To be specific, Ephesians 6:12 is usually interpreted as spiritual warfare and we Christians are called to it. In the warfare, the enemies we are fighting are not human with blood and flesh, but actual spirit-beings, which cannot be seen or touched, but their presence and power is real. Further, people in Myanmar are culturally person-focused and much less structure-oriented than the Western people. People do not care much about what organization or institutional structures (policies, rules and regulations, bylaws, and offices) are, but show more interest in who is the chief authority of the organization. Therefore, Wink's structural reading of the Powers language is very peculiar for his interpretation. The hypothesis is that examining the political context of Myanmar through the lens of Wink will expose the politics of Myanmar in a way that has never been done before.

Finally, this study is a Christian approach to nonviolence using a Christian theologian, even though the location in which this study situates is predominantly Buddhist. It is not unusual to use a Christian approach to expand its applicability to another context. Wink, as a Christian scholar, exegetes a biblical passage (Matt 5:38–42) to interpret and speak to the world both in affirmative and critical ways. Despite the contextual difference, the faith that Wink practiced is still the same that Christians in Myanmar share; therefore,

---

67. Wink, *Powers That Be*, 32.

it is assumed that Wink's ethical understanding of nonviolence must have something to speak to the context of this study.

2.2 Wink in Dialogue with Others: Toward a Constructive Frame

Bringing Wink's theology of nonviolence into dialogue with other scholars will enable us to discern which parts of Wink's view of nonviolence need to be affirmed, and which are to be integrated or reformulated. Wink's contribution to social ethics through his interpretation of the biblical language of the Powers is extremely valuable. For example, Robert Ewusie Moses's *Practices of Power*, the most recent work on the Powers language, says, "every work that addresses the biblical concept of powers must grapple with Wink's provocative thesis."[68] Of course, there are also some critical points to be made as there are commendable arguments Wink brings to the table. What follows in the discussion is, "What positive and negative comments do other scholars render Wink?" Likewise, "what can Wink offer in response to them?" More specifically, we will see the valuable thoughts of his ethical understanding of nonviolence through interacting with scholars who both agree and disagree with him. Following that, some critical points that he raises will be discussed, with the intention of constructing a frame for the study of politics in Myanmar.

2.2.1 The Powers as the Basis of a Christian Social Ethic

Wink formulates an ethical theory on the basis of the Powers language. How can this approach be justified? Or does this approach do justice to the biblical and ethical studies? How do other scholars respond to this approach? In general, some scholars have appreciatively argued for Wink's view, while others have not. First, we will highlight some scholars' appreciative arguments for Wink's interpretation. A great deal of recognition is given to Wink for his discovery of the spiritual aspect of an institution, which he calls its "withinness" or "interiority." For instance, Stephen Noll considers Wink's *Powers* trilogy as a rediscovery of "the spiritual inside of the generic order of the

---

68. Ewusie Moses, *Practices of Powers*, 34.

elements of the world."⁶⁹ Similarly, Nancey Murphy comments that Wink's discerning eye that distinguishes the spiritual from the material element, is unique in our individualistic culture. This reawakening of the awareness of the spiritual dimension helps us to be aware of the aspect of social entities which transcends the individuals involved in them.⁷⁰ For Robert E. Moses, Wink is right to be commended for challenging our modern obsession with materiality.⁷¹ Truly, it is untenable for people to believe in unseen spiritual things as the world is secularized. The word "secularization" describes the best way to talk about discarding the belief in unseen or spiritual things. In short, belief in the spiritual or unseen world is archaic and left in the premodern period. The idea of secularization is defined as "the process in modern societies whereby religious ideas, practice and organization lose their influence in the fact of scientific and other knowledge."⁷² Unseen things and scientifically unverified values are discarded in favour of scientifically tested facts.

Thus, Wink's rediscovery of the importance of the invisible and spiritual dimension of an institution when applied to the area of social institutions will be a paradigm through which to seek the socio-political context of Myanmar where the Powers are visibly and invisibly, physically and spiritually dominant.⁷³ How does Wink's interpretation of the Powers as simultaneously the outer and inner manifestations of an institution do justice to the area of the New Testament and theological studies? What specific critiques can we give him?

2.2.1.1 Hermeneutical-Methodological Critiques

As mentioned, Wink's *Powers* trilogy has had a significant impact on many Christian social ethicists. However, some critics fundamentally disagree with his interpretation of the Powers in terms of exegetical, hermeneutical and theological approaches. First, these critics point out that Wink lets his

---

69. Noll, "Thinking about Angels,", 25. See also Noll, *Angels of Light*, 25.
70. Murphy, "Social Science, Ethics," 32–33.
71. Ewusie Moses, *Practices of Powers*, 34.
72. Allan, "Secularization," 668.
73. In an interview with Wink, perhaps the last one before his death, Steve Holt introduces Wink's Powers trilogy as the work that unpacks the spiritual significance of political and societal institutions (the biblical "principalities and powers") and their role in systematic injustice, Holt "Confronting the Powers," 30.

worldview be his exegetical base to interpret the Powers language, not the text itself. Chloe Lynch indicates, "Wink's worldview is more inviolable to him than the Scripture."[74] In his dissertation, Landon Matthew Coleman also observes that, "For the most part Wink mocks the ancient worldview and its interpretation of the principalities and powers.... On the other hand, he tries to redefine and re-word the ancient worldview itself so that it supports his proposals."[75] From an African perspective, Kabiro wa Gatumu suggests that Wink's structuralist reading leaves us with numerous questions about whether it is logical to equate supernatural powers with the structures of human existence and the inner spirituality of an institution, and whether it is also reasonable to regard the "principalities and powers" as the inner and spiritual essence or gestalt of an institution or state.[76] Thus, the prime critique against Wink is the dominance of his worldview in interpreting the Powers language.

Another critical comment is that Wink commits a methodological error, "an illegitimate totality transfer."[77] According to this critique, Wink, after his studies of all the Powers-related terminology in *Naming the Powers*, concludes, "Unless the context specifies . . . we are to take the terms for power in their most comprehensive sense."[78] Thus, his conclusion is generalizing all Powers-related terms as imprecise, liquid, and interchangeable, therefore, they should be comprehensively understood. Upon this, Arnold critiques, "Because one term may have five different applications, it does not mean that all five applications may be used simultaneously."[79]

The third error that Wink commits according to his critics is personal belief. It is Wink's unbelief in the existence of personal spirit-beings that disappoints conservative scholars who presume the biblical or ancient worldview to be real, or who believe in the actual existence of spiritual entities. In his

---

74. Lynch, "How Convincing is Walter," 264.

75. Coleman, "Principalities and Powers," 100–101.

76. Kabiro wa Gatumu, *Pauline Concept*, 184.

77. D. A. Carson defines this error: "The fallacy in this instance lies in the supposition that the meaning of a word in a specific context is much broader than the context itself allows and may bring with it the word's entire semantic range." Carson, *Exegetical Fallacies*, 61.

78. Wink, *Naming the Powers*, 100.

79. Arnold, *Ephesians, Power and Magic*, 200.

observation about Wink's *Powers* trilogy, Gailyn Van Rheenen also wonders, "Why these Western theologians were forced to find a new paradigm for interpreting spiritual powers in the Bible? Could they not have interpreted the passages literally as personal spiritual beings?"[80] Arnold also indicates that Wink's argument would be reasonable merely for unbelievers of the existence of personal spiritual beings; however, for someone like him who believes in their existence, it is "unnecessary and even erroneous."[81] In short, the abovementioned critics are concerned with his worldview assumptions, his exegetical and methodological errors, and his unbelief in the existence of spiritual entities.

My disagreement with Wink's interpretation of the Powers particularly concerns his total disregard for the writers of the New Testament who viewed the powers as spiritual entities with intellect and will, whose actions affect human life on earth.[82] To use a personal illustration, I was brought up in Myanmar where belief in supernatural entities is common. For me, no logical or reasonable argument is necessary to affirm the actual existence of spirit-beings. For missionaries, pastors, and any sort of Christian ministers in remote parts of Myanmar, no affirmation or approval of the existence of spiritual entities is needed; their actual realities seem so obvious. In many villages of Myanmar, the witch doctor or sorcerer is still more authoritative than the village or town sheriff or headperson. The villagers are more prone to follow whatever the sorcerer asks them to do than what the sheriff or village-head does. Despite my personal belief of the Powers as personal, this research focuses on the interpretation of the Powers as structural in the context of Myanmar. Actually, the majority of Christians in Myanmar regard the Powers as spirit-beings. What they fail to look at is the structural dimension of the Powers. Therefore, this study asserts that reading the Powers as structural would help us comprehend the politics of Myanmar in a different way.

True, Wink admits his unbelief in the actual existence of spirit-beings. But this bias leads him too far that he fails to find another explanation for those Powers. Instead, he equates demons and evil spirits with Carl Jung's "psychic

---

80. Gailyn Van Rheenen, "Modern and Postmodern Syncretism," 180.
81. Arnold, *Powers of Darkness*, 199.
82. See also Ewusie Moses, *Practices of Power*, 34.

or spiritual power emanated by organisations or individuals."[83] His bias or unbelief in the actual existence of evil spirits compels him to be constrained to find another explanation.[84]

Moreover, Wink's mythical reading of human fallenness and the Powers language (demons, angels, gods, and evil spirits) has looked daringly modern that he seems forgetful to engage the ancient thought-form of viewing powers as personal spirit-beings. This imbalance between premodern and modern worldviews finally leads him to not just hermeneutical, but also theological flaws.[85] His hermeneutical and theological presuppositions are rampant in interpreting and formulating the theory of nonviolence throughout the *Powers* trilogy. Could he not interpret those Powers as he does now without discarding completely the actual existence of spirit-beings?

If Wink's theology of the Powers has such exegetical and methodical flaws, why does this study still use him as a lens to look at the politics of Myanmar? There are some reasons why this study adopts Wink's *Powers* trilogy. First, it is important to acknowledge that there is a wide range of sources upon which Christian ethicists establish their ethical exploration and arguments. In general, there are different sources or bases of Christian ethics through which ethicists argue, establish, formulate ethical frames and deal with the moral issues Christians are facing. The sources are, by and large, the Bible, Christian tradition, Christian experience, and reason or natural law. For the Bible-based ethicists, they appeal to the Scripture in reflecting how Christians should live, though there is no consensus on how it should be done since many passages in the Bible can be interpreted in more than one way.[86] For Christian tradition-based ethicists, what matters in Christian thought and practice is how the present church remains faithful to the original witness of the apostles.[87] Third, appeals to Christian experience which has a variety of forms, but essentially Christian life is regarded as existential commitment; that is, an individual Christian is moral, not simply because of acting morally,

---

83. Wink, *Naming the Powers*, 104.
84. See also Arnold, *Powers of Darkness*, 198.
85. O'Brien, *Letter to the Ephesians*, 469.
86. Spohn, "Scripture," 93; Gill, *Textbook of Christian Ethics*, 8.
87. Turner, "Tradition in the Church," 130.

but also because of intending to act morally.[88] The last group, reason-centred ethicists, believe the importance of Scripture, but they place more stress on the inherent *logos* of the natural world.[89]

According to this category of Christian ethical bases, Wink falls under the domain of the Bible as the source for Christian ethics. As noted, even among the Bible-based ethicists, there is a wide variety of different approaches and theories for interpreting the Bible.[90] Wink's approach to interpreting the Powers is evidently not a conservative approach, because he scraps the biblical-ancient worldview for its extraneousness to the modern context. As a biblical scholar, Wink has his own approach to interpreting the Scriptures, which he developed long before his *Powers* trilogy. This book is *The Bible in Human Transformation*, published in 1973.[91] There, Wink proposes a paradigm shift in the way we study the Bible – a turn from biblical criticism to being subservient to human transformation.[92]

In short, Wink's hermeneutics engages what the reader has with what the text says. Interpretation, for him, is not "a question of accepting or rejecting what is said in the text, but of self and social exploration in terms of the question which the text, possibly even in an inadequate or antiquated way,

---

88. Gill, *Textbook of Christian Ethics*, 12.

89. Pope, "Reason and Natural law," 148.

90. Robin Gill states the seven problems for using the Bible in doing Christian ethics. First, a particular passage can be interpreted in more than one way. For example, Augustine varied in his interpretation of Genesis 3, differing from his earlier allegorical interpretations to literalistic ones. Second, there are different voices on the authority of the Bible, posing questions such as "is the Bible infallible?" Third, "it is difficult to treat all parts of the Bible with equal seriousness and attention and not to be biblically selective." Fourth, there is a dispute regarding tensions between Old Testament and New Testament moral precepts. Fifth, should the words and actions of Jesus be given precedence over others? Sixth, how far can the teaching of Paul be reconciled with what can be known about the teaching of Jesus? Seventh, is the Bible still relevant to deal with a number of the most crucial present-day moral dilemmas, such as issues in the areas of technology, biotechnology, genetics and medicine? See Gill, *Textbook of Christian Ethics*, 8–10.

91. Wink, *Bible in Human Transformation*. Here Wink proposes a new paradigm, which he calls a dialectical paradigm. He is highly critical of the historical-critical method that scholars used at that time. For him, it dichotomizes between the subject and object, thereby becoming reductionist in approaching the text of the Bible.

92. Wink gives five reasons why he is dissatisfied with biblical criticism or the historical-critical method, see *Bible in Human Transformation*, 2–15. He states that his intention for the book is to enhance a mode of Bible study which facilitates transformation in human lives, Wink, iv. See also Thornton, "Book Review: Naming the Powers," 121.

has nevertheless been indispensable in helping us to recover."[93] In *Naming the Powers*, Wink follows the same hermeneutical approach, and makes it clear that his intention is not to remove the mythic dimension, but "rather juxtapose the ancient myth with the emerging postmodern (mythic) worldview and asking how they might mutually illuminate each other."[94] In fact, Wink is consistent in using a method he proposes in *The Bible in Human Transformation* for interpreting the scriptural passages in his later works. For example, in *Cracking the Gnostic Code: The Powers in Gnosticism*, Wink suggests that "ancient mythical language can and should be read, in the light of modern depth psychology, as a description of the interior dimensions of personal and social life."[95]

As examined, we have seen that Christian ethicists have diverse approaches in interpreting the Bible, despite using the same Bible as the source for Christian ethics. Wink has his own hermeneutical method in interpreting the Bible for ethical explorations; hence, it is unfair to consider his approach as faulty by another scholar's method alone. What is more, we have noted that Wink is consistent in the way he treats the scriptural passages throughout his writings in the same method he proposes. Wink's primary concern with hermeneutics is not about exploring objectivistic or historical reality but discovering an interface between what the text says and what the reader has in mind. In short, Wink's approach and interpretation of the Powers language is safe and reasonably valid within his own interpretive framework.[96] On top of that, the main focus of attention in this research is not on his hermeneutical approach to the Powers language, but on the social ethic that he advances.

---

93. Wink, *Bible in Human Transformation*, 67. He exemplifies this method in the book, *Transforming Bible Study*, where he practically applies the hermeneutical principle he proposes in *The Bible in Human Transformation*. To conduct a Bible study group, what is needed is a selected text and a group of people among whom some are biblically knowledgeable while others are not. No one in the group has a monopoly on discussion because it is the intersection of text with experience that evokes insights, no one need feel disadvantaged, see Wink, *Transforming Bible Study*, 37–38,

94. Wink, *Naming the Powers*, 104.

95. Wink, *Cracking the Gnostic Code*. Attridge, "Cracking the Gnostic Code," 267, review of the book.

96. Truly, Wink's interpretative frame can be criticized in numerous ways. But this part does not necessarily relate to the key component of this research.

Therefore, his hermeneutic may be disputable, but a social ethic that he offers is, as described above, applicable to the political context of Myanmar.

Despite the criticism given, Wink's interpretation of the Powers can still be justified by indicating two points. First, Wink's *Powers* trilogy was developed to formulate a Christian social ethic. He admits that reading William Stringfellow's *Free in Obedience* planted seeds in his mind of the possibility of constructing social ethics on the basis of the Powers.[97] The implication is that Wink did study the Powers language with the aim of creating a social ethic. In addition, the stimulus for Wink in articulating his notion of the Powers was his personal encounters with military dictatorships in Latin America, where he experienced human rights violations and oppression under military dictatorships.[98] Those experiences eventually led him to do an exegetical study of the Powers language. With the help of Stringfellow and his experiences in those South American countries, Wink launched his study of the Powers language in order to construct a social ethic. It is clear that his chief aim was to search for a social ethic rather than to seek the literal and historical meaning of the Powers vocabulary.

Second, in spite of his disbelief in the personal aspect of the Powers, Wink argues that they have a spiritual dimension. In order to maintain both structuralist and spiritualistic readings, Wink creates an "integral worldview." Put differently, as a shrewd scholar, Wink attempts to be a go-between for the ancient worldview and the postmodern. Despite this, Wink's integral worldview is not a new idea for the Asians. For instance, a Chinese way of thinking, known as the yin/yang figure, has infused the thinking of other Asians, such as Korean, Japanese, Burmese, and so on.[99] So, it is not an integral worldview itself that is insightful, but his implication of it in the area of

---

97. Wink, *Naming the Powers*, xi; Walter Wink, *Powers That Be*, 203. Stringfellow, though he was not a so-called academic theologian, caught Karl Barth's attention, a giant of theology in the twentieth century, during Barth's visit to the United States in 1962. Stimulated by Stringfellow's questions on the panel, Barth turned to the audience and said, "You should listen to this man!" See Wylie Kellermann, *Keeper of the Word*, 1.

98. In a four-month sabbatical in 1982, Wink and his wife, June, visited Argentina, Brazil, Bolivia, Peru, Costa Rica, Nicaragua, and spent most of their time in Chile. Wink started seeing those who were suffering from human rights violations and hunger under military dictatorships in those countries.

99. Yin/yang is a concept of describing the interdependent nature of quasi-opposite forces such as male and female, light and darkness, high and low, hot and cold, water and fire, life and

socio-political realities. For Asians, the "principalities and powers," needless to say, are considered to be supernatural beings that independently exist and interfere in human affairs. What they fail to do is to see the connection between these supernatural powers and institutions through the lens of yin/yang. The consequence is disintegration between them. In contrast, Wink's view is an enlightening thought, recognizing the spiritual and invisible dimension of an institution. Through Wink's eyes, the missing connection between the Powers and institutions can be bridged. Wink's argument for an intrinsic relationship between spiritual and physical is a lens for this research to look at the political context of Myanmar.

2.2.1.2 Theological-Philosophical Critiques

Wink is also criticized for his modern liberal theological positions, which, for some theologians, divert away from historic Christianity. The first is his view of God, angels, Satan, and heaven, which he adapted from process philosophy. Process theology has a view of God, which is similar to "panentheism," differing from theism and pantheism.[100] Panentheism is slightly different from pantheism. That is, God is in everything, he is present in all the world, but not limited by the world. Charles Hartshorne is often quoted to define the idea of God in process theism,

> The two "poles" or aspects of God are the abstract essence of God, on the one hand, and God's concrete actuality on the other. The abstract essence is eternal, absolute, independent, unchangeable . . . The concrete actuality is temporary, relative, dependent, and constantly changing . . . Hence, God's concrete knowledge is dependent upon the decisions made by the worldly actualities.[101]

In "panentheism," God's imminence or "withinness" in our world is given precedence over his transcendence. Stephen Noll indicates Wink's failure in

---

death. This view does not see these realities as opposites, but as complementary to each other. For example, there cannot be the bottom of the foot without the top.

100. Theism is mostly defined as the belief that God who is one infinite, all-powerful, all-knowing, completely good, exists and has created the universe, Evans, *Pocket Dictionary of Apologetics*, 114. Pantheism means all is God.

101. Cobb, and Griffin, *Process Theology*, 47.

providing for the transcendent role of angels, especially the holy angels. What is more, Noll continues to say, "Given Wink's world picture, this is not surprising: just as the angels are 'within' the world, so God also is wholly within the world (panentheism)."[102] In addition, Wink's attempt to view heaven as the metaphor of "withinness" or inwardness instead of otherworldly or "above" is liable to make a theological error. For this, Lawrence Osborn specifies that "treating heaven as the soul of the earth is a significant step towards the divinisation of the cosmos."[103]

In treating heaven, angels, and demons as metaphorical images, Wink, in one way or another, might be called as an advocate of the "emergent or emerging Christian movement,"[104] the movement that attempts to radically redefine the key concepts of Christianity, such as God, Jesus, heaven, hell, angels and demons, and so on. For example, a widely known emergent leader Rob Bell, in his book *Love Wins*, defines the concepts of God and heaven in three ways by looking at what Jesus means by heaven: first, "heaven is sometimes synonymous with the name God; second, the future when heaven and earth are coming together; third, heaven as present, *eternal, intense, real experiences of joy, peace, and love in this life*, with an emphasis on the third definition of heaven, and saying heaven is a present reality."[105] Somewhat similarly, the emerging movement endeavours to find the relevance of Christianity in the

---

102. Noll, "Thinking about Angels," 25. Panentheism is the view that God is in the universe, yet he is beyond it. There is a slight difference to pantheism, for which, God and the universe are strictly identical. But in panentheism, the universe does not exhaust God; however, it is part of the reality of God. It is true that Wink demonstrates that his integral worldview is in a way an implication of panentheism. The implication is "every creature is potential revealers of God." See Wink, *Powers That Be*, 20.

103. Osborn, "Angels," 44.

104. Here it is used as "emergent or emerging" inclusively because some see these two differently, but others don't. This movement is the most recent and growing Christian movement in the West, especially in the USA. This movement is also known as a form of postmodern Christianity. Robert E. Webber introduces a Christian movement led mostly by younger Christian generations in his book *The Younger Evangelicals* (2002). He is very optimistic about the future of Christianity that these leaders are bringing in. For Webber, these younger evangelicals are committed to witnessing the gospel which is biblically and historically rooted, and culturally connected in the twenty-first century, see Webber, *Younger Evangelicals*, 16–17. As a critic says, the weakness of Webber's book is its lack of systematic research. It is more a compilation of observations from a sympathetic observer than the results of an academic analysis, see Labanow, *Evangelicalism*, 4.

105. Bell, *Love Wins*, 58–59.

context of post-Christendom. In an introduction to the book *The Church in Emerging Culture*, Leonard Sweet presents that a classic work of Richard Niebuhr, *Christ and Culture*, itself has no relevancy in talking about the context of this time since it speaks in the modern context with an either-or or dichotomous mentality.[106] Wink expressed once that he wished he would get involved in a leading role for the movement.[107] In short, Wink is seen to some as moving away from an historic Christian teaching, which is fundamentally based on a particular interpretation.

More than that, Wink's theological enterprise throughout his life is apparently liberalistic with humanistic emphasis. His two books, *The Human Being: Jesus and the Enigma of the Son of the Man* and *Just Jesus: My Struggle to Become Human*, show the theological orientation that he had been pursuing in his life. It seems that whether Jesus is divine is not his concern. In *The Human Being*, Wink explores Jesus's life through a combination of the methods of historical-critical analysis and Jungian psychology with the intention of evoking Jesus as the archetype of the truly human.[108] Jesus, for him, was the perfect archetype of what it means to be fully human, thereby reminding us to embody what Jesus embodied.

Hence, he makes it clear that his understanding of Jesus's incarnation is different from the classic doctrine of the incarnation. Since his approach is "Christology from below," and he believes that the divinized Christ hinders human transformation. The major aim of the study is a theological precursor to the social ethics that he tries to formulate later. However, his Jungian approach in his Christology from below seems too strong, because he even suggests that Jesus himself was a Jungian.[109]

The second book, *Just Jesus* is a collection of Wink's autobiographical memoirs, from childhood to his death, where he honestly expresses his struggle to become truly human like Jesus who is, though not the best, but

---

106. Sweet, *Church in Emerging Culture*, 16–17.

107. Holt, "Confronting the Powers," 33.

108. Kelli S. O'Brien points out that Wink's historical-critical analysis is the least satisfactory, O'Brien, "Book Review: *The Human Being*," 455.

109. In the next chapter, we will see how this "Christology from below" leads him to argue for the *Christus Victor* theory of atonement at the cost of other theories.

his best.[110] His personal experiences are wide-ranging: growing under a strict disciplinary father and intellectual mother, a Pentecostal conversion, personal involvement in the Selma march, work with the Guild for Psychological Studies, Buddhist meditation, complicated relationship with academia, and so on.[111] Wink's concern is about Jesus's humanness, which inspires and motivates him to follow, as it is described that the whole book is his attempt to humanize Jesus.[112] In this regard, Wink's theology is fundamentally humanistic in its nature and socio-political in its focus. Featuring Jesus as merely human enables Wink to justify that whatever Jesus taught and lived out can be applicable to anyone. Similarly, dismissing the historic doctrine of Jesus's divinity helps Wink to include other non-Christian communities in such a way that Jesus is, like us, a mere man; thus, we all, regardless of religious differences, can join and resist the DS nonviolently.

Further, Wink critiques liberation theologians, suggesting that they are reductionists because they, in his view, regard the Powers as just institutions and systems, thereby dismissing their spiritual dimension.[113] However, Wink also becomes a reductionist by disposing of the transcendent and ontological aspects of heaven, God, angels and demons. When the transcendent nature of heaven, angels, demons and spirit world is made redundant from the discussion, what is left is nothing but the this-worldly sphere where humans are all held responsible for the existence of the DS.

Despite such theological presuppositions of liberal theology, this study takes Wink's *Powers* trilogy as a frame to look at the politics of Myanmar not because his liberal humanistic position is all convincing. This study, as described, indicates many disagreements with Wink's views on God in a panentheistic manner, angels, demons, his single-dimensional interpretation of Jesus Christ, and his purely mythical view of the Powers.[114] Wink's theory of the Powers, simply put, theologically raises many questions regarding

---

110. Wink, *Just Jesus*, 127.

111. In the '70s, Wink was denied tenure and academically shunned after publishing a book with the opening line: "Historical Biblical criticism is bankrupt," see Wylie-Kellermann, "Struggling to Become Human," 39.

112. Wink, *Just Jesus*, 15.

113. Wink, *Naming the Powers*.

114. In the following chapter, we will also see a discussion of Wink's understanding of atonement in detail.

hermeneutics, methodology, philosophy, and theology. However, Wink's structural interpretation is distinct from other structural interpretations in that he, as Arnold articulates, "Endeavours to probe more deeply into the meaning of the spiritual and reaches the conclusion that principalities and powers are 'the inner and outer' aspects of any given manifestation of power."[115]

The fundamental frame of his social ethics that this work espouses for engaging the political context of Myanmar is Wink's naming the world as the domination system, interpreting Jesus's teaching of "turning the other cheek" as the third way (nonviolence), and more persuasively, his ardent argument for nonviolence as the only path to transform the DS into the God's domination-free order. But, the most thought-provoking question that Arnold and Lynch pose at the end of their critiques of Wink's *Powers* is, "Can the Powers language be the fundamental basis for developing a Christian ethic?"[116] Truly it is the question that Wink should pay attention to, but as he is no longer living, he leaves us to deal with it. If the Powers are considered as "structures" like Wink and others suggest, there must be several implications for social ethics. Even if they are viewed as actual spirit-beings, like Arnold and Lynch suggest, those powers still have an influence on the structures.[117] For the former group, a Christian social ethic can possibly be built upon the study of the Powers language since the Powers are considered structural aspects; whereas for the latter, it is more complicated than the former group to say that the Powers can affect human institutions. For instance, Arnold describes two counter-statements: the Powers do their best to influence the structures, and at the same time, evil still resides in the structures only insofar as the people involved are evil.[118] If so, the onus of distinguishing between the evil affected by the demonic and the evil shaped by people is on him. Therefore, if the Powers are regarded as structural aspects, a study of social ethics can be constructed.

---

115. Arnold, *Powers of Darkness*, 198.
116. Arnold, 201; Lynch, "How Convincing is Walter," 266.
117. Arnold, *Powers of Darkness*, 204, 208–209.
118. Arnold, 204.

2.2.2 The Powers and the Domination System

Wink sees the radical plight of the human race as the domination system, which emerged because of the Powers' failings away from their divine vocation. How does Wink underpin the idea of the DS through biblical exploration? How does he compare the DS to other areas? And finally, how does he unmask the realities of the DS in the present world? Following that, a critical comment on Wink's structuralist reading of the Scriptures will be discussed. Duane A. Garrett observes that Wink is good at modifying the New Testament words to reflect appropriately his understanding of the gospel.[119] For instance, Wink uses a biblical word *kosmos* (world) to identify and intensify the idea of the DS. Through the words *kosmos* and *aiōn* (age), Wink affirms how humanity is both systemically and temporarily under the DS. By the word *sarx* (flesh), Wink also indicates the overriding values of the DS upon the human race. However, L. M. Coleman argues that Wink's replacement of John's references to *kosmos* and Paul's reference to *aiōn* with the DS is "flawed because he failed to justify the replacement."[120] In fact, Wink's argument for employing these terms is to highlight how the DS transcendently overpowers humanity, thereby showing that true liberation cannot emerge from the system itself, but only from something that transcends it.[121] Truly, the word *kosmos* describes evil in the New Testament, referring to the order of society and indicates that evil has a social and political character beyond the isolated actions of individuals.[122]

Not only does the DS echo the biblical concept of *kosmos*, it also epitomizes the characters of our contemporary world. As Ted Grimsrud observes, Wink's coinage of the term the DS "helps us understand our present context."[123] Hence, Wink's idea of the DS is matched against even secular thinkers and ethicists. Various social ethicists name what they feel is the most fundamental human plight, which affects all aspects of human life. Wink's DS can be illustrated with the ideas of two non-Christian thinkers, Gene Sharp and Michael Foucault. Gene Sharp observes that the four fundamental social illnesses

---

119. Garrett, *Angels*, 211.
120. Coleman, "Principalities and Powers," 94.
121. Satterwhite, "Christian Peace Maker," 227.
122. Mott, *Biblical Ethics*, 4.
123. Ted Grimsrud, "Introduction: Engaging Walter Wink," 5.

are dictatorship, genocide, war, and social oppression.[124] For Foucault, it is historical conditioning in which humanity, both individually and collectively, has been socialized. Sharp, as a political scientist, sees that it is the political power through which those illnesses, supposing the DS in Wink's term, can be cured. By political power, Sharp refers to "the totality of means, influences, and pressures – including authority, rewards, and sanctions – available for use to achieve the objectives of the power-holder, especially the institutions of government, the State, and groups opposing either of them."[125] For Sharp, the places in which power is located varies from society to society and from situation to situation – the places such as social groups and institutions such as families, social classes, religious groups, cultural and nationality groups, occupational groups, economic groups, villages, towns, cities, provinces and regions, and so on. Therefore, *loci* of power set limits to the ruler's power capacity. If power is mainly situated in governmental institutions, it would be very hard for the society to control the ruler. Hence, Sharp stresses the importance of strengthening *loci* of power in non-governmental institutions. Through the example of the French Revolution, he argues that effective *loci* of power can impose limits and controls over a ruler's power, but when they are weak, absent, or destroyed, the ruler's power will be uncontrolled.[126] In Wink's term, the power of the DS would always be mounting up as long as we respond to it in the first way (flight) or the second way (fight). As long as we fail to find an alternative or third way to engage the Powers, the DS will always be uncontrollable.

It might be too narrow to describe Foucault as a kind of historical determinist because Foucault never regarded himself to be so, as some of his opponents did. He firmly believed in human freedom. For him, the way in which individuals in their struggles, *can* freely constitute themselves as subjects of their practices or, on the contrary, reject the practices in which they are expected to participate. This indicates Foucault's strong proposal that there is always a way to escape from historical determinism or conditioning.[127]

---

124. Sharp, *Social Power*, 3.
125. Sharp, 27.
126. Sharp, 37.
127. Faubion, *Power*, 399. As a matter of fact, Foucault's ideas of power, politics, and truth are all intertwined. He argues that it is mistaken that power makes men mad, and that those

Although he believes in human freedom, this freedom is liable to the imprisonment of historical conditioning. Put differently, a system of restoration is indeed possible. But, that system of restoration can also eventually reveal its flaws, and society would have to make an effort to reconsider that particular penal system. Therefore, Foucault asserts that whenever an institution of power in a society is involved, everything is dangerous.[128] In this sense, even though a human being is psychologically or inwardly free, they are institutionally and socially under historical conditioning. In short, Foucault's historical conditioning bears a striking similarity to Wink's DS.

From a sociological perspective, Daniel Liechty sees the "principalities and powers" as "the unseen forces that often transform even our best and most humanistic intention into the service of violence and the system of domination into the world."[129] In Liechty's view, where Wink differs from a sociologist's view is that Wink, instead of establishing a social-scientific theory by interpreting the observed data, turns to an exegesis of mythology.[130] For Wink, it is the DS that discloses the archetypal shortcoming of the human world.

Psychologically, Wink reinforces his concept of the DS, especially through the eyes of Carl G. Jung. For Jung, egocentricity is a mode of being possessed or having an "autonomous complex,"[131] being unable to see the larger dimensions of the self.[132] But Wink separates himself from Jung by saying the ego is a web of internalized social conventions, a tale spun by the DS.[133] Jung emphatically regarded the ego as an autonomous inner complex, whereas, for Wink, this ego is also internalized by a heteronomous outer network of beliefs.

---

who govern are blind. For him, it is completely mistaken to believe that "Only those who keep their distance from power . . . can discover truth." In fact, the exercise of power itself creates and causes new objects of knowledge to emerge. *Therefore, the exercise of power perpetually creates knowledge,* Foucault, *Power/Knowledge,* 51–52.

128. Foucault, *Power,* 400.

129. Liechty, "Principalities and Powers," 47.

130. Liechty, 185.

131. According to Jung, "an autonomous complex" occurs when we are split-off from our consciousness. When this happens, complexes develop a seemingly independent, autonomous will and quasi-life of their own, which can potentially engulf and possess the total personality.

132. Wink, *Engaging the Powers,* 159. Wink acknowledges his indebtedness to Jung. In particular, Wink's *Unmasking the Powers* is an attempt to integrate or present a reading of theology from the Jungian perspective. This book can also be considered to be the fruit of reading the Bible from a psychological perspective.

133. Wink, 159.

Wink integrates a psychological understanding of ego with a theological view, deepening Jesus's teaching of self-denial as abandoning our egocentricity not as individuals, but as cultures, because our ego has been entangled within the DS and the process of dying to one's conditioning is never fully over.[134]

Further, Ray Gingerich engages Wink's DS in economic and political interests. Gingerich explicates that these interests can create an ethos, which is similar to the DS which dominates us as a church, a society, and as a nation.[135] Miroslav Volf also draws a parallel between his theology of exclusion and Wink's DS, thereby replacing the exclusion system with Wink's DS. Volf highlights, "Wink rightly points out to a complex transpersonal and systemic reality of evil which dominates, ensnares, and lures persons to dominate others."[136] Thus, Volf suggests that there is a connection between the exclusion system and the DS. Generally, Wink's DS bears a striking resemblance to the terms that Gingerich and Volf have named in identifying the fundamental human predicament of society. The contrast is that Gingerich's approach is politico-economic; Volf, socio-ethnic; and Wink, socio-political, respectively in their emphases.

As seen, in viewing Wink's DS in the light of other disciplinarian perspectives, we have found some similarities between socio-political, sociological, psychological and theological studies. Aside from the similarities, is there any distinction that Wink makes from those mentioned? What makes Wink different from others? What critical elements can be seen? To begin with, Wink's argument against the negligence of spiritual, social and structural dimensions in the Western context is substantial. In his understanding, there are two possible reasons why the West neglects the spiritual dimension – materialism and individualism. First, materialism displaces spiritual realities like angels, spirits, principalities, powers, and so on. As a result, "the wells of the spirit have run dry,"[137] complains Wink. Nancey Murphy also admits that

---

134. Wink, 161.
135. Gingerich, "Economics and Politics of Violence," 113.
136. Volf, *Exclusion and Embrace*, 87. See also his "Exclusion and Embrace," 53.
137. Wink, *Unmasking the Powers*, 2. In this second volume of the *Powers Trilogy*, Wink especially argues for the presence of the spiritual realities in the world. He asserts that the biblical terminology, the angel of nation and church, is not a celestial being; rather, he transposes it as the spiritualities of nation and church.

Wink's notion of the "withinness" is "one way of emphasising the fact that social groups have 'personalities' and 'moral character' over and above those of the individuals who make them up."[138] Put differently, the institutions we created, in turn, created us.

Second, Wink perceives that individualism forces us to react individually to every pain caused by institutions, thereby blinding us to the invisible forces that determine the choices of those who set policy and fire workers.[139] Glen Stassen rightly observes that Wink's DS shows the nature of power not only as an individual's property, but also as the DS with their spiritual justifications, ideologies, and drives.[140] In short, Wink's concept of the DS affirms the profundity of social evil – it is far deeper than we think, and more mysterious than we perceive because evil is spiritual as well as structural.

What is more, Old Testament scholar Walter Brueggemann's articulation of the difference between the ancient domination system and the alternative community that God gave the Israelites through Moses in his book, *Prophetic Imagination*, is much more biblically and theologically thorough and conscientious than Wink's DS.[141] Brueggemann contends that God, when he rescued the Israelites through Moses, willed them to be an alternative community with different social, political and economic values in total contrast to the surrounding cultures. For Brueggemann, it was King Solomon who countered completely the counterculture of Moses by establishing economics of affluence instead of the economics of equality, the politics of oppression instead of the politics of justice, and a controlled, static religion.[142] As a result of establishing a controlled, static religion, God and his temple have become part of the royal landscape, and God's sovereignty is fully subordinated to the purpose of the king. When the alternative community was removed and supplanted with a monarchical system, it was the time to launch a prophetic ministry, argues Brueggemann, because "the task of prophetic ministry is

---

138. Murphy, "Traditions, Practices," 190–191.
139. Wink, *Powers That Be*, 2.
140. Glen Stassen, "Kind of Justice Jesus Cares About," 160.
141. Brueggemann, *Prophetic Imagination*.
142. Brueggemann, 32, 33.

to nurture, nourish, and evoke a consciousness and perception alternative to the consciousness and perception of the dominant culture around us."[143]

Based on this statement, Marcus Borg suggests that Israel, which was liberated from the domination system of Egypt in her beginning, re-established the domination system by the emergence of kingship.[144] For Borg, the domination system of Israel continued into Jesus's time. As Borg argues, it is true that Brueggemann's concept of alternative community, biblically speaking, is an all-encompassing concept of social, theological, political, and economic areas. Wink's expression of the DS merely as a socio-political order, in this sense, does not do justice to the whole biblical narrative. The DS, in this study, is used to portray the human society which is fundamentally in opposition to God. Therefore, the DS should not be just socio-politically concerned, but also related to the theological dimension.

Wink's reading of the narrative of the fall of humans in Genesis 3 is mythical and structural. For him, the story of the fall is not a temporal event; instead, it is mythic, hence it is always present.[145] Because of this mythic interpretation of the Fall, Wink locates the origin of the DS in human history, claiming that the basic structure of the DS has operated for at least five thousand years from the time of the great conquest of the states of Mesopotamia around 3000 BCE. Since then, social systems have become rigidly hierarchical, authoritarian, and patriarchal.[146] Violence has also become the spirit of the DS. To a certain degree, Wink describes human sin as ontologically prior to all social systems and structures, yet he lays emphasis on the systemic or structural dimension of evil. Thus, he concludes that evil is fundamentally structural.

However, reading the fall in the biblical narrative from a structural viewpoint raises some questions. For example, what or whom should we attribute the blame in the cases of infamous despots like Hitler, Idi Amin, Gaddafi, two tyrants from Myanmar, Ne Win and Than Shwe, and so on? Is it the structural problem of that time because of which such despotic leaders emerged? Or was it they who built the structure to support their rule? Those questions

---

143. Brueggemann, 3.
144. Borg, *Conflict, Holiness, and Politics*, 12.
145. Wink, *Engaging the Powers*, 76–77.
146. Wink, *Powers That Be*, 40–41.

cannot be adequately answered in this section. There might be various possible ways to address these issues. One crucial tension in doing social ethics is a personal-vs-social dilemma. Both play a significant role in doing social ethics, and one should not be overstressed at the cost of the other. In other words, the personal dimension of sin should not be overlooked for the sake of the structural aspect in doing social ethics.

In this regard, a French sociologist and lay theologian Jacques Ellul (1912–1994) has a contrasting view to Wink's structural reading of the Bible. Unlike Wink, Ellul reads the Decalogue and regards the last commandment, "Thou shalt not covet," (Exod 20:17 KJV) as the crux of the whole commandment. For Ellul, the covetousness, which is more personal than structural, is the fundamental plight of humanity. Covetousness, therefore, becomes "the spirit of power or domination . . . and it is not just a simple moral question but utterly basic."[147] Put differently, Wink sees that the myth of redemptive violence is the spirit of the DS, whereas covetousness, for Ellul, is the spirit of power or domination. In Ellul's eyes, the basic human plight is more than the idea of redemptive violence – it is the human heart where the spirit of covetousness can hold sway anytime. Once covetousness seizes hold of the human heart, it becomes much stronger than the belief in the myth of redemptive violence. Thus, Ellul reminds Wink that it is not only the belief in redemptive violence, but a covetous heart and mind which can instigate all forms of violence.[148]

In the context of Myanmar, the gravity of personal sin is so evident that two successive military dictators, Ne Win and Than Shwe, have shockingly impoverished the country in numerous ways: economically, educationally, culturally, and politically. Of course, we cannot state that it is they alone who are responsible for all the atrocities and economic impoverishment. There

---

147. Ellul, *Humiliation of the Word*, 101.

148. As an addendum, I wish to point out the weak point of Wink's purely structural reading of the Powers. Wink has seen the Powers as an impersonal structural order that has inner and outer identities. This approach is not sufficient enough to scrutinize the Burmese politics because the despots who ruled the country have played a significant role. Like Clinton Arnold's view, if the Powers as personal spirit-entities can influence human affections and decisions, a logical conclusion is that the powers of darkness, to a large degree, did influence the two Burmese tyrants Ne Win and Than Shwe. Those influences led them to create oppressive dictatorships in their country. As further research, we can launch a study of how the evil forces or the powers of darkness have influenced the despotic rulers in Myanmar. The study could also focus on the practices of occults, astrology, numerology and spiritism.

were also structural aspects that buttressed their evil acts. For example, the traditionally inherited top-down leadership structure and the military doctrine of unquestioning obedience to any order given by a senior, are part and parcel of the military governing structure of Myanmar, which has a tremendous impact on other institutions.[149] These structural elements had to shape the lives of Ne Win and Than Shwe so significantly that they dared to commit such inhuman atrocities against all opposing political dissidents. Both structural and personal dimensions of evil are, in fact, intricately related in such a way that it is human beings who make institutions evil, and institutions, in turn, make human beings evil too.[150]

If Wink's DS and Ellul's view of covetousness are juxtaposed, the conflict between personal moral integrity and the "withinness" of an institution can be clearly perceived. We need an ethic that deals with both personal and social matters. There is no such ethic that seeks to treat social problems alone without correlating them with personal morality. A person with high moral integrity has potential to transform social evil, while also being affected by the social conditioning.[151] Even though Wink's view of the DS opens our eyes to discern the spirituality of human society and institution, it has its limitations in coping with personal moral integrity. For example, Mohandas K. Gandhi's personal morality, as his commitment to a nonviolent lifestyle grew, led his own people to regard him as a guru and even worship him as semidivine. His moral superiority moved the people of his country and even others from all over the world. This shows that personal moral merit does play a crucial role in treating social problems.

As this study seeks to scrutinize the politics of Myanmar through Wink's structural reading of the Powers, the emphasis will not be on a personal dimension of evil. The difference that Wink makes is the way in which he perceives a personal aspect of evil: having acknowledged the profound understanding of the depth psychologist and Eastern mystics on personal ego, still overlooks the fact that ego itself is a "web of internalised *social* conventions,

---

149. Saw Tun also explains the Burmese military mind-set in detail, Tun, "Military Mind-set."

150. This will be discussed at greater length in the last chapter of this study.

151. This will be discussed at greater length in the last chapter of this study.

a tale spun by the DS that we take in as self-definition."[152] Put differently, ego itself is a product of the DS as a result of internalizing the social conventions of the DS knowingly or unknowingly. This insightful opinion will also be a guiding point to look at the political culture of Myanmar. This insightful thought will help this thesis explore the nexus between personal and structural dimensions of evil in Myanmar.

2.2.3 The Powers and God's Domination-Free Order

Wink expounds the nature of the Powers in three ways: their creatureliness, fall, and redemption. The three statements – the Powers are created, the Powers are fallen, and the Powers shall be redeemed[153] – must always be held simultaneously. Understanding the Powers in this way, for Wink, helps him see the dual nature of all institutions. Wink succinctly writes: "God at one and the same time *upholds* a given political or economic system since some such system is required to support human life, *condemns* that system insofar as it is destructive of full life; and *presses for its transformation* into a more humane order."[154]

Here Wink's account of the Powers essentially agrees with his predecessors, like John Howard Yoder and Richard Mouw, whose readings of the Powers language, like Wink, are pre-eminently structuralist. Yoder did an exposition of the Powers language in a chapter of his classic book, *The Politics of Jesus*. For him, the Powers are pre-eminently institutions, structures and ideologies, but that does not necessarily mean that he rejects the literal meaning of the Powers language. Yoder looks at the literal meaning of the language and notes that the meaning of the Powers could literally mean demonic bondage, but he focuses more on the part of socio-political structures. He puts a great emphasis on their weight to operate human society. Thus, society and history, even nature, would be impossible without regularity, system, and order.[155]

Likewise, Richard Mouw also did a considerable amount of study on the Powers in his book, *Politics and Biblical Drama*. Mouw did his study with the

---

152. Wink, *Engaging the Powers*, 159, emphasis in original.
153. Wink, *Powers That Be*, 32.
154. Wink, 32.
155. Yoder, *Politics of Jesus*, 141.

aim to discover the political relevance of Christianity. He first looks at previous interpretations, and concludes that Paul believed in the realm of created spiritual powers. However, what needs to be asked, for those in the twentieth century, is "to what extent should we believe in the actual existence of the spiritual beings?" To draw a connection between those powers and human society, he contends that the Powers are operating behind the regular patterns and structures of social life. In doing so, Mouw does not mean that the political leaders are demon-possessed or communing with spirits.[156] While maintaining the ancient biblical view of the Powers, Mouw argues that Paul went beyond the Old Testament description of the spiritual powers by at least partially depersonalizing the Powers.[157] Thus, the Powers are nothing more than national or racial groupings, religious doctrine, moral rules, technology, sexual desires, altruism, and so on.[158]

However, Wink separates himself from Yoder and Mouw, who explain that the sovereignty of these Powers has been broken and disarmed by the cross of Christ. In contrast, Wink argues that God's liberation is not only for humankind, but also for the Powers themselves. This idea rejects both a dualistic myth of good and evil and viewing the Powers as intrinsically evil. Thus, Wink asserts that the Powers were originally good and essential for the survival of human society. Wink also differs from Yoder and Mouw who see, without paying much attention to its spiritual aspect, the Powers as primarily structural. What is missing in Yoder and Mouw is the spiritual element of the Powers.[159]

Generally, Wink's theological framework of the Powers – their creation, fall, and redemption – is of prime importance because its implication is an inspiring breakthrough to any resistance against the Powers. The simultaneity of the Powers' creatureliness, fallenness and redemption shows that

---

156. Mouw, *Politics and the Biblical Drama*, 88.
157. Mouw, 87.
158. O'Brien, "Principalities and Powers," 124.
159. See also the work on Yoder's theology of principalities and powers by Jamie Pitts, who did a revision of Yoder's theology by a French sociologist Pierre Bourdieu. There, he points out that Yoder's theology of the Powers lacks personal and spiritual dimensions. Through the eyes of Bourdieu, Pitts reconstructs the idea that, "if society only exists in relation to God, who is spirit, then spirit is constitutive of society itself . . . Spirituality is thus metaphysical, rooted in the spiritual being of God." Pitts, *Principalities and Powers*, 34.

transforming the DS is never-ending in this imperfect world. Thus, comprehending the simultaneous acts of this schema helps us to see a shining, but realistic future. First, knowing the Powers as God's creation teaches us not to be always pessimistic about social institutions; second, knowing them as fallen also enlightens us not to be always optimistic about them; and third, believing their redeemability infuses us with hope, even in quasi-hopeless situations; and finally, holding them together can integrate within us a hopeful, but realistic, critical, but creative outlook.[160] After framing the schema of the Powers, what Wink establishes is an alternative vision, which is antithetical to the DS. This alternative vision is the kingdom or the reign of God in biblical terms, yet Wink has re-invented it as God's domination-free order (the DFO). The control of the DS is too strong for all human races to resist; therefore true liberation from the Powers cannot come within the Powers system, but only by something that transcends it.[161]

The kingdom of God (the DFO in Winkian terms) has been a central theme to many Christian social ethicists. N. T. Wright suggests that, "once you lose the kingdom theme, which is central to the gospels, everything else becomes reinterpreted in ways that radically distort, that substitute a subtly different 'gospel' message for the one Matthew, Mark, Luke, and John are eager to convey."[162] Mark Chapman traces the two contradictory interpretations of the kingdom and their ethical implications through the studies of Albrecht Ritschl (1822–1889), Johannes Weiss (1863–1914), Rudolf Bultmann (1884–1976) and the liberation theologians of Latin America. The first interpretation is the kingdom as "wholly other" that has nothing to do with this present world. The second is the kingdom as the institutional church.[163] The former leads many Christians to ethically withdraw and isolate themselves from the world. The latter pushes Christians to participate in every area of society. The best representative for the former view is Johannes Weiss, Ritschl's own son-in-law. For him, Jesus's vision of the kingdom was wholly in the future and something which human beings could do nothing to bring about. An

---

160. Wink, *Powers That Be*, 32.
161. Wink, *Engaging the Powers*, 69.
162. Wright, *How God Became King*, 158.
163. Chapman, "Kingdom of God," 141.

American social gospeller Walter Rauschenbusch (1861–1918) represents the latter view of the kingdom. Rauschenbusch identified the kingdom of God with a particular social and economic system.

However, from the period during and just after World War II, scholars have begun to view the kingdom as both present and future. For example, George Eldon Ladd sums up his understanding of the kingdom with a threefold statement concerning the matter: "the *promise* of the coming kingdom in the Old Testament, its *fulfilment* through the life of Jesus, and its *consummation* at the end of history."[164] In the common usage, the kingdom of God is already present, but not fully consummated. In brief, it is *already*, but *not yet*. As a man of the twentieth century, the reign of God, for Wink, is not simply future, but also present. Wink suggests that, "we do not know how much of God's will can be realised in human affairs, but we must act as if the world can be transformed."[165] As a social ethicist, Wink also draws an implication: "Faith does not wait for God's sovereignty to be established on earth; it behaves as if that sovereignty already holds full sway."[166] However, Wink paraphrases the kingdom of God as God's domination-free order in order to accommodate his new coinage of the DS.

The question that Wink has to deal with in his paraphrasing is, "Is it justifiable to paraphrase the kingdom of God as God's domination-free order (DFO)?" By and large, biblical scholars agree that the kingdom of God is a central theme of the Bible and the message Jesus spoke in his earthly ministry. Though the phrase is only found in the New Testament, its idea is hidden in the teachings of the Old Testament. G. R. Beasley-Murray highlights the three points that the Old Testament contains the theme of the kingdom of God throughout the prophetic writings: first, Yahweh as the universal ruler; second, the righteousness that Yahweh and his people practice; and third, the peace that Yahweh establishes.[167] Beasley-Murray, after an exegetical study of the New Testament passages on the kingdom of God, concludes that, "according to Jesus, the coming of the kingdom of God is the determinative factor in

---

164. Epp, "Mediating," 52.
165. Wink, *Engaging the Powers*, 320.
166. Wink, 323.
167. Beasley-Murray, *Jesus and the Kingdom*, 20.

his ministry of word and deed; it culminates in his death and resurrection and leads to his Parousia at an undefined time."[168] Therefore, he draws the implication that, "Christian existence is set between an accomplished redemption and an awaited consummation."[169] Theologically speaking, the kingdom of God is such an all-embracing theme, ranging from the time of the Old Testament to the coming of Jesus and the end-times or his second coming. In a practical sense, the kingdom of God is all-inclusive, there are no hidden dimensions. As the document, "A Kingdom Manifesto for New Zealand" states, the kingdom of God is an alternative vision of the world where God, humans, animals, the eco-system, and the Powers are all reconciled to each other.[170]

Looking at the kingdom of God in this light, Wink's idea of God's domination-free order seems humanistic in nature, socio-political and economical in its focus, and egalitarian in its vision; therefore, it is less theological than the biblical teaching of the kingdom. That is, Wink's theology is, as noted, humanistic. His whole life itself is portrayed as a struggle to become human, and his doctrine of Christ is also Christology from below, stressing Jesus's humanness. As theologically a liberal, Wink sees the kingdom of God from a socio-political perspective and paraphrases it as God's domination-free order. The chart in which Wink lays out the differences between the DS and the DFO shows his theological presuppositions behind it.[171] Thus, converting the kingdom of God into God's domination-free order is a brilliant attempt to construct the theology of social ethics for Wink, but it puts some questions to biblical scholars discussed above. Therefore, Wink's idea of the DFO does somewhat make sense in a social and ethical sense but is not wholly biblical and theological.

2.3 Summary of the Chapter

In this chapter, I have analyzed Wink's *Powers* trilogy and discussed how it contributes to Christian social ethics. I have discussed Wink's *Powers* trilogy

---

168. Beasley-Murray, 338.

169. Beasley-Murray, 339.

170. *A Kingdom Manifesto for New Zealand*, compiled by Wyn Fountain, Brain Hathaway, Gordon Miller, and other evangelical and Charismatic church leaders in New Zealand and overseas, 1997.

171. Wink, *Engaging the Powers*, 46–47.

in an engaging way, not favouring Wink at the cost of other voices. At the same time, I have also critically engaged Wink's *Powers* in the light of other voices, showing that there are some things Wink could have paid more attention to. It is discovered that Wink's recovery of the interior or spiritual dimension of institutions revolutionizes the modern reductionists and materialists, who overlook or turn a blind eye to the unseen or spiritual aspects of human society. It is also discussed that Wink came to realize this spiritual dimension of our society through what he calls an integral worldview, which sees the outer and inner, material and spiritual, and without and within as inextricably and inseparably related to one another. With this view in mind, Wink interprets the Powers as not separate heavenly or ethereal entities, but the inner aspect of material manifestations of power.

This chapter also justifies some reasons why this study has taken Wink's *Powers* as a lens to explore the political context of Myanmar. A fundamental reason is that Wink's idea of the DS helps us see the persistent political violence of Myanmar throughout the nation's history and how oppressive it is. Likewise, Wink's view of the DFO envisions an alternative community, free of discrimination, domination, racism, classism, violence, exploitation, self-centredness, and contempt. Only through Jesus's third way or nonviolent engagement, will the DS be transformed into the DFO. It is assumed that the whole frame will be a great tool to critique and construct the politics of Myanmar.

Lastly, I have tried to engage Wink in conversation with other scholars in his interpretation of the Powers, the DS and the DFO. The chapter has pointed out that Wink's coinage of the DS is truly an illuminating insight in understanding this present age, and the DFO infuses hope within us. But the chapter also points out that many of Wink's ethical implications from his study on the Powers are anthropocentric or humanistic, socio-political and economical in focus. In the next chapter, we will engage Wink's proposal of nonviolence as Jesus's third way in dialogue with other scholars, and how it can transform the DS into the DFO.

CHAPTER 3

Jesus's Third Way or Nonviolent Engagement: A Critical Construct

In the previous chapter, aspects of the work of Walter Wink were examined in order to establish its relevance for Christian nonviolent engagement with society and culture in Myanmar. In particular, Wink's *Powers* trilogy, with its structural language of the domination system and the domination-free order, has proved useful in framing a lens through which to examine the political context of Myanmar. The last chapter examined Wink's work around those two structural descriptions. In this chapter, I shall analyze Wink's view of the nonviolent way, which he also calls the "third way" of Jesus, in such a way that these ideas may be used to constructively engage with the case studies of Martin Luther King Jr and Aung San Suu Kyi in later chapters.

This chapter also examines Wink's view of nonviolence in the light of other peace scholars. In this interaction, Wink will be reviewed from the standpoints of John Howard Yoder, Stanley Hauerwas, Glen Stassen, Miroslav Volf, Jacques Ellul and others. This critical engagement will affirm certain aspects of Wink's theory of nonviolence while rejecting other points of his theory. The aim of the interaction is to integrate Wink's theology with the wider scholarly context. Overall, the previous and present chapters provide an in-depth analysis of Wink's *Powers* trilogy so as to have a dialogue with King and Suu Kyi, in order to engage with the political context of Myanmar.

3.1 Engaging the Powers Nonviolently

If there are two radically different orders, the domination system versus God's domination-free order, and if the present world we live in is named the DS, how can the DS possibly be transformed? Is there a way to the DFO? If there is, what would that way be? Wink recognizes that there are two standard responses to evil, fight or flight, yet he rejects both responses. Instead, he contends that there is a third way, which is nonviolence. Nonviolence is neither fight nor flight, submission nor armed revolt, passivity nor violent rebellion, surrender nor revenge, withdrawal nor direct retaliation. Nonviolence, in Wink's view, is the third way, confronting or resisting evil in a non-evil way. He sees violence as the spirit of the DS and nonviolence as that of the DFO. We will expound what Wink means by the third way of Jesus, and how Wink's argument for the third way or nonviolence may be associated with Yoder's idea of "original revolution," Glen Stassen's "transforming initiatives," and Volf's "embrace."[1]

3.1.1 Jesus's Third Way

Wink's understanding of nonviolence as Jesus's third way is essentially an exposition of certain Bible verses (Matt 5:38–39a). Despite his critics, a majority of scholars affirm his exegesis. In this exegesis, Wink argues that the translation of the Greek word, *antistēnai* is "do not resist" or "resist not." According to this translation, the implication is that "one either resists or resists not."[2] Put differently, there are usually two standard responses to conflict: flight (passivity) and fight (violence). In contrast, Wink argues that the word should be translated as follows: do not resist *violently* and *revengefully*. In the comparative study of his *Transforming initiatives* and Jesus's third way, Glen Stassen supports Wink by quoting the two New Testament scholars, N. T. Wright and Donald Hagner, who side with Wink's translation.[3]

Wink continues to argue that in saying, "do not resist *violently* and *revengefully*," Jesus's intention is neither to be passive nor to be reactive violently. Rather, Jesus proposes a third way, which is neither submission nor assault, neither flight nor fight, but "a way that can secure one's human dignity and begin to change the power equation."[4] For Wink, Jesus gave the three examples,

---

1. Yoder, *Original Revolution*, 13–33; Stassen, *Just Peacemaking*, 53–88; Volf, *Exclusion and Embrace*.

2. Wink, "Neither Passivity nor Violence," 113–114.

3. Stassen, "Jesus' Way," 129.

4. Wink, "Neither Passivity nor Violence," 115.

which show how to practice the third way: turning the other cheek, rendering up the inner garment, and going the second mile. Richard Horsley, however, argues that Jesus is not a pacifist; instead, he sees Jesus as a revolutionary, but not a violent political revolutionary.[5]

Yet Horsley is uncertain whether Jesus taught nonviolence or not. For Horsley, Jesus's teaching in the Sermon on the Mount relates only to the people who were in oppressive conditions of poverty and debt in the Roman Empire. They were the people whom Jesus addressed and exhorted in order that they might "respond positively to each other and to be supportive of one another rather than divisive."[6] That means Jesus's ethic, according to Horsley, does not relate to the sphere of imperial political-economic relations. Glen Stassen points out that Horsley's argument is indeed concerned with Wink's lack of dealing with economic injustice. He contends that Wink's concern is mainly with the DS, but he does not deal with "the structure of justice that works to curtail domination by unchecked power."[7] Despite differing from one another, Wink and Horsley have a common stance, that is, they both do not regard pacifism as a form of purity, but as a means of winning justice for the oppressed.

Now we will discuss Wink's idea of the third way in the light of John Yoder and Glen Stassen, to show some correspondences between Wink, Yoder, and Stassen. First, Wink acknowledges Yoder as a predecessor and a great labourer in bringing the Peace Church witness against violence into the mainstream of theological discussion, yet he does not comprehensively cite him in his *Powers*.[8] In the first volume of the trilogy, Wink mentions that his exploration of the Powers language simply confirms the findings of his predecessors, including Schlier, Berkhof, Stewart, Caird, Morrison, William Stringfellow, and Yoder.[9] Thus, Yoder deserves to be included as a lens through which to consider Wink because of the legacies he bequeathed in regards to nonviolence and Christian pacifism.

---

5. Horsley, *Jesus and the Spiral*, 326.
6. Horsley, "Response to Walter Wink," 130.
7. Stassen, "Kind of Justice Jesus Cares About," 158.
8. Wink, *Powers That Be*, 204.
9. Wink, *Naming the Powers*, 35.

What parallels can be drawn between Wink's idea of Jesus's third way and Yoder's view of Jesus as the original revolutionary? According to Yoder, Jesus was a revolutionary in three ways.[10] First, Jesus refused all the prevalent ways to change the Roman Empire, and instead he obeyed God unto death, thereby overcoming evil with good, and defeating the Powers.[11] Next, Christ, through his incarnation, death, and resurrection, has brought in the new aeon. Lastly, Jesus has also created the church, the community of his disciples, to witness the gospel and follow his way. According to Yoder, this community exists not for the sake of "a simple moral rigor about not shedding blood but a robust alternative holistic social system."[12] Thus, Yoder's prime focus is to see the story of Jesus as a whole by looking at the historical context of Jesus's time, and establish how Jesus's revolution differed from his contemporaries. But Wink's concern is to show Jesus's way through the exegesis of the scriptural passage, Matthew 5:38–39. What is common for both Wink and Yoder is that they both recognize Jesus as the centre of their ethical exploration. However, Wink and Yoder differ from each other in creating the basis for social transformation. For Yoder, it is the church or community as an alternative social system to transform the present system of the world. On the contrary, Wink acknowledges that the church is called to nonviolence in order to express its fidelity; however, he regards it as one among many groups that struggle to humanize the Powers. Put differently, the church has no special role to play in the world in the process of transforming the DS into the DFO.

Second, Wink's third way of Jesus is analogous to Glen Stassen's *Transforming Initiatives*. Like Wink, Glen Stassen begins his ethical

---

10. In most of his study, Yoder used the early Christian church as the criterion to construct his pacifism. He believed that the first Christians were the real Christians. He argued that only studying their experience or making it a model will clarify what it means to be genuinely Christian at a later time, see Yoder, *Christian Attitude to War*, 42–43.

11. Yoder observed that there were four ways to respond to the repressive regime of the Roman Empire at the time of Jesus. The first was the way of the Herodians and the Sadducees who accepted the situation as it really was and attempted to save what they could by aiming at what was possible. The second was the way of righteous revolutionary violence, the path which the Zealots wanted. The third was the way of the Essenes who withdrew from the tension and conflict of the urban centre to maintain faithful copies of the text of the Old Testament. The last or fourth way was the option of "proper religion," represented among the community, the way of the Pharisees. They lived in an urban setting, but they separated themselves from others to be pure and holy, see Yoder, *Original Revolution*, 18–26.

12. Cited from Cook-Huffman, "Christianity and Nonviolent Resistance," 617.

exploration with the study of Jesus's Sermon on the Mount. Stassen asserts that throughout history, the interpretation of the Sermon was principally dyadic in its approach and called the antithesis "prohibitions" in its implications. According to the antitheses prohibitions, there are dyadic structures: one is traditional teaching and Jesus's authoritative antithesis. For example, the traditional teaching is "You shalt not murder," (Exod 20:13 ESV) and Jesus's authoritative teaching is to prohibit anger, thereby resulting in being reconciled.[13] For Stassen, there are not merely two options (e.g. eye for eye and violently resisting) but there is another way (to turn other cheek), which is neither fight nor flight, that Stassen calls "transforming initiative." Through the triadic structure, Stassen shows the presence of third alternatives, which, for him, are the ways of deliverance. These third alternatives are neither prohibitions nor high ideals but transforming initiatives. Therefore, Stassen asserts that, "seeing the triadic structure transforms our reading of the Sermon on the Mount so that it teaches the grace-based transforming initiatives that enable deliverance from bondage to vicious circles."[14] Within "transforming initiatives," Stassen explains it in three senses: "it transforms the person who was angry into an active peacemaker; it transforms the relationship from one of anger into a peace-making process, and it hopes to transform the enemy into a friend."[15] Therefore, Stassen himself draws a parallel between his transforming initiatives and Wink's third way of Jesus, thereby specifying the nature of the third way as "transforming initiatives that change our own way of relating to the enemy and that hope to change the enemy's way of relating to us."[16] What Stassen extends more in his exposition than Wink's is that not only Matthew 5:38–48 but the whole sermon has a transforming initiative structure.

In summary, Wink, Yoder, and Stassen all seek to establish their ethical exploration on the basis of Christology. To compare, Wink and Stassen are much more similar to one another than Yoder, because they both have established their argument on the Sermon on the Mount. However, what

---

13. Stassen, "Fourteen Triads," 268.
14. Stassen, 270.
15. Stassen and Gushee, 135.
16. Stassen, "Jesus' Way," 130.

makes Wink different from Stassen is that Wink examines only particular verses from the whole sermon (Matt 5:38–39a), whereas Stassen establishes a triadic reading to interpret the sermon. Yoder, instead of looking at a particular teaching of Jesus, views the narrative and drama of Jesus as a whole in order to establish Jesus as a pioneer of another revolution.[17] Nevertheless, their prime concern is to contend with the relevance of Jesus in formulating a social ethic in this contemporary world. Therefore, their conviction is that an authentic transformation, if Jesus's teaching is faithfully obeyed, is inevitable.

When we look at Wink's idea of Jesus's third way in the light of Yoder's original revolution and Stassen's transforming initiatives, the integration we can establish is based on Jesus's teaching and his person. Wink and Stassen advance their social ethics on Jesus's Sermon on the Mount, while Yoder's view does not focus particularly on any specific teaching of Jesus, but on Jesus himself. Jesus is truly an original revolutionary, as Yoder suggests, and at the same time, Jesus teaches us the principles of how to do revolution as Wink and Stassen propose. Seeing Jesus as a person and his teaching in such an integral way brings home to us the fact that Jesus was a revolutionary with revolutionary ideas.[18] Therefore, Stassen and Yoder do not discourage Wink's interpretation of the Sermon on the Mount; instead, they reinforce his interpretation.

3.1.2 Why Nonviolence?

What makes Wink different from other exponents of nonviolence? Why nonviolence rather than violence? Or why not violence? What does Wink mean by violence? Wink does not explicitly define what violence is and what it is not. The way he reasons is asking whether violence should be the last resort

---

17. In exploring theological influences on evangelicals in terms of political thought and action, J. Budziszewski observes that, "one of the reasons why evangelicals are drawn to Yoder is that he takes the story of Jesus seriously." To be more explicit, many evangelicals interpret the story of Jesus in the light of his teachings, whereas Yoder interprets the teachings in the light of the story, see the chapter "Four Shapers of Evangelical Political Thought," in Budziszewski, *Evangelicals in the Public Square*, 88.

18. It is not to understand the word "revolution" and "revolutionary" in this contemporary context, but it should be read and comprehended in the light of what Yoder argues. Jesus is not an armed revolutionary like Che Guevara; he is not a social prophet like Martin Luther King Jr, either, though there are similarities that we can find between King and Jesus. His revolution is more than social, political, and economic.

in the place where nonviolence fails. If so, he finds himself enmeshed in the belief that violence saves.[19] Violence, for Wink, is the violation of the nature of the DFO. In Wink's view, peace might be achieved by means of violence, but the peace attained will not enable the culture of the DFO to be cultivated. He sees violence as, "the ethos of our times . . . the spirituality of the modern world."[20] But Wink, in defending Jesus's use of the whip of cords in cleansing the temple (John 2:13–16), argues that even if violence is defined as injurious and lethal harm, Jesus scarcely can be accused of causing harm.[21] However, Wink seems unconcerned with defining the meaning of violence and nonviolence. Even distinguishing between force and violence does not appear to be reasonable to Wink. For some ethicists, force signifies a truly legitimate, socially authorized, and morally defensible use of restraint to prevent harm being done to innocent people, whereas violence means a morally illegitimate or excessive use of force.[22] Wink argues that violence, in the hands of duly constituted authorities, is still violence.[23] The real root of human society is not whether nonviolence works or fails, but "the long-term task of building a society founded on nonviolence."[24] In brief, defining the meaning of violence and nonviolence seems unimportant.

Glen H. Stassen and Michael L. Westmoreland-White define violence as "destruction to a victim or victims by means that overpower the victim's consent whether systemic and structural or individual, direct or indirect."[25] In Wink's eyes, violence is far more than harm or destruction; it is a belief in the myth of redemptive violence. Whether the means overpowers a person's consent or not does not count since the DS overmasters us. Generally, violence can be defined, in Wink's view, as the belief that violence saves, whereas nonviolence is seen as the transformative mode to transform the DS into the DFO. Therefore, violence reigns supreme over the DS, thereby becoming the

---

19. Wink, *Powers That Be*, 8.
20. Wink, *Engaging the Powers*, 13.
21. Wink, *Powers That Be*, 68–69.
22. Wink, *Engaging the Powers*, 236.
23. Wink, 237.
24. Wink, 236.
25. Stassen and Westmoreland-White, "Defining Violence," 21.

spirit of it; nonviolence lies at the centre of the DFO because it is the only transformative mode.

The main reason why nonviolence proponents – whether principled or pragmatic – argue against violence is because of the nature of its dynamic-destructive spiral. That is, violence begets violence. However, Wink's rejection of violence is based on far more than this vicious spiral. For him, violence is more than a means; it is a belief, a spirit, or spirituality – the spirit of the domination system. Thus, this section will look at Wink's ethical theory of nonviolence in the light of Yoder, Stanley Hauerwas, Jacques Ellul, and Miroslav Volf to explore the parallels and divergence between them. The following discussion establishes both the affirmation and re-formulation of Wink's ethical theory of nonviolence in the light of dialogue with other scholars in this area.

Yoder, as a prominent pacifist, also senses that there is a fundamental conceptual problem in human society, which is the just-war mentality. According to Yoder, the just-war mentality came into existence in the beginning of the Constantine period. On the contrary, Wink looks at the Babylonian myth of cosmogony, and then he indicates how the myth of redemptive violence has been steeped in human history. Yoder observes that everything with regard to Christian beliefs shifted from the time of Constantine: ecclesiologically, hierarchical system over people; eschatologically, the millennium was no longer forward-looking, but present-reality and the ruler became the model for ethical deliberations, and so on.[26] As a result, Christian morality was reduced so that everyone could practice it.

Another scholar who reflects and deepens Yoder's pacifism is Stanley Hauerwas, so I put Yoder and Hauerwas together since their views on nonviolence are fundamentally identical. Hauerwas's view of a fundamental conceptual problem in human society basically parallels Yoder's. Hauerwas assesses the assumption of American Christianity, that is, "Christians should have social and political power, so they can determine the ethos of society." In Hauerwas's eyes, this assumption is a mimic of "Constantinianism," which

---

26. For more, see "Constantinian Sources of Western Social Ethics" in Yoder, *Priestly Kingdom*. In many of his writings, Yoder reiterates the permeation of the Constantinian paradigm down to all Christians through the centuries.

used to happen when Christians ceased to become a minority and they accepted Caesar as a member of the church. Hauerwas refuses this notion, an opinion which is also shared and strengthened by Jerry Falwell, an American Christian fundamentalist because Falwell, somewhat like Niebuhr, was enthused with a passion to render all Christians involved in American politics for impacting Christian values.[27] According to Yoder and Hauerwas, the church as "messianic community"[28] has its own value. Jesus Christ is the Lord of this community and it finds its "rootage" in him, and its enablement in his resurrection.[29] The cross is the centre through which the church identifies its solidarity with Christ. For Yoder, the way of the cross is fundamentally non-resistant. Jesus, when he was unjustly tortured and crucified by the Powers, did not resist in any form of violence; instead, he obeyed God. The cross of Christ demonstrates God overcoming evil with good, thus this is always God's method in dealing with evil.[30] In Yoder's ecclesiology, the church is a counter-social entity and its existence itself is "a proclamation of the Lordship of Christ over the Powers, from whose dominion the Church has begun to be liberated."[31] Christians, as representative of the messianic community that follows Christ's way, have no room for violence in whatever circumstance.

One more scholar to interact with Wink is Miroslav Volf, Professor of Systematic Theology at Yale Divinity School. Volf's whole theology of nonviolence can be summarized with the two words, "exclusion" and "embrace." Somewhat similar to Wink, Volf argues that the fundamental human plight is exclusion, and violence stems from its effect. For Volf, the basic form of sin is excluding others because of their otherness. Put differently, to maintain our identity, we distance ourselves from others. It is a stern discrimination between the "we" or "us" syndrome and "they" or "them" syndrome. Looking

---

27. Hauerwas, *Hauerwas Reader*, 474, 463–464. Hauerwas's critiques of conservatives or neoconservatives and liberal Christians of the United States can also be seen in the chapter, "Life in the Colony: the Church as a Basis for Christian Ethics," in Hauerwas, *Resident Aliens*, 69–80. Hauerwas thus rejects both liberal and conservative Christianity in America.

28. "Messianic community" is one of the varied Christian pacifistic approaches, see Yoder, *Nevertheless*, 123–128. In this book, Yoder surveys the diverse positions of religious pacifism and at the end, he identifies his position as "the pacifism of the Messianic Community."

29. Yoder, *Nevertheless*, 124.

30. Yoder, *He Came Preaching Peace*, 19.

31. Yoder, *Politics of Jesus*, 153.

at how Jesus's table fellowships with outcasts, Volf asserts that Jesus changed the concept of sin: the real sinners are not the outcasts but the one who casts the other out.[32] He contends that the answer to exclusion is embrace. If a will to power is the heart of exclusion, then a will to love is the heart of embrace. Therefore, Yoder, Hauerwas, Volf and Wink all begin their studies with naming a fundamental human dilemma: for Wink, it is the DS; Yoder and Hauerwas, the Constantinian thought; and for Volf, exclusion.

The last theologian for the critical engagement is a French theologian, Jacques Ellul. Earlier we examined Ellul's view of the Decalogue against Wink's structural reading of the Powers. Here we examine the way Ellul regards violence and nonviolence. His approach to violence and nonviolence diverges from Wink's approach. First, Ellul does not consider nonviolence as an effective tactic for any social reform, a self-evident truth in itself, or a justifiable form as Wink does. Rather, Ellul suggests that nonviolence is a personal commitment, not a political stance. Violence is, for him, universal; therefore, it is a natural human state. To illustrate, natural laws are universal, and it is unnecessary to ask if gravity is good or evil. So is violence![33] For Ellul, even in the situation wherein there is no other way but the use of violence, "the Christian can never entertain this idea of 'last resort.'"[34] Second, violence, for Ellul, is the result of the broken communion between human beings and God. However, in the original created communion between God and the world, humans were the image-bearers of God's love and freedom in the world, over which they were granted dominion.[35] Third, Ellul asks, "how can a person be nonviolent in such a naturally violent world?" For him, only through union

---

32. Volf, "Exclusion and Embrace," 49. The two phrases that he has coined succinctly articulate his theology of embrace. First, it is "catholic personality," by which Volf refers to "a personality enriched by otherness, a personality that is what it is only because all differentiated otherness of the new creation has been reflected in it in a particular way." Second, it is "catholic foreignness," which is a kind of "distance that exists for the sake of transcending the exclusion of all other reality from the person's identity." Integrating the implications of these two terms are so crucial. Volf elaborates on the strength of this integration: "if the idea of catholic personality avoids any form of exclusivism, catholic foreignness rejects a monochrome character of one's own culture and confronts evil in every culture," 44.

33. Goddard, *Living the Word*, 180.

34. Ellul, *Violence*, 170. The idea of "last resort" is one of the criteria of *jus in bello* (just war theory), meaning that war should be made as a "last resort" in the situation where there is absolutely no other way out of it.

35. Goddard, *Living the Word*, 185.

with Christ who came into this naturally violent world, can a person be restored to communion with God so that they can break the ruptured world's way of life. Otherwise or apart from this union with Christ, Ellul contends that it is impossible to live nonviolently in such a violent world, because "the rupture from God prevents them from doing so."[36] Therefore, Ellul suggests, "we are invited to take part in a dialectic, to be in the world but not of it, and thus seek out a particular, a specifically Christian position."[37]

In conclusion, Yoder, Hauerwas, Ellul, and Volf are all alike in seeing nonviolence as specifically the essence of the Christian character. But, Ellul believes that violence is a consequence of the rupture in communion between human beings and God. Similarly, Yoder and Hauerwas consider violence as a persistent character of the world. For Volf, violence is a result of the exclusion system. In countering violence: for Ellul, it is the Christian who lives out God's Word and resists all "the world's forms of violence, while constantly confessing his/her own incapacity to fulfil this calling and seeking the forgiving grace of God";[38] and for Yoder and Hauerwas, it is the messianic community or the church which is called to choose, as Jesus did, the cross as an alternative strategy of strength, not weakness. Similar to Yoder and Hauerwas, Volf argues that it is the community of the crucified Messiah which is called to embrace others by the help of the Spirit, who is the Spirit of embrace in order to break the power of the exclusion system. In short, Yoder, Hauerwas, and Volf provide a range of views, with an emphasis on the role of the church, but Ellul focuses more on an individual Christian whose life is committed to Christ. Categorically stated, Wink's idea of the DS and the DFO is socio-political; Yoder and Hauerwas are countercultural, because the church, for them, is the counter-social entity to confront the system of the world;[39] Volf's exclusion and embrace is socio-racial in nature; and Ellul's vi-

---

36. Goddard, 186.
37. Ellul, *Violence*, 26.
38. Goddard, *Living the Word*, 197–198.
39. Stephen Bevans, in his book *Models of Contextual Theology*, divides six approaches to doing contextual theology: translation, anthropological, praxis, synthetic, transcendental, and counter-cultural. He places Stanley Hauerwas along with the later Lesslie Newbigin in the category of the counter-cultural model. According to Bevans, the counter-cultural model seeks primarily neither to translate the gospel in terms of the context (as the translation model would do), nor to facilitate new understandings to emerge from experience, culture, social location,

sion of nonviolence and Christians is more personal reconciliation with God or union with Christ than socio-political, because nonviolence, for him, is a matter of personal commitment.

Thus, what Wink significantly fails to consider in his social ethic is the role of the church. He does not treat fairly the important role of the church in pursuing his social ethic, whereas Yoder and Hauerwas's emphasis on the distinct nature of the church seems separatist or sectarian. These two polarities need to be examined so that this study may be relevant to the context of Myanmar where Christians are a minority. If Wink's view of the church is taken as a model, Christians have no distinct identity among Buddhists. In the same way, if Yoder's ecclesiology is modelled as a standard, Christianity would seem to be sectarian. Therefore, the question to be dealt with is why the role of the church is important in creating a social ethic. We will see this discussion in detail in the later part of this chapter.

3.1.3 Just War, Pacifism, Christian Realism, Just Peacemaking, and Nonviolence

As the subject of the study is the concept of nonviolence according to Wink, we need a critical interaction between him and other Christian traditions, such as just war, pacifism, Christian realism, and just peacemaking. First, we will look at the two conflicting theories – just war and pacifism, since they have been competing against each other throughout the history of Christianity. Second, a discussion on Christian realism and just peacemaking theories will follow, since these two are more recently developed theories on violence and nonviolence than just war and pacifism.

For just war theorists, the question is: why not violence? Is violence always wrong? Can violent means be justified in certain circumstances? Just war theorists believe that a particular war is just if it meets the ten moral criteria of the just-war position in deciding whether to go to war (the historic *ius ad bellum*), such as just cause, proper authority, right intention, last resort, reasonable chance of success, proportionate means, peace as the ultimate

---

and social change (as in the anthropological model), nor even to discover new meanings of the gospel from a faithful exercise of praxis (the praxis model), but to truly *encounter* and *engage* the context through respectful yet critical analysis and authentic gospel proclamation in word and deed. See Bevans, *Models of Contextual Theology*, 119.

aim, laws regarding how to conduct war (the *ius in bello*), non-combatant immunity, proportionality, and international treaties and conventions. Of course, there is, for just war advocates, a theological backdrop to defend their viewpoint. First, just war proponents believe that justice is an indispensable element without which no moral society can be established. For Christian exponents of the just war position, "Justice is cognizant of the fact that humans bear the image of God."[40] At the same time, it is also peace that proponents of just war theory seek – war not just for restoring justice, but also peace.

In Christian history, Augustine of Hippo (AD 354–430) is known as the father of the just war theory.[41] For Augustine, "war should be waged only that God may by it deliver men from the necessity and preserve them in peace."[42] Augustine believed that peace should be the object of our desire; therefore, war should be waged in order that peace may be obtained.[43] One more important thing to bear in mind is that Augustine's just war idea is centred on the implications of Christian love for non-combatant immunity and the protection of the innocent neighbour from unjust harm. Therefore, the combatants' intention in war is extremely important: "even in waging war, cherish the spirit of a peacemaker, that, by conquering those whom you attack, you may lead them back to the advantages of peace."[44] Putting love and peace together, we can conclude that if peace is the object of our desire, love would be the raison d'être for war.

For Thomas Aquinas and Martin Luther, the reason for just war is based on the teaching of Romans 13:1: "Let every person be subject to the governing authorities. For there is no authority except from God, and those that exist have been instituted by God" (ESV). They argued that governing authorities are instituted by God himself; thus, it is not for individual Christians and

---

40. Charles, *Between Pacifism and Jihad*, 120.

41. John Mark Mattox observes that there were pre-Augustinian philosophers who had used the idea of the just war theory. For example, Plato said, "the state must be organised for violent survival in an unruly world." Even in the East, the notion of just war theory could be traced. To illustrate, Laotse, Chinese philosopher wrote in the sixteenth century BC that, "war should be undertaken only with the utmost reluctance; and even then, it should never be continued beyond the point minimally required to achieve the purpose for which it was initiated," see Mattox, *Saint Augustine*, 1.

42. Augustine, "Letter CLXXIX," accessed 7 November 2017.

43. Augustine.

44. Augustine.

the church to interfere with the tasks of government. It is the government's role to take responsibility to punish the wrongdoers and to approve the good citizens. In answering the question of whether war is evil, Aquinas lists three conditions: sovereign authority, just cause, and right intention. In defining sovereign authority, Aquinas articulated,

> For it is not the business of the private individual to declare war (*Bellum*), because he can seek for redress of his rights from the tribunal of his superior. Moreover, it is not the business of a private individual to summon together the people, which has to be done in wartime. . . . And as the care of the common weal is committed to those who are in authority, it is their business to watch over the common weal of the city, kingdom or province subject to them. And just as it is lawful for them to have recourse to the sword in defending that common weal against internal disturbances, when they punish evil-doers, according to the words of the Apostle (Rom. xiii.4).[45]

Like Aquinas, Luther believed that it is not for Christians to attempt to rule the world by the gospel by abolishing all temporal law and sword. If Christians do so, they would be loosening the ropes and chains of the savage wild beasts and letting them bite and mangle everyone.[46] Since governing authorities are instituted by God, "Christians . . . do not fight as individuals or for their own benefit, but as obedient servants of the authorities under whom they live."[47] Like Augustine and Aquinas, Luther writes, "What else is war but the punishment of wrong and evil? Why does anyone go to war except because he desires peace and obedience?"[48] For Luther, the question of authority is the central one where use of the sword is concerned; only from its perspective can the justice of the cause be determined and the right intention be maintained.[49] In short, Augustine placed his argument for just war on the

---

45. Aquinas, *Summa Theologica*, 578.

46. See, "Temporal Authority: To What Extent It should be Obeyed (1523)," in Luther, *Martin Luther's Basic Theological Writings*, 436.

47. Luther, *Luther's Works*, 99.

48. Luther, 95.

49. Johnson, "Aquinas and Luther," 17.

basis of the overriding duty of Christians to love their neighbours, thus his view of war, peace, and love raises a question of logic: can peace be won by war and violence, which is the antithesis of peace? For Aquinas and Luther, it is Christians' responsibility to obey the authority since it is instituted by God himself. If Christians are to obey the earthly authority even in joining war, it is, by implication, Jesus's acceptance of war. Since war itself is one of the worst forms of violence, how could peace be established through it?

The questions for pacifists are: is pacifism a form of passivism? Is it a kind of isolationism? For nonviolent activists, is nonviolence a kind of nonresistance? Pacifism is, according to John Yoder, so diverse that it is impossible to give a single definition that covers all pacifists' positions.[50] Certainly, there are wide differences of opinion among pacifists themselves about their attitude toward a community at war.[51] Though there are various types of pacifism, they are not individually disconnected because there is some possibility of overlapping.[52] The word "pacifism," the belief that war and violence are always wrong, is originally derived from French *pacifisme* and *pacifier*, meaning "pacify."[53] For discussion, pacifism is the belief in social activism that goes against injustice without resorting to violence.[54]

In contrast with those traditions, Wink makes himself clear that his approach is different from these two conflicting theories: just war and pacifism. The contrast between just war and pacifism, for Wink, is that pacifism seems irresponsible in this violent world, whereas just war appears accommodating to the myth of redemptive violence. Thus, engaging Wink's proposal for the third way with just war and pacifism will help separate and strengthen Wink's approach for further analysis.

In general, there are chiefly two common concerns that both pacifists and just war theorists share. First, they both affirm the evils of war, its causes, conduct, and consequences. Second, the prevalent conditions of injustice

---

50. Yoder, *Nevertheless*, 10.

51. *Encyclopedia Britannica*, s.v. "pacifism," https://www.britannica.com/topic/pacifism.

52. Yoder, *Nevertheless*, 11.

53. *Oxford Dictionaries*, s.v. "pacifism," http://www.oxfordlearnersdictionaries.com/definition/english/pacifism.

54. John Yoder lists eighteen types of pacifism. Mohandas Gandhi and Martin Luther King Jr are also categorized as pacifists who used nonviolence as a method for social change. Yoder, *Nevertheless*, 48–52.

and oppression really disgust pacifists and proponents of just war alike. In response to the pacifists Willard Swartley and Alan Kreider, Arthur F. Holmes as a just war theorist, summarizes the commonalities that they both share:

> We agree in resisting the evils of war and violence. We agree in rejecting the idolatrous tendency in excesses of nationalism. We agree that their primary task is reconciliation and peacemaking. We agree in rejecting hate, retaliation and a vengeful spirit. We agree that the final solution lies in the power of Christ's gospel and the coming of his Kingdom on earth.[55]

According to Duane Friesen, the influence of a common biblical theology of shalom is the key factor for both pacifists and just war theorists.[56]

Despite the common vision of shalom society, fundamental differences lie between them. The first difference is a moral one: while pacifism rejects all forms of armed violent means to actualize shalom, just war theorists allow the proportionate and discriminate use of armed forms in certain circumstances. The second divergence is theological: understanding the tension of the kingdom of God – "already" and "not yet." According to Friesen, evangelical pacifism tends to focus on the "already" side of the polarity, whereas just war tends to look at the "not yet" side of the polarity. From the side of the peacemaking category, he sees that they both are in their own polarization. Thus, he concludes that what is needed is, "to accept the fact that there are differences among Christians, that no one position can contain the whole truth, and that each needs the other to correct its own inadequacies."[57] In Wink's eyes, each has its own extreme: pacifism is likely to be legalistic for the sake of moral pursuit, whereas the just war theory is prone to being another form of the myth of redemptive violence. In contrast, the third way of Jesus has found itself betwixt and between in the debate of just war and pacifism because it neither encourages a fight response (similarly just war) nor a flight position (pacifism).

---

55. Holmes, "Response to Willard Swartley and Alan Kreider," 61.
56. Friesen, "Convergence of Pacifism," 365.
57. Friesen, 372.

However, Wink's critique of pacifism arouses controversy among pacifists. As a pacifist, Ted Grimsrud responds, suggesting that Wink's understanding of pacifism is incomplete because pacifism is, in fact, not synonymous with passivism because pacifism is originally derived from Latin *pacis* (peace). For pacifists, peace or shalom in the Old Testament term is the highest value and the goal toward which all pacifists pursue and dream. Grimsrud sees peace as a holistic concept which covers all aspects of life, "well-being, wholeness, and health of the entire community on all levels."[58] Therefore, Grimsrud argues that nonviolence is, "part of the pacifist commitment" but that the term "is less all-encompassing and positive than the term 'pacifism.'"[59] It is true that the idea of pacifism, if looked at generally, is varied. As Tristin S. Hassell observes,

> The variety of pacifisms mirrors the diversity of normative theories about moral judgment making: consequentialist, deontological, and virtue-based; moreover, the varieties of pacifism and nonviolence each adopts a peculiar definition of justice, violence, and peace, and all are forced into answering questions about who it is that pacifism applies to and under what circumstances.[60]

Nonetheless, Wink's argument against pacifism is mainly the conviction of pacifists' non-resistance in the midst of injustice and repressive regimes. As discussed in his exegesis of Matthew 5:38–39a, Wink argues that translating the original Greek word, *antistēnai* as "resist not" is improper. For Wink, many Christian pacifists interpret this word as "resist not" to justify their position as non-resistant. Further, Wink's ethical exploration, as Grimsrud argues, cannot be confined to the concept of nonviolence. There are other key thoughts Wink has advanced, such as his comprehensive view of the world as the domination system, the pervasiveness of the myth of redemptive violence, and God's domination-free order. If peace is what pacifists are straining for,

---

58. Grimsrud, "Pacifist Critique," 56.
59. Grimsrud, 56.
60. Hassell, s.v. "Pacifism," in Chatterjee, *Encyclopaedia of Global Justice*.

the DFO is the dream of Wink. The DFO is also an all-embracing vision for all humanity if peace, as Grimsrud argues, is a holistic concept.

For Christian realists, is Christ's teaching of loving enemies feasible enough in such a sinful and imperfect world? Christian realism is a term mostly known through an American theologian, Reinhold Niebuhr. His ideas dominated and directed it, and his thought is the key to our understanding of it.[61] Essentially, Niebuhr's "Christian realism stresses the role of power in maintaining order and accomplishing political purposes, but he also insisted on the necessity of checking power with countervailing power."[62] In *The Nature and Destiny of Man: A Christian Interpretation*, Niebuhr expresses that sin is both religious and moral. It is religious because of human rebellion against God, and at the same time, it is moral and social because of human injustice. However, Niebuhr focuses more on the social and moral dimension of sin than religion, saying that, "the ego which falsely makes itself the centre of existence in its pride and will-to-power inevitably subordinates other life to its will and thus does injustice to other life."[63] In short, Ed Miller and Stanley Grenz give a succinct explanation of Christian realism,

> This theology was called Christian realism because, first, it entertained no illusions about the human situation as defined by sin; it was realistic about sin's inevitability and universality. Second, it found in the biblical and Christian perspective the most adequate account of sin, . . . and of the fallenness of humanity. It was a "pragmatic" endeavour because it was driven by an interest in practical solutions, or at least responses, to the sinful human situation.[64]

---

61. Lovin, *Reinhold Niebuhr*, 2.

62. Lovin, *Christian Realism*, 2.

63. Niebuhr, *Nature and Destiny of Man*, 179. In fact, Niebuhr's anthropological outlook was a product of his pastoral experiences among ordinary people in Bethel Evangelical Church in Detroit, Michigan. Against the historical backdrop in which liberal teaching on human innate goodness and political utopia was dominant, Niebuhr projected a view of human inborn wickedness based on the Scriptural teaching. He became such a sharp critic of reigning pacifism at that time, and civil rights movement led by Martin Luther King Jr. It is incorrect to consider violence as a natural and inevitable expression of ill-will, and nonviolence of goodwill; therefore, violence is intrinsically evil and nonviolence intrinsically good. See, Niebuhr, *Moral Man and Immoral Society*, 171–172.

64. Miller and Grenz, *Fortress Introduction*, 25.

What Niebuhr contended is that the Christian hope, therefore, can be found only in the grace of God amid man's sin, not in others such as natural law or human love. Likewise, he viewed the gospel as the source of divine mercy which can overcome a contradiction within our soul.

Hence, realistically, "Christian love must leave the evils of this life by means of just laws and, when necessary, by the use of force."[65] However, Niebuhr did not regard war as just; instead, he saw it as sin. What he argued is that war, when necessary, is to be held only for the cause of justice. Thus, as some scholars argue, he is pragmatic in this regard, focusing on what can be done here and now, rather than looking forward to what is to come. Wink, as a student of Niebuhr, was impressed by Christian realism in terms of the emphasis on grace, the Holy Spirit, and miracles. But he did not fully accept it as his own because it compromises the myth of redemptive violence for him.[66]

Lastly, there is a recently developed concept in the study of peace and war, which is known as the just peacemaking theory. These theorists do not give much attention to the issue of whether there is a so-called just war or whether making war can be justified. Instead, just peacemaking theorists seek to define and implement the praxis that prevents war and violent conflicts with the aim of creating peace.[67] Glen Stassen, as one of the theorists, argues that just peacemaking, unlike the just war theory, Christian realism, and pacifism, seeks the third option. That is, instead of asking either just war or pacifism, Stassen explores the question, "what initiatives are we to take for the prevention of war?"[68] In other words, the just peacemaking theory is closer to Wink's notion of Jesus's third way than just war, Christian realism, and pacifism. But its focus is more on the side of prevention and conflict resolution, than a change of institution itself, paying greater attention to negotiation, diplomacy, etc. On the contrary, Jesus's third way, for Wink, is basically to resist any system of domination nonviolently.

---

65. Niebuhr, "Christian Church is not Pacifist," 301.

66. Wink, *Engaging the Powers*, 279, 308.

67. Glen Stassen, as a proponent of just peacemaking, lists seven practices of the just peacemaking theory. They are: affirm common security, take independent initiatives, talk with your enemy, seek human rights and justice, acknowledge vicious circle, participate in peacemaking process, end judgmental propaganda or make amends, and lastly, work with citizens' groups for the truth. See Stassen, *Just Peacemaking*, 94–109.

68. Stassen, *Just Peacemaking*, 236.

Tracing these traditions, Wink shows that the third way or nonviolence goes beyond the former three views. On the one hand, he attempts to adhere to the pacifistic position with regard to principled nonviolence, yet he seems to be dissatisfied with pacifists' non-resistant position in the heat of conflict. On the other hand, he tries to adopt the position of just war in regard to siding with justice and being angered by injustice, yet he is poles apart from their use of violence. For him, the just war theory is in one way or another supportive of the myth of redemptive violence.[69] In short, he sides with pacifism with regard to principled nonviolence, but not with their non-resistant attitude. Wink seriously considers all form of injustice like the just war theorist and the Christian realist do, yet he by no means approves of the use of armed force.

To conclude, pacifists, just war theorists, and Christian realists are all debating with one another in favour of their own view. Some accuse the pacifist position as being idealism, while just war and Christian realism are considered to be too compromising in terms of morality. This quasi-unending debate between just war, Christian realism, and pacifism is a moot question. But what can be learned from just war and Christian realism is that sin is mysteriously rooted in the world. It is not just the DS, where the human race is caught. It is also a matter of the human heart where the egoistic attitude is deeply entrenched. This is where Wink's *Powers* Trilogy should be remade to include the mysterious dimension of sin, which is deep-seated not only in human society but also the human heart. However, what needs to be viewed with caution is that the use of violence should not always be justified on the ground of human imperfection.

3.1.4 Violence and the Cross

Today we highly regard tolerance, peace, and inter-religious dialogue as the imperative ingredients in such a culturally and religiously pluralistic society. Things pertaining to violence, any form of terrorism, and social or religious exclusion are considered to be the threats to social tranquillity. This affects Christianity. Thus, a number of theologians and biblical scholars have begun

---

69. It seems that the most unacceptable aspect of just war to Wink is not the list of criteria through which a particular war is justifiable or not. What embarrasses him is that the just war theory is another form of the belief in the myth of redemptive violence. See Wink, *Powers That Be*, 153.

to give greater attention to the study of peace, justice, nonviolence, and violence than before. The violent stories in the Bible become one of the serious subjects to them. In particular, believing Jesus's death as substitutionary atonement for human sin looks disgusting and totally unacceptable to many theologians. In studying nonviolence from a Christian perspective, the cross where Jesus was violently killed is such an enigma to Christian scholars. In *The Lost Message of Jesus*, the authors argue that the idea of divine forgiveness, unable to forgive without drawing blood, leads to a form of cosmic child abuse.[70] Therefore, it is essential for this study to discuss the cross and violence. Any Christian theological reflection on violence and nonviolence has to tackle the mystery of the cross – the God who saved humankind through the most violent death of his son, Jesus Christ.

My disagreement with Wink is the overemphasis on the *Christus Victor* theory of atonement at the cost of others, and especially that his severe criticism against the substitutionary theory is one-sided. In the following, I will discuss the way in which Wink argues for the *Christus Victor* so passionately that he disdains the historic Christian faith on substitution atonement. Wink also examines the violence in the Old Testament and the theory of atonement through the eyes of a Swiss Catholic theologian Raymund Schwager and a French anthropologist René Girard. First, Wink's view of Jesus's death only from the Girardian angle is a purely structural reading of the gospel. Wink reads the death of Jesus as the end of all sacrificial systems through the lens of Girard. In Girard's understanding, the sacrificial system of ancient time – Jewish or non-Jewish – is nothing but a form of organized violence for the sake of social serenity.[71]

---

70. Chalke and Mann, *Lost Message of Jesus*, 182.

71. According to Girard, we imitate others (mimesis) by desiring what others desire. This desire leads to mimetic rivalry by the time two or more people want the same thing at the same time. This rivalry causes the breakdown of the order of the social distinctions which Girard calls a "crisis of distinctions." To prevent the breakdown, a society has to find a scapegoat upon which or on whom all hatreds, resentments, and violent impulses are heaped. Girard posits that this is the way sacrifice becomes salvific for the society and the sacrificial system becomes the overarching principle of both religion and culture. Girard's idea of mimic desire is similar to a basic teaching of Buddha. In Buddhism, the root-cause of evil is *tanha*, which can be best translated as desire. To attain the *nibbana*, which is the ultimate goal of all Buddhists, one must extinguish *tanha* (desire). But Girard's view is only one-dimensional in the sense that he defines it from a structural point of view. Thus, he regards mimetic the desire as the root of violence

Thus, the sacrificial system became a preventive action to control the greater violence: a scapegoat is chosen to absorb all the violence in order to prevent a greater amount of violence. Jesus, through his willing obedience unto death, became a scapegoat. For Girard, what makes Jesus's sacrifice distinct from others is not his suffering and agonies, but it is Jesus's willing submission that unmasked the reality of the powers by denouncing the verdict passed on him, thereby revealing their judgment as a total miscarriage of justice. Put differently, the judgment passed on Jesus by the Powers itself, in turn, judged them. As John Yoder affirms, Girard's insightful contribution provides an understanding "both of the imperative for retaliation and of the way the cross breaks the chain."[72]

On the one hand, Girard's non-sacrificial reading of the sacrifices in the Old Testament is indeed enlightening in that it exposes the hidden nature of sacrifice in such a way that sacrifice is not just a religious offer to appease gods or spirits for blessings. It is also a form of scapegoating, putting all the blames upon a sacrificial victim, thereby freeing the community. On the other hand, this reading brings into question the whole sacrificial system of the Old Testament. That is, it is a moot point to contend that the whole sacrificial system in the Old Testament is merely a scapegoat mechanism. In particular, Wink's reading raises a question to the adherents of "penal substitutionary atonement,"[73] according to which Jesus, through his willing submission, was punished or penalized in the place of sinners, thus the justice be done, and God's forgiveness be experienced. For those who believe in the substitutionary atonement, Wink's reading of the Old Testament's sacrificial system through the lens of Girard is thoroughly one-sided because he neglects the important dimension of "sacrifice as God's appointed means to atone for the sins of his people."[74]

Despite the insightful contribution of Girard's reading, it does not encompass a wide range of the meaning of Jesus's death. As it is basically a

---

and the cause of the scapegoat mechanism. In contrast, Buddha viewed the desire as the root of all sufferings, which seems more comprehensive than Girard's.

72. Yoder, *War of the Lamb*, 177.

73. The most recent book that explains and defends the Penal Substitutionary Atonement is, Packer and Dever, *In My Place Condemned He Stood*.

74. Jeffery, Ovey and Sach, *Pierced for Our Transgressions*, 236.

structural reading, it trivializes the personal dimension of evil or sin. Volf points out that exposing the scapegoating mechanism will not suffice because people have a proclivity to "re-mask what has been de-masked when it fits their interests."[75] The problem of evil or sin is far more complex than the structural. Sin is not just out there, structurally and socially embedded, but also inwardly present within us.

Not only does Wink apply Girard's scapegoat theory in interpreting the cross of Jesus Christ, he also employs Carl Jung's psychoanalytic method for understanding it. For Wink, sin is alienation, which is not solely the result of our rebellion against God, but it is the way we have been socialized by alienating rules and requirements. Based on "You were dead in the trespasses and sins in which you once walked, following the course of this world," (Eph 2:1-2 ESV) *the* domination system, Wink regards sin as the result of socializing the culture of the DS. He insists that we are to be dead insofar as we have been socialized into patterns of the DS.[76] Thereby Wink verifies that the *Christus Victor* theory of atonement, according to which, what Christ has accomplished is neither to appease God's wrath nor to substitute our death, but precisely to overcome the Powers themselves. When sin is defined as merely being dead by the Powers, it would be justifiable for him to say that the *Christus Victor* is the only valid atonement theory.

The most recent scholar who passionately and brilliantly argues for the atonement theory is N. T. Wright, a world leading Bible scholar and the chair of New Testament and Early Christianity at the School of Divinity at the University of St. Andrews. In his book, *The Day the Revolution Began: Reconsidering the Meaning of Jesus' Crucifixion*, Wright proposes an approach to reconsider the death of Christ in the light of the whole biblical narrative because he exegetes the Old and New Testaments on the basis of Paul's statements in 1 Corinthians 15:3–4, ". . . that Christ died for our sins according to the Scriptures, that he was buried, that he was raised on the third day according to the Scriptures . . ." (KJV) Wright makes every effort to delineate what Paul means by "according to the Scriptures" in four chapters in part two of the book. As Frances Young reviews, Wright invites Christian scholars and

---

75. Volf, *Exclusion and Embrace*, 292–293.
76. Wink, *Powers That Be*, 90; *Engaging the Powers*, 157.

theologians to return to "the New Testament exegesis and a reclaiming of the accounts and categories through which the earliest Christians celebrated and affirmed the drama of the cross, scandal though it was."[77] Wright's thorough argument against is the view that God saves humankind through the death of Jesus Christ for our sin so that those who believe in him will go to heaven.[78] For Wright, this view is a Platonized goal and a moralizing diagnosis, which leads to the idea that an angry divinity is pacified by human sacrifice – Jesus's crucifixion.

In atonement theories, theologians advance their view on the basis of what the fundamental predicament and the ultimate goal of humanity the Bible talks about. Many view sin or moral failings as a fundamental problem and heaven as the ultimate goal. But Wright reconsiders from the perspective of the whole biblical narrative and argues that it is not sin or moral breaking but idolatry and the distortion of genuine humanness, and not heaven but a renewed human vocation within God's renewed creation.[79] In Wright's view, "works contract" does not refer to the idea that God told his human creatures to keep a moral code, which Adam and Eve failed to. Instead, Wright insists that it is a covenant of vocation – "its main task is image-bearing, reflecting the Creator's wise stewardship into the world and reflecting the praises of all creation back to its maker."[80] For Wright, it is not "a work contract but a covenant of vocation, it is not sin but idolatry, it is not heaven but renewed creation, are the central narrative of the Bible; therefore it is what Paul talks about 'according to the Scriptures.'"[81]

Seeing the cross from the whole biblical narrative, Wright contends that Christ's victory through the cross is centrally over the powers of evil, sin, death, and violence. In saying that, Wright does not mean to rule out other

---

77. Young, "Tom Wright," 381.

78. Wright, *Day the Revolution Began*, 4. This book was also published by SPCK with a little different subtitle, *Rethinking* instead *Reconsidering* by Harper Collins.

79. Wright, 73, 74.

80. Wright, 75, 76.

81. In his talk "The Cross" at Wheaton College, 2017, N. T. Wright articulated that many Christians read Paul's usage of the phrase, "according to the Scriptures" and interpret it in accordance with the narratives which are comparatively modern traditions. He insists that "according to the Scriptures" is far more organic and far more rooted than just a handful of isolated texts, see Wight, "The Cross" (YouTube video).

theories of atonement, instead he gives other theories space to make their proper contributions. In that sense, all other theories are not contradictory, but they all fit together. Taking one of them (for example, penal substitution) and interpreting out of its biblical narrative is, for Wright, perilous because God might be seen as a bullying headmaster who killed his one son for the salvation of humankind.[82]

In fact, Wright's *The Day the Revolution Began* is welcomed and criticized among many scholars and theologians. For instance, a Reformed theologian Michael Horton remarks that "the story he (Wright) tells is vital for us to hear; he exposes the wider redemptive-historical canvas that challenges tendencies to domesticate the gospel to a Platonised eschatology focused on the salvation of the individual believer from this world rather than the redemption of all believers with this world."[83] Many scholars and theologians welcome Wright's *The Day the Revolution Began* despite disagreeing with some of his arguments in the book.[84] Compared to Wink's argument for the *Christus Victor*, Wright is obviously more biblically and theological solid and robust than Wink's.

Though an advocate of *Christus Victor*, Wink's argument is based on Girard and Jung's views, thereby asserting that the idea of a God who is wrathful is intolerable. Thus, he rejects the historic Christian teaching of Christ's death as substitution for human sin. If he is correct, the teaching of the church through the centuries on the God of justice, who judges justly humankind is nothing but reckless. It is true that God is love, and his love is unconditional, but it does not mean that sin or evil that we commit does not matter to God. In this sense, Wink's view of God is distorted because he lays great emphasis on God's love at the expense of the justice, which is also an essential ingredient of God's attributes. How can the God who is just and holy receive humans who are unholy, evil, filthy? Put it in syllogistic reasoning, God is holy and man is unholy, therefore a bridge must be built to reconcile the holy and unholy. God is just, and injustice is evil, therefore the just God

---

82. See Wright, "Atonement Debate," (YouTube video).

83. Horton, "N. T. Wright Reconsiders."

84. Of course, Wright's *The Day the Revolution Began* deserves a lengthier discussion than now in this section. But the atonement theory is not such a central theological theme of this thesis though it is a part of it, suffice it to say that Wright's argument for the *Christus Victor* is much biblically and theologically richer than Wink.

must exercise justice for the evil that humans have committed; or God hates evil and evil must be treated, therefore God's treatment of evil must be just.

In reconciling between the holy and the unholy, the just and unjust, there must be someone or something which goes between so that the betweenness of the holy and the unholy, the just and the unjust, may be resolved. For Wink, the one who goes between the conflicting parties seems unnecessary. God is love, and at the same time, the biblical God also hates evil; therefore, his treatment of evil must reflect his justice. If not, God's love, justice, and holiness would contradict each other. But Wink argues that we are forgiven, now we can repent! God loves us, now we can lift our eyes to God. The enmity is over.[85] How does it happen? God is no longer vengeful, but he accepts us as we are. Where does Wink acquire this idea of God? For him, it was Jesus who introduced such a radical image of God. Wink argues that Jesus taught divine judgment not as an end but as a beginning, not to consume but to purify, not to destroy but to awaken people to the devastating truth about their lives.[86] If it were true, how could a God, who was vengeful before, turn into a forgiving God? Who or what made him to be so? Surely Wink must tackle these questions. Derek Tidball points out that justice is never, biblically speaking, an independent entity but always an expression of the character of a loving and holy God. The problem comes when we see the moral law of God through the eyes of contemporary statute law, according to which a judge discards all personal elements in the process of his judgment.[87] For Wink, penal substitutionary atonement seems to be a primitive idea of punishment. Hence, he seeks to "swallow up" the idea of divine wrath in the concept of divine love.[88]

As a matter of fact, Wink's approach is simply humanistic because humans are not innately evil. They become evil because of the socialization that they go through in the reign of the DS. As the Powers are outward and inward, material and physical manifestations of an institution, we are not only physically socialized into the patterns of the DS, but we are also spiritually internalized into the values and beliefs of the DS. As a consequence, humankind becomes

---

85. Wink, *Engaging the Powers*, 266.
86. Wink, 266.
87. Tidball, "Penal Substitution," 350.
88. Tidball, 351.

evil. Seeing the cross of Christ in this light, Wink interprets that what the cross does is simply to expose the Powers that turned away from the divine purpose, thereby bringing them back to the original divine purpose. This radically contrasts with the historic Christian doctrine of atonement which sees Christ's death as substitutionary for human sin.

Moreover, Wink goes too far by placing Jesus in the same category of the nonviolent revolutionaries as Oscar Romero, Martin Luther King Jr, and Mohandas Gandhi.[89] Wink sees that accepting arraignment, trial, crucifixion and death, Jesus stripped the scapegoating mechanism of its sacred aura and exposed it for what it was: legalized murder.[90] In that sense, Romero, King and Gandhi reflect the same truth that was revealed in Jesus.[91]

However, looking at the cross which is the salvific act of God merely from the perspective of violence and nonviolence diminishes the Christian gospel. The cross is God's judgment against evil and redemptive work for humankind; hence, it should not be equalized with the conflicts between humankind. Certainly, Jesus stood in solidarity with them in the sense of unmasking and resisting the injustice of the powers that be. Yet his death is indeed far greater than that. Supposing, if Jesus were merely a man like these activists, he would be nothing but a hero whose death unmasked the Powers that be of that time. Volf states that not all the people such as King, Gandhi and Romero are, like Jesus, innocent. According to Volf, "the tendency of persecutor to blame victim is reinforced by the actual guilt of victim, even if the guilt is minimal, and they incur it in reaction to the original violence, committed against them."[92] Hence, all humans are inclined to remake what has been unmade as it fits our interests. As a result, our society would always need such heroes in order that the never-ending operation of unmasking the Powers will be going on and on.

In short, Wink's exposition of Jesus's death, like Girard's, is just one dimensional, therefore diminishing the scope of God's liberation. If Jesus were taken as one of these social transformative agents, the implication would appear

---

89. Wink, *Powers That Be*, 86–87.
90. Wink, 86.
91. Wink, 87.
92. Volf, *Exclusion and Embrace*, 293.

that Christians are called to carry on the unfinished task of unmasking the Powers that Jesus, Romero, King, and Gandhi did not finish.

Rejecting the substitutionary atonement, Wink revisits the *Christus Victor* theory, according to which what Christ has overcome through his death is the Powers themselves, nothing else. Hence Wink avers that Christ, through his death, has released all those under delusion and enslavement of the Powers. With this view, Wink continues to define forgiveness in such a way that God has forgiven us for complicity in our own oppression and in that of others. This way of defining forgiveness trivializes the depth of divine forgiveness. Daniel Graham Reid points out that the idea of seeing Christ's death as a sacrifice for sin is sidestepped in the *Christus Victor* motif.[93] In fact, God's forgiveness toward humanity should be far broader than this because the Powers alone are not the guilty party for all evil. Lesslie Newbigin contends that seeing Jesus's death as a revolt against established powers discards the biblical account of the radical sinfulness of human nature. He proposes that the story of Jesus's death and resurrection should be interpreted in the light of the biblical account, not in our contemporary socio-political context.[94] In contrast, Wink interprets the cross not in the light of the biblical narrative but through the cultural and socio-political lens, which leads him to repudiate the historic Christian doctrine of the substitutionary atonement.

According to the critique of Kevin Vanhoozer, Girard and Schwager have equated God's salvation with the termination of the scapegoat mechanism and discarded the problem of guilt since the scapegoat mechanism has been unmasked.[95] Ronald J. Sider also rightly points out that, "some pacifists seem inclined to reduce the doctrine of atonement to a revelation of God's method of dealing with evil."[96] It is true that reading Girard enlightens us to see the cross as exposure of the scapegoat mechanism. However, Wink stresses this view so much that he depreciates other theories of atonement, especially the "substitutionary." Eventually, his structural reading of the gospel leads to the negligence of the personal dimension.

---

93. Reid, "Christus Victor Motif," 323.
94. Newbigin, *Foolishness to the Greeks*, 125–126.
95. Vanhoozer, "Atonement in Postmodernity," 382–390.
96. Sider, "Call for Evangelical Nonviolence."

So far, the discussion seems to lead us to conclude that the penal substitutionary atonement is biblically more justifiable than the *Christus Victor*. Certainly not. As church leaders throughout the ages have been arguing one theory over another, the meaning of the death of Christ is far broader than we can imagine. Therefore, the discussion does not aim to favour penal substitution over the *Christus Victor* or the *Christus Victor* over penal substitution. As mentioned earlier, any theological reflection on nonviolence is faced with the question of the cross where Jesus died. Wink, in tackling this question, favoured the *Christus Victor* over others in such a manner that other theories become flawed.

Of course, the *Christus Victor* theory of atonement contributes momentously to understanding the death of Jesus Christ. Christ's death can also be viewed from a structural point of view, seeing it as an answer to structural evil. T. Scott Daniels highlights that Girard's theory of scapegoat opens up new possibilities for understanding Christ as *Christus Victor*.[97] That is, Christ exposes the Powers to which humans are captive, thereby liberating us from the captivity of the Powers. Put it another way, Christ's death answers not just to the evils we individually have committed, but also to the Powers that overpower us. To quote Wink, it is true that we have rebelled against God, but that is not the sole source of our alienation. It is also the result of our being socialized by alienating rules and requirements.[98]

Therefore, the way in which we should tackle the problem is not either *Christus Victor* or substitutionary atonement; in fact, they should be complementary. Two early church fathers, Irenaeus of Lyons and Gregory of Nyssa, although they argued for the *Christus Victor* theory, admitted that this theory of atonement does not capture all of the significance of the cross. They both include other images and metaphors in their writings about the cross and never put forward a single model as though it captured the whole meaning of the cross.[99] Wink, in advocating the theory the *Christus Victor*, seems too daring and assertive in suggesting that other theories, especially penal substitution, are theologically risky except the theory to which he adheres. In

---

97. Daniels, "Passing the Peace," 136.
98. Wink, *Engaging the Powers*, 150.
99. Green and Baker, *Recovering the Scandal*, 124–125.

short, if the *Christus Victor* depicts Christ's death as exposure to the scapegoat mechanism, substitutionary theory explains how the cross has brought healing to an individual's guilt.

In doing so, two questions to be asked are: how can these two theories be reconciled? Or are they mutually incompatible? Gustaf Aulén, known as the foremost voice of the *Christus Victor* theory, argues that the first one is the predominant view of the early church. However, he suggests that these three theories are not indeed completely contradictory, but they have their own contrary emphasis. While the former sees Christ's work as primarily "a victory over the powers which hold mankind in bondage: sin, death, and the devil,"[100] the latter looks at that "which is done by Christ *as a man* in relation to God."[101] Likewise Alan Spence, on the basis of Aulén's study of three models, avers that atonement theories seem to be complementary to each other, yet they, if structurally and operationally analyzed, are competing with each other.[102] As a matter of fact, another fundamental reason these theories are competing is more than their emphases. Their emphases are principally the outcomes of their theological presuppositions. A good illustration would be if the fundamental human predicament is regarded as personal guilt, sin, alienation from God, we will emphasize the importance of how Christ's death brings about forgiveness of sin and reconciliation with God.

On the contrary, those for whom structural evil is the fundamental human dilemma underscore Christ's victory over the Powers through his death and resurrection. Neither of them is fallacious in viewing so. At the same time, neither of them entirely covers all the bases. The debate between the *Christus Victor* and "substitutionary theory" will surely be ongoing since each has its own theological backdrop upon which arguments ensue. Therefore, I am in disagreement with Wink regarding this debate of atonement theories and the view of the fundamental human predicament. First, Christ's death and resurrection should not be understood from a single theoretical framework.

---

100. Aulén *Christus Victor*, 20. In Aulén's discussion against the *Christus Victor* and the "satisfaction theory," Peter Albelard (1079–1142), as an advocate of "moral influence theory," argued that "Christ is the great Teacher and Example, who arouses responsive love in men; this love is the basis on which reconciliation and forgiveness rest" (96).

101. Aulén, 83.

102. Spence, "Unified Theory," 416.

Jesus's Third Way or Nonviolent Engagement

As it is the key theological tenet of Christianity, it must have rich and varied meaning. As structural reading goes, Christ's death and resurrection demonstrate the victory over the Powers. Likewise, Christ's death and resurrection also assure us of God's forgiveness of sin and reconciliation. Leon Morris rightly suggests that, "no theory (of the atonement) is adequate . . . We need the contributions of quite a few theories to express something of what the cross meant to the men of the New Testament."[103] This shows that each theory of atonement, though not completely, can partially shed light on the wide-ranging meaning of the cross.

Therefore, it is clear that I argue against Wink's sharp critique of penal substitution atonement in favour of the *Christus Victor*, but I agree in some measure with a view of *Christus Victor*, that Christ's death disarms the principalities and powers. Each model of atonement sheds light on something of the truth of the cross and resurrection, whether it is substitution or the *Christus Victor*, but some have more weight theologically and biblically as part of an integrated picture of atonement. As this study is a critical reading of the political context of Myanmar, Wink's structural interpretation of the Powers through the support of the *Christus Victor* is indeed convincing in that Jesus's death disarmed the principalities and powers. In part III, we will see what his structural reading of the Powers can bring out in the latent structural characteristics of the politics of Myanmar.

3.2 An Examination of the "What If" Dilemma

Hannah Arendt argues that Mohandas Gandhi's strategy of nonviolent resistance would cause nothing but massacre and submission if he were encountering Stalin's Russia, Hitler's Germany, and even pre-war Japan instead of England.[104] The what if questions are inevitable to all nonviolent adherents. What if someone breaks into our house? What if we were attacked by muggers? What if another race was committing an action of genocide against mine? What would we do if we were in such a situation? How do Wink,

---

103. Cited from Sider, "Call for Evangelical Nonviolence."
104. Arendt, "On Violence," 152.

Yoder, and Hauerwas respond to the what if dilemma? How does Wink deal with this dilemma differently from Yoder and Hauerwas?

For Wink, the what if dilemma itself shows the absence of nonviolence in the lifestyle and culture of our society, so we are confused if nonviolence is applicable to certain circumstances. In addition, neither violence nor nonviolence guarantees success. As violence fails, so does nonviolence. However, Wink admits that there are certain circumstances in which nonviolence seems impractical. In such circumstances, violence would be a kind of apocalyptic judgment that affects everyone. According to Yoder, there is an assumption behind the what if question. The question presupposes the individualistic notion: I alone can make a decision and the attacker seems pre-programmed to do all evils. Yoder's response reflects the way God responded to his son Jesus during the crucifixion.[105]

For Stanley Hauerwas, the question is not "should I or should I not have an abortion?" but, "what kind of person am I going to be if I do this or that?" Hauerwas argues that it essentially entails not basic principles or individual choice, but the traditions wherein we are nurtured. Therefore, Hauerwas asserts that, "nonviolent persons do not have to choose to use or not to use violence, but rather their being nonviolent means they must use their imaginations to form their whole way of life consistent with their convictions."[106] In a nutshell, Wink, Yoder, and Hauerwas have their own convictions on nonviolence. They are all alike in arguing that nonviolence is more than a means to achieve the desired result. For Wink, cultivating a lifestyle of nonviolence in all dimensions of our life is so important in the world where the belief in redemptive violence has been a pandemic. To cultivate such a culture of nonviolence, the essential requirement is the stories that can birth a living tradition.

Many scholars admit that it is controversial to regard Dietrich Bonhoeffer as a pacifist or just warrior in view of his involvement in the plot to assassinate of Adolf Hitler. If pacifism is defined as rejecting all forms of nonviolent coercion, then Bonhoeffer is surely not a pacifist, like many pacifists are.[107] Truly,

---

105. Yoder, *What Would You Do?*, 41–42.
106. Hauerwas, *Peaceable Kingdom*, 125.
107. Gides, "Dietrich Bonhoeffer's Theology," 13.

Bonhoeffer has left us confused in understanding his theology and life. His pacifism and his joining in the *Abwehr*[108] seem obviously self-contradictory. As André Dumas warns, "Bonhoeffer's ideas do not deserve to be accepted uncritically because he died for them."[109] For Bonhoeffer, Christ is the only object to which all his adherence and allegiance are pledged. What is more, Christian ethics is, according to him, neither a principle nor a doctrine, but obedience to Christ who defeated evil by enduring it. To follow Christ is also not merely to profess Christ doctrinally, but to obey whatever the costs. In short, Bonhoeffer may be variously interpreted – pacifist hero, a situational ethicist, and an advocate of violence. Consideration should be given to the price he paid for following Christ. However, his attempt at assassination cannot be justified because it is incompatible with Jesus's teaching on loving our enemies. He himself acknowledges his act as a sin.[110]

To conclude, Wink, Yoder, and Hauerwas as exponents of principled nonviolence affirm that violent means are unjustifiable for Christians who truly believe in Jesus and his teachings. Among these three, Yoder and Hauerwas appear more thoughtful and theologically solid than Wink because they critically explore the assumptions of this what if dilemma and provide fair critiques. For instance, just as Yoder points out the individualistic worldview behind the assumption, so also Hauerwas critically discerns that decision-making is more than an individual act. However, Wink's approach to this what if dilemma is somewhat futuristic in the sense that he suggests that the path to nonviolence is neither within easy reach nor an instant success. It is a culture that always needs to be cultivated. Wink, Yoder, and Hauerwas all do not leave their options open for violence since nonviolence is, for them, more than a choice. Nonviolence, for Yoder and Hauerwas, is a character and attitude, whereas, for Wink, it is also spirituality.

---

108. *Abwehr* means "counter-intelligence." It was a group of senior military men with civilian advisers in all fields of German life. Their sole purpose was to overthrow Hitler and the National Socialists (E. Robertson, *Shame and the Sacrifice*, 197).

109. Cited from Ertis-Kojima, "Significance of Dietrich Bonhoeffer Today," 83.

110. Wink, *Engaging the Powers*, 225.

3.3 The Powers, Church and Nonviolence

What is the role of the church in the struggle of the Powers according to Wink? What has the church got to do with the Powers? How should the church be prepared to engage the Powers? If nonviolence is the only alternative to transform the DS into the DFO, who or what is the most responsible for this transformation? What is Wink's view of the church in terms of the Powers and nonviolence? Now I will discuss Wink's view of the church in relation to the Powers and nonviolence in the light of Yoder and Hauerwas.[111] Then I will assess their ecclesiological viewpoint from the perspective of a mission theologian Lesslie Newbigin (1909–1998). Wink, Yoder, and Hauerwas, as western scholars, write their thoughts in their own context wherein Christianity is a predominant religion. In contrast, Newbigin, though being a westerner, worked as a missionary in India for nearly forty years. This interaction between these scholars aims to affirm Wink's ecclesiology on the one hand and reformulate it on the other.

In launching theological exploration, both Wink and Yoder seem to be somewhat similar to each other in the sense that the ultimate tension, for Wink, is between the DS and the DFO, while for Yoder, it is between the old and new aeons. Where they differ is how the DS or the old aeon may be transformed into the DFO or the new aeon. Wink believes that it is the DS that needs to be transformed into the DFO only through the nonviolent engagement of all sorts of socio-political groups; whereas for Yoder and Hauerwas, it is the old aeon that can be transformed into the new aeon only through God's new community, which is the church. Yoder distinguishes the role of the church from the other, worldly social groups because the church is the only social embodiment of the new aeon or the kingdom of God. But Wink makes no distinction between the church and the world in relation to transforming the Powers, because of the applicability of nonviolence to all religious contexts.

---

111. As some critics see Hauerwas as Yoderian, it is true that Hauerwas is ecclesiologically an enlarged expositor of Yoder. Put differently, Hauerwas has deepened what Yoder has begun. Thus, when I in some parts mention Yoder alone without describing Hauerwas, it does not mean that it is Yoder's view alone, but often that of Hauerwas as well.

Unlike Yoder and Hauerwas, Wink does not take the position that the church that Jesus built has a unique divine purpose. His view of the church is more superficial than Yoder, Hauerwas, and Newbigin. In an overview of early Christianity, Wink argues that the church regarded nonviolence as the only way, thereby seeing war as antithetical to Jesus's teaching. However, from the period of Emperor Constantine, a radical shift ensued. Many Christians, under the auspices of Constantine, began to see war, which had once seemed so evil, as a necessary evil to preserve and propagate the gospel. In Wink's eyes, churches through centuries have not been loyal enough to follow the footsteps of their master Jesus Christ who struggled to overcome the DS.[112]

Wink's key argument about the church in history is its incapability to decide upon whether domination is wrong or not, which is why he exerts himself to reinforce nonviolence as the vocation of the church. Thus, the church has nothing to do with any forms of violence in any circumstances. However, what is important for Wink is that the church is one among many groups that struggle to humanize the Powers. Even God does not rely exclusively on the church. Hence, the *raison d'être* of the church, like other socio-political groups, is to humanize the Powers for the welfare of humankind. Thereby he argues that the church is not called to create a new society, but "to delegitimate an unjust system and to create a spiritual counter-climate."[113] For him, the church is not distinct from other social groups.

However, Wink affirms that the primary task of the church, though it has many functions, is to unmask the Powers, that is, practicing a ministry of disclosing the spirituality of these Powers.[114] For him, the call to nonviolence is a vocation of the church – the vocation which is grounded in Jesus's teaching, the divine nature, the ethos of the kingdom and the power of the resurrection.[115] Therefore, the church is called to nonviolence to express its fidelity to Jesus's teaching; the call to nonviolence is not a matter of legalism, of an absolute ethical norm, or of salvation, but because God's grace invites us and enables us to do so.[116] In fact Wink, through this twenty-first century mindset, looks

---

112. Wink, *When the Powers Fall*, 11.
113. Wink, *Engaging the Powers*, 165.
114. Wink, 84–85, 164.
115. Wink, 216.
116. Wink, 217–218.

at the fact that Jesus himself was not entirely free of ethnocentric attitudes. The gospel was, for him, domesticated to androcratic (male-ruling) attitudes in the early church.[117]

Like Yoder, Wink discovers that the early church fell into the temptation of the power complex. Once it was the persecuted and oppressed, but it then became a persecutor instead when the Roman empire was Christianized.[118] Augustine (d. 430) was the one, for Wink, who promoted the idea of using violence, if necessary, as a loving obligation to defend the innocent against evil.[119] Wink's argument is that the church's entrapment into the web of the just war mentality from the time of the Roman emperor Constantine has been so powerful that the myth of redemptive violence has been, since then, prevalent throughout Christian history.

Truly, the church made numerous mistakes in its history. But does it mean that we should disregard the unique role of the church in society? Or, alternatively, should we regard the church as nothing but one of the religious entities? Of course not. Jesus himself did not demand his disciples to build a morally flawless community; instead, he commanded them to obey his teachings. It is evident that the church failed to obey Jesus's teachings many times in various periods. Hence, the church needs to be brought back to its initial call once it fails. What can bring back the church to its rightful place is nothing but the Scripture, where it finds its lord and master, Jesus Christ. The relationship between the church and Scripture is best described by the late Donald G. Bloesch,

> The church can bear a true witness to God's self-revelation in Christ but only insofar as its subordinates itself to Scripture and allows itself to be taught by the Spirit of God. The church can be a support for truth, but it is dangerously misleading to conceive of it as an incarnation of the truth. The church can be

---

117. For those who study ancient social, cultural and political values or beliefs, it has been a trap to critique ancient values in the light of contemporary context. There is no doubt that human civilisation is advancing on and on, technologically, medically, intellectually, and even some views on moral vision. Here, Wink's critique or comment on Jesus and the early church is so much presupposed with the modern worldview.

118. Wink, *Engaging the Powers*, 110–111, 212.

119. Wink, 212.

a helpful guide for people of faith, but it must never be thought of as guarantee for knowing the truth. The church is not itself the kingdom of God but a poignant sign and witness of the inbreaking of the kingdom into human history. The church is our mother and teacher in the faith but only insofar as it is open to being corrected and reformed by the wisdom of the eternal God as we see this manifested and embodied in Jesus Christ.[120]

Wink, instead of looking at the relationship between the church and Scripture, looks into the failures of the church in following Jesus's teaching on loving enemies, and ignores its important role in society. If God himself does not depend on the church as Wink argues, why did Jesus entrust his mission to the church? If the church has no significant role in unmasking the Powers, the question is, "where do other social groups, which struggle to humanize the Powers, learn how to confront the Powers?" If Jesus's God is interested merely in whether we behave in a way consistent with the divine order, does it mean that what counts to God is nothing but social service and philanthropic work? Wink's treatment of the church does not do justice to the biblical teaching on the important role of the church in society. Therefore, what necessitates this study is to recover the significant role of the church in confronting the Powers.

Unlike Wink, Yoder and Hauerwas have highly positioned the role of the church in creating their social ethics in such a way that the existence of church itself declares "the Lordship of Christ over the Powers, from whose dominion the Church has begun to be liberated."[121] For Yoder, the purpose of the church is to be the kind of humanity within which economic and racial differences are levelled so that it may become a structure and a power. Likewise, Stanley Hauerwas, as enormously influenced by Yoder, sees the church as a social ethic, polis and God's new language.[122] The church is called to be a new reality formed and shaped by the values and norms of the kingdom of God as seen in the life and destiny of Jesus.[123] As to the church as God's new

---

120. Bloesch, *Church*, 32.
121. Yoder, *Politics of Jesus*, 153.
122. Hauerwas, *Peaceable Kingdom*, 2nd ed., 99.
123. Hauerwas, *In Good Company*, 6.

language, Hauerwas uses the analogy of the new language that God created at Pentecost, a language that is more than words.[124]

In centring the church as the basis of a social ethic, Yoder, like Wink, is conscious of what the church wrongfully did in history. He calls it "Constantinianism," which is "the identification of church and world in the mutual approval and support exchanged by Constantine and the bishops."[125] As a result of Constantine's Christianization, the existence of the church, instead of being the obedient follower of Jesus Christ, is only to maintain the present order of things by using any cultic means at her disposal to legitimize that order. What is more, the just war mentality began to take root in Christianity as one of the results. Both Wink and Yoder see the mistake that the church committed in history. Wink, thus, concludes that the church has no special or peculiar qualities compared to other social groups. On the contrary, Yoder has taken a lesson from that mistake and suggested that the church should sidestep from it in order to be true to itself – God's new community. By and large, Wink seems very inclusive while Yoder and Hauerwas appear to be exclusive or sectarian in relation to understanding the relationship between the church and the world. What needs to be done, therefore, is to look for way to bridge the gap between Wink and Yoder. Put differently, how can the church be *in* the world, but not *of* it?[126]

Despite Yoder's seemingly exclusive view of the church and Wink's inclusive ecclesiology, Lesslie Newbigin goes between these two extremes. Somewhat like Yoder and Hauerwas, Newbigin views the church as a community that has committed to following the footsteps of Jesus Christ. The church is, hence, distinct because of its allegiance to Christ alone. In this sense, the church is different from the world because it has its own values and principles.

---

124. Hauerwas, *Christian Existence Today*, 53. The event of Pentecost can be seen Acts chapter 2.

125. Yoder, *Original Revolution*, 65. Yoder, in many parts of his writings, employs the term, "Constantinian or Constantinianism" in order to elucidate how the Christian church has been saturated by its ideology, i.e., "just war mentality" and diluted the radicalness of the Gospel of Christ with worldly ethical standards. His most lucid and clear exposition of the notion of "Constantinianism" can be found in the chapter, "the Meaning of the Constantinian Shift," in his book, *Christian Attitudes to War*, 39–54.

126. John 17:14. In her PhD dissertation, Elizabeth M. Mosbo VerHage notes that Yoder needs to flesh out his ecclesiology in order to reflect the dual nature of the Church – its identity and its mission.

However, Newbigin sees the church as being responsible for the world in three ways. First, Newbigin sees the church as the eschatological community with a vision of "the holy city into which all the glory of the nations will be brought and from which everything unclean is excluded."[127] Therefore, the church is called to commit without reserve to all secular work, but in doing so, the church is to work in the light of its own values and principles.

Second, Newbigin sees that the church is fulfilling the promise given by Jesus, "I still have many things to say to you, but you cannot bear them now. When the Spirit of truth comes, he will guide you into all the truth."[128] Newbigin believes that this promise is being fulfilled as the church goes on its missionary journey to the end of the time. During this journey, the church enters into dialogue with new cultures and "learns new things and provides the place where witness is borne to Christ as head of the human race."[129] Third, Newbigin sees the world through the lens of the cross. The cross, for him, depicts the balance of two poles: the infinite love of God and the unmasking of the dark horror of sin. Thus, he suggests that all true Christian thinking should maintain this two-edged magnetic field: the amazing grace of God and the appalling sin of the world. By implication, the church is called to cooperate with people of all faiths in struggling for justice and freedom, and at the same time, the church is also to be aware of the appalling sin of the world.[130] Hence, Newbigin's view of the church is more engaging than Wink's and Yoder's in the sense that the church plays a significant role in the process of transforming the DS into the DFO. The existence of the church is not for its own sake, but for the world's sake, hence Christians should collaborate with people of other faiths in the process of creating a domination-free order.

Integrally speaking, the nature of the church is, for Newbigin, particularistic, and at the same time inclusive. It is particularistic in the sense that Jesus is the only head or Lord of the church, and except him, there are no other heads or lords. Likewise, it is also inclusive in that all peoples on the earth are invited to join. For this dual nature of the church, Newbigin expressly states,

---

127. Newbigin, *Foolishness to the Greeks*, 136.
128. John 16:12–13 NRSV.
129. Newbigin, *Foolishness to the Greeks*, 139.
130. Newbigin, *Gospel in a Pluralist Society*, 181.

> The Church is the pilgrim people of God. It is on the move – hastening to the ends of the earth to beseech all men to be reconciled to God, and hastening to the end of time to meet its Lord who will gather all into one. Therefore the nature of the Church is never to be finally defined in static terms, but only in terms of that to which it is going. It cannot be understood rightly except in a perspective which is at once missionary and eschatological, and only in that perspective can the deadlock of our present ecumenical debate be resolved.[131]

To conclude, Wink and Yoder go to their own extremes in terms of the role of the church in relation to the world. For Wink, the church is nothing more than a sort of social institution among many others; in contrast, Yoder puts too much emphasis on the distinct existence of the church at the expense of its relation to the world. However, Newbigin sees a synthesis of the relationship between the church and the world in the context where Christianity is a minority. As this research aims to formulate a nonviolence theology with reference to the context of Myanmar where Buddhism is the state religion, Newbigin's paradigm is much more apposite to the Myanmar context than employing Wink and Yoder alone.

3.4 What's Next When the Powers Fall? Toward a Reconciliation

The inevitable question that we have to encounter when the Powers fall is, "How are we to treat or deal with the oppressors, victimizers, and human rights violators?" Put differently, how should the reconciliation or the broken relationship between the oppressors and the oppressed, victimizers and victimized be established or amended? Here the attempt in this section is to engage Wink's idea of reconciliation in the light of other peace scholars. Since transitional justice in post-authoritarian regimes is such an urgent and important subject in the global context, we should engage with this issue in this study.

---

131. Newbigin, *Household of God*, 18.

Reconciliation is often equated with compromise, the toleration of injustice, and obedience to the higher powers. For Wink, this is a false reconciliation;[132] Miroslav Volf calls it cheap[133] reconciliation. Wink suggests that to reconcile is to "re-establish love between two or more estranged parties."[134] So how can such love be restored? The process of reconciliation is the most difficult and complicated task. Wink is more concerned with the question of *how* rather than that of *who* the reconciler ought to be. For Wink, forgiveness is a mechanism through which reconciliation might be achieved. But forgiveness is, in fact, a personal psycho-spiritual exercise. What about the victims who suffered excruciatingly and were unable to forgive their perpetrators?

According to the study of peace building in post-conflict societies, there are two approaches to reconciliation: "interpersonal or individual reconciliation" (IR) and "national unity and reconciliation" (NUR).[135] The former seeks to reconcile victims and perpetrators on a personal level, whereas the latter focuses on creating a culture of human rights, based upon an inclusive and democratic notion of citizenship. Thus, the IR is mostly associated with either a religious paradigm or a medical/therapeutic one, while the NUR relates to socio-political institutions. For the IR, confession, repentance, forgiveness, and the restoration of broken relationships are given precedence over structural issues. In contrast, the emphasis, for the NUR model is placed on tolerance, peaceful coexistence, rule of law, democracy, human rights culture, conflict resolution, transparency, and public debate.

If forgiveness is considered as personal, Wink might be categorized as an advocate of the IR model. But Wink does not stop there in discussing reconciliation. He has a great regard for truth, peace, and issues of amnesty, which are all intricately related in the process of reconciliation. In the process, the unavoidable question is, "Should amnesty be granted to all perpetrators?" Desmond Tutu once asked, "Can it ever be right for someone who has committed the most atrocities to be allowed to get off scot-free, simply by

---

132. Wink, *When the Powers Fall*, 24–32.
133. Volf, "Forgiveness, Reconciliation, and Justice," 867–869.
134. Wink, *When the Powers Fall*, 16.
135. Borer, "Truth Telling," 32–33.

confessing what he or she has done?"[136] Wink suggests that truth precedes impunity, so "amnesty should be given only after all the facts are out and the victims have had their say."[137] Similarly, Tutu describes, "amnesty is granted only to those who plead guilty and accept responsibility for what they did."[138] This issue of amnesty is so crucial because it is a matter of false, cheap, or true reconciliation. Stephen Parmentier proposes four criteria: "searching for the truth about the past; ensuring accountability for the acts committed; providing reparation to victims, and promoting reconciliation in society."[139] Of course, no one can control the response of the perpetrators, but what can be done is to assess whether or not their response is false or not. Wink is not merely on the side of the IR model alone, he also takes the NUR model into consideration.

Although the NUR model discards some personal issues such as forgiveness, the reconciliation sought after would be incomplete without it. Forgiveness, in spite of its varied definitions from various (religious, social, or political) standpoints, is the dynamic of psycho-spirituality, thus, it can hardly be institutionalized in our legal system. Personal forgiveness is indispensable in doing reconciliation. The importance of forgiveness notwithstanding, it alone cannot bring us into the territory of reconciliation. Volf suggests that to achieve reconciliation is to be willing to embrace as well as forgiving indiscriminately. "There can be no embrace of the former enemy without forgiveness, and forgiveness should lead beyond itself to embrace."[140] Similarly, Wink proposes that forgiveness, despite being a component of reconciliation, is the first step because it requires us to instigate something – e.g. picking up the phone or meeting face to face and trying to work things out.[141] But for Volf, it is only through the will to embrace others uncondition-

---

136. Tutu, *No Future without Forgiveness*, 47. Tutu worked as a chairman in the Truth and Reconciliation Commission (TRC) – a court-like restorative justice body assembled in South Africa after the abolition of apartheid.
137. Wink, *When the Powers Fall*, 33–34.
138. Tutu, *No Future without Forgiveness*, 50.
139. Jones, Parmentier, and Weitekamp, "Dealing with International Crimes," 554–555.
140. Volf, *Free of Charge*, 190.
141. Wink, *When the Powers Fall*, 14.

ally while determining what is just and naming wrong as wrong, can a true reconciliation be achieved.

In addition to understanding forgiveness as the business of the perpetrated, Volf insists that it should also be an essence of Christian community if it faithfully follows its master, Jesus Christ, who not only taught about forgiveness, but demonstrated it in and through his life. Therefore, forgiveness is a concern of both individual and community. Wink has lacked discussion on this – communal or collective forgiveness. But Volf argues that this pursuit of embrace creates "a community of harmonious peace in an imperfect world of inescapable injustice."[142] He advocates that the creation of this community of embrace is very vital in our contemporary culture.

3.5 Summary of the Chapter

As the study seeks to achieve a better and more refined understanding of nonviolence, I have also done a critical interaction between Wink and other voices in this chapter with the intention of seeking a critical reflection between them. In this chapter, I have engaged Wink with other peace scholars to explore the similarities and differences between them. It is suggested that Wink's interpretation of nonviolence or Jesus's third way can be compared to Yoder's original revolution and Stassen's transformative initiatives. It is discovered that Wink's ethical exploration of nonviolence is socio-political in its focus; Yoder's original revolution is ecclesiologically centred; Stassen's transforming initiatives are peace-seeking. Despite their emphases, what they all have in common is that each establishes their social ethics on the teachings of Jesus.

At the same time, I have discussed how Wink's third way is different from just war, Christian realism, pacifism, and just peacemaking. Just war, for Wink, is too compromising, whereas pacifism is morally legalistic. Likewise, Christian realism seeks relevance at the expense of loyalty to Christ's principles, while just peacemaking is too result-oriented. In the most negative case, I have shown that Wink's ecclesiological comprehension of nonviolent resistance is limited. He views the church as having no important role in the

---

142. Volf, "Forgiveness, Reconciliation, and Justice," 873.

struggle because it is just one among other social groups. In every study of nonviolence, the following question is, "what is next after the Powers fall?" Finally, I have explored Wink's notion of reconciliation to affirm that reconciliation is the goal of nonviolence. For Wink, reconciliation is the complicating process in which forgiveness and truth play special roles. As part one has established a theoretical formulation of nonviolence based on Walter Wink's Powers by interacting with other peace scholars, part two will be an examination of two exemplars, Martin Luther King Jr and Aung San Suu Kyi. First, we will look at Martin Luther King Jr and his life, with an emphasis on his activism and moral view of nonviolence. Scholars scrutinize, argue, and establish their theory based on their predecessors or, for Christians, the Bible and traditions. If this is the way in which scholars do it, how do activists like King and Suu Kyi practice, enhance and advance their belief of nonviolence by their religious professions and traditions? We will see them in the following part two of the thesis.

Part II

CHAPTER 4

Martin Luther King Jr on Nonviolence

In part I, we have seen a critical engagement of Wink's *Powers* trilogy in the light of the views of other scholars. In part II, we will look at Martin Luther King Jr and Aung San Suu Kyi as practitioners of nonviolent resistance in their respective contexts, to bring them into a critical dialogue with Wink, which will be discussed in part III. As the research is in the field of practical theology, King is here a voice or exemplary role model for practicing nonviolence as a lifestyle, which is known as principled nonviolence.

Overall, this study seeks to develop an understanding of nonviolence from a Christian viewpoint in the political context of Myanmar, where Buddhism has been predominant throughout the history of the nation. Inviting King as a dialogue partner in this study appears to be extraneous to the context of Myanmar because King's struggle is predominantly against racism while the problem of Myanmar is chiefly military dictatorship. However, there is something in common between the context where King practiced nonviolence and the political context of Myanmar. The use of violence to maintain the status quo is common in both backgrounds – that of the United States in King's time and that of Myanmar. Thus, this chapter aims to look at how King formulated and practiced his idea of nonviolence at the peak of oppressive segregationism. Using King as an activist who practiced nonviolence from a Christian viewpoint, and Suu Kyi, a woman and exemplary activist who applied nonviolence from a Buddhist perspective, will enable this study to engage Christianity with Buddhism regarding nonviolence. Therefore, this chapter brings out a Christian voice through King for discussing nonviolence in the political context of Myanmar.

Further, King is known as an advocate of principled or philosophical nonviolence, whereas Suu Kyi's approach to nonviolence is pragmatic. For the former, nonviolence is not just a means or tactic to achieve a goal, but it is a principle to live out and a lifestyle to embody. For the latter, nonviolence is a means or tactic to achieve the desired end. Simply put, the former regards nonviolence as an end, while for the latter, nonviolence is a means to an end. By using King as a voice for principled nonviolence and Suu Kyi as that of pragmatic nonviolence, this research will be inclusive to cover the discussion of nonviolence both from the angle of interfaith dialogue (Christianity and Buddhism) and that of differing approaches to nonviolence. This chapter investigates how King came to become an ardent champion of principled or ideological nonviolence. In doing so, the discussion entails three parts: first, how King came to believe in the philosophy of nonviolence; how he practiced it and how that practice made his belief stronger; and finally, the way he profoundly advanced it from a Christian perspective. The exploration of King's life and influences will provide a voice for principled nonviolence (King) to engage with that of pragmatic nonviolence (Aung San Suu Kyi) in the light of Walter Wink in the following chapters.

4.1 Biographical Exploration: How King Came to Believe in Nonviolence

Martin Luther King Jr was not raised in the culture of nonviolence. In his time, violence was so rampant that the whole nation of the United States was dealing with suppressive racial injustice and racist attacks. His daily experiences of segregation, police brutality on his people (blacks), and seeing with his own eyes an incident of the Ku Klux Klan beating and savagely lynching a black man led him to hate whites vehemently. The question that was indelibly imprinted on his mind during his early years was how he could love people who hated him.[1] How could a person filled with intense hatred come to embrace nonviolence and teach his people to love the white oppressors?

---

1. Carson, *Autobiography of Martin Luther King*, 7–10.

King was able to cultivate the lifestyle of nonviolence in the heat of such racial hatred. In this chapter, we will see how King's quest for the answer to social evil during his early life and his academic studies led him to be an advocate of principled nonviolence. In tracing his life, we will observe the contextual situations in which King grew up and led the resistance so that a comparative analysis of both his context and the Myanmar context may be discussed.

4.1.1 Parental Influences

King was significantly influenced by his parents. In James Cone's words, "King *made* history, but he was also *made by* history."[2] The foundation for his principles began in his home where he was nurtured to esteem, respect, and value himself with a sense of "somebodiness."[3] The parental influences on King were so huge that he eventually blended the character traits of each his parents. In fact, his father and mother were seemingly contradictory personalities. His father Michael King[4] was tough and self-determined. He was known as "a strict disciplinarian."[5] When his children broke rules, he would often whip them.[6] Despite being raised in the condition of abject poverty, Michael King worked hard to provide for his family. He taught his children to rely on themselves without giving any excuses.[7]

What is more, Michael King had a robust spirit of protest. As a pastor, he never limited his pastoral ministry to the spiritual dimension alone. Throughout his pastoral ministry, he preached sermons that dealt with both the mind and the emotions of the congregation, while also addressing their material condition.[8] Furthermore, Michael King never felt satisfied with the injustice and discrimination which devalued the blacks. As a pastor, he

---

2. Cone, *Martin & Malcolm & America*, 20.

3. Carson, *Autobiography of Martin Luther King*, 3.

4. His father changed his and King Jr's names from Michael King to Martin Luther King (Sr and Jr) in 1934, after coming into contact with, and being influenced by, leader of the reformation Martin Luther.

5. Garrow, *Bearing the Cross*, 34.

6. Stephen B. Oates mentions that it was not unusual to discipline physically one's children in America in the 1930s. Parents and principals alike spanked children as a matter of course, Oates, *Let the Trumpet Sound*, 8.

7. Cone, *Martin & Malcolm & America*, 22.

8. Burrow, *Extremist for Love*, 50.

appealed to his congregation to participate in protests he led. Observing King and his father's life, Burrow Jr remarks that King inherited not only the protest tradition from his father, but also the way of thinking about and doing ministry.⁹ That pastoral legacy which King received from his father Michael King was formative in his later intellectual quest for an answer to the racial injustice of that time. In short, King received a legacy from his father in two areas: the protest spirit and an idea of Christianity that views spiritual and social dimensions in an integral way.

Unlike his father, King's mother Alberta Williams King was raised in a comfortable home and educated at Spelman College. King's impression of his mother was very different from that of his father. Alberta was, unlike her husband, soft-spoken and easy-going. She was also a deeply committed Christian.¹⁰ While Michael King was forceful, outspoken, and bossy, Alberta King was submissive to her husband and took a backseat to him. Her hand in the family seemed invisible. King described his mother as the one who worked behind the scene showing motherly care, the lack of which would have been detrimental to her family.¹¹

Like her husband, Alberta never complacently adjusted to the system of segregation. That was a characteristic that both shared. Besides, it was Alberta who "instilled a sense of self-respect in all of her children from the very beginning."¹² Showing much care for all her children, she created a family where love was ever present. Therefore, King, in one of his letters to Alberta during his studies at Crozer Theological Seminary, wrote that he had "the best mother in the world."¹³ Most of all, King learned how to be inwardly strong and courageous under the care of his mother.

Interestingly, the personalities of Alberta and Michael King were poles apart from each other. While the former was soft, the latter was tough. Alberta was slow to anger, but her husband was a stern disciplinarian. In a sense, their differences seemed to complement each other, instead of contradicting. Put differently, Alberta King filled something Michael King lacked, and vice

---

9. Burrow, 52.
10. Carson, *Autobiography of Martin Luther King*, 3.
11. Carson, Luker, and Russell, *Papers of Martin Luther King*, 360.
12. Carson, *Autobiography of Martin Luther King*, 3.
13. Carson, Luker, and Russell, *Papers of Martin Luther King*, 161.

versa. What if King had been raised under the hands of parents who were both either strict disciplinarians or too forgiving and soft? If it were so, we might probably be reading about another King who might be either a disciplinarian or too forgiving. Martin Luther King Jr, under the influences of such parents, had been well prepared both inwardly and outwardly for his future nonviolent resistance. As a result, King's character became a combination of the two quasi-antithetical personalities.

How far did parental influence on King go? What was their influence on him in regard to the spirit of nonviolence? Was the spirit of nonviolence something he was already familiar with? Does it have anything to do with his family upbringing? In his writing, he traced how he came to be acquainted with the idea of nonviolence only when he began his studies at Crozer Seminary. His wife, Coretta, also said, "The spirit of nonviolence was not inherited from Martin's family."[14] However, R. Burrow Jr contends that this comment is only partially correct. In Burrow's understanding, it is true that King's father and his paternal grandparents did not teach him to be nonviolent, yet his mother and maternal grandparents certainly did.[15] Another scholar Lewis Baldwin also supports this view that King's first direct contact with pacifism was through his mother.[16] Alberta King's gentleness, her motherly care for her children and even for the members of Ebenezer Baptist Church is where King first encountered the idea of nonviolence. Nevertheless, King did not naturally and effortlessly become nonviolent. Instead, he had been wrestling for some time in developing a nonviolent lifestyle. The dangers that he faced – his life was threatened several times, his house was bombed, and finally he gave even his own life for what he believed – proved that the journey he went through was a tough one.

Another impact on King was apparently the church his father pastored. For him, the church was a second home and Christianity was something that he grew up in.[17] Black theologian James Cone observes that, "the church at that time was a dominant institution in the social life of Atlanta's

---

14. Scott King, *My Life with Martin Luther King, Jr.*, 77.
15. Burrow, *Extremist for Love*, 10.
16. Cited from Burrow, *Extremist for Love*, 10.
17. Carson, Luker, and Russell, *Papers of Martin Luther King*, 361. See also Carson, *Autobiography of Martin Luther King*, 6.

African-American community, serving as the source for leadership development and also providing the moral values which leaders used to achieve justice for blacks."[18] If his family was the place where he learned about self-worth and the value of being human, church (Ebenezer Baptist Church) was the place where he experienced the spirit of community, as Cone observes.[19] Perhaps, his vision of "beloved community,"[20] to a certain extent, originated from the church where he grew up and the church he went on to pastor.

Despite the parental nurturing and religious upbringing, King was still struggling to find a satisfactory solution to the racism of that time. What is worse, he had been entrapped in the circle of reactive hatred for some years. His personal experience and witnessing of the segregation at that time led him to a spirit of hatred.[21] That spirit remained ingrained in his mind from an early time until he fully submitted to the philosophy of nonviolence. Under such an oppressive system of segregationism, it took some years for King to embrace the lifestyle of nonviolence. King's journey to nonviolence, or how he cultivated a lifestyle of nonviolence in the midst of racial injustice, implies that there is always the possibility of resisting any form of injustice.

4.1.2 Intellectual Quest

King began his intellectual journey from 1944 to 1955. Even though he majored in systematic theology, the question of how he could love the people who hated him seemed to forcefully lead him to "seriously search for a method to eliminate social evil,"[22] and he read widely in the areas of both philosophy and

---

18. Cone, *Martin & Malcolm & America*, 20.

19. Cone, 25. The Jim Crow Laws were the laws of segregation practiced at the time of Martin Luther King Jr. From Delaware to California, and from North Dakota to Texas, many states could impose legal punishments on people for consorting with members of another race. The most common types of laws forbade intermarriage and ordered business owners and public institutions to keep their black and white clientele separate. For instance, "Buses: all passenger stations in this state operated by any motor transportation company shall have separate waiting rooms or space and separate ticket windows for the white and coloured races; Nurses: no person or corporation shall require any white female nurse to nurse in wards or rooms in hospitals, either public or private, in which negro men are placed," *Jim Crow Laws*, from: https://www.nps.gov/malu/learn/education/jim_crow_laws.htm.

20. King, *Where Do We Go from Here*, xi.

21. Carson, *Autobiography of Martin Luther King*, 7–12.

22. King Jr, *Stride Toward Freedom*, 78.

theology.[23] Here the aim of this chapter is not chiefly to discuss each aspect of this in detail, but to trace how King progressively came to the conclusion that nonviolence is the best solution to transform the system of racism. Most of all, how did King intellectually go through different philosophers and theologians until he read Mohandas K. Gandhi's writings?

Henry David Thoreau

Martin Luther King's first encounter with the idea of nonviolence was through reading Henry David Thoreau's "On the Duty of Civil Disobedience."[24] Thoreau, as an abolitionist, wrote the essay to argue against slavery and the Mexican-American war at that time. The argument in the essay is that an individual should not allow any government to override or atrophy their conscience. For Thoreau, what matters most is to refuse cooperation with any evil system whether it is government or not.[25] Put differently, his concern is that we need to fight not merely against injustice, but also against complacency about any form of injustice. Thus, the idea of refusing cooperation with an evil system fascinated King, so he read it several times. In short, Thoreau's "Civil Disobedience" paved the way for King's first intellectual journey towards nonviolence.

However, King himself differed from Thoreau in two ways. First, Thoreau did not believe in nonviolence for philosophical reasons, while King did.[26]

---

23. Carson, *Autobiography of Martin Luther King*, 14.

24. Thoreau, "Civil Disobedience," 15–36.

25. The essay was originally a speech given by Thoreau against slavery, and an excoriation of the Mexican-American war at that time. The influence of this essay is immense in that it had a great impact not only on King, but also on Mohandas Gandhi. However, Gandhi suggested that Thoreau's impact on him had been overstated: "The statement that I had derived my idea of civil disobedience from the writings of Thoreau is wrong. The resistance to authority in South Africa was well advanced before I got the essay of Thoreau on civil disobedience," cited from Carson, Luker, and Russell, *Papers*, vol. 5, 149. Henceforth, this will be cited as King's *Papers* vol. 5. Looking at his essay as a whole, Thoreau seemed to be pessimistic about order, state, and government, which is why he placed individual's rights over the government, because the power and authority of the state or government is derived from these individuals. Therefore, he wrote, "I heartily accept the motto, — 'That government is best which governs least;' and I should like to see it acted up to more rapidly and systematically. Carried out, it finally amounts to this, which I also believe, — 'That government is best which governs not at all;' and when men are prepared for it, that will be the kind of government which they will have. Government is at best but an expedient; but most governments are usually, and all governments are sometimes, inexpedient," pp. 29–30.

26. Cited from Watley, "Against Principalities," 21–22.

The second is their view of law. Thoreau seemed to be more like an anarchist, while King believed in the rule of law. Nevertheless, Thoreau's essay of "Civil Disobedience" was first and foremost an eye-opener for King in his journey towards the philosophy of nonviolence.

Walter Rauschenbusch

King's first theological breakthrough came through Walter Rauschenbusch's *Christianity and the Social Crisis*.[27] Rauschenbusch helped him see that Christian involvement in social welfare could be theologically justified. Rauschenbusch (1861–1918) was the pastor of "the Second German Baptist Church in New York City."[28] What King learned from reading Rauschenbusch is the inseparability of the spiritual and social dimensions of human life. That is, the gospel touches not only a spiritual but also a social factor. In fact, this is not a brand new idea that King came up with. He had learned this idea from his father already. However, his conceptual understanding of the interdependence of spiritual and social aspects was not theologically upheld. Rauschenbusch justified the theological position by interpreting a biblical theme, the kingdom of God. For Rauschenbusch, the kingdom of God is an all-embracing theme without which Christianity would be individualistic, having no relation to the social order. Hence, Rauschenbusch asserted, "This doctrine (the kingdom of God) is itself the social gospel."[29] Through reading Rauschenbusch – especially the chapter, "the social aims of Jesus" in *Christianity and the Social Crisis*, King established a theological basis for the social concern that he had since his childhood. Through the help of Rauschenbusch, King's conviction regarding the inseparability of spiritual and social dimensions was theologically espoused:

> The gospel at its best deals with the whole man, not only his soul but his body, not only his spiritual well-being but his material well-being. Any religion that professes to be concerned about the souls of men and is not concerned about the slums that damn them, the economic conditions that strangle them and

---

27. Rauschenbusch, *Christianity and Social Crisis*.
28. Koller, "Emphases in Preaching," 21.
29. Rauschenbusch, "Kingdom of God," 165.

the social conditions that cripple them is a spiritually moribund religion awaiting burial.[30]

Moreover, Rauschenbusch enlightened King to see the relationship between church and the kingdom of God. He saw the kingdom of God as an ideal society wherein people lived together and experienced brotherhood in cooperation, love and justice. For him, a man himself with the help of God would be able to build such a society.[31] Reading Rauschenbusch brought home to King that, "the church should take a direct, active role in the struggle for social justice."[32] Additionally, it was also through Rauschenbusch's eye that King came to see the centrality of love in social ethics. For Rauschenbusch, love is the fundamental virtue in the ethics of Jesus. He asserted "love is the society-making quality."[33] Perhaps, it was the first time King noticed the central role of love in Christian social ethics.

Nevertheless, King did not accept every idea that Rauschenbusch argued. First, Rauschenbusch, in King's view, was trapped in "the nineteenth century cult of inevitable progress."[34] Thereby Rauschenbusch became an uncritical religious utopian. The second point that King disagreed with is Rauschenbusch's attempt to identify the kingdom of God with a particular social and economic system. That, for King, was "a temptation which the church should never give in to."[35] However, many scholars have seen that King's criticism of Rauschenbusch was not completely fair. Unlike the optimistic liberals of that time, Rauschenbusch acknowledged human weaknesses and frailty. He argued that, "if there were no evil, . . . the Kingdom of God will still be the end to which God is lifting the race."[36] Similarly, Robert Cross also confirms that Rauschenbusch did not believe that "human nature was fully perfectible, only that man might become more Christ-like by seeking to

---

30. King, "Pilgrimage to Nonviolence," in *A Testament of Hope*, 37–38; see also King, *Strength To Love*, 150.

31. Hordern, *Layman's Guide to Protestant Theology*, 94.

32. Quoted from Nojeim, *Gandhi and King*, 177.

33. Rauschenbusch, *Christianity and the Social Crisis*, 55.

34. King, *Stride Toward Freedom*, 78.

35. King, "Pilgrim to Nonviolence," in *A Testament of Hope*, 37; also in *Strength to Love*, 150.

36. King, "Pilgrim to Nonviolence, *in A Testament of Hope*, 171.

build Christ's kingdom."[37] In *A Theology for the Social Gospel*, first published in 1917, Rauschenbusch discussed sin more seriously than most of his liberal counterparts. There, he argued that the advancing of the kingdom of God is not simply a process of social education, but a conflict with hostile forces. Therefore, the strategy of the kingdom of God involves a study of the social problem of evil.[38] In this regard, King did not do justice enough to critiquing Rauschenbusch's theology of the kingdom of God. Despite these disagreements with Rauschenbusch, King had a theological breakthrough through Rauschenbusch's influence in his journey to nonviolence.

Karl Marx

In tracing King's intellectual journey, many scholars do not pay as much attention to Karl Marx's influence as they do to that of Rauschenbusch, Mohandas Gandhi, Reinhold Niebuhr, and Anders Nygren.[39] However King, in retrospect, largely discussed Marx's teachings especially *Das Kapital* and the *Communist Manifesto*. There, King spelled out some reasons why he rejected Marx's philosophy and some points at which he found it challenging.[40] More importantly, King described communism in a number of his speeches and writings since it was a dominant counter-political ideology against capitalism. For example, he even preached a sermon with a title, "Can a Christian Be a Communist?"[41] What is more, the Federal Bureau of Investigation (FBI) labelled King as a self-professed Marxist. According to the FBI, King did not profess this publicly because doing so would sully his reputation. Adam Fairclough surmized that that critique was, perhaps, a product of the racism that permeated the Bureau under its chief, J. Edgar Hoover, who loathed King.[42] True, King, in the last two years before his death, worked passion-

---

37. Rauschenbusch, *Christianity and the Social Crisis*, xx.
38. Rauschenbusch, *Social Principles of Jesus*, 148.
39. For example, Rufus Burrow Jr, in *Extremist for Love*, mainly discusses the intellectual impacts of Walter Rauschenbusch and Reinhold Niebuhr on King. John J. Ansbro focuses his discussion on King's concept of *agape* love, which he adapted from the Swedish bishop Anders Nygren. Michael J. Nojeim in *Gandhi and King*, comparatively examines King and Gandhi, thereby unearthing Gandhi's impact on King.
40. King, *Stride toward Freedom*, 79–83.
41. Carson, Luker, and Russell, *Papers of Martin Luther King*, 445–454.
42. Fairclough, "Was Martin Luther King a Marxist?" 118.

ately for social and economic equality. Hence, it is necessary to look at how communism or Karl Marx, to a certain extent, inspired King's passion for nonviolence despite the fact that he rejected its rudiments.

At the time of King, the ideological feud between communism and capitalism was politically so pervasive that a number of wars broke out. For instance, the Vietnam War was a repercussion of that feud.[43] Communism, at that time, was considered to be the common enemy to fight against in the so-called democracy-flourishing Western countries. In the speech, "Beyond Vietnam," King reflected communism as a challenge, saying, "It is a sad fact that because of comfort, complacency, a morbid fear of communism, . . . the Western nations that initiated so much of the revolutionary spirit of the modern world have now become the arch anti-revolutionaries."[44] Every tenet of communism was seen as evil or threatening. King read Marx's *Communist Manifesto* and *Das Kapital* so as to discern where he should agree and disagree with him.

Most of all, King rejected the ethical relativism and atheism of communism. So, he regarded communism as a serious rival of Christianity. Truly, it is menacing because communism devalues what Christianity values, especially theistic worldview. That led many Christians to react defensively and offensively against everything pertaining to communism. Pointedly stated, communism became nothing but evil itself. This approach seemed not fair to King because it was too offensive as well as defensive. If all humans have been searching for the truth in several ways, an atheist is no exception to this quest.[45] So, it is crucial to look at communism in brief.

Karl Marx, the father of communism, was born in 1818 and raised in a Jewish home in Germany. For economic reasons, his parents had converted from Judaism to Protestant Christianity. That experience was a formative factor for him in becoming materialistic. It is, in his eyes, not God that mattered,

---

43. The Vietnam War (1954–1975) was a war between the communist government of North Vietnam, inspired by Chinese and Soviet communism and that of South Vietnam, supported by the United States. It is also known as the "American War" in Vietnam. In the *Encyclopedia of Britannica*, it is said that the war was also part of a larger regional conflict and a manifestation of the Cold War between the United States and the ex-Soviet Union and their respective allies, Ronald H. Spector, "Vietnam War, (1954-75)" *Encyclopedia Britannica*, from http://www.britannica.com/EBchecked/topic/628478/Vietnam-War.

44. Carson, *Autobiography of Martin Luther King*, 341.

45. Pandit, *Did Marx Kill God*, 1.

but money. Marx deliberately argued that money, since it has the potential to appropriate all objects to itself, is the object *par excellence*. He illustrated the omnipotence of money: "I am ugly, but I can buy myself the most beautiful woman."[46] Thus, Marx invested a great effort in looking at politics from a materialistic eye. For instance, he employed Hegel's dialectic method but discarded all the supernatural or metaphysical elements to materialistically interpret human history and later formulate his idea of a revolutionary utopia. Unlike Marx, King was raised in a family in which Christian faith was deeply entrenched, and the church where his father pastored was, as noted, also like a second home to him. His upbringing led him to easily believe in the God of love. King delineated his idea of God who is able, in *Strength to Love*. This God, in his understanding, is "at work . . . not outside the world . . . Like an ever-loving Father, God is working through history for the salvation of his children."[47]

Even so, King was enormously impressed with Marx's passion for social justice. He discerned a positive side of communism, which is, for him, the revolutionary spirit. Communism, in his understanding, is "a judgement against our failure to make democracy real and follow through on the revolutions that we initiated."[48] About the concern for social justice, King believed that Christians are bound to be in accord with communism. He continued to say that even though Christians do not accept communists' creed, they must admire their zeal and their readiness to sacrifice themselves to the very utmost.[49] So, later King's passion for economic justice, because of the gulf between abject poverty and superfluous wealth, led him to criticize the lopsided view of capitalism from a socialistic or communistic view. In Michael Nojeim's view, "King's radicalism evolved into what can be referred to as 'Christian socialism' or 'democratic socialism.'"[50]

In an address, King proposed an idea on the possibility to integrate communism and capitalism: "You can work within the framework of democracy to bring about a better distribution of wealth; you can also use your powerful

---

46. Singer, *Marx*, 18; Lochman, *Encountering Marx*, 59–60.
47. King, *Papers*, vol. 6, 512.
48. Carson, *Autobiography of Martin Luther King Jr.*, 341.
49. King, *Papers*, vol. 6, 148–149.
50. Nojeim, *Gandhi and King*, 302.

economic resources to wipe poverty from the face of the earth."[51] It is very obvious that King had been, perhaps unknowingly, impacted by the vision of communism and socialism in terms of equitable distribution of wealth. That vision was reawakened and reinforced in a much deeper way when he left for Norway and Sweden in 1964 to accept the Nobel Peace Prize. There he was amazed and inspired by the democratic socialist tradition.[52] In short, communism helped King see the negative side of capitalism; it also inspired in him a strong sense of socio-economic equality.

Another insight that King learned from reading Marx is the dialectical method of interpreting human history from a materialistic perspective. It is well known that Marx was massively indebted to a German philosopher Georg Wilhelm Hegel.[53] Marx, by using the dialectical method of Hegel, formulated the idea of communism. According to Hegel, dialectic is progressive. In any development, there are three different moments (for some scholars, they are a thesis, an antithesis, and a synthesis) that keep up the spirit of its journey. However, Hegel's creation of this dialectical principle is not to interpret human history materialistically; rather, he attempted to view the accessibility of the infinite or to employ the Kantian term, the thing-in-itself.[54] In contrast, Marx de-spiritualized or de-absolutized the Hegelian dialectic so that it might be assimilated to interpret human history materialistically.

Even though King did not accept Marx's dialectical materialism, he seemed impressed with Marx's argument of a revolutionary idea via Hegelian dialectic. As mentioned in King's personal upbringing, he was reared at the hands of parents with two different personality types. His early upbringing itself led him to be inclined towards the principle of dialectic thinking. So, reading Marx convinced him that capitalism and communism each bear a

---

51. King, *Papers*, vol. 3, 416.
52. Carson, *Autobiography of Martin Luther King*, 254.
53. I will discuss Hegelian dialectic in more detail later.
54. Hegel, like some of the previous philosophers, had a view of the absolute. But his idea differed from Kant's. To distinguish between their different views on the absolute is to divide them into *transcendent* and *immanent metaphysics*. The former defines the absolute as entirely different from totality and therefore as transcendent. The absolute, in this view, is categorically not part of this world. In contrast, the latter sees the absolute as a totality differentiating itself, Markus Gabriel, "The Dialectic of the Absolute: Hegel's Critique of Transcendent Metaphysics," in Limnatis, *Dimensions of Hegel's Dialectic*, 80–81.

partial truth. For King, capitalism was so concerned with an individual enterprise that the collective dimension of humanity was neglected. Likewise, Marxism focused on collective enterprise at the cost of individual enterprise. The conclusion that King made is very Hegelian in method: "the kingdom of God is neither the thesis of individual enterprise nor the antithesis of collective enterprise, but a synthesis which reconciles the truths of both."[55]

Friedrich Nietzsche

King had an intellectual and emotional crisis prior to his conviction concerning *agape* love. That crisis was so severe that King hardly believed in the power of love. It was Friedrich Nietzsche whose writings left King with despair concerning the power of love. Nietzsche, known as anti-Christian, seriously attacked Christian values and teachings in order to reinvent the new values and culture that are fundamentally opposed to Christianity. For him, it was Christianity that created imaginary causes such as God, soul, ego, free will, and imaginary effects such as, sin, redemption, grace, punishment, and forgiveness of sins. Most of all, he viewed that Christ on the cross is the most sublime symbol – even today.[56] In his eye, "Everything that happens, happens in accordance with strife."[57] For him, life is a dynamic interplay of strife. Though he himself was a son of a pastor during his childhood, later in his life, he opposed Christianity and invented a morality which is radically hostile to it. All the attempts he had been making were to confront humanity with the most difficult demand ever made of it.[58] As an existentialist, he did not endeavour to erect new idols or ideals. In his view, humanity is called to actively involve themselves within life's dynamic nature in us. One of the well-known ideas that he advanced is "will to power." For him, it affirms life through the enhancement of opposing activities or values. In contrast, the "will to truth," an opposite of will to power, according to Nietzsche, requires unconscious submission, a weakness of will and repressed creativity. While will to power represents the new world order that he liked to create, will to truth represents Christianity that seeks comfort, peace and safety. Thus,

---

55. King, *Stride toward Freedom*, 83.
56. Nietzsche, *Will to Power*, 128.
57. Quoted from Huskinson, *SPCK Introduction to Nietzsche*, 3.
58. Friedrich Nietzsche, *Ecco Homo* in Kaufmann, *Basic Writings of Nietzsche*, 673.

Nietzsche vehemently opposed the values of Christianity. Love, pity, and meekness are nothing but hurdles to those whose lives are committed to the will to power. Therefore, it is no wonder that King was bewildered by reading such anti-Christian philosopher Nietzsche. As John J. Ansbro observes, reading Nietzsche's critique of Christianity confused King with the idea that Jesus's teaching in the Sermon on the Mount is only the ethics for the conflict among individuals, not necessarily for social implication.[59] However, King's confusion did not last long, and in reading Gandhi his doubt about love and its wider implications were diminished.

Mohandas K. Gandhi

King came to know Mohandas Gandhi through hearing the address given by Dr Mordecai Johnson, president of Howard University, who had just returned from a trip to India. Johnson's message was, indeed "profound and electrifying" to him.[60] Through reading Gandhi's works, his doubt about the power of love gradually faded away. His confusion regarding Jesus's teaching of loving enemies was also solved. Most importantly, King was convinced that nonviolence or practicing the love of enemies is the answer to social evil. Although he intellectually owed his beliefs to others such as Davis, Niebuhr, Marx, Rauschenbusch, and the like, Gandhi is the one who satisfied his desire of searching for social justice.[61]

Gandhi is known with the title, "Mahatma," meaning "Great Soul." Scholars note that Christianity played a special role in the life of Gandhi. Gandhi religiously claimed to be Hindu, yet he was inspired a great deal by Jesus and his Sermon on the Mount. For Gandhi, the sermon vividly depicted his ideas of nonviolence. In the sermon, Jesus gave his disciples the otherworldly norms and values to transform the current world. Similarly, Gandhi viewed nonviolence as a countercultural value to change the power of violence. For

---

59. Ansbro, *Martin Luther King*, 7.

60. Carson, *Autobiography of Martin Luther King*, 23.

61. Carson, 24. W. Watley notes an interesting trilogy of intellectual linkages in the thoughts of Henry David Thoreau, Mahatma Gandhi, and Martin Luther King Jr. King was influenced by Thoreau and Gandhi. Gandhi was influenced by Thoreau and had an abiding interest in the struggles of American Blacks. Thoreau was influenced by the great Hindu works, the Bhagavad-Gita, and the sacred Upanishads, and was a strong opponent of slavery. Put differently, "it is intriguing how the lines of Eastern and Western thought interlace in the formation of King's social philosophy," Watley, "Against Principalities," 29–30.

Gandhi, liberation through nonviolence is inclusively physical, material, social, political, and economical.

However, the theory of Christ's death as a sacrifice for the sins of the world was deplorable to Gandhi. He saw Jesus merely as "a martyr, an embodiment of sacrifice and a divine teacher, but not as the most perfect man ever born."[62] In his autobiography, Gandhi mentioned how he was often given a number of books about Christianity, yet none of them except Tolstoy's *The Kingdom of God Is Within You* struck him. He did not regard Christianity as a perfect religion or the greatest of all religions.

At the same time, he was also critical of some teachings of Hinduism, especially the concept of untouchability. In regard to religions, Gandhi was a free thinker, though he followed the traditions of Hinduism and some parts of Christian teaching. But Gandhi, as a self-professed Hindu, established his idea of nonviolence on the basis of Hinduism. For him, life persists in the midst of destruction. So he argued that there must be a higher law than that of destruction – the law that society would be well-ordered, intelligible and enabling a life worth living. He believed that that law is love – the law of love through which to conquer an opponent.[63] He felt that the more he abided by this law, the more he felt delight in life. In short, reading Gandhi – the man with a strong conviction of love, reopened King's eyes to seeing the importance of *agape* love. Despite the fact that King saw another world through the lens of Gandhi, it does not mean he was converted to Gandhi's religion, Hinduism.

Gandhi's philosophy of nonviolence is largely based on the doctrine of *ahimsa* which is derived from Hindi, meaning a combination of the two words "*a*" (none or without) and "*himsa*" (violence). Approximately translated, it refers to nonviolence, noninjury, or tolerance. For Gandhi, *ahimsa* meant much more than nonviolence. It meant we are neither to offend anybody nor to harbour an uncharitable thought, even in connection with one who may consider oneself to be our enemy.[64] What is more, Gandhi's view of God and truth is typical of Hinduism. For him, God and truth are inseparable because

---

62. Gandhi, *Story of My Experiments*, 136.
63. Gandhi, "My Faith in Nonviolence," 45.
64. Todd, *Mohandas Gandhi*, 42.

truth is the most important name of God.⁶⁵ The idea of *satyagraha* ("*satya*" means truth, whereas "*agraha*" means firmness, meaning in compound word "insistence on truth" or "holding firm to truth") – the term through which Gandhi decoded his philosophy of nonviolence – highlights Gandhi's whole religious and social perspective.⁶⁶ For Gandhi, all people have only two ways to follow: either *himsa* (violence) or *ahimsa* (nonviolence). Gandhi's conviction for *ahimsa* is so strong that he considered it as the only means to know God who is truth and identified it as a positive and active state of love. Thus he wrote, "When you want to find Truth as God, the only inevitable means is love, that is, nonviolence, and since I believe that ultimately the means and the ends are convertible terms, I should not hesitate to say that God is Love."⁶⁷

In contrast to Gandhi's exposition of nonviolence on the basis of Hinduism, it was Christianity that was always fundamental to King's life. It was neither Gandhi nor his idea of love that basically shaped King. But, "King's faith derived from such a love having been made flesh in Jesus of Nazareth."⁶⁸ Lerone Bennett wrote: "King's genius . . . was not in the application of Gandhism to the Negro struggle, but in the transmuting of Gandhism by grafting it onto the only thing that could give it relevance and force in the Negro community, the Negro religious tradition."⁶⁹ In his own words, King succinctly wrote, "Christ furnished the spirit; Gandhi showed how it would work."⁷⁰ Thus, everything King thought and did is not an exposition of Gandhi's *ahimsa*. For instance, God, for King, is personal – the one who works in human history. King believed that faith in God who is more powerful than anything

---

65. Ansbro, *Martin Luther King, Jr*, 3. In his writings, Gandhi used Truth with a capital T. The implication is that God and Truth, for Gandhi, are synonymous. Significantly, Gandhi did not regard God as personal. God, for him, is a force, the essence of life, pure, undefiled consciousness, truth, goodness, light and love. He sees God as the unseen power pervading all things, the sum total of life, and the indefinable, the formless, the nameless. However, it does not make any difference to him whether one regards God as personal or impersonal, see Richards, *Philosophy of Gandhi*, 2, 3.

66. Gandhi, *Story of My Experiments*, 318–319.

67. Quoted from Ansbro, *Martin Luther King, Jr.*, 4.

68. Slack, *Martin Luther King*, 34.

69. Bennett, *What Manner of Man*, 4,

70. King, "An Experiment in Love" in *A Testament of Hope*, 17. See also Scott King, *My Life with Martin Luther King, Jr.*, 72.

played a significant role throughout his life.[71] Yet, Gandhi's idea of God is more Hindu-theistic than Christian. For him, all embodied life is, in reality, an incarnation of God. Human beings are seen as the divine sparks.[72] So Gandhi believed that the most religious people live out most of the divine spark in them. During his life, Gandhi aspired to see God face to face, and God seemed very personal to him. But he did not claim to have seen God face to face.[73] In contrast, King's emphasis was more on the justice and love of an all-powerful God – the God who sustains the universe and by his presence, King believes, the ultimate triumph of good over evil will be realized. Moreover, what made King distinct from Gandhi is his contribution to the Christian concept of *agape* or "disinterested love," "redeeming good will for all men." For Dennis Dalton, the idea of *agape* is quite similar to Gandhi's spirit of inclusiveness.[74]

In conclusion, Gandhi's influence, albeit enormous, was specifically in terms of nonviolence. While Hinduism was the source for Gandhi to explicate his idea of *ahimsa*, Christianity is, for King, the foundation on which to construct his view of nonviolence. But Gandhi's firm belief in love and strenuous commitment to nonviolence removed King's despair regarding the power of love and replaced in him the conviction that love is the only power. King re-gained his belief in the power of love by reading Gandhi so that he reread Jesus's Sermon on the Mount in such a way as to strengthen himself in the idea of the sermon.

Reinhold Niebuhr

In the first chapter, I have already sketched a critical interaction between Niebuhr's "Christian Realism" and Walter Wink's "third way of Jesus." Here

---

71. King, *Strength to Love*, 106–114.

72. Gandhi, *Selected Writings*, 30.

73. Despite the fact that Gandhi never made the claim of having seen God face to face, the inner voice was for him the voice of God. It was not a voice that came from a force outside of him. For Gandhi, a power beyond us has its locus within us. It is superior to us, not subject to our commands or wilful action, but it is still located within us. According to him, one acquires the capacity to hear this voice when the "ego is reduced to zero," See Suhrud, "Gandhi's Key Writings," 86. The use of the phrase, "inner voice of God," that Gandhi frequently used indicates how he was influenced by Tolstoy's *The Kingdom of God is Within You*.

74. Dalton, *Mahatma Gandhi*, 185. I will discuss the role of *agape* love in more detail in a later section.

we will mainly look at how Niebuhr's writings profoundly bolstered King's theology of nonviolence in a particular way.

Reinhold Niebuhr is known as a theologian, though he did not like to be called so.[75] According to John C. Bennett, he has done more than any other American to change the climate of theology.[76] Despite being previously influenced by liberal Christian thought, Niebuhr's pastoral works at Bethel Evangelical Church in Detroit from 1915 to 1928, eventually opened his eyes to seeing the impracticality of liberal Christianity. *Moral Man and Immoral Society* was the result.[77] Niebuhr was a pacifist before, but later he became a sharp critic of pacifism.

Niebuhr had a strong view of sin. For him, the human predicament is fundamentally sin which has a profound dominance over individuals and society. So the religion of modern culture is a superficial religion for it attempts to find meaning without having discovered the perils to meaning in death, sin and catastrophe.[78] With profound consciousness of man, he continued to critique those who optimised human history at all cost, saying that an optimism which depends upon the hope of the complete realization of highest ideals in history is bound to suffer ultimate disillusionment. With this view, Niebuhr argued that the pacifistic movement is unrealistic. Pacifists, for him, are simply "social idealists who are profoundly critical and sceptical of the use of physical force in the solution of social problems."[79] Niebuhr, from a pragmatic perspective, did not focus much on the means by which to achieve a certain end; rather, he looked at the end result. For him, what matters is not whether Christians should cling to pacifism or not because the Christian gospel refuses simply to equate the gospel with the "law of love."[80] He argues that there is not the slightest support in Scripture for this doctrine

---

75. "It is somewhat embarrassing to be made the subject of a study which assumes theology as the primary interest. I cannot and do not claim to be a theologian," Reinhold Niebuhr, "Intellectual Autobiography of Reinhold Niebuhr," in Kegley and Bretall, *Reinhold Niebuhr*, 1–24, especially, 3.

76. Bennett, "Reinhold Niebuhr's Contribution," 58.

77. Rasmussen, *Reinhold Niebuhr*, 45.

78. Niebuhr, *Christianity and Power Politics*, 1–2. See also McAfee Brown, *Essential Reinhold Niebuhr*, 7.

79. Childress, "Reinhold Niebuhr's Critique," 471.

80. McAfee Brown, *Essential Reinhold Niebuhr*, 102.

of nonviolence.[81] As a Christian realist, he denied any form of absolutizing any doctrine or teaching.

Niebuhr's sole basis for the argument of using violent resistance is the universality of sin, and so the conclusion was that war as a particular expression of sin can be justified. John C. Bennett argues that it was Niebuhr's assumption that "war, horrible as it is, may be preferable to surrender to a totalitarian system."[82] From this point of view, Niebuhr pointed out that Gandhi's nonviolent resistance against British overlords worked well because the British had reachable consciences. But he conjectured that the Gandhi method would presumably not have worked against a fanatic like Hitler.[83]

Moreover, Niebuhr argued that the pacifists' view of *agape* love is also too idealistic; for him, such a love can never be practiced in the world where sin is all-pervasive. For him, humans are sinners, thus justice can be achieved only by a certain degree of coercion on the one hand, and by resistance to coercion and tyranny on the other.[84] Truly, Niebuhr agreed with the pacifists in that he considers the law of love to be the law for the whole of humanity, including the political sphere. He wrote, "as God is love, the essence of human nature is also love . . . there can be no principle of harmony short of love."[85] But Niebuhr differed from pacifists in regard to how love should be carried out. Like pacifists, he believed that a simple endeavour to love in the personal realm is reasonably effective for overcoming evil. Despite this, Jesus's *agape* love is, for Niebuhr, a religious ideal and it has nothing to do with a normative ethic in a corporate or political realm. In the political area, Niebuhr talked more about justice than love. An ethic of love is a kind of perfectionism. Those who live by an ethic of love are always limited by their selfishness. Love can never be perfect.[86] It is impossible for humanity to live together without justice that includes all with whom we might join to form a communal society based on fairness that requires sacrifice.

---

81. McAfee Brown, 107.

82. Bennett, "Reinhold Niebuhr's Social Ethics," 123.

83. Niebuhr, *Christianity and Power Politics*, 168. See also Bingham, *Courage to Change*, 110.

84. Cited from Werpehowski, "Reinhold Niebuhr," 209.

85. Niebuhr, *Nature and Destiny of Man*, vol. 1, 146–147.

86. Lemert, *Why Niebuhr Matters*, 99.

In short, Niebuhr is neither a proponent of nonviolence nor of just war; he placed himself betwixt and between the debate of just war and nonviolence, agreeing with parts of each argument. He called himself a Christian realist. The term "realist" itself describes what sort of man he is. As a practically oriented pastor, Niebuhr used to examine the context before applying any means to reach any end – whether violence or nonviolence. He seemed uninterested in establishing any kinds of absolute.

Now the question is, "how did Niebuhr, as a sharp critic of pacifism and nonviolence, shape King's idea of nonviolence?" According to the order of King's intellectual journey, King, after the serious study of Gandhi, was already convinced that nonviolence was the method that he would adhere to. When reading Niebuhr, his conviction was challenged and somewhat shaken again. At first, he was confused and wondered if he should follow either Gandhi or Niebuhr. But as Charles Lemert comments, "confusion, it seems, had a maturing effect on King."[87] As King used to do previously in his intellectual journey with philosophers, he attempted to learn something valuable both from Gandhi and Niebuhr. The result is that King's first confusion indeed disappeared, and his view of nonviolence was strengthened more than ever. King's biographer Taylor Branch notes that his nonviolent tactics were influenced far more by Niebuhr than by the other oft-cited source. King also admitted that reading Niebuhr's critique of pacifism left him "in a state of confusion."[88] If Gandhi indeed influenced King in terms of using *satyagraha* (soul-force) in resisting political dominance. King had much to learn from Niebuhr because they both formulated their social ethical view in the same context of the United States. For instance, in *Moral Man and Immoral Society*, Niebuhr observed the danger of mixing the wrongdoing and the wrongdoer in resistance, saying,

> In every social conflict, each party is so obsessed with the wrongs which the other party commits against it, that it is unable to see its own wrongdoing . . . Individuals are never as immoral as the social situations in which they are involved and which they

---

87. Lemert, 92.
88. King, *Stride toward Freedom*, 86.

symbolise. If opposition to a system leads to personal insults of its representatives, it is always felt as an unjust accusation.[89]

King, in drawing the principles of nonviolence, clearly states that the ultimate goal of nonviolence is not to defeat the opponent, but to establish reconciliation. In Charles Lemert's view, these words of King could be taken directly from Niebuhr.[90] However, it is not just Niebuhr's idea, but also Gandhi's, because he used to make a distinction between individual Englishmen and the system of imperialism which they maintain.[91] But some aspects of Niebuhr's thought regarding sin and the relationship between love and justice greatly helped King to see the whole picture of the human being.[92] King, before a serious reading of Niebuhr, was mostly packed with the liberal doctrine of anthropology. Later he read Niebuhr and saw the presence and power of sin both at individual and societal levels. At the same time, King felt that Niebuhr was so preoccupied with the sinfulness of human nature that his view of grace and forgiveness seemed to be weakened. In addition, King, though he might be called an apostle of *agape* love, also learned from Niebuhr about the relationship between justice and love: "Justice at its best is love correcting everything that stands against love."[93] In short, reading Niebuhr enriched King's understanding of nonviolence. Niebuhr's discussion about the relationship between love and justice also helped him see the inseparability of love and justice.

Georg Wilhelm Friedrich Hegel
Interestingly, Hegel was the last philosopher that King read in his intellectual odyssey, but the principal method through which King used to articulate the

---

89. Niebuhr, *Moral Man and Immoral Society*, 248.

90. Lemert, *Why Niebuhr Matters*, 96.

91. Niebuhr, *Moral Man and Immoral Society*, 249. There Niebuhr himself discussed how Gandhi also drew lines between the crime a person committed and the person themselves.

92. A historian David Chappell argues that King had already had an idea of human imperfection or flawedness before he came to be acquainted with Niebuhr. King's essay on Jeremiah, "the rebel prophet," written in 1948, showed some originality in academic work. He saw that evil is mysteriously rooted in individual humans and society. Echoing Jeremiah and Job, King wrote that history shows "the just suffering while the unjust prosper." Evil is rampant in the universe: "Only the superficial optimist who refocuses to face the realities of life fails to see this patent fact." Therefore, Chappell concludes that King's relationship to Niebuhr is not a question of roots, but a question of affinities, Chappell, *Stone of Hope*, 45–48.

93. Carson, *Autobiography of Martin Luther King, Jr.*, 325.

idea of nonviolence is mostly Hegelian. Hegel's influence on King is not principally philosophical, but methodological in thinking. According to Hegel, something is identified – it is grasped at its point of origin; then something negative strikes, which, in turn, leads it to the next step where something of the earlier moment is retained still.[94] For Hegel, this is the way all meaningful things evolve. Even the Absolute Spirit itself is not static, but a process, so dynamic. For Hegel, progress appears as an advancing from the imperfect to the more perfect; but the former must not be understood abstractly as only the imperfect, but as something which involves the very opposite of itself – the so-called perfect – as a germ or impulse.[95] This dialectic process, in Hegel's eyes, is something that drives human history; so history is a product of dialectics – a product (or synthesis) that has come out of the two contradictories.

Hegel's analysis of the dialectical process helped King see that growth comes through struggle. King's *magnum opus*, *Strength to Love* is the most vivid expression of his indebtedness to the Hegelian dialectical process. There he began with the statement: "truth is found neither in the thesis nor the antithesis, but in an emergent synthesis which reconciles the two."[96] A year before he was assassinated, King mentioned, "the old Hegelian synthesis *still offers* the best answer to many of life's dilemmas."[97] Looking at all his intellectual discoveries, King was not essentially a creative theologian or an originator of ideas. He just made the best use of the Hegelian dialectic in articulating his own standpoint, skilfully synthesizing between two contradictories, such as between liberalism and neo-orthodoxy, or communism and capitalism. Like John Howard Yoder remarks, "King was not an academic. He was a product of the white Anglo-Saxon school, and he was intelligent, critical, and synthetic

---

94. Akash and Mohapatra, *Reading Hegel*, 6. A number of scholars interpret Hegel's dialectical principle in the form of the triad or three-steps of thesis, antithesis, and synthesis. However, Roland Hall argues that this way of interpretation is mistaken because Hegel did not actually use the terms. In fact, even though Hegel evinced a fondness for triads, neither his dialectic in general nor particular portions of his work can be reduced simply to a triadic patter of thesis, antithesis, and synthesis, *Encyclopaedia of Philosophy*, s.v. "Dialectic" (Farmington Hills, MI: Thomson Gale, 2006).

95. Hegel, *Philosophy of History*, 73.

96. King, *Strength to Love*, 9; see also King, *Testament of Hope*, 491.

97. Cited from Seay, Jr, "Theologian of Synthesis," 52.

in thinking."[98] But when it comes to nonviolence, King never compromised. For him, no synthesis could be established between violence and nonviolence.

Personalism

Not only was King influenced by great thinkers of his time, but a prevailing philosophy of that time also had a great impact on him: personalism. This might be defined as,

> The thesis that only persons (self-conscious agents) and their states and characteristics exist, and that reality consists of a society of interacting persons. Typically, a personalist will hold that finite persons depend for their existence and continuance on God, who is the Supreme Person, having intelligence and volition. Personalists . . . tend to be non-utilitarian in ethics and to place ultimate value in the person as a free, self-conscious, moral agent, . . . holding that a good God will not allow what has intrinsic value to lose existence, they believe in personal survival of death.[99]

This definition makes crystal clear King's belief in the God who acts in human history; about his conviction of human intrinsic worth; his assurance of moral absolutes; and his buoyant hope that justice will finally prevail. Personalism, for him, is "the theory that the clue to the meaning of ultimate reality is found in personality."[100]

Two recent scholars, David Garrow and David L. Chappell, strongly stress the influence of Niebuhr's realism on King, and downplay that of personalism. For them, Niebuhr's influence on King seemed more substantial than the philosophy of personalism.[101] But, their argument is not convincing if we look at King's life and writings closely. King himself described personalism as a "basic philosophical position."[102] Since personalism was his basic philosophi-

---

98. Yoder, *War of the Lamb*, 60.
99. Cited from Bengtsson, *Worldview of Personalism*, 31.
100. King, *Stride toward Freedom*, 88.
101. Burrow, *Extremist for Love*, 42.
102. Carson, *Autobiography of Martin Luther King, Jr.*, 31.

cal foundation, it is necessary to look at how this philosophy significantly enhanced his view of nonviolence.

George Washington Davis, a professor of Systematic Theology, introduced personalism to King. Davis believed that, "God and history belong together."[103] For him, God has a purpose for the human race, and history moves toward a goal. That helped King see God as a personal being who acts in human history. His belief in personalism was truly a source empowerment throughout his nonviolent struggle. Reflecting his experience of the Montgomery boycott, King asserted that God still works through history to perform his wonders. It seems as though God has decided to use Montgomery as the proving ground for the struggle and triumph of freedom and justice in America.[104]

To be specific, personalism convinced King in two ways: theologically and anthropologically. Theologically, it gave him metaphysical and philosophical grounding for the idea of a personal God, thereby affirming his belief in a personal God. In his doctoral dissertation, King argued against both views of Paul Tillich and Henry Nelson Wieman, who rejected God as a personal being. For Stephen B. Oaths, King chose to write his thesis on the divergent theisms of Tillich and Wieman in order to deepen his understanding of personalism.[105] For Tillich and Wieman, seeing God as a person is to limit God's absoluteness. God, for Tillich, is transcendent; nothing can compare with what he is like. On the contrary, Wieman's view is somewhat pantheistic, seeing God as the One who is in everything. Tillich stressed the transcendent nature of God, whereas Wieman focused on His immanent nature. Against their views, King argued that if God is not personal, it is unreasonable to speak of God's goodness; it is also impossible to say that God is love because outside of personality, love loses its meaning.[106] Due to the personal nature of God, he can love, be good and mindful of every individual. James Cone also highlights that King's faith in the personal God deepened his commitment to justice and sustained him in his struggle, allowing him to be free from fear for his life or for his family.[107]

---

103. Washington Davis, "God and History," 36.
104. King, *Stride toward Freedom*, 51–52.
105. Oates, *Let the Trumpet Sound*, 46.
106. King, *Papers*, vol. 2, 513.
107. Cone, *Martin & Malcolm & America*, 125.

Anthropologically, his belief in personalism assured King of a "metaphysical basis for the dignity and worth of all human personality."[108] Paraphrasing Martin Buber, King asserted, "Segregation substitutes an 'I-it' relationship for the 'I-thou' relationship and relegates persons to status of things."[109] Blacks were trivialized as a thing or property of traditional southerners of that time. That social milieu restrained blacks from fostering self-esteem and self-worth. Obviously, self-esteem and self-worth could not be constructed among the blacks unless they had a solid philosophical and theological basis. King, therefore, devotedly embraced personalism.

Despite the fact that King learned about nonviolence from various intellectuals during his academic life from his undergraduate to his doctoral studies, his academic honesty was called into question for plagiarism. The papers that have a number of instances of plagiarism are those written during the Boston years (1951–1955). Critics point out that King's documentation is frequently sloppy and sometimes outright plagiarism.[110] As Philip Yancey describes, "why does someone like him who masters in choosing words and prose feel the need to steal someone else's?"[111] His plagiarism disappoints scholars, and gives an opportunity for his opponents to disdain all his work. But is this critique too much of a generalization? Should we discard everything King did on the basis of this mistake?

Nevertheless, King's intellectual search for the solution of racism is a decisive phase in his life. Greatly indebted to Gandhi in learning nonviolence as a method, King did not fully adopt it as it was. Instead, he reconstructed its theoretical frame in the light of the scriptural teachings. In addition to Gandhi, there is a range of other intellectuals, like Niebuhr, Hegel, and Rauschenbusch, who broadened, deepened and refined his understanding of nonviolence. At that time, his discovery was merely on an intellectual or theoretical level. He was still inexperienced in a practical sense.

As this research also locates Wink, King and Suu Kyi in the context of military despotism, exploring King's notion and practice of nonviolence in the

---

108. Carson, *Autobiography of Martin Luther King, Jr.*, 31–32.
109. King, *Strength to Love*, 160.
110. Chappell, *Stone of Hope*, 51.
111. Yancey, *Soul Survivor*, 18.

socio-cultural milieu of his time will bring out a concrete notion of principled nonviolence. Likewise, analyzing Suu Kyi's notion and practice of pragmatic nonviolence in her own background in next chapter will also generate a concrete concept of pragmatic nonviolence. After these two views are critically engaged in the light of Walter Wink, we can draw some political implications for Christians in Myanmar. Now we will see how King began to work out his conviction of nonviolence practically in the civil rights movement.

4.2 Involvement in the Civil Rights Movement

The question of how he could possibly love the people who hated him was intellectually resolved during King's college years. The time eventually came for King to test if what he learned was effective. But at that stage, King was not yet fully committed to the principles of nonviolence. How did he become an advocate of principled nonviolence? I will discuss how King's belief in nonviolence strengthened his practice and how practicing nonviolence, in turn, refined his faith in it through the civil rights campaigns he led. In the discussion, I will not detail each campaign King led, but I will survey all the campaigns to scrutinize the key events in which King practiced what he learned from his academic studies. This analysis will expose the mounting tension between the power of nonviolence and that of racism.[112]

The first campaign was the Montgomery Bus Boycott that took a year from 1955 to 1956 with the aim of establishing the Alabama bus laws as unconstitutional. That boycott succeeded more than its initiators expected. Equality in the Alabama bus laws was instituted, and it also resulted in a revolutionary change in their evaluation of themselves.[113] The self-esteem and self-worth that ebbed away under segregation were reclaimed through the accomplishment of the Montgomery movement. In addition, King and

---

112. Segregationism at the time of King was, in short, a racial problem. Yet it affected other non-racial factors. According to a sociologist Aldon D. Morris, segregationism affected three areas: economic, political and personal oppressions over blacks. Economically blacks were concentrated in the lowest-paying and dirtiest jobs. Next, they were systematically marginalized from political rights. Third, segregation restricted blacks from personal freedom. So, Morris calls it the tripartite system of domination. Morris, *Origins of the Civil Rights*, 1–2. In such a context, King rose up and led the movement until he was assassinated.

113. Cited from Garrow, *Bearing the Cross*, 81.

the black community discovered the effectiveness of nonviolent resistance – a method that all the blacks can work with.

Before the Montgomery movement, the practice of nonviolence seemed to be new both to the black community and to King.[114] Thus at first, King wondered if the boycott method was Christian or un-christian, moral or immoral; but later he sensed that the method might be used to establish justice in business.[115] Regarding this, some scholars argue that the reason King and his fellows adopted nonviolent resistance was not primarily because of their theological and philosophical convictions about it, but because it was the only tactic the black people had to use.[116] John C. Bennett wrote, "King did not choose nonviolence; nonviolence chose him."[117] Truly, the blacks at that time were powerless and dominated by the white majority, and there was no available weaponry to fight back against the whites. If the blacks had been militarily sophisticated, no one knows what kind of revolution they would have embarked on.

Nonetheless, if Bennett's argument were taken to be true, all of King's intellectual, religious, and personal odyssey in the direction of nonviolence before would have been nothing but merely a myth. This criticism also contradicts what King said, that, "persons who used the nonviolent method of protest either because they were afraid or because they lacked the instruments of violence were not truly nonviolent."[118] In that sense, the Montgomery movement was the best window of opportunity for King to demonstrate what he had learned throughout his life. However, if the blacks were militarily sophisticated, war against the whites might have broken out already before King was born. On top of that he would not necessarily be attracted to finding an alternative way to solve racial injustice since the fight would already be there; instead, he might become one of the armed fighters against segregationists.

After the Montgomery Boycott, King was fully devoted to nonviolence as a way of living in a world where violence was prevalent. King's life shows that nonviolence requires greater intellectual conviction than just a physical

---

114. Otten, *Bonhoeffer and King*, Kindle location 5221 of 10261.
115. Carson, *Autobiography of Martin Luther King*, 53.
116. See Watley, "Against Principalities," 86.
117. Quoted from Watley, "Against Principalities," 86.
118. King, *Stride toward Freedom*, 90.

exertion. It entails the whole life commitment: intellectual, mental, and volitional commitment. Looking at the period around the 1950s, owning guns and knives among southern blacks and whites was as common as owning the clothing on their backs.[119] Revenge against the violence of the white racists often occurred. What made the situation worse were the incidents of black-against-black violence and homicide. As King believed, nonviolence is not a method for cowards, but the way of the strong. Only strong persons could be truly devoted to nonviolence, leaving no place for violence. Only after his active involvement in the civil rights movement did King enable himself to be fully committed as an advocate of principled nonviolence.

The second campaign that King led was the Albany movement (1961–1962). Despite the success of the first campaign, the Albany movement represented a failure. To be precise, the campaign failed without having gained anything it aimed for. The main mistake that King and his people made was not what they did wrong, but what they failed to do. Put simply, it was unpreparedness and a lack of planning for the campaign. However, the blessing in disguise is that King's stature became a force that could not be ignored.[120] Simply put, the Albany movement led King to become a well-known public figure.

King, with great care and a thoughtful plan, led the third campaign (the 1963 Birmingham movement) to a great success. Birmingham was probably the most segregated city in the United States at that time, a place where violent attacks against blacks often happened.[121] Under the administration of the police officer Bull Conner, the protesters were brutally attacked during demonstrations. The Birmingham movement remarkably enriched King's theology in such a way that he saw how evil was deep-seated in American society, individually as well as collectively. There he learned to differentiate just laws from unjust laws, and to defy unjust laws. There he also came to see that a real hurdle to the civil rights movement was neither white supremacists nor the Ku Klux Klan, but the white moderates who preferred order to justice. For them, peace is an absence of tension, instead of the presence of

---

119. Burrow, *Extremist for Love*, 201.
120. Nojeim, *Gandhi and King*, 234.
121. King, *Why We Can't Wait*, 42.

justice, so they reprimanded the use of nonviolent direct action. King was frustrated by the criticisms of those white moderates more than those of the white supremacists.[122] Overall, the Birmingham campaign led King to become a sharp critic of the white moderates who opposed the nonviolent direct action that he was leading.

In 1965, King led another historic campaign, known as the Selma March. If the Albany event represented the nadir of the civil rights movement, the Selma March was its zenith. The greatest gain that came from the Selma campaign was the August 1965 passage of the Voting Rights Act, which essentially eradicated the Jim Crow Laws. What is more, the Selma movement had proved the power of nonviolence resistance.[123] The Selma success was not, nevertheless, bloodless. Many ruthless beatings happened, especially on the notorious Bloody Sunday, 7 March 1965.[124] Besides, Selma's unique contribution was that several whites joined the march. So King saw the Selma March as a foretaste of the Beloved Community.[125] It is truly reasonable to comment, as the King scholars do, that the Selma movement convinced King to see the beginnings of his dream of the Beloved Community.[126] The Selma success truly empowered and fortified his conviction of the power and effectiveness of nonviolence.

As the civil rights movement was growing, King extended the movement from racial to socio-economic justice. In the inception of the civil rights movement, the campaigns King led prior to Selma basically aimed for racial integration. Everything King and the blacks were endeavouring to do was racially concerned. But the next march, for the Chicago Freedom Movement (in 1966), was different because King expanded the movement by dealing with an economic issue – especially the gap between the rich and the poor.

---

122. King, "Letter from Birmingham City Jail," in, *Testament of Hope*, 293–297.

123. Nojeim, *Gandhi and King*, 244.

124. King recalled that "the days can never be forgotten when the brutalities at Selma caused thousands all over the land to rush to our side, heedless of danger and of differences in race, class and religion." King, *Where Do We Go*, 9. What made the march serious in the eyes of many was the fatality of a white man Rev James J. Reeb of Boston from a serious blow to his head on 11 March, see Garrow, *Bearing the Cross*, 405.

125. "Beloved community" is the term coined by Vincent Harding who wrote an introduction of King's book, *Where Do We Go from Here: Chaos or Community?*, xi.

126. Nojeim, *Gandhi and King*, 244; Cone, *Martin & Malcolm & America*, 218. The idea of Beloved Community will be discussed at greater length in the later part of this chapter.

He discerned that the issue that the northerners were facing was different from that of southerners. The appalling encounter King experienced was the physical devastation of the area, Los Angeles' Watts. James Cone states that it was there that "King began to see that there are literally two Americas, one beautiful, rich, and primarily white, and the other ugly, poor and disproportionately black."[127] That experience led him to work for the economic advancement for black people within the system. Moreover, King was awed that most of the urban young did not accept nonviolence as the primary method for gaining their freedom.

More than that, King encountered opposition from his own constituents, especially the Black Power movement. It was a social movement which aimed to realize the autonomy of blacks. Black Power means blacks exercising group power in all areas of life – political, economic, and socio-cultural. But it was, in King's opinion, another form of domination. For the advocates of black power, any means whether nonviolence or violence, could be used to achieve their goals. On the contrary, King persistently held on to nonviolence, and expressed his commitment to nonviolence by saying that, "if every Negro in the United States turns to violence, I'm going to stand up and be the only voice to say that it is wrong."[128]

The Black Power movement, nonetheless, illuminated King to see that "sharing power with blacks was not an item on the white agenda."[129] King came to analyze the word "power" in a positive way too. Power, for him, is the ability to achieve the purpose or the strength to bring about social, political or economic changes. He was aware of the danger of using power alone without associating it with love, thereby repudiating the concept of Friedrich Nietzsche's "will to power."[130] Unlike Nietzsche, King contended that power

---

127. Cone, *Martin & Malcolm & America*, 222.

128. Cited from Cone, *Martin & Malcolm & America*, 225–226. See also King, *Where Do We Go*, 63.

129. Cone, *Martin & Malcolm & America*, 232.

130. Here Nietzsche's concept of "will to power" is often mistakenly construed. J. Keith Hyde argues that it is a misinterpretation to view Nietzsche's "will to power" as a maudlin endorsement of brute strength. In fact, that overlooks the subtler nuances of his thought. He points out that Nietzsche once criticized the futility of unleashing brute force: "while a crude injury done him certainly demonstrates our power over him, it at the same time estranges his will from us even more – and thus makes less easy to subjugate," Hyde, *Concept of Power*, 56. For Nietzsche, life and its experiences are regarded as a dynamic interplay of opposing forces,

should be accompanied by love. In short his understanding of power, love and even justice was well honed through analyzing the philosophy of Black Power. The insight he gained is, "Power at its best is love implementing the demands of justice. Justice at its best is love correcting everything that is against love."[131]

As the Black Power movement led him to clarify the relationship between power and love, King's experience in the slums of Chicago also revived what he had read from Marx's writings about communism versus capitalism during his doctoral studies at Boston University. Many scholars view the Chicago movement as a failure because it did not produce an enforceable open housing law; James Cone argues that Chicago was one of King's great successes, in that it created the most important development in his perspective on America.[132] When he saw the plight of poverty-stricken people in the slums of Chicago, what he learned from Marxism became a powerful tool to dissect the economic issues of that time. The real problem in Chicago was not racism, but poverty and unemployment. It was motioned in the proposal for nonviolent action as follows:

> Educational opportunities in Chicago, . . . were hardly adequate to prepare Negroes for metropolitan life. A labor force of some 300,000 have found little beyond low paying service occupations open to them, and those few who possessed skills and crafts found their rank rapidly being depleted by automation and few opportunities for advancement and promotion.[133]

King, despite the unsuccessful Chicago campaign, continued to launch a new project, which was known first as the Washington Spring Project, and later as the Poor People's Campaign. The campaign sought to dramatize poverty in the United States. For Michael Nojeim, King's vision of reform in America reached full blossom, thereby seeking congressional passages of legislation: first, a minimum annual income for all Americans; next, a federal government

---

creating conflict and tension. Lucy Huskinson also observes that the wrestling of opposing forces, for Nietzsche, exhibits the discord necessary for all existence: "everything that happes, happens in accordance with this strife." Huskinson, *SPCK Introduction to Nietzsche*, 3.

131. King, *Where Do We Go*, 37.
132. Cone, *Martin & Malcolm & America*, 224.
133. Quoted from Facing History and Ourselves, *Eyes on the Prize*, 121.

commitment to achieve full employment; and finally, production of at least half a million low-cost housing units per year.[134] However, King was tragically assassinated on 4 April 1968, before the campaign was launched. In brief, King's intellectual discovery of nonviolence during his college years led him to practice it, and his experiences, in turn, honed his understanding of nonviolence. King's belief and practice of nonviolence, in the context where various forms of violence were rife, grew stronger than ever as he persisted in leading the movement. He developed a lifestyle of nonviolence in such a context.

To look at his later life, two or three years before his assassination, King seemed to be struggling to cope with depression and frustration. In the comparative analysis of King and Malcolm X, Dennis Dalton points out that King's later life relates, in impersonal tones, the success of a method, not any journey of the self. It is remarkable how little King's ideas developed in the 1960s compared to his early writings.[135] Towards the end, King suffered severe bouts of depression and agonized over pre-occupations with death.[136] It seems that King was losing his heart or had burned-out in leading the movement.[137] Or, he had a premonition of his own death, and he was so pre-occupied with it. In short, various attacks (both physical and verbal), serious accusations from his opponents and the portent of his death led him gradually to be psychologically deteriorated. However, King's life was too short. King's whole activist life was a little over twelve years (1955–1968) while Gandhi lived for almost seventy-nine years. When King died, he was just thirty-nine. As Robert Holmes observes, King's death cut short a life that was probably nowhere near realizing its potential for moral leadership.[138] His premature

---

134. Nojeim, *Gandhi and King*, 254.

135. Dalton, *Mahatma Gandhi*, 183–187.

136. See Garrow, *Bearing the Cross*, 622; Abernathy, *And the Walls Came Tumbling Down*, 42; Oates, *Let the Trumpet Sound*, 459, 472–473.

137. Dalton observes that Malcolm had been a criminal, an addict, a pimp, a prisoner, a racist, and a hater; he had really believed the white man was devil. However, two days before his death, all this had changed. In commenting to Gordon Parks about his past life he said: "That was a mad scene." And Malcolm was free. No one who knew him before and after this trip to Mecca could doubt that he had completely abandoned racism, separatism, and hatred, Dalton, *Mahatma Gandhi*, 184.

138. Holmes, *Ethics of Nonviolence*, 252.

death leaves questions behind, such as, "How long could King persistently lead the Civil Rights Movement for social change?"

King's deep conviction of nonviolence notwithstanding, his reputation for philandering disgusted many conservative Christians and moralists. It was factually correct that King did have sexual misconduct. The FBI taped numerous episodes in King's hotel rooms. His closest colleague and friend Ralph Abernathy also revealed that King had extramarital affairs until the eve of his death.[139] Under the FBI's electronic surveillance, King's sexual misconduct was found out. Philip Yancey observes that King's moral failing became an excuse for anyone who wanted to avoid his message.[140] True, it seems unsound for many conservative Christians to regard King as a prophet. For instance, Yancey's *Confession of a Racist* sparked a storm of anger among some conservative Christians.[141] How should King's sexual misconduct be considered? Should we say, like Mike Royko, *Chicago Daily News* columnist, who asserted that, "King's personal affairs had nothing to do with national security or his probity as a civil-rights leader."[142] Or should we, like conservative Christians, regard him merely as a social activist whose moral failings made him unqualified? In fact, King's life (both private and public) itself reflects his own anthropology which he adapted from the liberal teaching and Niebuhr's doctrine of human being. King's unswerving commitment to nonviolence and his love for the people of America (whites and blacks) reflected the liberal teaching of human being, according to which humans are inherently good. Like Niebuhr's pessimistic view of human nature, King's sexual misconduct manifests human sinfulness. In short, his life reflects a blend of two contradictory anthropologies.

We have seen that all the campaigns King led did not succeed. A few such as Albany and Chicago Freedom Movement failed, whereas many campaigns (Montgomery and Selma) largely succeeded. The police's brutal crackdown

---

139. Yancey, *Soul Survivor*, 18.

140. Yancey, "Confessions of a Racist."

141. See Yancey, *Soul Survivor*, 38–40. There presidents of Bible colleges raised the question, "how can a womanizer and plagiarizer become a prophet?"

142. In fact, the FBI's hateful vendetta against King was flagrantly illegal and unconstitutional. Acting Attorney General Nicholas Katzenbach was also shocked when he found out about the FBI's dossier on King, and he took the matter directly to the President. But Johnson made no effort to rein Hoover in, Oates, *Let the Trumpet Sound*, 315, 316.

and arresting of many protesters including King during the Birmingham March stirred up the conscience of the whole America, and there came powerful and massive subsequent campaigns (Washington March and Selma), and the civil rights movement reached its peak. This confirms the discovery of Erica Chenoweth and Maria J. Stephan about the effectiveness of nonviolent resistance; nonviolent campaigns are, in general, more effective than violent campaigns in contexts where either type of resistance has the potential to succeed.[143] Chenoweth and Stephan discover this finding from the comparative analysis from many nonviolent campaigns that had been gone through from 1900 to 2006. The results show that nonviolent campaigns are more likely succeed in the face of repression than are violent campaigns.[144]

Somewhat similarly, Wink also contends that nonviolence generally works where violence would work, and where it fails, violence too would fail.[145] What is more, nonviolence sometimes works where violence would fail. Reading King's life and the influences upon him helps us see that it is possible to find a solution for social illness even in the severity of racial discrimination.

King's belief in nonviolence was, until his active involvement in resistance, merely intellectual conviction. During the civil rights movement, he became a strong advocate of principled nonviolence. In the next chapter, we will explore how Aung San Suu Kyi became a practitioner of pragmatic nonviolence in a context where violence has been a means to seize power. In both contexts, the use of violence to maintain the status quo is a reigning political culture. Both King and Suu Kyi, amid such a culture, have clung to their belief in nonviolence. As King and Suu Kyi are both practitioners of nonviolence, their views are not as profoundly and systematically articulated as Wink's. When King's nonviolent resistance against segregation is viewed and interacted with Wink's framework, we can see that first, King was socialized in a segregated social milieu. Later during his college years, he became re-socialized intellectually by studying a number of theologians and philosophy, and eventually

---

143. Chenoweth and Stephan, *Why Civil Resistance Works*, 152.
144. Chenoweth and Stephan, "Why Civil Resistance Works," 19–24.
145. Wink, *Engaging the Powers*, 239. Wink illustrates that neither violence nor nonviolence might have been effective in Stalin's Russia, and neither has succeeded so far in Myanmar, 239. It was 1992 when his book, *Engaging the Powers* was published. Now we can say that nonviolence has worked in some measure in Myanmar.

he became fully convinced of nonviolence for social injustice. At last, King began to practice what he believed by leading the civil rights movement until his death. We will discuss the critical interaction between Wink, King and Suu Kyi in detail in later chapters.

4.3 King's Principles of Nonviolence: A Critical Examination

So far, I have argued that King's philosophy of nonviolence is not merely an outcome of his personal upbringing and his intellectual enterprise, but also of applying what he studied and discovered throughout his life in all the civil rights movements he led. Through an intellectual quest, King reached the conclusion that nonviolence was the best way to handle the socio-political injustice at that time. All the things he learned were being refined as he experimented with them during his nonviolent struggles. As a result, King formulated six principles, which were in one way or another a refined comprehensive view of his philosophy of nonviolence. His speeches and writings are an exposition of these six principles. What follows is a critical examination of each of these six principles and how they are interconnected.

4.3.1 Nonviolence as a Method of the Strong

The first principle of nonviolence is that it is not a method of the coward, but of the strong. Scholars point out that this is an echo of Gandhi.[146] For Gandhi, fear and cowardice are unacceptable, so he said, "cowardice and *ahimsa* do not go together any more than water and fire."[147] On the surface, the way of violence when fighting against oppression seems more courageous than that of nonviolence because using arms also requires a great deal of physical strength. In contrast, the nonviolent method is sometimes considered as passive or nonaggressive because it is not a physically aggressive force. As a matter of fact, what is required for a nonviolent resistance is far greater than physical energy, so here King was referring not to physical strength, but

---

146. Chakrabarty and Carson, *Confluence of Thought*, 61.
147. Quoted from Richards, *Philosophy of Gandhi*, 35.

inner and spiritual force. Therefore, King argued that cowardice and fear are stumbling blocks to be surmounted if nonviolence is to be practiced.

Because of this, King spent a great deal of time in analyzing fear. For him, there are four antidotes to fear: first, recognition of the reasons behind our fear; second, courage as the supreme virtue; third, love as something that can vanquish fear; and fourth, faith in the God who is in control. Prior to his analysis of fear, King had personally encountered a frightening moment, so he knew first-hand how fear could emotionally paralyze a person. This incident became known as his divine experience in the kitchen.

This divine experience is perhaps the best illustration to portray why King believed nonviolence is the method of the strong, not cowards. It happened during the Montgomery Bus Boycott. One night, King got a phone call before he went to sleep. An angry voice on the phone threatened that he would be killed if he marched to Montgomery. Terrified, he was unable to remain in bed any longer. So, King got up and went to the kitchen for a cup of coffee. Though he had heard this kind of threat before, on this occasion he was losing his heart. Finally, he could think of nothing else to do but to bow over the kitchen table and pray to the God whom he believed was a personal being.[148] After the prayer, King heard God, through an inner voice, speak to him telling him to stand firm. In that moment, he experienced the presence of God in a way that he never had felt before. All his fear was wondrously faded away and his soul began to be filled with all the strength and courage to face anything. That experience was so crucial to him, that King could then not only master his fear, but also his conviction of nonviolence grew stronger than before.

Therefore, King, like Mohandas Gandhi,[149] was so convinced that a coward could never become truly nonviolent unless he mastered the fear inside himself. If people choose nonviolence simply because they are afraid or merely because they lack the instruments of violence, they are not truly nonviolent, but instead are cowards. Like Gandhi, King understood that it was the spell

---

148. Carson, *Autobiography of Martin Luther King*, 77.

149. The oft-quoted statement of Gandhi is this: "where there were only a choice between cowardice and violence, my advice is violence."

of fear that had to be broken.[150] This principle raises a question, "how can those under the extreme oppression overcome the fear?" For instance, fear is a day-to-day reality in the lives of the people of Myanmar, whose minds and hearts had been conditioned through the "leadership by terror" for more than five decades.[151] How can such a people be motivated to become courageous for nonviolent resistance? Robert Holmes rightly puts it that people, like Gandhi and King, in such situations were not afraid as they engaged in nonviolent resistance.[152]

4.3.2 Nonviolence as a Path to Reconciliation

King's second principle of nonviolence was that the chief aim of nonviolence is to end enmity and win friendship, or reconciliation between nonviolent resisters and their antagonists. This principle is also an adapted idea from Gandhi. Gandhi believed that friendship was a key concept in attempting to heal the enmity between Indian Muslims and Hindus of that time. An intense conflict between Indian Hindus and Muslims was prevailing across the country, especially around the time that India was about to gain independence from Britain.[153]

In the same vein, King's ultimate purpose for nonviolent resistance was far greater than achieving desegregation; it was integration. It was the creation of the Beloved Community where all racial, social and economic boundaries are broken down. To illuminate his vision, King distinguished key terms such as segregation, desegregation, and integration. Segregation, for him, is a system that denies blacks equal access to public spheres, while desegregation is eliminative and negative because it only discards the legal and social prohibitions. On the contrary, King strongly proposed the notion of integration.

---

150. To quote Jawaharlal Nehru, Gandhi was convinced that, "the dominant impulse in India under British rule was that of fear, pervasive, oppressing, strangling fear, that it was against this all-pervading fear that Gandhi's quiet and determined voice was raised: Be not afraid," cited from Dalton, *Mahatma Gandhi*, 163.

151. The phrase "leadership by terror" is adopted from Manfred Kets de Vries's *Lessons on Leadership by Terror: Finding Shaka Zulu in the Attic*, which is the in-depth case study of the life of Shaka through the lens of psychoanalysis, Kets de Vries, *Lessons on Leadership*.

152. Holmes, *Ethics of Nonviolence*, 212.

153. Gandhi, *Selected Writings*, 178. Once Gandhi undertook a penitential fast for twenty-one days to appease the warring Hindus and Muslims and to revive their friendship, Majmudar, *Gandhi's Pilgrimage of Faith*, 180.

He defines integration as "creative, therefore, more profound and far-reaching than desegregation; it is the positive acceptance of desegregation and the welcomed participation of Negroes into the total range of human activities."[154] To employ Hegelian dialectic, integration is neither thesis (segregation) nor antithesis (desegregation), but it is a synthesis (integration). Therefore, the ultimate goal of the civil rights movement, in King's view, was not desegregation, but integration because it is only through such integration, that the Beloved Community can possibly be created.

What role does nonviolence play in creating integration and the Beloved Community? King's idea of integration and the Beloved Community is connected to that of the inseparability of means and ends. For King, the means we utilize are crucial. In his understanding, it is logically out of the question to attempt to foster such a community by means of violence, because violence can only breed more violence. Since the end that King sought was reconciliation and the Beloved Community, the means to reach it could only be nonviolent. Violence has, therefore, no place in the Beloved Community, which itself is the product of nonviolence. So King adopted the means of nonviolence because our end is a community at peace with itself.[155]

If nonviolence is the means to bring about the end (the Beloved Community), then love is the crux of the community. For King, this community is all-inclusive of Hindus, Muslims, Christians, Jews, and Buddhists. He envisioned that the call for such community is "a call to all humans for an all-embracing and unconditional love."[156] Love, as the overarching principle of all the subjects King talked about, is central to the notion of the Beloved Community. This love is best expressed in interpersonal relationships. Only through this type of love will opponents be transformed into friends.[157] In *Where Do We Go from Here*, King's vision is articulated, "We still have a choice today: nonviolent coexistence or violent co-annihilation. This will be mankind's last chance to choose between chaos and community."[158] For King,

---

154. King, "Ethical Demands for Integration," in *A Testament of Hope*, 118.
155. King, "An Address before the National Press Club," in *A Testament of Hope*, 102–103.
156. King, *Where Do We Go from Here*, 201.
157. King, "Facing the Challenge of a New Age," in *A Testament of Hope*, 140.
158. King, "Where Do We Go from Here?" in *A Testament of Hope*, 633.

the end that nonviolent resistance seeks is not the defeat of his opponents, but reconciliation with them.

4.3.3 Nonviolence as the Weapon against Evil

Seeking reconciliation as the end, nonviolent resistance is not directed against people, but against evil itself; not against those who work within the system, but against the system itself. This principle also reflects Gandhi's *ahimsa*. In Gandhi's view, "man and his deed are two distinct things . . . Hate the sin and not the sinner."[159] From the beginning of the civil rights movement, King discerned the difference between the whites that worked within the system and the system. He made it crystal clear that their fight was not against the segregationists, but the segregation; not against whites, but against the notion of white supremacy. Put it another way, the struggle was not between whites and blacks, but between justice and injustice, between the forces of light and the forces of darkness, and between interracial harmony and racism.[160]

However, it is impossible to completely dissociate an evil social system from the personal moral responsibilities of the individuals who maintain it.[161] Of course, depersonalizing evil is quite unwarranted. Systemic evil can lead humans to behave in evil ways, but that (systemic) evil does not come out of nothing. It is a human product. In fact, one reason why King depersonalized racism was his understanding of human nature. He believed that a human has a potentiality to become good or evil. This belief of King was a result of retaining a balance between two theological positions – the liberal optimistic view of human nature and that of Reinhold Niebuhr.

---

159. Quoted from Dalton, *Mahatma Gandhi*, 239. Gandhi encouraged his people to distinguish evil from evildoers; that is, not to non-cooperate with evil, but to love English people who discriminated against Indians on the basis of race. *Ahimsa*, for him, is more than shunning violence or harm, but doing good even to the evildoer. *Satyagraha*, for Gandhi, distinguishes between people and systems; one may hate the system but not the people who are involved with the system, Richards, *Philosophy of Gandhi*, 51.

160. Some Christian scholars suggest that King's perception of the fight against evil itself is similar to the biblical idea of fighting against powers and principalities, Heiltzel, *Jesus and Justice*, 63; Watley, "Against Principalities," 301. King, of course, did not use this biblical vocabulary of powers and principalities. Yet if principalities and powers were construed as socio-political structures, it is true that King's nonviolent resistance was not against people, but against principalities and powers.

161. Niebuhr, *Moral Man and Immoral Society*, 249.

King's understanding of human nature seems still optimistic in that he believed that human nature can be changed. Human nature can, for him, respond to goodness because a human being is not totally depraved. But the questions that need to be asked are: why were a number of whites so complacent and even antagonistic to the movement? Should we lay the blame for this on the system or condemn the racial bigots? Can evil that a person has committed be exclusively separated from themselves? Who invented the segregation system? In fact, humans commit evil because external evil has influenced them, and at the same time, because evil is already inside humans. From sociologist Peter L. Berger's viewpoint, society is a human product and at the same time, a human is also a product of society.[162] Of course, the idea of hating sin, but not the sinner is revolutionary. Yet it is truly complicated in practice. The role of justice and rule of law should be considered in this principle since truth, justice, and forgiveness are indispensable ingredients in restoring a friendship or reconciliation. As Niebuhr points out, it is impossible to completely disassociate an evil social system from the personal moral responsibilities of the individuals who maintain it.[163] Therefore, it seems idealistic to depersonalize evil in an absolute sense, because it is people who maintain an evil social system. Evil has been an unsolved mystery throughout human history.

However, Niebuhr admits that it is morally and politically wise for an opponent to mingle sin and the sinner. In social reform, what matters is to reduce animosities and preserve rational objectivity in assessing the issues under dispute. The more the egoistic element can be purged from resentment,

---

162. Berger, *Sacred Canopy*, 3, 4. James M. Dixon summarizes that the individual and society are dialectically related through the processes of externalization, objectivation, and internalization. Man creates society through interaction. Society becomes an objective fact through the typifications of habitualized actions and through language. Man, in turn, accepts these objective facts and internalizes them. It is in the order of objectivation that religion enters in. The second order of objectivation – legitimation – is an explanatory and justifying process for institutions and on the highest level of legitimation – that of symbolic universes – it is such a process for the whole social order. Religion is a symbolic universe of meaning beyond and prior to everyday life that aims at ordering and protecting man and his social reality from the marginal experiences of life, especially the most fearful and radical –death, Dixon, "*The Sacred Canopy*," 40–41.

163. Niebuhr, *Moral Man and Immoral Society*, 249.

the purer a vehicle of justice it becomes.[164] The idea of hating evil and not the evildoer, albeit seemingly impossible, is an essential characteristic of social activism for nonviolent change.

4.3.4 Nonviolence and Redemptive Suffering

If nonviolent resistance is against evil, not people, the inevitable outcome for those resisting is suffering. So, King asserted that nonviolent resistance calls for a willingness to suffer without revenge. This principle was also adapted from Gandhi.[165] Like Gandhi, King stressed the inescapability of suffering in nonviolent resistance and interpreted it in the light of biblical tradition. David Chappell traces King's view of suffering suggesting that, as a Christian theist, King had a "dilemma." Out of the study of Jeremiah and Job, King came to see the just suffering while the unjust prosper. For him, the ultimate solution for problem of evil is not intellectual but spiritual; so, the Christian answer to evil is ultimately contained in what he does with evil, itself the result of what Christ did with evil on the cross.[166] That idea that unearned suffering is redemptive is King's gloss on the sacrifice of Jesus, his guide to the path of following in His footsteps.[167] Most of all, his personal trails also taught him the value of unmerited suffering.[168]

King acknowledged suffering as a powerful social force in both violent and nonviolent resistance. However, how it becomes a creative and a powerful force is different in these two contexts:

> Violence says that suffering can be a powerful social force by inflicting the suffering on somebody else and you achieve some end by inflicting suffering on another . . . The nonviolent say that

---

164. Niebuhr, 249–250.

165. For Gandhi, "nonviolence in its dynamic condition means conscious suffering," Gandhi, *Selected Writings*, 48. Self-suffering or sometimes suffering even unto death, according to Gandhi, is indispensable in the quest of truth. Nothing like self-interest can replace self-suffering. Suffering is a key element to understand Gandhi's soul-force. John Howard Yoder affirms that Gandhi's view of suffering is a Christian truth as well as a Hindu truth. See Yoder, *For the Nations*, 127

166. Clayborne Carson, "Introduction," in King, *Papers of Martin Luther King Jr. Vol. II*, 17.

167. Chappell, *Stone of Hope*, 50.

168. Martin Luther King, "Suffering and Faith," in *Papers of Martin Luther King Jr., Vol. V*, 444.

> suffering becomes a powerful social force when you willingly accept that violence on yourself so that self-suffering stands at the centre of the nonviolent movement and the individuals involved are able to suffer in a creative manner, feeling that unearned suffering is redemptive, and that suffering may serve to transform the social situation.[169]

So, suffering can be redemptive if someone seeks to transform it into a creative force. King also views suffering as the way of Christ and the cross.[170] For him, nonviolent activists willingly allow themselves to be the victims of violence, as they are convinced that their suffering and cross-bearing will result in the redemption of social institutions. King compared his life to a cross-bearer that bore their cross to die upon.[171] Only through bearing the cross can reconciliation occur and the broken community be restored.

4.3.5 Nonviolence and Inner Strength

The fifth principle of nonviolent resistance is that it "avoids not only external physical violence but also internal violence of spirit."[172] Like Gandhi, here King deepened the scope of nonviolence by intermingling physical with mental or psychological dimensions. In Gandhi's *Satyagraha*, the use of violence in any form, whether in thought, speech, or deed, is exclusively proscribed. *Satyagraha* resists the will of a tyrant wholeheartedly but never by resorting to hatred or violence.[173] King also asserted that nonviolent resisters refuse not only to shoot their opponents, but also refuse to hate them. For him, hate never degenerates hate, rather it intensifies its existence in the universe. Only through love, can the chain of hate be loosened and broken. This principle affirms that nonviolence requires a force which is stronger and more demanding than an external or physical force. It is a force, being generated from inside or the human soul. King expounded this principle by extensively employing the idea of *agape* love. Love, for King, is concerned with

---

169. King, *Testament of Hope*, 47.
170. King, *Stride toward Freedom*, 170.
171. Carson, *Autobiography of Martin Luther King Jr.*
172. King, "An Experiment in Love," in *A Testament of Hope*, 19.
173. Richards, *Philosophy of Gandhi*, 50.

internality – something operating in the human heart by the divine hand. In King's eyes, *agape* love is the love that seeks not one's own good, but the good of others. It is also the love that recognizes the fact that all of life is interrelated. Thus, nonviolence demands more than physical force; it requires inner strength that draws on *agape* love.

4.3.6 Nonviolence and Justice

The last principle of nonviolence, for King, is that the forces of the universe bend toward justice. In other words, it is a hope that justice will prevail. In his view, it is the God who empowers him to stand firm on the grounds of nonviolence in the midst of adversities. His belief in such a God was crucial in his ability to withstand every threat and difficulty on his way to freedom and justice. With such a faith, King asserted that we, through nonviolent engagement, might become co-workers with God.[174] As a Christian, King justified his position using the stories of Jesus's crucifixion and resurrection. The Good Friday was not the end, as Easter Sunday dawned. Nevertheless, King did not confine the applicability of this principle to Christians alone. Instead, he believed that it also works out in the lives of the devotees of nonviolence who do not believe in a personal God, but still believe somehow that there is something in the universe (be it as an unconscious process, an unmoved mover, or a personal God) that works for the unfolding of justice.

In summary, King shared Gandhi's ideas of nonviolence in drawing these six principles. In a sense, these are not his original ideas that he developed himself; rather he adapted from Gandhi's ideas in such a manner that he Christianized them all. If Gandhi were discarded in reading these six principles of King, it would sound purely Christian – there seems to be no Hindu-toned characteristics. Both King and Gandhi are activists who practiced what they believed in. They were not academics, yet they were critical and synthetic thinkers. John Yoder observes that as both Gandhi and King were the products of white Anglo-Saxon schools, they were skilled at integrating what they learned from those schools into what was going on in their respective contexts.[175]

---

174. Quoted from Ellingsen, *Reclaiming Our Roots*, 363.
175. Yoder, *War of the Lamb*, 60.

Like Gandhi, King tried his best to make religion the foundation of his movement. Gandhi foundationally based all his arguments for nonviolence on Hinduism, whereas King formulated his view of nonviolence on the basis of Christianity. Essentially, both Gandhi and King articulated their political mission at enormous personal sacrifice by pursuing religion-driven social action, and they trod the same pathway at the ends of their lives.[176] Their lives shed light on the integral relationship between politics, morality, religion and social concern; once one is removed for sake of others, what is left would be a deformity. What makes them different, by and large, is that they adhered to a different religion (Hinduism and Christianity), upon which they formulated their principles of nonviolence, and through which they articulated their views and actions. As discussed, these six principles of nonviolence, though each has its own significance, are clearly interrelated. As an exponent of principled nonviolence, King formulated these six principles to guide and navigate his actions, and through them he lived his life. In the next chapter we will look at Suu Kyi, as a pragmatic nonviolent practitioner and highlight her view of pragmatic nonviolence, so that King and Suu Kyi may interact with each other to draw some practical implications in order to engage with the political context of Myanmar.

King's principles parallel those of Wink and Suu Kyi. For instance, the method of nonviolence, for King, requires an enormous deal of courage. Wink also presents three stages (flight, fight, and nonviolent). If a person wants to move from the first stage (flight) to the third (nonviolent), they have to go through the second stage (fight). Only after having courage to fight back (second stage), can they move to the third, nonviolent resistance. In the same way, Suu Kyi also stresses the importance of courage or freedom from fear in nonviolent resistance, which we will detail more in the next chapter.

4.4 What Would You Do?

The unavoidable question for all advocates of nonviolence is: "what would you do if someone entered your house and attacked your family?" Unlike many theorists of nonviolence, King's response to this what if dilemma was

---

176. Chakrabarty and Carson, *Confluence of Thought*, 190.

not primarily philosophical. Instead, it was his personal experiences which brought him to firm conviction and commitment to nonviolence. So, I would like to highlight how his experiences led him to become an advocate of principled nonviolence, and then I will look at his response to the what if questions.

During the Montgomery Boycott, King's use of nonviolence was still tactical, employed as a method for resistance – nothing more. In fact, King was intellectually convinced that nonviolence was the best solution to deal with the social illness at that time; however, he was not fully ready yet in a practical sense. Therefore, he still carried a gun with him for self-defence. In Rufus Burrow's comment, King still adhered to the idea of retaliatory self-defence.[177] Through serious conversations with his close friends and colleagues, Bayard Rustin and Glenn Smiley, King finally renounced all tactics of self-defence. In retrospect of Montgomery, King wrote,

> The experience in Montgomery did more to clarify my thinking in regard to the question of nonviolence than all the books I had read. As the days unfolded, I became more and more convinced of the power of nonviolence. Nonviolence became more than a method to which I gave intellectual assent, it became a commitment to a way of life.[178]

King's wife, Coretta, also stated that:

> In the early years, when he first preached nonviolence Martin would be asked the inevitable question put to all men of his belief, "What would you do if someone were attacking your wife?" He would answer them, "I am not sure, but I hope I would not respond with violence." Later, as his ideals of nonviolence were tested in fire, he was able to answer more surely, confident out of his terrible experiences, that he would not strike out.[179]

Thus he adopted nonviolence as a way of life is, not merely a result of philosophical speculation, but through practice and experiences. Further, King was

---

177. Burrow, *Extremist for Love*, 291.
178. King, *Stride toward Freedom*, 169–170.
179. Coretta King, *My Life with Martin Luther King*, 274.

often asked whether self-defence was necessary for the movement. The question, "What would you do if someone attacked your wife and children?" seems inapt and totally irrelevant to King and those living at that time, because under the oppression of white supremacists, violence was a daily experience for the blacks. It was not "what if someone attacks," but how attacks should be responded to. Thus, the idea of self-defence, instead of being a what if, was a real issue. After his resolute commitment to nonviolence as a way of life, it is ridiculous to ask the question of self-defence to someone like King, because nonviolent activists see the misery of their people so clearly that they volunteer to suffer on behalf of others and put an end to their plight.[180]

In addition, King did not see a huge difference between defensive violence and aggressive or retaliatory violence. He argued that "when violence is tolerated even as a means of self-defence there is grave danger that in the fervour of emotion the main fight will be lost over the question of self-defence."[181] King asserted that he is ready to bear violence because violence creates more problems than it solves. The chain of violence (e.g. violence breeds violence) can never be broken down by violence. Only a refusal to hate or kill can put an end to the chain of violence in the world and lead us toward a community where all humankind can live together without fear.[182] In short, King eventually reached the conclusion that any form of violence, even a kind of defensive violence, is undesirable.

4.5 Summary of the Chapter

In this chapter, I have discussed King's theory of nonviolence by exploring how he discovered that nonviolence was the best method for seeking social justice, and his implementation of it afterwards. It took a long journey for King to find the satisfying answer for the social illness of his time. To divide King's pilgrimage to nonviolence into three scenes, his life before educational enterprise may be seen as a foundational period, because his parents'

---

180. King, "Nonviolence: The Only Road to Freedom," in *A Testament of Hope*, 57.
181. King, 57.
182. King, 58.

influence and personal experiences led him to become a passionate seeker for the answer to racial injustice.

In the second place, his passion for social justice, inherited from his childhood, inspired him to untiringly continue his search for the answer by reading several great philosophers and theologians. Reading their works intellectually enriched him, but none satisfied him like Mohandas Gandhi. Reading Gandhi opened King's eyes to see that Jesus's ethical teaching in the Sermon on the Mount could be applied not only on an individual level, but also in a corporate area. However, King did not become a Gandhian or a devout follower of Gandhi. King reconstructed what he learned from Gandhi from a Christian perspective so that what he was doing might be apposite to his own context. Thus, King's philosophy of nonviolence is basically an exposition of the Gandhian method of nonviolence from a Christian perspective.

However, it took some time for King to reach a complete commitment to nonviolence or to become a proponent of principled nonviolence. In other words, the way he reached a total commitment to nonviolence is evidently not by way of philosophical speculation, but through the struggles he was experiencing. Despite his unswerving commitment to nonviolence, we have observed that King was not a morally perfect hero. Plagiarism in a number of his writings and extramarital affairs became stumbling blocks for many conservative Christians and moralists to support the campaigns he had been leading. His life itself reflects the anthropology he adhered to, that is, King believed that humans are neither totally deprived nor basically good. Instead, he retained the balance between the liberal optimistic view of human nature and Niebuhr's pessimistic notion of human imperfectability.

As King was convinced of nonviolence as the only way to achieve racial integration, he developed six principles of nonviolence. As examined, these principles are interconnected. To dissect all of these principles, what can be observed is that *agape* love is the most overarching and unifying principle of the whole philosophy of nonviolence. It is also discovered that the principles of nonviolence are originally not his own, but Gandhi's; however, he reformed them in the light of biblical teachings and Christian worldview. This chapter has also brought out a Christian view through King's notion of nonviolence to engage a dialogue with Aung San Suu Kyi and Walter Wink so that an integrated lens may be created to investigate the political context of Myanmar. This investigation will bring out the implications for Christian engagement with politics in Myanmar.

The next chapter will be an analysis of Suu Kyi's Buddhist understanding of nonviolence. How King discovered nonviolence and applied it in the violence-filled context of that time will, to a certain degree, also reflect Suu Kyi's nonviolent (spiritual) revolution in the political context of Myanmar where seizing power by means of violence has continued throughout its history. Although what they resist against is different, how they persist in their resistance is the same. The next chapter will present this similarity in detail, so that the critical interaction between King and Suu Kyi may be investigated in the later part of this study.

CHAPTER 5

Suu Kyi on Nonviolence

The previous chapter discussed Martin Luther King Jr's ethic of nonviolence by looking at his familial and intellectual upbringing, his nonviolent resistance in the civil rights movement, and an articulation of his principles of nonviolence, thereby categorizing him as a champion of principled, philosophical or ideological nonviolence. This chapter examines Aung San Suu Kyi and her understanding and practice of nonviolent resistance. This research has taken King to be a voice for Christians and principled nonviolence for which the way of nonviolence is not just a means to achieve a target, but an end. Similarly, the study has also chosen Suu Kyi to be a voice for Buddhists and pragmatic nonviolence, which regards nonviolence as a means to attain a goal. Further, this research aims to contribute something to the Christians of Myanmar who live in the country where Buddhists are a majority. Thus, through using Suu Kyi as a voice for pragmatic nonviolence to interact with King as practitioner of principled nonviolence, an integrated lens will be developed so that political implications for Christians in Myanmar may be drawn.

This chapter will focus on her personal and intellectual upbringings, her entry into the political arena of Myanmar, the struggles she has been through, and her articulation of nonviolence from a Buddhist perspective. At the same time, it is also necessary to discuss the current situation and how she is dealing with the politics of Myanmar at present so that we may discern how she persists in sticking to the principles she has practiced before. This chapter analyzes Suu Kyi's view of nonviolence with the aim of presenting Suu Kyi as a Buddhist voice in the dialogue with King and Wink, with special reference to Myanmar.

5.1 Parental Influences

One of the questions that people across the world often ask Suu Kyi is how she had been coping with the maltreatment and the brutal schemes of the regime during her house arrest. In considering this question, it is important to trace how she became such a woman of iron will. In doing so, her personal upbringing – how she was raised by her parents – needs to be examined. Parental influences on Suu Kyi are truly immense. This chapter begins with an introduction on her father Aung San who died when she was only two. It is not strange to see a father's influence on his children. But in the case of Suu Kyi, it appears to have been more than usual. How could Aung San, who died when his daughter was two years old, influence her in such an unusual way? To deal with this question, it is necessary to sketch the life of Aung San, because he is such a legendary character imprinted in the minds of the people in Myanmar.[1]

Born at Natmauk village on the 13 February 1915, Aung San was recognized as the founder of the Burma Independence Army, which later became the Burma Defence Army, and is now the Myanmar Defence Army or *Tatmadaw*.[2] Since high school, the political affairs of the country captivated Aung San.[3] When he became a student at Rangoon (now Yangon) University, Aung San was actively involved in political activities. Because of his political engagement, he was expelled from the university on two occasions.[4] Aung San's contemporary Dagon Taya notes that he found no interest in other things except politics.[5] What made him unique from others is his character. Many people who knew him in person identified him as an ill-mannered, unsocial, rude and straightforward character. On the surface, these characteristics were indeed unappealing to anyone in the socially sensitive world. Indeed, Aung San did not pay as much attention to outward social interactions as he did to inward qualities such as courage, honesty, and integrity. He was unsocial,

---

1. By "people in Myanmar," I mean all citizens from all different ethnic backgrounds.
2. In a literal sense, the word *Tatmadaw* means the king's royal troop. It is the word that has been used for a long time in Burmese history.
3. Naw, *Aung San and the Struggle*, 12.
4. San, *Political Legacy*, 40.
5. Dagon Taya, "Politics was His Sole Existence," in Muang, *Aung San of Burma*, 26.

but honest; straightforward in speech, but benevolent; ill-mannered, but sincere; and dared to sacrifice his life for the sake of his country. His recorded speeches, which are well known among the people in Myanmar, are the best illustration of his character. For those who do not know Aung San's personality, his speeches might seem rude, harsh, or even insulting. However, the majority of the population of Myanmar deeply admire and applaud his speeches, even today.

Furthermore, Aung San's popularity was not only among his ethnic group the Burmans,[6] but he was also hugely appreciated and trusted by other ethnic minorities. According to a Chin ethnic leader, *Bogyoke* Aung San was a unifying factor in the historic conference.[7] Simply put, Aung San's honest interest and concern for the ethnic minority groups appealed to their leaders.

Being a daughter of such a legend of Myanmar has had a remarkable impact on Suu Kyi in many ways. She studied her father Aung San from various sources such as published materials, her extended family members, and the people who knew him personally. It seems that as she studied her father, and came to know more about him, she had greater esteem for him. Thus, some critics decry that Suu Kyi is obsessed with her father. For instance, Michael Aung-Thwin, one of her personal acquaintances during her studies in Japan, commented that she was always talking about her father.[8] Later, Aung-Thwin's critique became the then military junta's propaganda against Suu Kyi.

However, the word "obsessed" seems too severe for her. Even Michael Aung-Thwin mentioned that he would be too if his father were as famous as hers.[9] As a matter of fact, Aung-Thwin's comment is simply personal. When he remarked so, Suu Kyi was not yet such a famous icon across the globe. To this critique, Suu Kyi herself also responded that it is not obsession, but

---

6. Burman is the dominant racial group among seven other minor ethnicities.

7. Vum Ko Hau, "The Spirit of Panglong," in Maung, *Aung San of Burma*, 150. The Conference is known as the Panglong Gathering where most of the ethnic leaders attended with the aim of building union for the country.

8. Farrelly, "Professor Michael Aung-Thwin." Both Suu Kyi and M. Aung-Thwin completed their research at the Centre for Southeast Asian Studies, Kyoto University in 1985–1986. At that time, Suu Kyi was with her younger son Kim doing her research, but her husband and older son Alexander were in Nepal, doing his research.

9. Farrelly, "Professor Michael Aung-Thwin."

respect and admiration.[10] Besides this, the conclusion that can be drawn is that if Aung San were an obsession for Suu Kyi, the majority of the population of Myanmar would be obsessed with him, too, because Aung San has left an indelible imprint in the psyche of the majority of the population in Myanmar. Jesper Bengtsson also discerns that this accusation is particularly strange if one considers that almost everyone in Myanmar regarded Aung San as a hero.[11]

Most importantly, being a daughter of Aung San has birthed a sense of responsibility in Suu Kyi: a responsibility to do something for the people of Myanmar. For Suu Kyi, it is more than her father's influence, it is a sense of duty for her country people as well. Being a daughter of Aung San has, therefore, made her destined to serve her country, Myanmar. She acknowledges that one of the important reasons why she has taken part in the democracy movement is because of the love she has for her father. For her, loving her father and the country Myanmar are inseparably linked.[12] In this sense, Suu Kyi may be a moral heir of her father, Aung San.

In fact, Aung San was more than a father to her; metaphorically, he was like an idol whose ghost had possessed his daughter, Suu Kyi. If this is called "obsession," she was, of course, obsessed with her father. She expressed it in an early interview, "When I was young I could never separate my country from my father . . . even now it is difficult for me to separate the idea of my father from the concept of my country."[13] When she was in Japan, a man Aye Chan confronted her by saying, "In Burma there are Shans, Karens, Kachins, Chins and so on. They all make up Burma. Burma doesn't belong just to the Burmans."[14] The flush ran over Suu Kyi's face. Perhaps, it was first time Suu Kyi encountered the voice of ethnic minorities. For Michael Aung-Thwin, Suu Kyi was a divisive figure, forever harping on about her father.[15] In this sense, Suu Kyi's regard for Aung San is more than her love and admiration. It leans towards obsession and perhaps deifying or treating him as a god of the nation. Truly, Aung San was considered by many people in Myanmar as

---

10. Kyi and Clements, *Voice of Hope*, 83.
11. Bengtsson, *Aung San Suu Kyi*, 70.
12. Wintle, *Perfect Hostage*, 249.
13. Popham, *Lady and the Peacock*, 239.
14. Wintle, *Perfect Hostage*, 219.
15. Wintle, 219.

the founder and national hero of modern Myanmar, but not all the ethnic minorities (Karens, Kachin, Chins, Shans, Rakhain, and so on) would agree. For many ethnic minorities, Aung San is just a leader with the same superiority mentality of Myanmar. What makes him different is that he showed more concern for minorities than other nationalistic politicians during that time.

Like Aung San, her mother Khin Kyi also had an enormous influence on Suu Kyi. After Aung San's unexpected demise, Khin Kyi, without remarrying, took on all the household responsibilities and raised all of her three children. Patricia Herbert, who lived in Rangoon in the Ne Win years, said, "Khin Kyi was such a dignified woman with a very distinctive voice... it was a very clear voice, very authoritative without being domineering: you paid attention to what she said, and I think in that sense she must have had a huge influence on her daughter."[16] It was Khin Kyi who instilled in the mind of her children a strong memory of their father.[17] Ma Than É, a close friend, mentor and adult role model for Suu Kyi, also wrote that it was Khin Kyi, who "impressed upon the children their obligation to Burmese social and moral values and brought them up in the Buddhist faith."[18] In that regard, Suu Kyi has become the person her mother Khin Kyi wanted her to be.

Khin Kyi is also known as a strict disciplinarian with "a warm-hearted personality."[19] Suu Kyi, under the nurture of such a mother, developed characteristics, such as courage, honesty, and discipline. Khin Kyi's influence on her daughter Suu Kyi was not limited merely to character and attitude, she also implanted a love for the country Myanmar and its people in her daughter's mind, regardless of religious and ethnic differences. Suu Kyi recalls how her mother raised her up: "From my earliest childhood my mother taught me this idea of national unity (to live together in harmony in the midst of ethnic diversity); not by merely talking about it but by including it in everyday work."[20] In one of her speeches, she gives a personal illustration:

---

16. Popham, *Lady and the Peacock*, 167.
17. Lintner, *Aung San Suu Kyi*, 31.
18. Ma Than É, "A Flowering of the Spirit: Memories of Suu and Her Family," in Aung San Suu Kyi, *Freedom from Fear*, 280.
19. Kyi and Clements, *Voice of Hope*, 86.
20. Aung San Suu Kyi, "The Need for Solidarity among Ethnic Groups," in *Freedom from Fear*, 219.

we always had people from various ethnic groups living with us. At that time my mother was working with nurses. Nurses from all over the country would come to Rangoon to attend classes on childcare. She would invite those from ethnic minorities to stay at our home. Since my youth, then, I was taught to live closely with people from other ethnic groups.[21]

Another noticeable influence that Khin Kyi had on her daughter Suu Kyi was in teaching her to value and maintain traditions of Myanmar. Many of those who are acquainted with Suu Kyi affirm that she, despite growing up in the Western context, could keep in touch with the aspects of customs, traditions of Myanmar and even the Burmese language. Put differently, her upbringing in the UK was unable to inhibit her love for the country; instead, she has lived up to her mother and father's expectations in regard to loving the country, and valuing and maintaining the customs and traditions of Myanmar. Suu Kyi, under the rearing of such a mother has inherited a sense of duty and courage to do what is right, as well as indiscriminate love for the country and its people. This personal upbringing under such parents is a decisive factor that empowered Suu Kyi to lead, unfalteringly, the nonviolent resistance against the then military regime.

5.2 Intellectual Upbringing

If the parental influence has outfitted Suu Kyi with a sense of responsibility and love for her country, how did her education furnish her to cherish and embrace freedom, justice, and human rights? How much does Suu Kyi's educational enterprise prepare her for the nonviolent resistance? Generally, Suu Kyi has a very good educational background. She completed her basic education at the English Methodist High School (EMHS) in Yangon, Myanmar, until her mother moved to New Delhi, India, as an ambassador for Myanmar in India. She continued her college education at Lady Shri Ram College, India. There she came to be familiar with Mohandas Gandhi's nonviolence philosophy. Being fascinated by Gandhi's nonviolence, Suu Kyi

---

21. Aung San Suu Kyi, 220.

read not only Gandhi's writings, but also those of the philosophers who had influenced Gandhi.[22] So, Gandhi is the first person through whom Suu Kyi was intellectually illumined and inspired to resolutely commit to nonviolence.[23]

In 1964, Suu Kyi continued her undergraduate degree, in Philosophy, Politics, and Economics at St. Hugh's College in Oxford. The choice of degree reveal her desire to dig deep into politics, philosophy and economics. According to Ang Chin Geok, the reason Suu Kyi chose to study economics is not because of her interest in it, but because economics seemed a useful subject for a developing country.[24] Another biographer of Suu Kyi also mentions that her interest is not in politics, philosophy and economics, but in English, Japanese or forestry. Thus, Suu Kyi seemed to be experiencing a clash between what she wanted to study and what she thought she ought to study for the sake of her country Myanmar. Perhaps as a result of this, in some areas of study her grades were average, not outstanding.[25] Nevertheless, this educational background expresses how her heart was devoted to her country even before she had any chance to do something for the country. After completing her Bachelor of Arts in 1967, Suu Kyi went to New York, USA, and worked at the United Nations for three years while she was doing her postgraduate studies. During this time, she developed an appreciation for famous nonviolent activists, like Gandhi and Martin Luther King Jr.[26] In short, Suu Kyi's educational enterprise was a stepping-stone in preparing her for when the time would come for her to do something for her country Myanmar.

Further, it is not only the education itself she pursued, but also the sociocultural context where she studied. Both the education she undertook and the learning environment where she had been nurtured highly value and practice the ideas of freedom, justice, democracy and human rights as universal norms. Ethnically she is a Burman however, culturally and intellectually she is more western. Well-versed in the concepts of democracy, freedom, justice, and human rights, she is eloquent and articulate in interpreting them in speech and writing by using cultural symbols, tales, and concepts of Myanmar

---

22. Hasday, *Aung San Suu Kyi*, 47.
23. Hasday, 44.
24. Ang Chin Geok, *Aung San Suu Kyi*, 26.
25. Popham, *Lady and the Peacock*, 194.
26. Ang Chin Geok, *Aung San Suu Kyi*, 29.

and Buddhism. During her studies at Oxford, she met Michael Aris whom she married in 1972. They have two sons – Alexander and Kim. Until she got involved in politics in Myanmar, she and her family spent time in England, the US and India.

5.3 Entry into the Myanmar Politics

Looking at her early life, Suu Kyi did not have the desire to become a politician. All she wanted was simply to contribute something to her country – in particular, simply to start several libraries in Myanmar.[27] How could a woman with such a vision turn out to be a nonviolent activist, politician and a voice of freedom across the world as well as throughout Myanmar? What pushed Suu Kyi to enter the politics of Myanmar?

On 2 April 1988, Suu Kyi arrived in Yangon, Myanmar, to attend to her ailing mother in Yangon Hospital. Until then, she did not have any intention to get involved in the politics of Myanmar. Coincidently, this was during the student protest that began in March 1988 and increased in intensity in August. In the hospital, she saw numerous protesters being battered and wounded by gunshots. For a woman who loves and feels responsible for her country, it was unbearable to see the regime's brutal attacks against the protesters. Eventually it led her to join the movement and become involved in politics. Unfortunately, the junta denounced Suu Kyi as an opportunist politician who used the Four Eights as the best chance to become a national heroine.[28] In one sense, the regime's reprimand was somewhat sensible because it was not Suu Kyi's initial desire to become a politician. But the denunciation was unacceptable for the following reasons. First, Suu Kyi felt a deep responsibility to do something for Myanmar. For such a woman, encountering the army's brutal attacks against the protesters was agonizing. At the same time, she began to notice that the need of Myanmar was more than establishing libraries. The country needed a thorough reform of its political structure. Thus, she states

---

27. Pederson, *Burma Spring*, 43.

28. The 1988 uprising is known as the Four Eights. In fact, the protest began on the 12 March 1988 and reached its peak on the 8 of August 1988.

that she has taken part in the democracy movement in Myanmar because of her love of the country and a sense of responsibility toward its people.[29]

However, Suu Kyi was politically naïve; she had no experience whatsoever. She did not have a passion for it as her father had. Politics was of no interest to her, though she read Philosophy, Politics, and Economics in undergraduate studies at Oxford. Instead, her passion was to become a writer. Though she loves the nation Myanmar, most of her life was spent in the West. The woman who lacked political passion happened to engage in the politics of Myanmar. During her undergraduate studies at Oxford, she did not take any part in the university's political life. When she was informed about "the struggle of the Greenham Common women besieging the US military base in the English countryside in protest, her response was that these women would be better advised to go home to their families and their duties as wives and mothers."[30] How could such a woman efficiently and effectively engage in the politics of which she has no interest or familiarity?

5.4 Political Life of Suu Kyi (1988– the Present): A Survey

This research looks at two personalities, Martin Luther King Jr and Aung San Suu Kyi. While the former passed away almost fifty years ago, the latter is still alive, therefore it necessitates a survey of Suu Kyi's ongoing struggle for freedom and democracy. Suu Kyi, although born in Myanmar, grew up in a very different political context in the UK where law, human rights, and democratic values are more respected, practiced, and cherished than in Myanmar. As such a woman, how could she resolutely develop a nonviolent resistance against one of the worst repressive regimes in the world? In this survey, I will focus on how Suu Kyi persists in struggling for democracy against one of the most brutal despotic military regimes in the world by looking at major events that she encountered, not by narrating her life chronologically.

---

29. Kyi and Clements, *Voice of Hope*, 165.
30. Popham, *Lady and the Generals*, 229.

5.4.1. The Military Regime and Suu Kyi

The key phrase to depict the conflict between the junta and Suu Kyi is indeed the power struggle. As a matter of fact, the conflict between the junta (known as the State Law and Order Restoration Council [SLORC] / State Peace and Development Council [SPDC]) and Suu Kyi is not something between the powerful and powerless, but between two powers. Each has its own power.[31] The power of SLORC/SPDC is institutional, whereas Suu Kyi's power is personal. The regime does not have what Suu Kyi has, and vice versa. It led to a fierce fight between them. The discussion of this power struggle will shed light on understanding Suu Kyi's commitment to nonviolence.

Being a daughter of Aung San and her rhetorical skill in public speeches enabled Suu Kyi to win instant fame within a short time when she entered politics. As her popularity was growing across the nation and the globe, the regime's bitter hatred toward her became fiercer. Under such an attitude, Suu Kyi received various reproofs from them, most of which are too subjective and even prejudicial; therefore, those may be called stinging rebukes. First, the regime accused the National League for Democracy (NLD) in particular and other party politicians in general of practicing personality politics. For the then junta, these politics would lead the nation to disunity. Thus, they justified their coup by stating that the army is the only true father and mother to the public because it is the only genuine institution that has no special regard for any personality. Does Suu Kyi actually practice personality politics?

To deal with this question, I would like to clarify two Burmese words – *a-na* and *awza* – which can both be translated as "power." Despite the fact that these two words are power-related, I would like to name *a-na* as "authority" and *awza* as "influence" to analyze the concept of power in Myanmar. An *a-na* is institutional, dictatorial, and centralized, whereas *awza* is distributed and corporate. While the former is seen as top-down, the latter is inter-relational. According to Gustaaf Houtman, the former does not cope with

---

31. After Ne Win resigned from power, the military regime by the name of the State Law and Order Restoration Council (SLORC) came to power. SLORC was dissolved on 30 March 2011 by Senior General Than Shwe and it was renamed the State Peace and Development Council (SPDC).

awza (influence) through incorporation, but rather using exclusion.[32] This strategy made the *awza* (influence) leader more *awza* or influential, and at the same time, the *a-na* (authority) leader more authoritarian. Houtmann argues that in leading the public, the junta is strictly based on *a-na*, but Suu Kyi primarily relies on *awza*. As a result, the more the regime holds on to *a-na* (authority), the more they become authoritarian. In contrast, Suu Kyi's *awza*, as she bears the attacks of the regime, grows stronger. A political activist said, "We admire and love Suu Kyi and accept her policies because of her *awza*."[33] In this regard, Suu Kyi's leadership looks like personality politics since Suu Kyi, in leading the people, focuses more on *awza* than *a-na*.

To take a closer look, Suu Kyi does not actually want a personality cult, but the cultural context of Myanmar seems to prevent her from avoiding this. There is a Myanmar saying, that only when a person is admired and loved enough, will people accept what they believe (*lu ko khin hma tayar myin*). The meaning of this saying may be interpreted differently depending on the context, but essentially it means that when people love and admire a person, they will heartily follow that person. It is impossible to force or coerce people to willingly follow someone. The concept of this saying is culturally entrenched in the minds of the Myanmar people. Suu Kyi, being a daughter of Aung San and having her personal charisma, has been so much admired

---

32. Gustaaf Houtman, "Sacralizing or Demonizing Democracy?" in Skidmore, *Burma at the Turn*, 134–135. Houtman has expanded the discussion of *awza* and *a-na* in detail in his book, *Mental Culture in Burmese Crisis Politics*, 157–167. In fact, a political scientist and Sinologist, Lucian W. Pye, pioneered a study of the Burmese concept of power by analysing the term *awza*. His study focused on three words: *pon*, *awza*, and *ahnadeh*. The first refers to the idea of grace, charity, election, destiny; the second, a kind of power; and the third, a warm physical sensation towards others, see Pye, *Politics, Personality and Nation Building*, 147–148; with Mary W. Pye, *Asian Power and Politics*, 103–104. But, Pye's analysis of the Burmese concept of power focused only on *awza* alone. His study did not include the word *a-na*, which is also very salient in understanding the Burmese concept of power.

33. This is the interview completed by Jessica Harriden herself for her book, *Authority and Influence*, 221. Jessica Harriden, from the western perspective, compares Suu Kyi's *awza* with Max Weber's "charismatic authority," see, *Authority of Influence*, 20. For Max Webber, there are three different types of authority: traditional authority, legal-rational authority, and charismatic authority. The first type is exercised by custom and ancient practices; the second, exercised by formal rules which have been established by proper procedure; and the last, the charismatic leader is obeyed because followers believe he or she possesses an extraordinary character that trumps existing rules or prevalent customs. See Bruce and Yearley, *Sage Dictionary of Sociology*, 14. Truly, the leadership Suu Kyi expresses is very similar to the charismatic type.

and loved; therefore, her *awza* (influence) is so immense that she becomes a personality cult whether she likes it or not.[34]

In addition, Suu Kyi is a globally prominent person, compared to other political dissidents in Myanmar. The United Nations, the foreign media and journalists have reverently focused on her. This international attention inflamed the SPDC's and ex-Senior General Than Shwe's animosity towards her. Than Shwe once countered a United Nations envoy, saying, "Why do you focus on only one individual when there are fifty-four million people in my country?"[35] This question seems aggravating to the international communities. However, it is brusquely true in the sense that all the international communities, in particular the West, have taken a keen interest in Suu Kyi, ignoring other dissidents and opposition forces who worked sacrificially and suffered excruciatingly for the country Myanmar, perhaps even more than Suu Kyi did. Zauddin Sardar, as a cultural critic, assesses that the reason behind the West's focus on Suu Kyi and the Asian female leaders, like Benazir Bhutto (the eleventh Prime Minister of Pakistan) is their embodying of the character of the West. Their educational upbringings at Oxford and their excellent English in expressing a language of democracy, human rights and modernization capture the West.[36] Sardar is right that the West's intense focus on a single woman, Suu Kyi, is somewhat disturbing in the sense that their interest, albeit sincere, seems to ignore other political dissidents. The greater attention the international community paid Suu Kyi, the angrier the regime became. That heightened the regime's attack on Suu Kyi which became more severe than ever. In short, because of the demanding situation of global as well as local populations, Suu Kyi is unable to evade personality politics, though she does not yearn for it.

---

34. A Dutch, Burma scholar, Gustaaf Houtman, articulates how Suu Kyi's followers highly position her even as the "Angel of University Avenue" (the name of the street where her house is situated) and as a "female bodhisattva," in "Sacralizing or Demonizing Democracy?" in Skidmore, *Burma at the Turn*, 133–153.

35. Rogers, *Than Shwe*, 52.

36. Sardar, "Kept in Power*,*" 24. In my understanding, it is true that the West's focus on Suu Kyi is too much. As a result, many political activists who sacrificed so much more than Suu Kyi appear to be ignored. Suu Kyi does notice that there are a number of activists who have suffered much more than she has.

On the other hand, the regime's way of administering the nation itself is another form of personality politics. For instance, the first military government created by Ne Win and existing from 1962 to 1988 is known as the Ne Win era; and similarly, its succeeding regime (1988–2015) is called the epoch of Than Shwe. In the era of Ne Win, everything was under his control. He ruled the country as a monarch. Likewise, Than Shwe followed in the footsteps of Ne Win with regard to exercising power. Of course, each had its so-called political tag with the former as the BSPP (Burmese Socialist Programme Party) and the latter as the SLORC and SPDC. Nonetheless, the whole system of each was based on a single personality. In that sense, personality politics is the system of the regime as well as that of Suu Kyi. However, the difference lies particularly in the way of producing the personality cult: Suu Kyi becomes an influential personality through *awza* (personal power) while Ne Win and Than Shwe seek to become dictatorial personalities with the aid of *a-na* (institutional power).

As the regime's attempt to vilify Suu Kyi was unsuccessful, the accusations against her became sharper, more unreasonable and even preposterous in some cases. To illustrate the point, the two state-owned daily newspapers, the *New Light of Myanmar* and *Working People's Daily*, often launched vitriolic attacks against Suu Kyi. According to their denouncement, Suu Kyi was nothing more than a prostitute who had three foreign husbands, with whom she practiced all the wifely duties. She was also said to be a traitor because the international community supported every act she did. What is more, she was accused of being one who was destabilizing the country.[37] The junta used to attack her whenever an opportunity arose. For instance, the junta encouraged her to go back to the UK when her husband Michael Aris was dying. But Suu Kyi knew that the regime would never allow her to re-enter Myanmar if she did so. The regime then made an awful attack against Suu Kyi apropos of her family. The regime accused her of being disloyal to her family because she left her husband and two sons in the UK and remained alone in Myanmar simply to seek political power. They questioned, "Should

---

37. Than Shwe's regime often attacked Suu Kyi through their mouthpiece, the newspapers, almost every day.

she be more devoted to her family than to her country if there is only one option available?"

Of course, family is always what Suu Kyi had in mind. To look at her real life, Suu Kyi is a woman whose devotion to her family is doubtless. For example, she had plenty of photographs of Michael, Alexander and Kim, but she kept them upstairs in her private room at no. 54 University Avenue, Yangon, away from prying eyes. Feeling the separation from her family dreadfully, she once said, "Of course I regret not having been able to spend time with my family . . . One wants to be together with one's family. That's what families are about."[38] She went on to say, "I would like to have been together with my family. I would like to have seen my sons growing up. But I don't have doubts about the fact that I had to choose to stay with my people here."[39] Simply put, she had a tough choice in choosing between family and the nation; and she has prioritized the latter over the former. Indeed, she did know that the dilemma she was facing was an either/or situation.

The harshest attack from the SPDC was that the ideas Suu Kyi was introducing such as human rights, democracy and freedom were incompatible with Burmese culture. In response to this, Suu Kyi compared it with Buddhism and its ideals of a righteous monarch. Specifically, through using various examples such as the ten duties of a king, *mettā*, *thitsa*, and so on. Suu Kyi articulated the compatibility of Buddhism and politics. In her writings, speeches and conversations, what is evident is an attempt to integrate politics and religion, thereby demonstrating the compatibility of freedom, democracy, human rights and Buddhism. Stephen McCarthy, in his essay "Buddhist Political Rhetoric of Aung San Suu Kyi," concludes that Suu Kyi's Buddhist political rhetoric was "a product both of her unique circumstances and her conscious decision to combine Buddhism with politics in a way that her father Aung San had not."[40] To sum up, the power struggle between Suu Kyi and the regime is one-sided: the junta attacked Suu Kyi more than Suu Kyi did the regime. The conflict between *a-na* (institutional power) and *awza*

---

38. Wash, "Aung San Suu Kyi."
39. Wash.
40. McCarthy, "Buddhist Political Rhetoric," 79. Further discussion on Suu Kyi's attempt to integrate politics and Buddhism will follow later, but here I discuss mainly how the junta's view about the incompatibility of human rights and Burmese culture is reasonable.

(influence), interestingly, shows the necessity to have both. There are things that *a-na* alone cannot do and vice versa. Each mutually requires the other. Only through synthesizing *a-na* and *awza*, will there be an effective state that truly reforms the country of Myanmar.

5.4.2 Physical Attacks on Suu Kyi

As observed, the regime's repugnance grew harsher as Suu Kyi gained popularity and found favour with national and international communities. This led the regime to attack Suu Kyi even physically. In other words, the government's attack went beyond simply trying to make her lose heart and give up; they attempted to assassinate her. Among the attacks, the Danubyu and the Depayin incidents are most significant because they indicate two things: the inhumane audacity of the regime to conserve power and Suu Kyi's unswerving commitment to nonviolence in the heat of heartless violence.

Danubyu is a town in the Irrawaddy Delta about one-hundred kilometres north-west of Yangon. It was on 5 April 1989 while campaigning in the Irrawaddy District. She and her colleagues, while walking into the Danubyu, were stopped and told to return to the town from which they came. Suu Kyi courageously walked straight up to the soldiers who were aiming at her and ready to shoot. Fortunately, the order to open fire was declined.[41] The Danubyu incident had a great impact on Suu Kyi in terms of the public and the junta's views of her. After Danubyu, Suu Kyi became more renowned for her courage than before. Her courage appealed to many young activists, and so many young people rallied alongside her for the movement. Meanwhile, the military junta also realized how Suu Kyi was determined to strive for democracy regardless of death-threats. For the people living under such a brutal regime for decades, it is indeed an act of courage, and therefore immensely inspiring and challenging.

After the Dnubyu, the military placed Suu Kyi under house arrest until 1995. From 1995 to September 2000, she got involved different political activities. Then she was put under house arrest again from 2000 to May 2002, the year she was released again. That was the year when the second well-known incident took place. It was known as the Depayin massacre, and it broke

---

41. See the more detailed story in Jesper Bengtsson, *Aung San Suu Kyi*, 82–83.

out on 30 May 2003. Depayin was a town located in the Shwe Bo district, Sagaing Region. While Suu Kyi and her colleagues were closely approaching Depayin, thugs numbering about three thousand with bamboo sticks, iron bars, and knives stopped their caravan and began to attack them.[42] According to one witness,

> The attackers beat women and pulled off their *longyi* (skirts) and their blouses. When victims, covered in blood, fell to the ground, the attackers grabbed their hair and pounded their heads on the pavement until their bodies stopped moving. The whole time, the attackers were screaming the words, "Die, die, die..." There was so much blood. I still cannot get rid of the sight of people, covered in blood, being beaten mercilessly to death.[43]

Their target was to kill Suu Kyi, but her bodyguards saved her. The Asian Human Rights Commission states that more than seventy victims were massacred in the incident.[44] What matters most is that that incident was well thought-out and ordered by the then Senior General Than Shwe.[45] According to the Asian Legal Resource Centre, the massacre at Depayin clearly amounts to a "widespread or systematic attack directed against [a] civilian population, with a knowledge of the attack, and is, therefore, a crime against humanity."[46]

In short, the Danubyu and Depayin incidents expose the regime's determination to seize power regardless of complaints from local and global communities. It showed their single-mindedness in their efforts to retain power and their willingness to do anything if their power is endangered. On the other side, Suu Kyi and the NLD are also too dogged to sacrifice whatever cost to bring in democratic values to Myanmar. Put differently, they manifestly represent the most extreme encounter between violence and nonviolence throughout the history of Myanmar. Those incidents have widely

---

42. The USDA was the organization established by the then junta and has now become the political party, Union Solidarity and the Development Party, of the current government (USDP).

43. Zaw, *Face of Resistance*, Kindle location 443 of 2829.

44. Htoo, "Depayin Massacre."

45. Popham, *Lady and the Peacock*, 361. Aung Lynn Htut was a former senior officer in the Military Intelligence and number two in the Burmese Embassy in Washington. After his boss Khin Nyunt was purged, he sought political asylum in the United States in 2005.

46. Cited from Duthel, *Aung San Suu Kyi*, 331.

publicized the ruthlessness of the regime and the fearlessness of Suu Kyi and the NLD as well.

Truly, Suu Kyi deserves the credit for her great perseverance in the face of vicious attacks from the ex-junta and her firm commitment to nonviolence. However, the only reason she became locally famous is, as mentioned, simply because of her father Aung San. As a western product, her dealing with the then regime was at first confrontational. The international community's immense focus on her also disgusted the senior general Than Shwe and his accomplices. That added fuel to the flames of their rage against her. Once she was a housewife but she has become a celebrity. A woman who wanted to be a writer is now a politician. The question that occurs to me is, can such a woman be an efficient and effective politician? And can she restore the country from the culture of dictatorship to that of democracy? If so, to what extent? Before we respond to these questions, we will look at her understanding of nonviolence.

5.5 Principles of Nonviolence: A Critical Examination

So far, I have briefly examined the life of Suu Kyi, how she began to be involved in politics in Myanmar, and how she faced and nonviolently fought against the military regime without losing hope in a better future for Myanmar. How could Suu Kyi stick to the nonviolent method to fight against such a dictatorial regime? Why is she so convinced about nonviolence?

5.5.1 Why Not Violence?

If Aung San is a personality who has immensely influenced her, why did Suu Kyi not follow in his footsteps in regard to using the means of forceful resistance for the sake of freedom? It is necessary to look at reasons behind Suu Kyi's preference for nonviolence. Why did she not follow armed action like her father? The first reason is the age difference between Suu Kyi and Aung San when each began their political careers. That is, she was over forty-four when she began her democratic movement, whereas her father was only eighteen when he entered politics.[47] This age difference matters. Regarding knowledge, international experiences, education, and life experiences, Suu Kyi was far better equipped than her father, Aung San. Moreover, the different socio-political contexts in which they worked is also crucial. Aung San lived in the wartime during the two world wars. Many countries were at war, so the only single option at that time was to defend oneself by any means possible or die. It seems that for Aung San, armed force was the best solution. On the contrary, Suu Kyi lives in a time where people across the globe have become conscious of terrors, violence, and technologically advanced weapons. People in this time have become more aware of the advantage of nonviolence and the disadvantage of violence than those in the time of Aung San. History, to a particular extent, also affirms how nonviolent resistance, as a technique, has overcome dictatorial governments, and so Suu Kyi has more advantages in acquiring the strength of nonviolence than her father, Aung San had.

More significantly, there is a fundamental reason Suu Kyi and the NLD follow the path of nonviolence. For them, violence perpetuates a cycle of violence. In other words, violence increases violence. It creates a tradition of changing the political situation through force of arms.[48] If the military regime were overthrown by means of violence, people would be mentally conditioned to believe that violence can be defeated by violence alone, and thus the tradition of violence would never end. In Suu Kyi's words, "if you want to change a system where might is right, then you have to prove that right is might."[49] However, Suu Kyi does not condemn violent activists who have been fighting against the regime for many decades. In a BBC Reith lecture, she asserts that she has taken the path of nonviolence for practical and political reasons, not for a moral reason.[50] Through this, she has publicized her positive attitude toward violent activists in Myanmar.

---

47. Kyi and Clements, *Voice of Hope*, 85.
48. Suu Kyi, "Securing Freedom."
49. Kyi and Clements, *Voice of Hope*, 115.
50. Suu Kyi, "Liberty." Many argue that even Gandhi, to a certain degree, supported violent means to fight for justice and freedom. But the question is, "Does it mean that Gandhi really advocated the use of violence when he said so?" In my understanding, Gandhi placed his emphasis not on supporting the use of violence, but in stressing the importance of courage for all nonviolent activists. Gandhi understood that the way of nonviolence requires greater

However, it seems that Suu Kyi does not appreciate the use of armed force. In the lecture, she expresses it in the words, "if I were to support violence, it would only be because I believed that a short burst of violence, if you like, would prevent worse things happening in the long run. Only for that reason would I ever support violence if I were to support it."[51] Has she even practiced this? At present, she and NLD have become the government of the country. From the inception of her government, Suu Kyi has been faced with the historically long-rooted Rakhine-Rohingya conflict. She organized a team and appointed former General Secretary of the United Nations Kofi Annan to lead the team in examining and reporting the conflict situation. A recent event was the military fighting against Rohingya terrorists who attacked some security forces there. As a result, the international community has started to criticize the military and the NLD government for such a disproportionate attack against the Rohingyas. What the international community does not give proper regard to is the relationship between the military and the government. Suu Kyi and her government do not have any kind of power whatsoever upon the military because the constitution allows the military to stand on their own.

So far, Suu Kyi has been handling that Rakhine-Rohingya conflict with great sensitivity and delicacy, since it is such an enduring issue; it is not just racial, but religious. The issue is not that simple to deal with. There is no overnight solution to it. As it is a long-lasting conflict, it would surely take time to cope with it effectively. So the question is, should Suu Kyi condemn the military attacks against Rohingyas? What if Suu Kyi condemned the military attacks against Rohingyas? To answer the question generally, she would receive a big applause from international community, but she would definitely lose her favour with the majority population of the country. Whatever she chooses will cause her to lose one support – either local or international community. Apparently the situation impaled Suu Kyi on the horns of a dilemma, forcing

---

psychological effort than that of violence. Here, it seems that Suu Kyi has mistakenly quoted Gandhi's statement in order to affirm her stance.

51. Suu Kyi, "Dissent." Like Suu Kyi, Desmond Tutu once showed himself as different to Martin Luther King Jr, stating that he is a "peace-lover" not a pacifist. Tutu understands that violence, for some of his people, is the only alternative because of the harsh conditions of the apartheid, Bernard Hill, *Theology of Martin Luther King*, 116.

a choice between local and global support. The way in which she responded to the Rakhine-Rohingya conflict is neither fully yes nor no; instead she chose a middle-of-the-road response. That is, she stays silent on that issue. This discourages the international community, and gradually she has begun to fall into their disfavour. This shows that she has become a politician who seeks to compromise instead of choosing one over other.

In ethical terms, there is a difference between a greater and a lesser evil. According to this theory, when given two bad choices, the one that is not as bad as the other should be chosen over the one that is a greater threat. This is, by implication, a position of pragmatic nonviolence. It is still the position of "the end justifies the means." Her pragmatic view of nonviolence allows her to give fair credit to those who have fought for freedom through the use of armed force: including her father, Aung San, his comrades, and all the political activists. In short, Suu Kyi, in spite of personally leaning towards being a proponent of principled nonviolence, is politically aligned with pragmatic nonviolence and even violence. Put another way, it is a compromise which Suu Kyi came to learn from the inception of her political engagement. She has begun to learn how to compromise in her political dealings from the time she resolved to be a politician instead of being an icon of human rights.

5.5.2 Nonviolence as a Buddhist Ethic

Every reader of Suu Kyi is aware of how Buddhism plays a significant role in her life and political thought. Despite the contextual differences, Suu Kyi, like Martin Luther King Jr and Mohandas Gandhi, is highly skilled at making religion the foundation of her resistance.[52] For her, to be a Buddhist is to

---

52. Though Buddhism plays a central role in Suu Kyi's life, it did not seem that she practiced regularly prior to her political struggle in Myanmar. She considered herself to be a destined person to Myanmar, yet she was not that well-trained in Buddhism. It was her late husband Michael Aris who was well-versed in Buddhism. He did part of his PhD on, "A Study on the Historical Foundations of Bhutan with a Critical Edition and Translation of Certain Bhutanese Texts in Tibetan," which later was published as *Bhutan: The Early History of a Himalayan Kingdom*. Justin Wintle describes that whether Aris was a Buddhist in a strict sense is uncertain, yet his knowledge of Buddhism and its many different schools and sects enabled him to be accepted as a kindred spirit by Buddhist scholars in South-East Asia, the Himalayas and China, see Wintle, *Perfect Hostage*, 391–392. Michael Aris, though he came from Catholic family background, spent many of years in studying Buddhism in Bhutan. Suu Kyi learned scholarship and Tibetan Buddhism from her husband. She began to practice Buddhism in her life after she was put under house-arrest.

practice its teachings in all areas of one's life: there should be no fragmentation between what one believes and what one practices. Through integrating politics and Buddhism, Suu Kyi first and foremost attempts to construct nonviolence as a Buddhist ethic. This makes her different from her father, Aung San. For Aung San, politics is mundane or this-worldly, whereas religion is a spiritual or otherworldly affair. Thus Aung San opposed the proposal of making Buddhism the state religion while draughting the Burma constitution in 1947.[53] In contrast, Suu Kyi views politics and religion as inseparable. For her, it is neither idealistic nor naïve to talk about *mettā* in politics, but in fact, it makes practical sense.[54] For example, practicing *mettā* as the basis of the relationship between the NLD members would make people come to realize how Buddhism is intricately connected with the political enterprise. Her intention is to let people see that "politics is about people . . . love and truth can move people more strongly than any form of coercion."[55]

What makes Suu Kyi and Aung San radically different in their views on religion and politics? In fact, the contexts where they developed their political rhetorics make them different from each other. Stephen McCarthy examines the idea that Aung San developed his perspective during his study at Rangoon University, whereas Suu Kyi's view transformed noticeably while under house arrest in isolation. That is, her fusion of Buddhist meditation practice with her general, more developed Buddhist thought produced her distinctive form of political rhetoric.[56] According to McCarthy, the political contexts made Suu Kyi and Aung San different in the way they relate religion to politics. Of course, Suu Kyi's practice of Buddhist meditation during house arrest has significantly influenced her desire to integrate politics and Buddhism. However, it is not the only decisive factor. There is another factor that is equally important. Knowing the political importance of Buddhism, she interprets the politics of democracy in the light of Buddhist ideas to win

---

53. The 1947 constitution was implemented from the years 1948 to 1962, when Ne Win usurped the power of the parliamentary democratic government. Then Ne Win re-drafted the constitution, approved it in 1974, and enforced it until his resignation from politics in 1988. In 1988, the SLORC took power and they suspended the 1974 constitution. Under the SLORC, the 2008 constitution was drafted again and approved in 2008.

54. Kyi and Clements, *Voice of Hope*, 45.

55. Suu Kyi, *Letters from Burma*, 17.

56. McCarthy, "Buddhist Political Rhetoric," 79.

the predominantly Buddhist population. In contrast, Aung San, in favour of other minority religions, rejected the proposal for making Buddhism the state religion. This difference makes a radical distinction between Suu Kyi and her father.

Further, integrating politics with Buddhism is not an easy task. For example, the first post-independence prime minister, Prime Minister Nu struggled a great deal in doing so. Nu was a devout Buddhist, and in the time of his presidency, Buddhism became the state religion. Nu is also known as one who attempted to become a *Bodhisattva* (a being striving for Buddhahood).[57] But being a devout Buddhist, for Nu, clashed with the political tasks, such as using the armed forces.[58] However, Suu Kyi does not see things in this way; for her, there is no conflict involved in being both a Buddhist and a politician. She believes that a person can be a politician and a good Buddhist at the same time. The difference, according to Suu Kyi, lies in the fact that while she does not purposefully aim to be a *Bodhisattva*, Nu did. To delve deeper into this issue, one can ask what if Suu Kyi had been the Prime Minister in the time of Nu? In Nu's time, there were the civil wars between the state army and other minority ethnic groups and also the wars between the state army and communist insurgents. Currently, it is still a little early to objectively critique how far Suu Kyi can insist on synthesizing politics and Buddhism, in which previous politicians, like Aung San and U Nu, had hardly seen its possibility.

Despite the fact that integrating politics with Buddhism is controversial, Suu Kyi views nonviolence as a Buddhist ethic by the Five Precepts. The first precept is to refrain from killing (killing of all living beings – animal as well as human). The second is to restrain from stealing; the third, to avoid sexual misconduct; the fourth, to refrain from false speech; and the fifth, to desist from drinking and using drugs that cloud the mind. Most Buddhists associate

---

57. *Bodhisattva* refers to an ordinary person who takes up a course in his or her life that moves in the direction of buddhahood, an enlightened one. Actually, anyone who directs their attention and their life, to practicing the way of life of a buddha is a bodhisattva, as described in Uchiyama, "What is a Bodhisattva?"

58. The word *Bodhisattva* is defined differently by two wings of Buddhism – Mahayana and Theravada. For the former, it refers to the one who postpones attainment of Nirvana in order to alleviate the suffering of others; while for the latter, it means the *arhat* or the one who has attained Buddhahood. But the term in Sanskrit literally means the one who seeks awakening (Bodhi) – thus, an individual on the path to becoming a buddha, see *Encyclopedia Britannica*, s.v. "Bodhisattva," from http://www.britannica.com/- EBchecked/topic/70982/bodhisattva.

killing and sexual misconduct (rape) with violence. In short, Buddhism rejects any form of violence. But Suu Kyi broadens the idea to suggest that it is not just not killing that deals with violence; robbing (stealing) is also a form of violence because it violates someone else's right to own property. In that sense, theft, for Suu Kyi, is also a form of violence. Likewise, telling lies is violence because it violates another's right to hear the truth. With this view, Suu Kyi sees the use of intoxicating drinks and drugs as a form of violence. By having alcoholic beverages, one is harming oneself. Hence, Suu Kyi insists that nonviolence or *ahimsa* is at the root of the Five Precepts.[59]

In brief, notwithstanding her upbringing in the West, her interpretation of nonviolence and politics from the viewpoint of Buddhism is convincing enough to the Buddhist population of Myanmar. She skilfully integrates her ideas with local resources to let the public know that Myanmar desperately needs a revolution that is spiritual in its nature. So, she articulates the idea of nonviolence through the eyes of Buddhism with the use of existing stories, values, tales, and worldviews of the people.

However, Suu Kyi is a shrewd politician, knowing the right time, the right place and the right thing. In her life before political engagement in Myanmar, religion was not her concern. Practicing Buddhism seemed not fascinating to her. Married to a Christian man, being brought up in the secular context, religion seemed to be an otiose matter that a person does in their private life. Her main concern was more with her father than religion. Perhaps she might have been quite knowledgeable about Buddhism and its teaching, but lacked practice in her daily living. Only after being involved in the politics of Myanmar, has she begun to practice Buddhist meditation.[60]

On the surface, Suu Kyi seems to contradict herself regarding her pragmatic position on nonviolence and Buddha's teaching of the five precepts. The teaching of the five precepts is clearly a form of nonviolence. Yet Buddha once explained the danger of dogmatic thinking and improper learning of dharma in the parable of the raft. His teachings are compared to a raft, which could be used to cross the river, but not to cling to after crossing the river. Likewise, Buddha taught that his teachings are, like a raft, for crossing over with – not

---

59. Kyi and Clements, *Voice of Hope*, 64–65.
60. Suu Kyi, "Benefits of Meditation and Sacrifice."

for seizing hold of.[61] Thus, Suu Kyi's pragmatic position on nonviolence is somewhat compatible with the teaching of Jesus.

5.5.3 *Mettā* as the All-Embracing Principle of Nonviolence

As a Buddhist, Suu Kyi believes that *mettā* (loving-kindness) is the key foundation in practicing the teachings of Buddha in every aspect of life. In her understanding, *mettā* is the only right way for her to change the course of the nation's history. Using *mettā* and other Buddhist terms, metaphors, and illustrations in the Myanmar context, Suu Kyi expresses her thought, struggle, and vision for the future of the nation. Her conviction is that Buddhism is pertinent enough to apply to the political context of Myanmar, where so-called Buddhist dictators have been present for a long time.

First, Suu Kyi, unlike traditional Burman Buddhists, has somewhat a different view of *mettā*. For instance, she looks at some forms of practices of *mettā* in Myanmar and concretizes the notion in a revolutionary manner. In the traditional Myanmar Buddhist community, *mettā* is mainly practiced in religious circles instead of in day-to-day relationships. In particular, practicing *mettā* in our relationships is less common than "sending or extending *mettā*" to other living beings as a form of religious exercise.[62] In contrast, Suu Kyi has attempted to implement the notion of *mettā* in her daily or political career in having a relationship with her colleagues and the regime. Thus love or *mettā*, for her, is not an abstract idea, but something she and her colleagues practice in their everyday relationships. They work as a family and show real concern and affection for each other regardless of any pressures or difficult situations. So *mettā*, as the basis of their relationship, becomes something through which they can stand together and face the repression and dangers.

In addition, Suu Kyi's view is that if we practice *mettā* through friendship and affection, it will be much easier for us to offer the same affectionate

---

61. O'Brien, "The Buddha's Raft Parable," https://www.learnreligions.com/the-buddhas-raft-parable-450054.

62. The conception of "sending or extending *mettā*" to other living beings is the commonly practiced ritual. That is, sitting in front of the Buddha idol, a person recites a spell and says, "let every living being from all corners – east, west, south and north – be free from all kinds of harm, diseases, and be at peace." This is what a Myanmar Buddhist calls "sending or extending *mettā*."

friendship to the people who may think of themselves as our enemies.[63] In fact, what she is doing is an attempt to justify that there is a way to become a devout Buddhist and at the same time, a politician. In that sense, Suu Kyi's view of *mettā* is revolutionary to some traditional Myanmar people because the practice of *mettā* can also be seen not only as one of the religious rites but also as an act in politics.

With this understanding, Suu Kyi sees *mettā* as active, and opposite to passive *mettā* and simply sitting there saying, "I feel sorry for them."[64] Unlike passive *mettā*, active *mettā* means doing something about the situation – something one can do to save someone else at the cost of one's life.[65] So, she openly expresses her desire for all people from all walks of life – monks, nuns and lay people alike – to take part in the movement. Nonviolent acts, done out of such *mettā*, are active, compassionate actions.

From a purely religious perspective, one can ask, "Does she politicize Buddhism?" Of course, the answer depends on one's view of religion and politics. If religion is recognized as a purely spiritual business, Suu Kyi is apparently politicizing Buddhism. On the contrary, if religion is regarded as being inclusive of all aspects of life, her call can be justified. Suu Kyi knows the essential role of Buddhism in the political history of Myanmar. From the time Buddhism came into Myanmar, it has been an intrinsic value in politics. Kings in the monarchical period highly regarded Buddhism as the state religion. In the same vein, the post-independence governments such as Nu and Ne Win also considered Buddhism to have a special role in politics. According to Donald Eugene, Nu also tried to demonstrate that Buddhism and democratic socialism were completely compatible and indeed complementary.[66]

Similarly, the then military government also legitimated their rule by using Buddhism because democratic values, for them, are contradictory to those of Myanmar. Buddhism has always been a vital force to legitimize the rules of all monarchs and post-independence governments since the day Buddhism came into the country. Suu Kyi's predecessors legitimized their

---

63. Kyi and Clements, *Voice of Hope*, 160.
64. Kyi and Clements, 43.
65. Kyi and Clements, 43.
66. Smith, *Religion and Politics in Burma*, 312.

rules with the aid of Buddhism, so Buddhism was a means of legitimacy. On the contrary, Suu Kyi views Buddhism as a means to examine if a ruler is loyal to Buddha's teachings. Buddhism, for previous governments, is a means of legitimacy, whereas for Suu Kyi, it is a means of investigation. Thus, Suu Kyi's use of Buddhism in politics had been in conflict with that of the then junta. What makes Suu Kyi different from the regime is that the latter focuses on the outward form of Buddhism, while the former looks at the teachings of Buddha; the latter interprets Buddhism from a nationalistic viewpoint, and the former portrays Buddhism through humanitarian eyes.

Moreover, Suu Kyi believes that genuine *mettā* distinguishes between what a person does and what that person is. Simply put, *mettā* distinguishes evil from evildoers. For her, it is important to focus on what people do, rather than on what people are.[67] With regard to this, she quotes a story of Angulimala – a man, known as a serial killer in the time of Buddha.[68] Among Myanmar Buddhists, Angulimala is a well-known man who tried to kill even Buddha. Before meeting Buddha, he had already killed a number of people. The evil Angulimala had committed was so great that no one in his time believed he could be redeemed. When he heard Buddha saying to stop killing, he was

---

67. Kyi and Clements, *Voice of Hope*, 66.

68. The name of Angulimala was not his original name. His name was Ahimsaka, meaning "the harmless one." He was born with a dark fate, so he would one day become a robber. To deter that fate, his father sent Ahimsaka to the University of Taxila in order to study under a well-known Brahmin Guru. He was a brilliant student, thus becoming a favourite of the guru and enjoying special privileges. That fame led Ahimsaka to be envied by his fellow students. They developed a stratagem to suggest that Ahimsaka had seduced the teacher's wife and had also boasted that his wisdom was superior to his teacher. The teacher believed that ploy and asked Ahimsaka something impossible (to get 1,000 human fingers) to get the master's approval – the approval that Ahimsaka needed to complete his training. So he became a bandit, killing pilgrims and traders passing through the wilderness, and collecting fingers. To be able to count the number of fingers, he strung them on a thread and hung them on a tree. But he couldn't do that again because birds began to eat the flesh from the fingers. So he began to wear them around his neck as a garland. That was how he came to be known as *Angulimala*, meaning "garland or necklace of fingers." According to the tradition, the Buddha perceived with his divine eyes that Angulimala had acquired 999 fingers, and was desperately seeking the thousandth. So he came to meet Angulimala. When Angulimala saw the Buddha, he drew his sword and ran towards the Buddha. Although he was running as quickly as possible, he was not able to catch the Buddha who was walking calmly. Eventually, he screamed at the Buddha to stop. Then the Buddha turned and spoke to Angulimala saying that he, the Buddha, had already stopped. He had stopped killing and harming people, and now it was time for Angulimala to do likewise. Those words struck Angulimala so deeply he threw away his sword and followed the Buddha, later becoming a monk.

struck and enlightened, recognizing that what he was doing was wicked. Even when such an evil man Angulimala understood what he did was wrong and genuinely repented, Buddha took him as one of his followers. In Suu Kyi's view, this story indicates that the evil Angulimala committed was horrendous, but the Buddha was able to separate what he was from he did.

Suu Kyi's further attempt to see politics through the eye of Buddhism is to seek common ground for other religions to stand together, and she believes that it is the idea of *mettā*. For her, *mettā* or love is so central to the teachings of every religion. As an example, she quotes a Christian Scripture verse, "perfect love casts out fear,"[69] thereby identifying "perfect love" with *mettā*. The question to ask is, is the idea of Christian love essentially identical with the Buddhist's view of *mettā*? Hermann Oldenberg notes the significant differences between Buddha's idea of *mettā* and Christian love:

> One may compare the great figures here and there. Here saint Francis or Vincent de Paul, who practiced love of God and love of neighbour to help the least of the lowly, the most deeply suffering of all sufferers, out of the warmest personal attachment. There Sariputta or Ananda, who sits down in the loneliness of the Indians forest to contemplate the *maitri* (*mettā*) and out of the cool quiet of Nirvana, to which he knows himself close, extends his good will toward people animals, and all creatures from one region of the world to another – the good will of one who has sought and achieved "not to love anything in the world." Are these not the citizens of two different worlds?[70]

Besides, despite using a quasi-similar term, love for a Christian and *mettā* for a Buddhist, each defines it in accordance with their belief system. For Christianity, love is defined in the light of the personal God; in contrast, for Buddhism, *mettā* is expressed impersonally since it views the universe as an impersonal and purposeless order of physical-mental proportions. Winston L. King shows a striking contrast between them: due to its personalistic

---

69. 1 John 4:18 ESV. Adoniram Judson (1788–1850), an American Baptist missionary in Myanmar, in translating the Christian Bible from the original languages (Hebrews and Greek) into Burmese, used the word *mettā* for the word "love."

70. Quoted from Luz and Michaels, *Encountering Jesus*, 83–84.

conception of the universe as governed by a supreme God, a Christian thinks, feels, speaks, and acts in interpersonal terms. In contrast, a Buddhist thinks, feels speaks, and acts in what the West calls impersonal.[71] Thus, each religion seemingly has a universal expression of love or *mettā*, but they define it in their own terms.

In spite of the different interpretations of love or *mettā*, both Buddhism and Christianity believe that a better world would be possible if the way of love and *mettā* was valued and followed. For Christians, the better world may be called the kingdom of God; while for Buddhists, it would be the world wherein humans are enabled to seek self-liberation. If Suu Kyi means *mettā* in this sense, it is indeed a common ground for Buddhists and Christians to stand together and act for the betterment of the world. Furthermore, practicing *mettā* is, in Suu Kyi's understanding, able to liberate us from the bondage of fear. In her well-known essay, "Freedom from Fear," Suu Kyi characterizes the politics of Myanmar as based on fear.[72] Fear captures the ruling regime as well as the public. While the government and the public fear might be different, they both fear something. For the regime, it is the fear of losing power, but for the public, it is a fear of incarceration, fear of torture, fear of death, or fear of losing someone or something. But Suu Kyi optimistically wrote, as Matthew Walton observes, that fear, despite its insidious form, can be overcome by the courageous.[73] According to her, the root of fear is a lack of *mettā*: "fear is rooted in insecurity and insecurity is rooted in a lack of *mettā*."[74] Where there is no *mettā*, there will be no security and vice versa. This insecurity eventually leads to fear. Therefore, only through *mettā* can fear be overcome because it alone can liberate people from the captivity of fear. In brief, *mettā* is the key element in defining and interpreting Suu Kyi's concept of nonviolence.

---

71. King, *Buddhism and Christianity*, 98.
72. Suu Kyi, *Freedom from Fear*, 180–185.
73. Walton, "Buddhism, Politics," 118.
74. Kyi and Clements, *Voice of Hope*, 29.

5.5.4 Nonviolence as a Revolution of the Spirit

The term "spirit" or "spiritual" is a subject of crucial importance in understanding Suu Kyi's idea of nonviolence. If *mettā* is at the core of nonviolence, what is its nature? For Suu Kyi, nonviolence is more than a method to fight injustice; it is a revolution of the spirit. In her eyes, a genuine revolution is not just an attempt to replace one government with another, but to change a "political system, which is guided by certain spiritual values."[75] The unhappy legacies of authoritarianism cannot be easily removed.[76] So nonviolence as spiritual revolution seeks to transform the values of the old system with those of the new system. In her essay, she brilliantly explains what she means by a revolution of the spirit, saying,

> Without a revolution of the spirit, the forces which produced the iniquities of the old order would continue to be operative, posing a constant threat to the process of reform and regeneration. It is not enough merely to call for freedom, democracy and human rights. There has to be a united determination to persevere in the struggle, to make sacrifices in the name of enduring truths, to resist the corrupting influences of desire, ill will, ignorance and fear.[77]

It is a revolution of the spirit through which Suu Kyi seeks to change the political system. This revolution is also spiritual in nature because she perceives how Myanmar has been subjected to monstrous repression, and so the revolution needed is more than political and social. It must be a movement of the spirit.[78] As she believes in the inseparability of religion and politics, she also demonstrates how politics is spiritually connected. In the conversation with Alan Clements, Suu Kyi states, "spirituality and politics cannot be separated, ultimately; they both deal with the everyday life of people. And at the core of life – at the core of spirituality and politics – are the same qualities, that of human freedom and human dignity."[79] Because of the integral

---

75. Kyi and Clements, 81–82.
76. Suu Kyi, "In Quest of Democracy," from *Freedom from Fear*, 178.
77. Suu Kyi, *Freedom from Fear*, 183.
78. Kyi and Clements, *Voice of Hope*, 82.
79. Clements, *Instinct for Freedom*, 79.

nature of politics and spirituality, a nonviolent struggle goes beyond the political enterprise. Therefore, in Suu Kyi's understanding, the first thing that nonviolent activists need to do is to liberate themselves from the bondage of fear. Thus it requires courage. Throughout her essay, "Freedom from Fear," Suu Kyi emphasizes the importance of courage for nonviolent activists. For those who are on the horns of a dilemma – forced into a choice between passivity and cooperation with the prevailing system, the path to liberation is simply to depend on themselves. In the Buddhist vocabulary, it is *atta hi attano natho* ("one is one's own refuge").

Courage is an indispensable ingredient to enable this spiritual revolution. Courage requires the use of mental power as well as that of physical power. What Suu Kyi stresses is the latter form of courage. But it is, for Suu Kyi, not a naturally inborn gift for the majority. It is something that, "comes from cultivating the habit of refusing to let fear dictate one's actions."[80] Thus, the first step to becoming courageous is to confront our own fear, taking courage to shift our eyes from our own needs and to see the truth of the world around us. Not only does it take courage to see the truth of oneself and the world, but there are also two other aspects of courage – the courage to feel one's conscience and the courage to act. Only through the realization of courage, can an actual spiritual revolution take place.[81]

Further, this spiritual revolution also calls for not only courage but also moral integrity. Suu Kyi understands that the deterioration of moral consciousness among the Burmese people is because of the corruption that has pervaded various sectors of society for several decades. The freedom or liberation she talks about is not just from political oppression, but also from moral

---

80. Suu Kyi, *Freedom from Fear*, 184. Suu Kyi herself had a hard time in living with fear while she was a child. She was afraid of the dark. To deal with this fear, she trained herself by staying in dark, some times for some days. After training herself for a while, her fear of the dark was gone. She used to tell this childhood experience in her writing and conversations with others. Perhaps, that experience might be unimportant to those in the western countries. But for the people in Myanmar, fearing the dark or ghosts is so common. Many Myanmar children, including myself, grew up with those horror myths and tales. When I was a child, some of the older playmates used to tell such horror stories and haunt me and my other playmates. It was indeed terrifying to us. So when Suu Kyi said, she had that experience, and described how she overcame such a fear, it shows her courage. Only those who have feared something or someone understand how paralyzing fear can be.

81. Clements, *Instinct for Freedom*, 76–77.

corruption. So, she insists that Myanmar needs a spiritual revolution because it resists moral defilement as well as political oppression. With the emphasis on a spiritual revolution, Suu Kyi has sensed that the need of Myanmar is far greater than democracy, freedom, and human rights. In order for spiritual revolution to be realized, "there has to be a united determination to preserve in the struggle, to make sacrifices in the name of enduring truths, to resist the corrupting influences of desire, ill will, ignorance and fear."[82] In short, only through this spiritual revolution will the forces that produced the iniquities of the older order be overcome. But participating in such a spiritual revolution is not playing a zero-sum game; rather, its ultimate aim is to seek a win-win situation or reconciliation.

The question arises, did Suu Kyi use nonviolence because she had no other option? Now she has power, will she still use nonviolence in dealing with other political dilemmas? Looking at what she said and did during her resistance against the then regime, it seems that she was a devout nonviolent activist. For example, she was so convinced that nonviolence is the Buddhist way. What is more, the tradition of changing politics through violent means through the history of the nation has perpetuated the political culture of Myanmar; therefore, only through nonviolence will that tradition be transformed into truly democratic principles.

To our surprise, Suu Kyi has changed so much from the time she resolved to be a politician instead of a public icon. From that time onward, Suu Kyi has learned to negotiate and compromise with the army generals rather than sticking to the principles of nonviolence. As briefly discussed, her silence in the Kachin war and Rakhine-Rohingya conflict apparently show that she liked to compromise rather than stick to what she believes. As a politician, she has to learn to gratify the majority rather than siding with the minority. Therefore, the answer to the question, "will she still choose the nonviolent path now that she has power?" is perhaps yes, but not in an absolute sense because her government has no power whatsoever upon the army and the police. The power struggle between the army and her government has been tense since the inception of her government. Therefore, it is not that easy to say that Suu Kyi would take whatever means – violence or nonviolence

---

82. Suu Kyi, *Freedom from Fear*, 183.

to cultivate the democratic culture in Myanmar. What can be sure is that she is now a politician, therefore she would act and practice politics like a politician, not like a heroine of human rights. This is the major change that she has since she has power. This change is truly immense that she has been losing her reputation for democracy and human rights. For example, the British city of Oxford, where she studied, revoked the Freedom of the City of Oxford award that she received in 1997 for her refusal to condemn the human rights violations.

5.6 Dialogue, Forgiveness, and Reconciliation

The end of the nonviolent struggle in the stories of Mohandas Gandhi in India, Martin Luther King Jr in the United States, and Nelson Mandela in South Africa is not retributive justice, but restorative justice; and not just to end enmity, but also to restore friendship. Reconciliation is indeed a vital component in the philosophy of nonviolence. In the context of Myanmar, the reconciliation needed is not just between the military regime and the opposition parties, but also between the army of the state and the ethnic minority groups. Ethnic rebellions that began post-independence are still going on in the present day in spite of the government's various attempts for peace talks. Knowing this situation, Suu Kyi asserts that, "the main impetus for struggle is not an appetite for power, revenge and destruction but a genuine respect for freedom, peace and justice."[83]

The first step towards reconciliation, in Suu Kyi's understanding, is a dialogue. Dialogue, for her, is not a debate. It is not a question of losing face. It aims to find the best solutions for the country.[84] She exemplifies this by decoding the word "parliament," which means "talk" in French; so talking, for her, is so essential because it is "better to shout at each other than to kill each other."[85] She believes that the answer to Myanmar's problem is dialogue. Through dialogue, misunderstanding and differences may be resolved; and from there, an agreement and consensus between the opponents may be

---

83. Suu Kyi, "In Quest of Democracy," from *Freedom from Fear*, 179.
84. Cited from Silverstein, "Idea of Freedom," 227.
85. Suu Kyi, "The Need for Dialogue," from *Freedom from Fear*, 255.

reached. When an agreement is reached, national reconciliation could possibly be realized. But unfortunately, the ex-junta showed no interested in such a dialogue, and so they replied that they would like to negotiate with her on the terms under which she would leave Myanmar. So a dialogue never happened in the time of the previous military government.

Further, Suu Kyi looks at and interprets reconciliation from a Buddhist perspective. She argues that the practice of *mettā* is a determining factor for reconciliation to be realized. For her, there are numerous ways to show *mettā* not only in a religious milieu but also in a socio-political setting. She suggests that Buddha's way of reconciliation is certainly sacrificial: when the Buddha reconciled two fighting groups, he would go out and stand between them so that he would get injured first before they could hurt each other. So, Buddha's way of reconciliation is neither one against the other, nor showing favour for one; instead, he placed himself betwixt and between them in the conflict. This way of expressing *mettā* will protect others at the sacrifice of one's life.[86] Hence, the road to reconciliation is painful and sacrificial because it demonstrates the active *mettā*.

In the process of such reconciliation, Suu Kyi perceives an inseparable nature of truth and forgiveness – no truth telling, no forgiveness; no forgiveness, no reconciliation. If reconciliation is the end to be pursued, truth telling is a means and forgiveness a way to achieve true reconciliation. Thus, she shows the importance of the role of truth in that, "denying the truth will not bring about forgiveness, neither will it dissipate the anger in those who have suffered."[87] If the truth is withheld, how can forgiveness possibly occur? Put differently, reconciliation can never be realized apart from truth telling. Correspondingly, without truth telling, forgiveness can never be experienced. Even if reconciliation without truth telling and forgiveness happens, it would be, to quote Miroslav Volf, "cheap reconciliation."[88] This sort of reconciliation will never heal the wounds of the public who suffered under the former regime.

---

86. Kyi and Clements, *Voice of Hope*, 43.
87. Kyi and Clements, 38.
88. Volf, "Social Meaning of Reconciliation," 8.

According to the two models of reconciliation, Suu Kyi's understanding of reconciliation is more on the side of the Interpersonal or individual Reconciliation (IR) between victims and perpetrators on a personal level) than National Unity and Reconciliation (NUR) (creating a culture of human rights on the basis of inclusive and democratic notion of citizenship).[89] But she does not neglect the latter at the cost of the former. For example, Suu Kyi makes every effort to establish a rule of law, which is strange and un-practiced in the politics of Myanmar. At the same time, she also puts great emphasis on a culture of democracy, human rights, and so on. Being aware of the great need of the country, Suu Kyi does not favour one model at the cost of the other. The country Myanmar, in her understanding, needs a reconciliation that aims at personal as well as structural dimensions.

As noted, a dialogue between Suu Kyi and the previous regime never happened. Probably, this dialogue seemed undesirable and detrimental to the junta because it would have required a huge deal of willingness and courage, if necessary, to change what one feels is true, and to accept what one strongly opposes. The history of the democratic movement since 1988 shows how the regime mulishly refused to open dialogue. Likewise, in the eyes of the top generals, whatever Suu Kyi did and said seemed mere threats to them; to them, she is simply another power-hungry politician. For example, the then Senior General Than Shwe regarded Suu Kyi as nothing but a Western product and therefore, extraneous to Myanmar. Thus, Suu Kyi's idea of dialogue is theoretically perfect, yet for the junta, it seems simply unfavourable. In other words, the dialogue, which Suu Kyi talks about as a path to reconciliation, appears to be impossible in the political context of Myanmar. Thus, the reconciliation which Suu Kyi expected is truly comprehensive, but seemed unrealistic to the regime. Even though such a reconciliation did not happen during the era of the previous military government, the present political situation of the nation Myanmar is probably the most appropriate time to instigate national reconciliation: reconciliation between the military and all other political parties.

---

89. For more detail see pp. 105–106.

5.7 Rule of Law and Nonviolence

What is palpable from what Suu Kyi has written and said is that she is not an anarchist; indeed, her conviction of the rule of law is robust enough.[90] In particular, she has repeatedly mentioned that it is extremely important for the government to establish the rule of law. What does the rule of law mean? What does Suu Kyi mean by rule of law? It would be inadequate to talk about the rule of law without articulating its meaning. Stephen Bloom suggests that without a concrete definition of the rule of law, it might be just "a political slogan rather than a tangible goal towards which objective progress can be measured."[91] Of course, Suu Kyi has something particular in mind regarding the rule of law. She has described it in her well-known essay, "Freedom from Fear" that, "Just laws can prevent corruption and at the same time it can also help to create a society in which people can fulfil the basic requirements necessary for the preservation of human dignity without recourse to corrupt practices."[92] For Suu Kyi, law is something to protect individuals and ensure a harmonious and peaceful society. In her eyes, there is a distinction between unjust and just laws. Suu Kyi, when she talks about law, refers to the laws that are just and giving everybody equal protection. Everybody – including both the government and the governed – is subject to such laws; no one should be above the rule of just laws. Thus, Suu Kyi calls for every individual in the country to be prepared to stand up for justice: that is, not to say what is just is unjust and what is unjust is just.

In current Muslim-Buddhist conflicts in the Rakhine State, Suu Kyi, unlike other political leaders, points out that the root of such conflicts is the absence of the rule of law in those places. In other words, where there is no rule of

---

90. In Myanmar, the rule of law is translated into *Ta Ya U Pa Day Soe Moe Yae*. This translation perfectly conveys the idea of rule of law: to analyze the words, *Ta Ya* refers to just, impartial, or fair; *U Pa Day* simply refers to law; and last, *Soe Moe Yae* means rule, dominion, or supremacy. To re-combine these three words, the phrase refers to the rule of law that is just. Obviously, the Myanmar phrase does cover the idea of rule of law more than the English word does. In English, the phrase only depicts the rule of law – merely law without "objective" or unspecified law. In contrast, the Myanmar phrase inclusively covers the law which is just.

91. Stephen Bloom, in *The Irrawaddy* newspaper, discerns the threat of talking about the rule of law without explaining what it means, Bloom, "'Rule of Law' in Burma."

92. Suu Kyi, *Freedom from Fear*, 183.

law, injustice and violence will always prevail. As a nonviolent activist, Suu Kyi believes that establishing rule of law, to a certain degree, can diminish the prevalence of injustice and violence. Thus, nonviolence reinforces the establishment of the rule of law. However, the challenge is regarding the people of Myanmar's negative views towards the law. According to the Myanmar Rule of Law Assessment, "the people of Myanmar, through history, have seen the law and law enforcement as the enemy."[93] This shows that for the population of Myanmar, law is detrimental. To be specific, the law or justice system that the Myanmar people have encountered throughout history is based on heredity status. Michael Aung-Thwin suggests, "Hereditary status in the 12th and 13th century was a legal principle upon which the concept of justice were based . . . social status rather than objective factors determined punishment."[94] The late Maung Maung Gyi, as a political scientist, also describes two contrasting concepts: first, law of status, which means "an individual does not exist as an independent entity but as a component of a unit, either in family or in society,"[95] and second, the rule of law. The former sees law as personal, whereas the latter sees it as impersonal. For the former, law is subjective and hierarchical; but for the latter, it is objective. According to Maung Maung Gyi, ruling figures throughout post-independence time were so steeped in the former that they could not appreciate the noble principles embodied in the rule of law.[96]

During the years of the military rule (1962–2015), Myanmar's legal system existed as an exploitative institution designed to maintain order, police politics, and extract resources from those swept up in it.[97] "Law and order," in Myanmar, is a collection of four words: *ngyein* ("being still or quiet"), *wut* ("crouched"), *pi* ("pressed"), *byaye* ("flattened"). Each has nothing to do

---

93. New Perimeter, et al., *Myanmar Rule of Law Assessment*.
94. Aung-Thwin, *Pagan*, 125.
95. Gyi, *Burmese Political Values*, 170.
96. Gyi, 170–173.
97. Cited from Prasse-Freeman, "Conceptions of Justice," 89. Even President Thein Sein's government was hardly said to be a civilian government because the majority of the ruling figures in it were ex-military. The 1988 uprising brought down Ne Win's military government, and the successive military junta came to power with the self-designated name, the State Law and Order Restoration Council (SLORC), which later changed to the State Peace and Development Council (SPDC). Notably, there is a huge contrast between "law and order" and "the rule of law."

with the ideas of law or rule. Nick Cheesman remarks that law and order in Myanmar is "a concept that reinforces existing political relations through exogenously imposed order."[98] Even worse, the military rule has obfuscated the notion of the rule of law with their arbitrary use of power or "law and order." Now the NLD has become the newly elected governing power, and Suu Kyi has been appointed to be State Counsellor to have a role in leading the country. The serious challenge that Suu Kyi and her government must face is to cope with the traditional concept of the law of status and to replace it with the notion of the rule of law. Therefore, the most serious confrontation they face is a corrupted and exploited legal system within various institutions of the government.

However, Suu Kyi's reiteration of the importance of rule of law is a form of generalization. For example, Suu Kyi, as noted, views that it is the lack of the rule of law which is the root cause of the Rakhine-Muslim conflict. In fact, the conflict is much deeper than rule of law. There are other factors hidden in the conflict, such as racial and religious. Buddhism and race play such an important role in Myanmar; they are inseparable. The protection of Buddhism is considered as a responsibility for all Buddhists. Population growth of Muslims in the Rakhine area is seen as a threat to Buddhists. This is seen as a major threat to Buddhist nationalists in Myanmar. There are some nationalist monks who said how military dictatorship is actually good for the religion, Buddhism. So, they do not like the country being opened to the outside world because it would make their religion less dominant.[99] Suu Kyi's view of Buddhism is not in conformity with that of Buddhists in Myanmar and the fact that she wants to internalize Myanmar's social and cultural life.[100] Can such a religiously enthusiastic people who have a negative attitude to law be possibly harnessed by rule of law? Can the racial and religious prejudice that is deeply and historically long-enduring in the hearts of Buddhists in Myanmar be healed by rule of law? Since Rohingyas are seen as illegal or unlawful immigrants from Bangladesh, rule of law is not the key to solution.

---

98. Cheesman, *Opposing the Rule of Law*, 31.
99. Jordt, "Breaking Bad in Burma."
100. Jordt.

So the root problem is not rule of law but whether Rohingyas should be seen as one of the ethnic groups in Myanmar.

One of the founding members of the NLD, the late Win Tin, noticed that "the people of Myanmar cannot regard Bengali [internationally known as Rohingyas] because they are not our citizens at all, everyone knows here that."[101] The real issue is that Rohingyas claim themselves as a race and the natives of the country. The term "Rohingyas" itself creates problem among the people of Myanmar. Therefore, they are not mentioned as Rohingyas in local medias within the country; instead, they are called Bengali, because the people of Myanmar consider them as illegal immigrants or interlopers from Bangladesh. Even in the speech about Myanmar's humanitarian catastrophe on 19 September 2017, Suu Kyi used the term "Muslim community" instead of Rohingyas. It is such an oversensitive issue within the nation. Looking at the problem from inside and outside viewpoints, it is not rule of law that can heal the crisis. What must be dealt with is, should Rohingyas be regarded as a race and natives of the land?

5.8 A Proponent of Principled or Pragmatic Nonviolence?

As mentioned, there are two approaches in the study of nonviolence: pragmatic and principled. To critically review Suu Kyi's position regarding nonviolence, I would like to point out some contradictory points between what she has stated in the Reith Lecture, "Securing Freedom: Liberty" ("I do not hold to nonviolence for moral reasons, but for practical and political reasons . . .")[102] and what I have discussed above. The discussion above shows *mettā* as an all-embracing principle; her commitment to practicing Buddha's basic teaching of the Five Precepts in all dimensions of life; and an integral relationship between politics, spirituality, and morality.

What is more, having faith in freedom from all forms of fear and in freedom from moral defilement, Suu Kyi is apparently situated more on the

---

101. Irrawaddy, "Using the Term 'Rohingya.'" In this study, I use the term "Rohingya," in order for non-Myanmar readers to understand.

102. Suu Kyi, "Liberty."

principled or philosophical side of nonviolence. Despite the fact that she holds on to nonviolence for political reasons, not because of moral beliefs, Suu Kyi's practice of Buddhism is explicit enough to identify her as an exponent of principled nonviolence. On the surface, practicing nonviolence for political reasons sounds like pragmatic nonviolence. However, it could also be argued that it is her attempt to include others who do not follow the nonviolent path in resisting the former government. That means Suu Kyi apparently does not want to exclude other activists who fought against the regime in the name of principled nonviolence. If she did so, she would spontaneously exclude all the independence fighters against the British Empire, including her father Aung San as well. From this viewpoint, Suu Kyi, despite her claim to be an advocate of pragmatic nonviolence, is more on the side of principled nonviolence.[103]

5.9 Suu Kyi after 2010: A Look at Her Current Political Life

This research looks at Martin Luther King Jr and Suu Kyi via Walter Wink's *Powers*. Both King and Wink have passed away, but Suu Kyi is still a living figure. This necessitates looking at Suu Kyi's present political life in this research. Since her release from house arrest in November 2010, she and the NLD had been working with the current government, widely composed of ex-generals that previously attacked her and the NLD before. In the recent general election, which was held on 8 November 2015, her NLD won by a landslide victory so that they were able to form a new government. The power transfer at the end of March 2016 went peacefully. In short, the genuine civilian government, which is publicly elected, has to govern the nation in March 2016. I will explore Suu Kyi's political dealings from the year she was released from house arrest to commencing her full political involvement. The exploration focuses on how Suu Kyi, as a proponent of nonviolence and one who seeks the integration of politics and Buddhism, has started to transform the political system that has been perverted under the two successive military juntas into a system that echoes democratic principles and values.

---

103. Whether Suu Kyi is an advocate of principled or pragmatic nonviolence will be discussed in the next chapter.

Before exploring Suu Kyi's current political life, I would like to survey the political changes that have happened since 2010 in order to examine Suu Kyi's political dealings in the present political context of Myanmar. On 7 November 2010, the military regime launched a general election in accordance with the new constitution, as approved in the referendum in May 2008. That election was nationally and internationally regarded as a sham. The ex-general Thein Sein became the president of Myanmar. From the beginning of his presidency, Thein Sein gave a number of pledges, like seeking the national reconciliation between the state military and other ethnic insurgents; the elimination of poverty; trying to be a clean government, and so on. He also promised that Myanmar was now "moving from an authoritarian system to a democratic one and that the reform his government has undertaken is irreversible."[104] Truly, he is mostly known as a moderate among military generals. For example, Czech Foreign Minister Karel Schwarzenberg, after meeting Thein Sein, said, "I was so impressed with the meeting with your president because he was very frank and very open and we had a very open discussion."[105] Some positive changes have happened indeed. Many long-term political dissenters were released. The press had more freedom than before. The first public impression of Thein Sein was during the suspension of the hotly controversial China-funded dam project (known as Myitsone Dam project) in Kachin State on 30 September 2011. This project was contracted between the Ministry of Electric Power No. 1 and the China Power Investment in December 2006.[106]

Despite these positive changes, there are some critical points to be made. First, Thein Sein's government did not tolerate political protests. For example, the police's violent raid on Letpadaung copper mine protesters raised the question of the credibility of Thein Sein and his government.[107] According

---

104. Quek, "Myanmar Reforms Irreversible."

105. Campbell, "EU Sanctions End."

106. It is this Myitsone dam project that set fire to the fight between the Kachin Independence Army and the Burmese military that has continued since 2011. Domestic campaigns against the project were also held, and local media open criticized the lack of transparency in that project.

107. It was the protest against the mine project operated by a Chinese company (Wanbao Mining) and the Union of Myanmar Economic Holdings Limited (UMEHL), a massive military-owned company. The protest broke out because of the dispute between local villagers, and the government and Wanbao over land grabs and environmental damage.

to one BBC reporter, dozens of protesters were injured and more than one-hundred people were arrested.[108] The population felt that the influence of Than Shwe behind Thein Sein's government was still there. According to some political analysts, Than Shwe remained a dominant force in the country and kept in regular contact with the top brass from the military, in the government and the parliament, and notably the military.[109] The present commander-in-chief, Min Aung Hlaing and other military leaders, including ex-president Thein Sein were a handpicked team of Than Shwe. Hence, even Thein Sein, despite his presidency, did not have control over the armed forces. Suu Kyi, in one of her interviews, remarks that the generals still manipulate power.[110]

On 9 July 2012, Suu Kyi along with her colleagues took their oaths and officially began to attend parliament for the first time as lawmakers. Scholars, critics and observers were keenly watching how Suu Kyi was able to work constructively with the present government in the process of democratization. People were aware that she, to a particular extent, adjusted herself to the political environment. It is clear that Suu Kyi is a woman of principle, and committed to her beliefs without reservation. But she also adapted her position to a certain degree in working with the pseudo-civilian government of Thein Sein. To illustrate, Razali Ismail, a special envoy of the United Nations for Myanmar recalled the first meeting with Suu Kyi in Insein prison right after the Depayin incident. Her first words were: "I want justice, Raz."[111] However, after a year, Razali met her again. During that meeting Suu Kyi's attitude towards the regime was quite changed, because despite the events at Depayin, she was ready to meet the generals for the sake of the people. Ismail remarks that, "Suu Kyi had come a long way to realize that democracy can only be done through the generals;" and he continued, "this realisation of hers is in stark contrast to the imperious, principled, and unbending Suu Kyi I had met over twenty meetings ago."[112] However, it does not mean that, according to Ismail, Suu Kyi had compromised on the principles she always stood for, but that she had broadened her outlook to accept certain things in

---

108. BBC News, "Myanmar Riot Police Beat Student Protesters."
109. BBC News, "Burma Leader Than Shwe."
110. CBS News, "Suu Kyi."
111. Zaw, *Face of Resistance*, Kindle edition, Location 466 of 2828.
112. Zaw, Kindle edition, Location 466 of 2898.

working with the government as long as it helped the people.¹¹³ In one sense, Suu Kyi, albeit a woman of principle, has adapted to the Myanmar cultural context after struggling for many years.

With regard to her adaptation to the context of Myanmar, there are both negative and positive responses to her and the NLD in relation to Suu Kyi's entry into the government as an MP, and her quasi-neutral stance regarding the Rakhine-Rohingya conflict and the war between the state army and the Kachin Independence Army (KIA).¹¹⁴ For some critics and sceptics, Suu Kyi's and her party's decision to enter the April 2011 by-election seemed as though they were compromising too much with the regime. The basic disagreement was in their distrust towards the current government. According to Hillary Clinton, Suu Kyi knew the consequences she would face if she entered government. Suu Kyi would no longer personify the people of Myanmar's dreams of peace and happiness and prosperity because she understood how hard it is to balance one's ideals and aspirations with the demands of practical politics.¹¹⁵

Regarding the fight between the military and KIA and the Rakhine-Rohingya conflict, people waited eagerly for Suu Kyi's response to these issues,

---

113. Zöllner, *Beast and the Beauty*, 405.

114. The Rakhine-Rohingya conflict is a violent fight between two racial groups: Arakanese and Rohingya. Rakhine (formerly Arakanese) is one of the nationally recognized ethnic groups in Myanmar, who live in Rakhine State, northern part of Myanmar. Concerning religion, they are strong Buddhists. Rohingya is, according to the Myanmar people, known as the people who migrated to Myamar from Bengal (today, Bangladesh) during the period of British rule. These people are mostly Muslims. The Myanmar people see the Rohingya as "immigrants to Myanmar" and thus they are not eligible for citizenship. While the majority of Rakhine live in the southern part of the state, Rohingyas mostly live in the northern part. The first attack happened in June 2012. According to the narrative, a young Buddhist woman in Rakhine was raped and murdered by two Muslim men. Subsequently, retaliation followed and non-Muslim men stopped a bus and killed eight Muslims on board. Following this, the series of aggressive conflicts got out of control. Thawnghmung, "Contending Approaches," 323. The war between the Kachin Independence Army (KIA) and the government army is a long-lasting war, which has sometimes stopped for some years by a cease-fire agreement. In fact, armed rebellion against Myanmar state began in 1961. In 1994, a ceasefire was agreed to, and it was relatively peaceful in the Kachin state. The fight began in June 2011 less than three months after the nominally civilian government took power. What has caused the outbreak of the war was that the government sent the army troops to guard the three dams under construction near the Chinese border. An agreement was made regarding this move. But the KIA suspected that the army was bringing more troops in than what had been agreed upon. So conflict began and the fight launched. As a result, an estimated 100,000 Kachin people have been displaced, with many fleeing across the border into China, see Wai Moe, "Struggle for Peace," 265.

115. Cited from Popham, *Lady and the Peacock*, 400.

as she is a public icon. But Suu Kyi's response is that it is not a time to use her moral leadership, but to look at the root cause of the problems.[116] This reaction did not satisfy many people. Her silence in the face of these cries for help caused observers and activists to wonder about her underlying motives. For Maung Zarni, Suu Kyi is no longer a political dissident trying to stick to her principles. She's a politician, and her eyes are fixed on the prize, of holding a majority Buddhist vote.[117] In the case of the Rakhine-Rohingya conflict, Peter Popham discerns that Suu Kyi is now on the horns of a dilemma: "If she were to speak out loud and clear against the attacks, she would win the applause of people in the West."[118] But it would be the quickest way for her to lose the support of the majority of the population of Myanmar since anti-Muslim prejudice is so common among the Myanmar people. Thus, Suu Kyi is a shrewd politician with an ambition to become the president of the nation, who knows how to compromise; she should no longer be regarded as an icon of democracy and human rights.

During the previous government (2010–2015), many observers and critics considered that Suu Kyi, due to her desire to become the president, became a self-interested politician. The question is, is Suu Kyi a self-interested politician like these critics say? Despite the national and international support, it is clear that Suu Kyi's words would not be as powerful as the president and his ruling team in this Rakhine-Rohingya riot. Besides, the ethnic conflict in the Rakhine State is not an issue that can be solved within a short period, because it is a problem that has been present for many decades. In addition, it is believed that some military figures that are hostile to Suu Kyi, cunningly organized this conflict so that this situation would force her to speak out.[119] In doing so, they hoped to defame her reputation. This seems reasonable because the way Thein Sein's government handled this riot was unlike the way they deal with the political protests against them and seemed too lenient.[120] If this

---

116. BBC News, "EU Chief Barroso."
117. Quoted from Gecker, "Suu Kyi's Silence."
118. Popham, "Why Does Aung San Suu Kyi Not Speak UP?"
119. Popham.
120. For example, a number of protests against education legislation broke out in Myanmar. According to the critics of the National Education Bill, this legislation was intended to keep the management of higher education in government hands, thereby stifling academic freedom. Haung Sai, a member of the National Network for Education Reform, who took part

is so, as Peter Popham observes, Suu Kyi's silence may be seen as a sign of shrewdness.[121] Although her silence might be somewhat frustrating to the international community, silence might be the wisest way to respond to the situation. Therefore, it seemed impossible for Suu Kyi, as merely a parliamentarian, to effectively deal with the issues such as fighting between the state army and the Kachin armed groups, and the Rakhine-Rohingya conflict.

On the one hand, it is true that Suu Kyi should be seen as a politician instead of an icon. In her meeting with Hillary Clinton, she expressed that she would rather be seen as a politician than as an icon.[122] As Ronan Lee concludes in the essay about Rohingya, truly Suu Kyi is "appearing more and more like just another politician and less like the international icon of democracy, freedom and human rights that she once was."[123] In short, Suu Kyi, whose personality is disciplinarian and perfectionist, has decided to become a politician, and this decision leads her to compromise her principles in numerous ways so that she might possibly work with the generals. Peter Popham rightly critiques that the criticism of Suu Kyi was rare until many months after her release (in 2010). However, as she came to politics, she came into focus. The world began to see through the startling beauty and the years of imprisonment to the person within.[124]

Political changes in Myanmar have been so rapid that it has been a challenge to keep up with the latest occurrences. The power transfer went peacefully on 30 March 2016. The first genuine civilian president after fifty-three years, Htin Kyaw, was elected. His government created a powerful new role, known as State Counsellor, for its leader, Aung San Suu Kyi. This new role was created for Suu Kyi so that she may be able to work both in the executive and legislative branches of government.[125] According to the constitution drafted by

---

in the protests, told Al Jazeera, "the authorities were clearly in force and geared up to end as violently and as quickly as they could." She continued, "The politics brutality was too much and we are getting more determined to make sure the reforms we want are seen through," see Aljazeera, "Myanmar Police Crack Down." During the NLD government, many protests against the government still broke out. The path to realization of democracy still seems a long way to go.

121. Aljazeera, "Myanmar Police Crack Down."
122. Ebbighausen, "Aung San Suu Kyi's Sacrifice."
123. Lee, "Politician, Not an Icon," 330.
124. Popham, *Lady and the Generals*, 227.
125. McLaughlin, "Suu Kyi's State Counsellor."

the previous military regime, Suu Kyi is banned from becoming the president of Myanmar because her two sons are not citizens of Myanmar. Hence, she picked Htin Kyaw, one of her most trusted friends, to be president. Besides working as state counsellor, she is also the Minister for Foreign Affairs and in the President's office.

As a matter of fact, Suu Kyi wanted to become the president of the country. Before the 2015 general election, she repeatedly stated that she was interested in becoming president, though she knew that the constitution does not allow her to do so. That desire contradicts what she often said in her speeches on leadership. For example, she gave an address on "Democracy and Expectations on Young Leaders of the World" in the University of Tokyo on 17 April 2013. There she mentioned,

> When I was released in 2010 after the election . . . I made it quite clear that one should not think in terms of position but in terms of responsibility. I said that I was not interested in giving particular positions to anybody, young or old. I would think of it as giving people a responsibility with the party, giving them a chance to take up certain responsibilities. And this is how I would like young leaders to look upon their tasks in life.[126]

If position does not matter in leadership, why did she want to become president? As Popham questions, can position and responsibility be complementary?[127] Can they be totally separated? If she thinks of responsibility alone, why did she and the NLD create a position of State Counsellor? Why did she desire to become president? In this sense, Suu Kyi has contradicted herself. Placing an emphasis on responsibility at the cost of the position or vice versa is truly a one-sided view. Truly responsibility alone is inadequate, as is position. As was mentioned in the discussion of *awza* and *ana*, they both are necessary to accomplish something in the political realm. Supposing somebody has *awza*, but no *ana*, what can they do? During the military regime, Suu Kyi possessed a great deal of *awza* but she had no *ana*. Consequently, she was unable to do things which only a person with authority

---

126. Suu Kyi, "Tokyo University," YouTube video, 23:25.
127. Popham, *Lady and the Generals*, 224.

could do. Now she and her government created a position of State Counsellor because it is indispensable for Suu Kyi to have *ana*, without which she would be legally unable to accomplish anything. In spite of knowing herself the indispensability of *ana* or "position," she still claims that what matters is responsibility, not position. To illustrate, a person has a strong sense of duty, but no position in an institution. How could such a person work in that institution? Responsibility and position should go hand in hand.

Suu Kyi's government has begun their work for almost one term (five years) with the expectation of reforming one of the least developed countries, Myanmar. At the start of her government, and to some extent throughout all her first term, people in Myanmar were not sure to what extent she can go on her spiritual revolution for the people of Myanmar. Ingrid Jordt, by examining the correlation between Buddhism and politics, comments that Suu Kyi's "revolution of the spirit" does not look capable of achieving the genuine democratic transformation she had in mind. Rather, its notable success is being subsumed by the traditional tug-of-war legitimacy between Sangha (Buddhist monk) and state.[128] True, Suu Kyi's interpretation of Buddhism from a humanistic or secularized perspective is not well accepted by the traditionally bound people of Myanmar, for whom religion, race, and politics are all inseparably linked. However, what Jordt fails to see is the religious and ethnic minorities who have begun to play a crucial role in the politics of Myanmar. Though Burman is the ethnic majority, there are still seven other ethnic groups who have been disregarded and mistreated by the two military regimes throughout the nation's history. Thus, Jordt's comment on the basis of Burman's integral view of race, religion and politics is just partially correct, not completely.

In short, it is still too early to comment either negatively or positively regarding how capable Suu Kyi and her government would be to lead the country, one of the least developed and most corrupted nations in the world, into democratization. Yet, numerous challenges await the new government. To list some of them, the new government is faced with the challenges to cope with ethnic conflict, the demand of a federal state, grinding poverty, the educational system, and amendment of the constitution. However, a glimmer

---

128. Jordt, "Breaking Bad in Burma."

of hope for Myanmar has arisen. Time will tell whether the new government under the leadership of Suu Kyi will be able to fulfil the hope of people.

5.10 Summary of the Chapter

In the previous chapters, I looked at Walter Wink's *Powers* trilogy and Martin Luther King Jr's view of nonviolence. This chapter has examined Aung San Suu Kyi's understanding and practice of nonviolence in the light of her life and struggle for democracy in Myanmar. The next chapter will seek to integrate the views of Wink, King and Suu Kyi with the aim of constructing a lens by which to read the political context of Myanmar. The reading will help to draw political implications for Christians in Myanmar.

The chapter has shown that Suu Kyi's love for her country was birthed from her parental influence. Though she was raised and educated in the Western context, her love for the country never grew cold. Therefore, the Four Eights incident led her to become a nonviolent activist. Suu Kyi is also shrewd in defining and interpreting politics, nonviolence, and morality in the light of Buddhism. She regards politics as multi-faceted, and therefore politics, religion and morality are all interconnected.

With this in mind, Suu Kyi makes an effort to revolutionize a historically-rooted idea of politics as a dirty game. She asserts that a person can be a good politician and a faithful Buddhist at the same time. With this faith, Suu Kyi views political work from the Buddhist perspective, saying that saints are sinners who go on trying.[129] Now she has begun to lead the country as state counsellor with the newly formed government for almost five years. As a new government, immensely difficult challenges awaited them. How could her government possibly cope with a legacy of corruption in all sectors of the country? How could she face challenges without giving up her values and her spirit of revolution? So far, the people of Myanmar have not realized the changes in the way expected. What has been going from the time they have begun to rule to the present is that majority of population of Myanmar are feeling being governed by two opposite governments – military and civilian. I will discuss these questions in the last chapter in the light of Walter Wink

---

129. Kyi and Clemets, *Voice of Hope*, 126.

and Martin Luther King Jr. The next chapter examines a critical interaction between Wink, King and Suu Kyi in the areas of leadership, religion, and ethical exploration of nonviolence.

Part III

CHAPTER 6

King and Suu Kyi in Dialogue with Walter Wink

In the part I, I have presented the introduction of the thesis and a critical commentary of Wink's *Powers* trilogy and his view of nonviolence. In part II we examined Martin Luther King Jr and Aung San Suu Kyi as exemplary nonviolent activists in the light of their supporters and critics. In this part III we will read the politics of Myanmar via the eyes of Wink, King and Suu Kyi to draw political implications for Christians in Myanmar. In order to make this reading possible, we need to establish an integrated lens of Wink, King and Suu Kyi.

This chapter seeks to engage Martin Luther King Jr and Aung San Suu Kyi through Walter Wink's *Powers* in order to complement and correct each other. In doing so, all their voices will be heard equally, assessed critically, and corrected and complemented mutually with an intention to sharpening each other through interaction. This critical dialogue focuses on three areas: leadership, religion, and the ethics of nonviolence. Wink will be a principal voice in the dialogue with King and Suu Kyi, since this research takes Wink as a theologian and King and Suu Kyi as exemplary practitioners of nonviolence. This chapter will be a guide for the following chapter of this study, which explores leadership, the role of religion, and the political ethics that could be practiced in Myanmar.

6.1 Nonviolence and Leadership: A Correlation

What does nonviolence have to do with leadership? On the surface, nonviolence appears to be merely a tactic to achieve something. Whether principled or pragmatic nonviolence, there are some robust philosophical presuppositions behind the idea of nonviolence. If we examine those presuppositions, nonviolence can be seen to voice concerns about leadership. To ask a more specific question, can a nonviolent activist or one who believes and practices nonviolence become a tyrant or dictator? Alternatively, does nonviolence have anything to do with the abuse of power? My aim here is, through looking at King and Suu Kyi via a Winkian eye, to discern some reasons behind the notion of nonviolence that oppose the very foundation of tyranny and call for true liberation from all despotic rules. In working towards this aim, King and Suu Kyi will be the voices, and Walter Wink the lens through which to look at them.

As discussed in the second and third chapters of this study, Wink identifies two opposing forces in this world: the domination system (DS) versus God's domination-free order (DFO). Each stands in total contrast to the other in exerciing power, in politics, and in relationships. In the DS, power is exercised to control, destroy, and even take a life if needed; thus, it is usually either win or lose, domineering and competitive. This contrasts with the DFO where power functions to give, support, and nurture; therefore, it is typically win-win, based on partnership, and cooperative. Politics in the DS is seen as the conquest of all opponents, autocratic, and authoritarian; whereas, the politics in the DFO is considered to be diplomatic, democratic, enabling, and decentralised. The DS seeks to practice ranking, domineering hierarchies, racism, and a rigid "we/they" division in relationship with others. In contrast, relationship in the DFO seeks to nurture cooperation, equality of opportunity, and to be inclusive of all people, thereby being flexible in dealing with relationship issues.[1]

In whichever kind of leadership – political, economic, social or religious – power is an indispensable feature without which the exercising of leadership is impossible. The role of power is vital because politics is, to every degree, a way of exercising power both in individual and collective ways. Both Martin Luther King Jr and Aung San Suu Kyi understand power differently. For King, power is an ability to achieve a particular purpose. For Suu Kyi, power is a responsibility to do one's best for those who have entrusted themselves

---

1. Wink, *Engaging the Powers*, 46–47.

to you. But Wink, instead of defining what power is, contrasts two kinds of power. Power, for him, is not to be over but to be with; not to take life, control and destroy, but to give, support, and nurture life; not a zero-sum game but a win-win solution; not to dominate but to partner; not merely to compete but to compete and cooperate.[2] Wink's understanding of the nature of power reflects the philosophical backdrop of nonviolence; King's idea of power is too general, while Suu Kyi's is relational. That is, if power were seen as an ability to achieve a goal and a responsibility to do one's best, the questions of "how" remain: how should a leader achieve a goal? How should a leader fulfil the responsibility? A leader can reach a goal by fraudulent means, and responsibility can also be met by dishonest means. Wink's view of power enlightens us to deal with the questions of how – the important thing is not just what to achieve, but also how to achieve a goal. In other words, it is not just to have a goal to attain or responsibility to fulfil, but to have the right means to reach a goal or fulfil a responsibility.

Further, Wink continues to seek the role of power in the DS and the DFO. He highlights that the DS has constrained us from evolving and transforming our civilization into a better future. Thus our destiny, under the DS, is not governed by free choice. Instead, the DS teaches us to value and use power to achieve above our goals. The DS overpowers all institutions in making decisions and selecting leaders. As a result, people have become slaves of their evolving systems.[3] Leaders, despite leading their institutions, have no control over the DS; instead, the DS is in control.[4] Hence, no leader in the DS is resistible to the power of corruption because they are inured to the vicious cycle of the DS. In contrast, power in the DFO is not the power over, but power with; not domination, but cooperation. Looking at King and Suu Kyi from this perspective, it is the DS itself into which they put every effort to transform the system into the beloved community for King or the

---

2. Wink, 46.

3. Wink, 42.

4. Here Wink appears to be a political determinist. It is, to a certain extent, true because of his emphasis on the overwhelming presence of socialization, which greatly impacts on those who lead and govern. In this sense, he sounds politically deterministic. On the other hand, he is liberationist in the sense that there is another order, which he calls "God's domination-free order," antithetical of the DS. Thus, there is a possibility to transform the DS, that determines us in numerous ways, into the DFO.

culture of democracy for Suu Kyi. Similarly, the power that King and Suu Kyi understand and practice is not the power of domination, competition, win or lose; but it is the power that gives, supports, and nurtures life; thus, it is cooperative, and win-win.

Both King and Suu Kyi resist the reigning domination system in their respective contexts: for King, it was segregation, while for Suu Kyi, it was military dictatorship. Both segregationism and dictatorship are so thoroughly deep-seated that no one who is trapped in the system is capable of transforming it. To resist the system, King and Suu Kyi did not abide in the reigning culture of their settings. Instead, they conceptualized the notion of power in the context of their visions: King envisioned it in the light of his American dream and beloved community, while Suu Kyi saw it in the light of responsibility and freedom from fear (freedom from the fear of losing power and fear of the scourge of power). Seeing power in this way, for both King and Suu Kyi, is indeed revolutionary in the contexts where they work.

Power over or power to control and destroy, to quote Wink's *Powers* trilogy, is the spirit or inner form of leadership in the DS. In King's time, segregationist leaders exercised their power to control and dominate the blacks through the idea of white supremacy. Thus, King and the civil rights movement were, in the eyes of segregationists, a threat that obstructed the spirit of their domineering leadership and was trying to eliminate the spirit of the system. In a nutshell, King's nonviolent resistance challenged segregationists to change their way of exercising power. Likewise, Suu Kyi revolutionizes the idea of power in the land where it is seen merely as a privilege or license to do whatever one wants. The might is right idea is predominant in the political culture of Myanmar, hence what matters most is not whether we do the right things or not, but whether we have power. No one and nothing, even the law, is above the powers that be or those on top. In this context, Suu Kyi considers power as responsibility and the rule of law – a view that is entirely contradictory to the reigning culture of the politics of Myanmar. Suu Kyi, therefore, asserts that what has corrupted politicians of Myanmar is not power itself, but fear of losing power and fear of the scourge of power. For the powers, it is a fear of losing power; whereas for the public, it is a fear of the scourge of power. Thus, Suu Kyi invites both parties to be free from fear. In Suu Kyi's eyes, both the powers that be and their subjects are all trapped in the bondage of fear.

Freedom from this spirit of fear is of supreme importance because Suu Kyi believes that only through this would power to control be transformed into power with or power to nurture.

More importantly, King and Suu Kyi developed the concept and practice of power against the backdrops of a system of segregation and a dictatorship. So the question is, how could King (as the one who was raised in the culture of segregation where power was hierarchical and manipulative) and Suu Kyi (as the one who grew up in the culture of a dictatorial regime) cultivate in themselves a habit of power with or power to nurture? Wink looks at how people can train themselves to be free from the corruption of power through a biblical vocabulary. This is a kind of rebirth.[5] However, according to Wink, this rebirth is not just a private or inward movement alone. It also includes the necessity of dying to whatever in our social surrounding has shaped us in negative ways – dying to the socially formed ego. It means to die to things like racism, false patriotism, greed, and homophobia. To be more precise, we must die to the DS in order to live authentically. For Wink, that socially formed ego is not just an inner or private attitude, because the ego itself is a web of internalized social conventions of the DS.[6]

Dying to powers means, positively speaking, surrendering our egos to the redemptive initiatives of God. To be more specific, dying to powers means to step out of the DS where violence is always the ultimate solution, into the world of the DFO, in which nonviolence is at the centre. From this Winkian perspective, King and Suu Kyi comprehend power not in accordance with the reigning culture of their times, but with the view of another world: the beloved community for King, and democratization for Suu Kyi. In the Winkian sense, they both applied the idea of dying to the socially formed ego because despite living under the DS, they do not support this approach to power.

The white supremacy in the States and the view of power as privilege in Myanmar are both dominant leadership cultures. Both King and Suu Kyi

---

5. Rebirth is a significant term in evangelical theology. It is synonymous with regeneration, which is defined as, "an inner re-creating of fallen human nature by the gracious sovereign action of the Holy Spirit," see Elwell, *Evangelical Dictionary of Theology*, 1000. Among evangelicals, it is mostly seen that it is an individual's divine experience which radically and internally changed the individual from the inside out.

6. Wink, *Powers That Be*, 94–95.

learn to read culture as a text, and to read the signs of the times – the cultural Zeitgeist – and their effects on life. Against such cultures, they redefined power in the light of their respective dreams. As nonviolent activists, they both disregard the reigning culture of power because they know that power in nonviolence is fundamentally different from power in violence. Whether from a principled or pragmatic approach, nonviolence has no place for domineering power, which is controlling, destructive, and aggressive. Looking through Wink's lens, King and Suu Kyi demonstrate that through the power they exercise, they do not seek to dominate and lord it over their peoples, but to nurture and support them. King and Suu Kyi, though they differ in approaching nonviolence from their respective religious viewpoints, are both convinced that nonviolence outlaws any form of oppressive power because it only allows power that supports and nurtures.

In terms of leadership style, both King and Suu Kyi are recognized as charismatic leaders who inspire, motivate and challenge their peoples. Max Weber first introduced the concept of charisma in explicating various forms of authority. He defines charisma as, "a certain quality of an individual personality virtue which he is set apart from ordinary men and created as endowed with supernatural, superhuman, or at lease specifically exceptional powers or qualities."[7] Both King and Suu Kyi demonstrate their charisma in many ways. For example, they are both skilled at conveying their ideas, beliefs, and vision through public speeches and writings. Many scholars acknowledge King to be one of the great orators in American history. According to some witnesses of his oratory, "when he was behind a podium, he became charismatic."[8] Likewise, Suu Kyi's first speech, "Speech to a Mass Rally at the Shwedagon Pagoda," not only won the hearts of the great crowd, but also of the key opposition politicians.[9]

What is more, both King and Suu Kyi express their charisma through identifying with their peoples. For instance, King, to experientially comprehend the real conditions of slum life in the ghetto, moved to Chicago's West Side with his family and stayed there for some time. There he learned from

---

7. Weber, *Theory of Social and Economic Organization*, 358–359.
8. Phillips, *Martin Luther King, Jr*, 88.
9. Suu Kyi, *Freedom from Fear*, 192–198.

first-hand experiences how a pressure-cooker ghetto life really was. That fascinated and inspired many blacks living there, and caught great media attention.[10] One of his speeches in Chicago crystallized his leadership:

> I choose to identify with the underprivileged. I choose to identify with the poor. I choose to give my life for the hungry. I choose to give up life for those who have been left out of the sunlight of opportunity. I choose to live for and with those who find themselves seeing life as a long and desolate corridor with no exit sign. This is the way I'm going. If it means suffering a little bit, I'm going that way. If it means sacrificing, I'm going that way. If it means dying for them, I'm going that way, because I heard a voice saying, "Do something for others."[11]

During her life in the UK, Suu Kyi used to garnish herself with the traditional costume as an expression of her identification with the people of Myanmar. Even though Suu Kyi is educationally a product of the West, she is fluent in the Burmese language and can masterfully articulate her ideas by using local resources (such as sayings, metaphors, illustrations, and images) without referring to Western intellectual traditions.[12] This greatly appealed to many of the people of Myanmar. As a result of identifying with her people, Suu Kyi received love, admiration and respect from her people and from those across the world. This kind of leadership can be compared to the idea of "incarnational leadership" which is now promoted among Christian scholars. The word "incarnation" is a theological term that refers to the act of God coming to earth in human form as Jesus. Based on this concept, incarnational leadership is defined as, "an attempt to imitate the self-emptying act of Jesus as the Word made flesh that came to dwell among us."[13] Therefore, incarnational leadership promotes a leadership approach that values those of the people

---

10. Oates, *Let the Trumpet Sound*, 408; see also Nojeim, *Gandhi and King*, 249.

11. David J. Garrow, *Bearing the Cross*, 524.

12. Nonviolence guru Gandhi also wore simple sandals and a loincloth, thereby identifying himself with the daily costume of a male worker in India. Gandhi, though educated in the West, was skilful enough in articulating his idea through the cultural and religious symbols, metaphors, sayings, tales, and so on.

13. Bekker, "Values of Incarnation Leadership."

who are being led with active humility. Therefore, King and Suu Kyi, through identifying themselves with the people, were able to get a closer look at and better understand the real lives and struggles of their people.

Furthermore, leadership in nonviolence seeks to nurture and support people, not to overpower them. Nonviolent leaders refuse to use any form of violence in any situation for they have identified with the spirit of the DFO. As Wink illustrates that in the crucifixion, Jesus rejected the use of violence, even as a last resort, and instead trusted God with the outcome, as he endured the cross.[14] Similarly King and Suu Kyi, in their leadership, have exercised a great deal of power in leading their people, where the power they exerted is transformative and supportive, not domineering and overbearing. They have also repudiated violence as a last resort; instead, they endured all the threats and attacks of their opponents. In that sense, the ideas of dictatorship, authoritarianism, totalitarianism, despotism, and tyranny have nothing to do with nonviolence, because they all seek power to control, but nonviolent leaders seek to get rid of this idea and transform enmity into friendship.

Despite the great moral leadership of King and Suu Kyi, their charisma led their people to idolize them, and eventually, they inadvertently created personality cults. The civil rights movement that King led could not find a replacement for him after his assassination. Similarly, who will replace Suu Kyi after her retirement since she is eighty years old? Further, she has felt that the younger generation seems to be too ambitious or craving position instead of responsibility. As discussed in the last chapter, she stresses the importance of responsibility in leadership at the expense of the role of the position. For her, what counts is not a position but responsibility. As Peter Popham observes, there is Suu Kyi's suspicion – anybody who wants to lead is a priori proof that they are not of the right moral calibre. That is because they have not given evidence that they are of that calibre.[15] Position and responsibility, as noted, should be interdependent.

In addition, how did King and Suu Kyi demonstrate their leadership? Did their belief in nonviolence influence their leadership styles? It makes us hesitant to give a fair critique to King's leadership because of his untimely death.

---

14. Wink, *Powers That Be*, 69.
15. Popham, *Lady and the Generals*, 225.

However, King had a team, the Southern Christian Leadership Conference (SCLC) that was composed of five executive directors, and in which King was president. The SCLC, in spite of the word Christian, "was also open to all, regardless of race, religion, or background."[16] The people in the leadership team were not yes-men who obeyed whatever King said without questioning. He also had a research committee, a kind of brains trust that would advise King on a structured basis. King himself found the meetings with the committee stimulating and refreshing.[17] His social environment did not allow him to become authoritarian; it limited the use of power for his own sake. Not only did King have a good social environment, he spent time building alliances. Having understood that it was impossible to achieve a major social transformation by working through his own organization (SCLC) alone, King strategically established trust and built personal relationships with the leaders of the national civil rights groups. He advocated the creation of alliances of many kinds – political, social, religious, intellectual, economic, and cultural. He was convinced that significant social change is best achieved in groups.[18] As a team leader, King's practice of power reflects Wink's view of power: it is power with others, partnership and cooperation. He was target-oriented, which is why he did not care much about the differences of ideas, race, or religion.

In contrast, Suu Kyi's profile in the previous chapter suggests that she is a woman of principle, a disciplinarian, and a perfectionist. However, she began to change from the year 2011 when she became a parliamentarian. A disciplinarian and a woman of principle turned into a politician who learns to compromise. For example, her silence in the fight between the army of Myanmar and Kachins and the riot between Rakhine and Rohingya disappointed the local and international community. A western journalist also pointed out that as far back as 1988, Suu Kyi demanded students oppose the regime through nonviolent resistance. Later, she remained silent about the escalating violence of Buddhist's in Myanmar against Muslims.[19] The one who

---

16. Southern Christian Leadership Conference, "SCLC History."
17. Oates, *Let the Trumpet Sound*, 291–292.
18. Philips, *Martin Luther King, Jr*, 138–139.
19. Hunter, "Aung San Suu Kyi's Quest."

is masterful in articulating the idea of democracy, human rights and freedom becomes now a politician who seeks compromises. Unlike King, she does not have a team of experts with whom she works out plans for the country. Peter Popham describes how Suu Kyi has lacked experience in working as a team:

> There is a photograph of Suu at a meeting in Delhi in November 2014 with Narendra Modi, the Indian prime minister. Mr Modi is accompanied by ten men in suits, plus an interpreter. Suu is accompanied by her female aide, Dr Tim Mar Aung. The satirical blog Burma Tha Din Network, which posted the photo, captioned it, "Aung San Suu Kyi and her policy team meet with the Indian Prime Minister and his policy team." This wasn't satire, it was the bizarre truth.[20]

What is worse, Popham continues to point out Suu Kyi's detachment from her party by the way she treated her small entourage during her visit to England in June 2012. They were put up in hotels at the expense of the UK government, but Suu Kyi told them firmly not to use the hotel minibars or the laundry. Overall, Popham points out three problems with her leadership: her silence in the Rakhine-Rohingya conflict, the disorganization in her office, and her alleged high-handedness. Popham is right in pointing out the second and third characteristics of Suu Kyi's leadership style, but not the first. The riot between Rakhine and Rohingya is, as discussed, indeed more complex and complicated than the international community thinks. This conflict ought not to be examined merely through the lens of outsiders. The disorganization and lack of management skills is indeed disappointing to us. What has been confounding is that she gave an address on the leadership mindset in Singapore Management University on 22 September 2013 with an emphasis on the importance of team management and leadership. There she mentioned,

> Teamwork is not something that is taught in our country because we don't have an educational system that promotes teamwork. Leadership becomes more of a difficulty and more of a responsibility. Because what we are talking about is leaders, not

---

20. Popham, *Lady and the Generals*, 244.

commanders... Leaders lead. Commanders command; they expect the commands to obey whether or not they are reasonable. Leadership means convincing those whom you aspire to lead that the way you have chosen is the right one. It has to be a choice. They have to choose to follow you. That is what leadership is about.[21]

The question that occurs to me is, why does she not practice team leadership and management if she knows its importance? It seems that she does not exercise what she believes or says – is it a form of self-contradiction or hypocrisy? If she believes in team leadership, why does she not create a team who can support, cooperate, and correct her if she does something wrong? Perhaps, the disorganization in her office and her alleged high-handedness co-habits. What pushes Suu Kyi to be such a woman might be fame, honour, and respect that local and international communities have rendered her, and the titles such as Nobel Peace Laureate, the heroine of human rights and freedom, the icon of democracy, and so on. The idolization of the people across the country and the globe brings out self-sufficiency and high-handedness in her. Other people seem less capable, skilled, reliable, knowledgeable or perhaps less noble than her. Compared to King, Suu Kyi's leadership is too personality-based, not team-oriented; spontaneous, not scheduled. To look at her practice of power from the angle of Walter Wink, she evidently has failed to nurture and develop a cooperative work with others regardless of racial, religious and cultural differences. Despite the fact that she refuses the practice of personality cult, she could not exert herself to break through the labyrinth of public admiration.

6.2 Religion: Engaging Buddhism with Christianity

Belief in God or the word "religion" is, according to the new atheistic movement, synonymous with an irrational delusion and a social toxin.[22] Religion,

---

21. Suu Kyi, "SMU Ho Rih Hwa Lecture."
22. Richard Dawkins's *The God Delusion*, Christopher Hitchens's *God Is Not Great*, Sam Harris's *The End of Faith*, Daniel C. Dennett's *Breaking the Spell*. These leading atheists vehemently argued against all kinds of religious beliefs in various ways.

according to the late Christopher Hitchens, is, "violent, irrational, intolerant, allied to racism and tribalism and bigotry, invested in ignorance and hostile to free inquiry, contemptuous of women and coercive toward children."[23] After the events of 11 September 2001 in the USA, religion and God-professing faith communities have been severely attacked by atheists and non-religious secularists. The questions being raised are, is religion or belief in God still relevant to the pluralist society of the twenty-first century? Or should all religious institutions and belief in a supernatural God be discarded?

Looking at King and Suu Kyi in the light of these questions, it is evident that religion, particularly Christianity and Buddhism, is not as destructive as the new atheists claim. Of course, religion has been used as a channel to uphold the systems of injustice throughout human history. In King's time, Christianity was an instrument to buttress racial prejudice. White supremacists interpreted the Bible from a racist perspective. All the racially discriminative Jim Crow laws were also backed up by the prejudiced interpretation of the Christian Bible.[24] Intriguingly, King did not rely on other religious sources to resist against that discriminatory culture. Instead, he recovered a biblical Christianity with the principles of freedom, equality, and human dignity. It was one version of Christianity against another. Thus, the way in which King came to see and critique the problems of his country, was using the prophetic tradition of the Old Testament. His historic speech, "I Have A Dream," featured a number of quotations from prophetic books in the Old Testament. For example, the phrase, "justice rolls down like waters and righteousness like a mighty stream" is an almost exact adaptation of Amos 5:24. King, in short, supported his resistance through recovering the prophetic tradition of the Old Testament.

In a similar way, the ex-military regime craftily exploited Buddhism to secure their power because they knew that it could be used as a powerful tool to legitimize their rule. Although Suu Kyi was raised in the UK

---

23. Hitchens, *God Is Not Great*, 56.

24. In US history, the Jim Crow laws were the laws that enforced racial segregation in the South between the end of Reconstruction in 1877 and the beginning of the civil rights movement in the 1950s. The word "Jim Crow" was the name of a minstrel routine performed beginning in 1828 by its composer, Joseph Jefferson. Later the term came to be a derogator epithet for African Americans, see Urofsky, "Jim Crow Law."

where Christianity was culturally rooted, and was married to Michael Aris, a Catholic Christian, she did not generate her thought of resistance against the regime on Christianity.[25] She is described as a socially engaged Buddhist because she has reconstructed the political values of Myanmar in the light of Buddhist traditions and the teaching of Buddha. Therefore, Suu Kyi's nonviolent resistance was also Buddhism against Buddhism. Thus, what matters is not religion itself, but how it is interpreted.

In Wink's view, religion can be a part of the DS. For instance, Wink indicates that what killed Jesus was not irreligion, but religion itself.[26] It was not lawless or irreligious people, but upholders of the religious orders (Judaism) of that time, who killed Jesus. However, Jesus's crucifixion exposed the true nature of that religion. Jesus, though he was crucified, embodied the genuine form of what religion should be. Religion under the DS imprisons humanity instead of liberating it. Jesus, in Wink's understanding, liberates the religion that had been institutionalized by the society of that time by absorbing all the violence directed at him, thereby exposing and unmasking the powers that unfairly judged him.[27] When Jesus liberated the people from the religion of the DS, he did not do it from a non-Judaist viewpoint. He did not disregard the forefathers (Abraham, Jacob, Moses, and so on) of Judaism; instead, he reinterpreted them in the context of the kingdom of God, or God's domination-free order.

From the Winkian perspective, King and Suu Kyi did not act much differently to the way Jesus did in the sense that the main philosophical sources through which they supported and promoted their struggles were all familiar to their peoples. In Jesus's time, the religion of Judaism was, under the DS, powerful enough to kill Jesus, who was the embodiment of true religion. In brief, the religious leaders of Jesus's time, being ignorant of the spirituality of their religion, were overpowered by their religious system; but Jesus knew the essence of Judaism, so religion for him was a powerful source of liberation

---

25. Here, I have identified the UK as the then Christian country because during the years (1964–1988), when Suu Kyi lived and studied in the UK, the influence of Christianity was still dominant. Nowadays, the UK has become a religiously pluralistic country, turning from a Christian to a post-Christian country.

26. Wink, *Powers That Be*, 83.

27. Wink, 85–86.

for the oppressed. In this sense, religion, whether Judaism, Buddhism or Christianity can either be used well or misused.

Hence, both Buddhism and Christianity, as religions, are paradoxical in their nature. That is, they can either be a tool for suppression or an instrument for liberation. As noted, the Christian Bible was often employed as a means to buttress the segregation in King's time. Likewise, Buddhism was a powerful tool used to legitimize the military rule. In that sense, both Christianity and Buddhism, like other religions, are identical in nature. In the study of religion and the racial problem in the USA, Michel O. Emerson and Christian Smith indicate the paradoxical nature of religion: "religion has tremendous potential for mitigating racial division and inequality."[28] When the DS overpowers religion, it becomes a mechanism to enslave people. However, Christianity can be a liberating dynamism to bring in God's domination-free order for someone who does not operate in the realm of the DS. In the same way, Buddhism can become an emancipatory mechanism to transform the politics of Myanmar if we repudiate the reigning culture of the DS, like Suu Kyi does. In Wink's view, King and Suu Kyi are the ones who lived outside of the zone of the DS, so religion (Christianity and Buddhism), for them, is the most powerful mechanism to transform their nations.[29]

If religion can be used as a tool either for oppression or emancipation, what would be the key to unlock the true nature of religion that liberates, not oppresses? Is there any means or secret through which we can interpret any religion – Christianity or Buddhism, in an emancipatory manner? To ask precisely, what are the keys through which King, Suu Kyi and Wink unlock the liberating messages of their religious writings? For King, it was the same religion of Christianity that the segregationists adhered to, and through which they justified the segregation system. Likewise, Buddhism was the religion through which the ex-regime validated their rule.

First, where did King learn the revolutionary idea of social justice? A historian of modern America, David L. Chappell, sheds light on the intellectual root of the civil rights movement. For him, the movement was not driven by liberal faith in human reason, but by a prophetic tradition that

---

28. Emerson and Smith, *Divided by Faith*, 153.
29. Wink, *Powers That Be*, 65.

runs from David and Isaiah in the Old Testament, through to Augustine and Martin Luther to Reinhold Niebuhr in the twentieth century.[30] Though he was indebted to Gandhi in terms of the nonviolent method, his primary philosophical source was not Gandhi, but prophetic tradition, the church where he grew up, and his philosophical and theological predecessors.

David Chappell also concludes that King masterfully communicated with the world beyond his church, who bought much of his church with him into the mainstream, and who reminded his church and the mainstream how much they had in common.[31] Despite the fact that the religion that the segregationists and King practiced was the same, King, unlike the former group, had a different hermeneutic to interpret the Scriptures, and that hermeneutic was originally adapted from the prophetic tradition. Put differently, King did not read the Bible and understand it through the lens of the cultural presuppositions; instead, he took an interpretative lens out of the Bible itself and used it to understand the Scriptures.

Somewhat like King's case, Suu Kyi practiced the same religion, Buddhism, that the ex-regime practiced, yet their interpretation of Buddhism was different. As discussed in the previous chapter, Suu Kyi articulated the relevance of democratic values with traditional Buddhism in the essay, "In Quest of Democracy."[32] Being racially a Buddhist of Myanmar, but culturally and intellectually a western product, Suu Kyi interprets Buddhism through the lens of western values on human rights, human dignity and human worth, thereby justifying democratic principles to Buddhism. What makes Suu Kyi different from King is that King interprets the Bible through the narrative within the Bible, thereby critiquing the Christianity practiced among the whites. For Suu Kyi, the democratic principles that she adopted in the West become a lens to interpret Buddhism. Put another way, the lens through which Suu Kyi sees and understands Buddhism is originally western, so her approach is, unlike King, not a Buddhism through Buddhism but Buddhism through a western eye. Thus, Buddhist cultural conservatives do not appreciate her interpretation of Buddhism.

---

30. Chappell, *Stone of Hope*, 3.

31. Chappell, 48.

32. Suu Kyi, *Freedom from Fear*, 167–179.

Furthermore, Christianity and Buddhism provide King and Suu Kyi with a comprehensive ethos for their philosophy of nonviolence. Despite being a product of western culture and education, Suu Kyi has formulated and articulated her political outlook and nonviolent struggle against the regime from a Buddhist perspective. The regime cunningly confronted her in several ways. One of their criticisms was that democratic values and principles are incompatible with the Burmese culture. Against that, Suu Kyi persuasively reinterpreted the relevance of democratic values and principles for the people of Myanmar in the context of Buddha's teachings.[33] All her writings and interviews shed light on the integral relationship between being a Buddhist and a politician. Likewise, Christianity became the backbone of the culture of segregation in the time of King. The Bible, for segregationists, does not oppose slavery; and in fact, through direct and indirect examples, supports it.[34] As a result, segregationists took it for granted that segregation was authorized by their religion. What King did was to reinterpret Christianity in favour of justice, freedom, and love. As a man from a Christian family, a son of a pastor, and a pastor himself, Christianity had always been the source from which he developed and articulated the ethical principles of nonviolence.

As the religions King and Suu Kyi practiced were sources for their philosophies, they were also psycho-spiritual sources for them. For instance, King's experience of the divine presence in the kitchen,[35] his belief in the God of the Bible, and his conviction of Jesus Christ as the one who died and rose again hugely inspired, motivated, and empowered him to continue tenaciously and persistently in the struggle for freedom and justice. Similarly, Suu Kyi, during house arrest, trained herself through way of Buddhist meditation. According to her, spending time in meditation led her to increase her mindfulness in her everyday life.[36] Most of all, King and Suu Kyi withstood a great deal of maltreatment in their struggles, yet they never sought revenge. They also

---

33. Suu Kyi, "In Quest of Democracy," in *Freedom from Fear*, 167–178.

34. Emerson and Smith, *Divided by Faith*, 34.

35. See chapter 2 where I have narrated the story of how King sensed the presence of the Divine in the kitchen while he was overwhelmed with fear.

36. Suu Kyi, "Benefits of Meditation and Sacrifice." "Mindfulness" is a step on the Noble Eightfold Path in Buddhism. It can also be translated as "attentiveness." Mindfulness is called *Sati* in Pali and *Smriti* in Sanskrit. The system of mindfulness built around the concept is mainly analytical, in contemplating the diverse factors in the body, the sensations, the thought-

refused to compromise their nonviolent approach. Wink believed that King and Suu Kyi reflected the same truth that was revealed in the life of Jesus, who never succumbed to the perspective of his persecutors by seeking revenge.[37]

In addition, what is striking in the comparison between King and Suu Kyi is their respective religious contexts. Christianity, for both black and white Americans, was deeply ingrained in the whole country in the time of King, and Buddhism, for the majority of Myanmar's people, is seen as the national religion. Both King and Suu Kyi identified with the religion of the majority of the population. Hence, when they justified their struggle on the basis of the religion, it was not difficult for the public to accept it because the religions both King and Suu Kyi presented were not strange to them. Supposing that King was a Buddhist and Suu Kyi, a Christian, how would their peoples respond to them? Perhaps, this question is too speculative. Since Suu Kyi is a Buddhist and King, a Christian, the question seems extraneous.

Nonetheless, this issue is important because Suu Kyi's struggle was one of Buddhists against Buddhists and King's resistance was of Christians against Christians. Both the junta and its opposition, Suu Kyi, are Buddhists; therefore, the fight between them is principally a power struggle. In the same way, King's resistance against segregation was also predominantly social and racial since both King and his opponents were Christians. To illustrate this point in a clearer way, King's contemporary Malcolm X also fought for his black fellows. However, unlike King, he was a Muslim. Of course Malcolm X also did his best, as King did, for the desegregation or the liberation of the blacks. Nonetheless, he was less well-known, recognized, or honoured, than King. Did the people of America support King more than they did Malcolm X on the basis of religion? To a great extent, this is true. Malcolm X's critique of Christianity was fierce. He classified Christianity as white nationalism, and Islam as black nationalism; Christianity enslaves blacks; Islam liberates them. He saw Christianity as the root of segregationism. James Cone suggests that

---

processes and phenomena, but goes further in a higher synthesis of consciousness, in *Samādhi*, see Humphreys, *Popular Dictionary of Buddhism*, 198.

37. Wink, *Powers That Be*, 111.

Malcolm X's unrestrained critique of Christianity led him to be ignored by white Christians and receive less attention from black Christians.[38]

Likewise, if Suu Kyi were a Christian, would the Buddhist majority assist her as much as they do now? In the context of a Buddhist majority, Christians and Muslims are often disadvantaged in politics and culture. Since the 1962 military rule, government servants who are Christians have been disadvantaged in the promotion to key positions. This shows that religious identification in politics plays a crucial role for both King and Suu Kyi. This also raises the question of whether an individual from a minority religious background can become a leader like King or Suu Kyi. Should Christians and Muslims change their religious position to win public support? Would Christians or Muslims be able to win public recognition without changing their religious position? Perhaps King and Suu Kyi might not be able to deal with this question.

Finally, the most powerful and compelling argument that King and Suu Kyi made during their struggles was the integral relation of politics, morality, spirituality, and religion. The prevailing idea in the time of King was that Christianity was primarily concerned with spiritual things, such as how to get to heaven, and had nothing to do with life here and now. The role of a pastor was predominantly to care about the spiritual maturity of the congregation, not to interfere with the social and political affairs. King, through the eyes of his father and Walter Rauschenbusch, revolutionized this one-sided view of Christianity through arguing for the inseparability of the social and the spiritual from the perspective of the kingdom of God.

Likewise, Suu Kyi's understanding of the integral nature of politics, spirituality, and Buddha's teaching of *mettā* is also revolutionary in the political context of Myanmar. The politicians before her, such as the late U Nu, the first prime minister post-independence and also a devout Buddhist, felt it was impossible to be a politician and, at the same time, a good Buddhist. For them, political business and religious duties seem incompatible and opposite. Thus Suu Kyi, when talking about morality, *mettā*, and *thissa* ("truth") in politics, was often confronted with the question, "why so much religion in politics?" For many politicians, it is too idealistic or naïve to talk about *mettā*

---

38. Cone, *Martin & Malcolm & America*, 173, 296.

in politics, as she described in conversation with Alan Clements.[39] Against this dominant presupposition, Suu Kyi argues that politics is about people, so it is inappropriate to separate people from their spiritual values. With this view, Suu Kyi explored Buddhist principles and some relevant cultural values with a view to integrating religious values in her politics. In doing so, Suu Kyi revolutionized the idea that a person can become a good Buddhist, and at the same time, a good politician. In short, both Suu Kyi and King were deeply convinced of the integral link between politics and religion. For both of them, religion was not to be used to maintain power, but to be a liberating force.

6.3 Ethics of Nonviolence: Engaging King and Suu Kyi Via Wink's Eyes

So far, I have explored the connection between leadership and nonviolence in the lives of King and Suu Kyi from the Winkian perspective. I have also looked at how religion has a significant role in the concepts of nonviolence for King and Suu Kyi, via Wink's *Powers*. Now I will examine King and Suu Kyi and the ethical principles of nonviolence from the Winkian perspective.

6.3.1 Why Not Violence?

Violence done in the name of religion, political ideologies, and racial issues are widespread in today's world. Against this backdrop, scholars and leaders from religious, secular, social, and political circles voice various opinions. What is increasingly evident in societies nowadays is the search for peace – how we can possibly live in harmony in the midst of cultural, racial, religious, and philosophical diversities.[40] In this context, the words "peace" and "nonviolence" are thrilling and comprehensive for scholars to articulate in

---

39. Kyi and Clements, *Voice of Hope*, 45. Often Suu Kyi was asked if it is reasonable to talk about *mettā* in political business. In her essay, she recalled her experience that people cheerfully contributed hard work and money to the late Buddhist monk, known as Thamanya Sayadaw because they believed their contributions would not be in vain, but benefit the public. Thus, she concludes that it is totally relevant to talk about *mettā* in the political context. What happened in Thamanya proved its relevance, see Suu Kyi, *Letters from Burma*, 12.

40. In academic, social and international levels, a number of centres for peace and conflict studies have been mushrooming over the last decade. In the United Nations, peacemaking, peace-building, and peacekeeping are strongly emphasized and operated directly under the supervision of the Secretary-General.

their studies. They become such popular and frequently used words which can be heard and seen in political, social, and religious contexts. Tolstoy in Russia, Gandhi in India, Martin Luther King Jr in the United States, and more recently, Mubarak Awad[41] in the Middle East, the Dalai Lama in Tibet, and Aung San Suu Kyi in Myanmar, become the models of nonviolence. Why do King, Suu Kyi and Wink denounce violence and encourage others to do so?

Before dealing with this question, we need to define violence. Defining violence and nonviolence is not as easy as we might imagine. Glen H. Stassen and Michael L. Westmoreland-White define violence as, "destruction to a victim by means that overpower the victim's consent."[42] To cover both structural and individual dimensions, P. Iadicola and A. Shupe define violence as, "any action or structural arrangement that results in physical or nonphysical harm to one or more persons."[43] Despite not using the words individual and structural, the former definition inclusively covers both aspects. The phrase, "by means that overpower" implies using a personal or institutional power, weapon, or any object. The latter definition also entails a number of dimensions, such as structural and personal, physical and nonphysical, psychological, or mental. However, both definitions fail to engage in the spiritual or inner nature of violence, as they both see violence simply as a means or an action. In seeing violence as a spirit of the DS, this study needs to investigate the spiritual or inner nature of violence that runs deep in our society. Hence, defining violence as an action or a means does not necessarily fit with this study. In this context, violence is viewed with the belief that violence can save, can establish order, peace and justice, and can achieve a desired goal. Put differently, violence begins with the human psycho-spiritual domain since it is a belief.

What King and Suu Kyi have in common is their belief that "violence breeds violence." King believed that the beloved community could never be realized through violence, and Suu Kyi believed that bringing about change through violence perpetuates the tradition of violence. For King, nonviolence

---

41. Mubarak Awad is a Palestinian, born in Jerusalem, in 1943. He founded "Nonviolence International," a non-governmental organization with the mission of promoting nonviolent action, a culture of peace, and seeking to reduce the use of violence worldwide, see their website at: http://nonviolenceinternational.net.

42. Stassen and Westmoreland-White, "Defining Violence," 18.

43. Cited from Barak, *Violence and Nonviolence*, 26.

is the only way to establish the beloved community; in Suu Kyi's view, nonviolence is the best way to protect the people, and in the long run, it alone can ensure the future stability of democracy. They also both believe that violence contrasts sharply with their convictions of *agape* and *mettā*. Suu Kyi sees evil as stupidity, whereas King regards it as sin. Stupidity is *avijjā* (ignorance or *moha*), greed (*lobha*), and anger (*dasa*). In Buddhist terms. *Avijjā* is nescience or ignorance, unknowing, or delusion, which is the primary root of all evil and suffering in the world. This also puts a veil over our mental eyes and prevents us from seeing the true nature of things. When we are darkened with *lobha*, *dosa*, and *moha*, whatever we do will harm ourselves and other people.

For King, the reality of sin is on every level of human existence.[44] King regards sin as separation, thereby arguing that segregation is an existential expression of tragic human separation on the basis of colour, an expression of their awful estrangement, their terrible sinfulness.[45] He believes that sin is deeply rooted in human society. Even the way of nonviolence or realistic pacifism is, in King's understanding, not purely sinless; it is the lesser evil. In general, Suu Kyi's view of evil or stupidity is individualistic in the sense that *avijjā* or stupidity is a characteristic that can be mainly seen in an individual. In contrast, King discerns the collective nature of sin in human society. To conclude, stupidity as *lobha*, *dosa*, and *moha* is the root of violence for Suu Kyi, and the reality of sin is the origin of violence for King.

According to the Winkian outlook, the views of King and Suu Kyi concerning the root cause of violence are not particularly explicit. For Wink, the world in which we live is under the domination system (DS). In the DS, violence is the method of change. It was the ethos, or spirituality, of the DS. Wink calls it "the myth of redemptive violence" in which humans are habituated and conditioned to accept violence. Peace through war, security through strength, victory through combat, and order through military suppression are the core convictions of the DS; they form the solid foundation on which the DS is

---

44. King, unlike systematic theologians, does not define what sin really means. It seems that he, as influenced by Niebuhr, sees that sin has come in as a result of human revolt against or turning away from God. Consequentially, humans deny their creatureliness, and instead they desire to become like God.

45. King, *Testament of Hope*, 293–294.

founded in every society. Briefly stated, the myth of redemptive violence is so embedded in human history that people cannot see its true nature.

Unlike Wink, King and Suu Kyi pay attention to the vicious circle of violence, but they do not seem interested in why this circle exists. Wink answers that the myth of redemptive violence is the engine of that circle. As long as we fail to recognize the existence of the DS and do not look for an alternative, we will always be lost in the labyrinth of the DS. To recall the question of why not violence, Wink answers that any attempt to change certain things through violence can never liberate us from the DS, because violence itself is the spirit of the DS. Violence multiplies violence, and changing a political system via violence will never end the tradition of violence; instead, it will prolong it. Why does violence breed violence? Why does violence perpetuate a tradition of violence? Wink gives an answer to these two questions – the questions that King and Suu Kyi fail to deal with – it is simple, because the belief in redemptive violence is the inner spirituality of the DS. To combat the spirituality of the DS, what we need is an alternative, and that is nonviolence.[46]

6.3.2 Nonviolence and Love: Engaging King's *Agape* and Suu Kyi's *Mettā* through Wink's Loving Enemies

King, as noted, is an activist for principled nonviolence, whereas Suu Kyi is a proponent of pragmatic nonviolence. Despite this difference, they both had the conviction that the nonviolent path is more than a means; hence they talked a huge deal about *agape* and *mettā*, knowing that without this their resistances would be soulless and lifeless. Scholars may interpret King's nonviolence in various ways, but what cannot be sidestepped is his emphasis on *agape*. Likewise, Suu Kyi adapted a Buddhist term, *mettā*, to identify her idea of nonviolence.

Wink, however, specifies that the kind of love necessary in nonviolence is the "love of enemies." Wink's idea of "loving enemies" is fundamentally theocentric. He believes that God is all-inclusive. He forgives us so that we may repent of our evil deeds. He also loves us so that we may lift our eyes to him. God does not hate those whom we hate. Since God is compassionate toward us, he must also treat our enemies the same way. Therefore, Wink

---

46. Wink, *Powers That Be*, 42, 113.

concludes that we are to be like God, having a love that is all-encompassing, loving even those who have the least claim or right to our love. As God can never be domesticated or nationalized, Wink asserts that we are to regard the enemy as beloved of God as much as we can.[47] For King, *agape* is a love that is shown to all kinds of people, both friends and enemies. When we love others, we do so not because of their racial, economic, or political significance, but because God loves them. In this love, we love those who do an evil deed while hating the deed that they do. So *agape* love is transforming and redeeming.[48] In that sense, King, as a Christian, does not differ from Wink.

However, Suu Kyi, as a Buddhist, is non-theistic and self-reliant in defining *mettā* and nonviolence. As Buddhism is a non-theistic religion, the name God is not mentioned in Suu Kyi's writings and interviews, and even if it is mentioned, it refers to the Judeo-Christian concept of God. But it does not mean that Buddhism is an atheistic religion. In the context of Myanmar, the majority of Buddhists believe in the existence of supernatural deities. Truly, their concept of God or gods differs from the Judeo-Christian notion of God, but they accept the existence of a deity. In that sense, Buddhists of Myanmar are not atheists. The focus of Buddhism is the liberation of oneself from *dukkha*, meaning suffering, pain, and the state of being unsatisfied. Depending on God for one's personal liberation is foreign to Buddhists like Suu Kyi.

As noted, Wink and King, as Christians, build their argument for *agape* and "loving enemies" on the Judeo-Christian concept of God. However, belief in such a God seems, for Suu Kyi, unnecessary. Looking at these perspectives, on what grounds do they say that we should love our enemies? For King and Wink, we should love our enemies because God loves them with the same love he has for us. But for Suu Kyi, we should have *mettā* towards our enemies because it is the way of Buddha. Suu Kyi's *mettā* is, unlike the Christian view of love, purely anthropocentric and horizontal; there is no theological or vertical dimension. This is a fundamental difference between Christianity and Buddhism.

In short, Buddhism and Christianity are theologically irreconcilable because of fundamental differences in their worldviews – e.g. Christianity is

---

47. Wink, *Engaging the Powers*, 263–271.
48. King, *Papers*, vol. 3, 327.

theistic, while Buddhism is not. Yet, it does not mean that King, Suu Kyi and Wink are contradicting each other in their ideas of nonviolence. These differences do not necessarily imply dissension. As discussed above, King's *agape*, Suu Kyi's *mettā*, and Wink's "loving our enemies" fundamentally correspond to each other. For Christians, we are to love our enemies because God loves them just as he loves us. For Suu Kyi, we should love our adversaries on the basis of being human.

However, Wink's exposition is much more accurate, articulate, and deeper than King and Suu Kyi when it comes to the idea of *mettā* or *agape*. Wink suggests that one's enemy can be a gift. How can someone's enemy possibly be a gift to them? Wink indicates that some common characteristics of our enemies can also be found in us. In that sense, enemies can help us "see aspects of ourselves that we cannot discover any other way than through our enemies."[49] Wink highlights that the enemies are therefore not an obstacle on the way to God, but they can be the way to God. Thus, loving our enemies can result in a double transformation: transforming ourselves, as well as transforming our enemies. In discussing the role of enemies, Wink does not differentiate between "we" (us as lovers) and "they" (our enemies as haters). According to this false dichotomy, it seems that we are destined to love, while our enemies are destined to hate. In contrast to this idea, Wink has discerned the commonality between our adversaries and us. Therefore, Wink deepens King's *agape* and Suu Kyi's *mettā* and advances from these ideas to suggest that the nonviolent resistance should aim to transform our repressed attitudes as well as those of our enemies.

6.3.3 Principled or Pragmatic?

As noted earlier, King was an activist for principled nonviolence, while Suu Kyi takes the pragmatic position. I have analyzed Suu Kyi's idea of nonviolence and put her in the pragmatic category on the basis of her statement, "I have not chosen nonviolence for moral reason, but for political ground."[50] R. J. Burrowes, in his study of Gandhi's idea of nonviolence, distinguishes the principled from the pragmatic approach: the former believes in the inseparability

---

49. Wink, *Engaging the Powers*, 273; *Powers That Be*, 170–171.
50. Suu Kyi, "Securing Freedom."

of means and end, while the latter is not concerned about this; the former views nonviolence as a way of life, but the latter does not. Followers of the principled approach see the conflict as a shared problem with their opponents and are willing to accept suffering at the hands of their opponents. However in the pragmatic approach, the conflict is seen as having incompatible interests with their opponents, and they are more inclined to inflict suffering on their opponents rather than to accept it themselves.[51] Burrowes' distinction between the principled and the pragmatic approach sounds too sharp. In his analysis, Suu Kyi cannot be characterized as pragmatic anymore because Suu Kyi does care about the delicate relationship between means and end. What is more, Suu Kyi sees the person and their deed as separate, and therefore never inflicts suffering on her opponents.[52]

Robert L. Holmes, unlike Burrowes, categorizes the principled nonviolence in two ways: absolute and conditional. If nonviolence is regarded as an absolute, the distinction between the principled and pragmatic approaches can be sharply drawn. But there is another sort of principled nonviolence, which is conditional. According to this kind of nonviolence, violence may sometimes be justified in a narrow range of cases. Violence may be used to prevent worse things from happening in the long run. By and large, both the principled and the pragmatic approaches justify nonviolence as the right means. The rationale, for the principled approach, will be moral, but for the pragmatic it will be social, political, economic, nationalistic, etc.[53] Holmes' distinction is perhaps more appropriate, which suggests that Suu Kyi's basis for nonviolence is practical rather than political or moral. Nevertheless, Suu Kyi's idea of nonviolence is still somewhat different from the characteristics of the pragmatic or conditional. To be precise, there is a quasi-contradiction in Suu Kyi's nonviolence. She makes two statements that allude to the fact that she is an exponent of pragmatic or conditional nonviolence: holding nonviolence for political reason and allowing a short burst of violence to prevent worse things from happening in the long run.[54]

---

51. Burrowes, *Strategy of Nonviolent Defence*, 99.
52. Kyi and Clements, *Voice of Hope*, 172, 180.
53. Cicovacki, *Ethics of Nonviolence*, 172.
54. Suu Kyi, "Securing Freedom: Liberty."

Despite these statements, she has never employed violence on a personal level and has made every effort to abide by Buddha's teachings of *mettā* in her life. The characteristics of principled nonviolence are manifested in her attempt to abide by Buddhist principles in her worldly dealings. If we look at her in this way, we can understand these two statements in a new light. When she describes that she has chosen nonviolence for political reason, she is pointing out her willingness to include other political activists who fought the regime through the use of armed forces for many decades. Similarly, when she talks about allowing a short burst of violence, she acknowledges human imperfection. Therefore, Suu Kyi should not be categorized as purely pragmatic or conditional. She may be best described as a proponent of politically pragmatic nonviolence. That is, personally she adheres to the Buddhist principle of nonviolence; however, she is pragmatic for political reason so that she may treat others who are different from her in using arms to fight against the regime as friends. Despite personally holding to the idea of principled nonviolence, Suu Kyi does not exclude others who do not share her principle. Thus, it is best to depict her as an advocate of pragmatic nonviolence for political reason.

It is clearly evident that King was a proponent of principled nonviolence. He renounced all kinds of violence. Nonviolence is, for him, not only a means to achieve something but an end itself because nonviolence is a way of life. The last sermon he delivered, "I See the Promised Land," explicitly described his firm position regarding principled nonviolence. There he asserted that the choice before us is no longer violence or nonviolence, but nonviolence or nonexistence. King, according to Holmes' categorization, is an exponent of absolute principled nonviolence.

Like King, Wink admits that there are situations so extreme that one cannot conceive of any alternative to violence. He confesses that he does not know if he could be nonviolent in a maximum-security prison like Sing Sing.[55] To be specific, it is a situation where an oppressive power has squandered every opportunity to do justice, and the capacity of the people to continue is gone.

---

55. Sing Sing is a maximum-security prison operated by the New York State Department of Corrections and Community Supervision in the village Ossining, in the US. The prison is located about thirty miles north of New York City on the east bank of the Hudson River.

Then the violence visited on the nation is a kind of apocalyptic judgment.[56] But Wink insists that the church has no business legitimating the violence of war; instead, she is obligated to try to mitigate the violence. In that sense, Wink should also be categorized in the group of principled nonviolence. In short, Holmes' category is far better than Burrowes' because it best describes the position of these three personalities – Wink, King and Suu Kyi. According to Holmes' category, Wink and King stand for absolute principled nonviolence, whereas Suu Kyi, for conditional principled nonviolence.

In a nutshell, King among them is the strongest exponent of principled nonviolence compared to Wink, and Suu Kyi is a shrewd politician who personally endeavours to abide by Buddhist teachings in her life, but she makes compromises with others for political reason. Wink, despite being an advocate of principled nonviolence, is aware of certain complex situations where there is no alternative except violence. To juxtapose each other, Wink's position is much more convincing than King and Suu Kyi because King seems to be too dogmatic for his overemphasis on nonviolence, while Suu Kyi seems to be compromising her principles for political relevance.

6.3.4 Principles of Nonviolence: King and Suu Kyi Via Wink's Eyes

Whether following an absolute principled or others-friendly idea of nonviolence, there are certain principles of nonviolence that King and Suu Kyi stick to. Wink also believes that some principles are time-tested and operationally proven, such as the congruity of means and ends, and respect for the rule of law. Here I will establish a dialogue between King, Suu Kyi and Wink in order to discuss it in the next chapter in which political implications will be examined for the context of Myanmar.

Means and Ends

For King and Suu Kyi, the end does not justify the means. They both believe that the means we employ must be congruent with the ends we pursue. Violence can never create the beloved community, nor can it uproot the tradition of the existing regime. It also cannot implant the democratic values in

---

56. Wink, *Engaging the Powers*, 239–240.

soil where a dictatorship has reigned for many decades. King was convinced that violence, hate, and revenge could do nothing except cause destruction; only through nonviolence, can friendship be established. In the same vein, Suu Kyi believed that changing a political system via violence perpetuates the tradition of violence. Wink also shows a number of examples to prove the consequences of violence in history. To be specific, Joseph Stalin in the Soviet Union, Mao Zedong in China, and Ahmed Ben Bella in Algeria are examples of the negative effects of attaining power through violence, as these leaders caused the extermination of millions of people. Violence is addictive: once the path of violence has been chosen, it cannot be easily renounced by the new regime.[57]

King, Suu Kyi and Wink all have a firm grasp on the labyrinth of violence. However, Wink goes further than King by suggesting that violence is not just a descending spiral, but it also begets the very thing it seeks to destroy. Likewise, Wink explains that the use of violence can perpetuate the tradition that change can only be realized through violence because it is the spirit of the DS. Without changing the inner part of a particular system, a true transformation cannot be achieved. Additionally, from the Winkian perspective, the beloved community that King had been looking forward to and the democratization that Suu Kyi has worked towards are parts of the DFO. Thus the means they employ must be compatible with and reflect the desired ends they pursue.

In that sense, both King and Wink oppose a teleological ethic or consequentialism, which focuses on the end result rather than the means. Put another way, Wink and King believe that certain kinds of acts are wrong in themselves, and thus morally objectionable. For instance, they all think that violence is morally undesirable; therefore, it cannot authentically achieve the desired end. Violence as the spirit of the DS cannot create the DFO because they are incompatible with each other. Furthermore, if democratic values are peace, freedom, and justice, the way to embrace those values should not be through violence. In the case of Suu Kyi, though she holds the position of pragmatic nonviolence, she has a strong conviction that bringing about change through violence has been a tradition in the politics of Myanmar

---

57. Wink, *Powers That Be*, 113.

throughout its history. She desires to end this tradition; therefore, she uses nonviolence as her political tactic.[58] She knows that violence is not the right means to terminate that tradition. In this regard, she seems to be, like Wink and King, closer to a deontological or principled approach to nonviolence.

The debate regarding teleological and deontological ethical methods is unending among ethical theorists. Teleological theorists see deontological theory as, "one that either does not specify the good independently from the right or does not interpret the right as maximising the good."[59] At the same time, deontologists believe that "the right is not to be defined in terms of the good, and they reject the idea that the good is prior to the right."[60] By and large, the debate between them might be largely a comparison of emphasis (rather than actual disagreement regarding specifics). But in the case of violence and nonviolence, King, Suu Kyi and Wink have discerned that their ultimate concern is not merely to change a socio-political system, but to end the vicious cycle of violence, and transform the interiority of the DS into the DFO. It, for them, is not a matter of choice or a matter of either good or right, but rather good *and* right. Teleological and deontological ethicists attempt to define "good" and "right" independently instead of looking for their common ground. However, King, Suu Kyi and Wink look at the relationship between them instead of focusing on their independence. In this sense, it would not do justice to categorize them into an ethical taxonomy, because their understanding of violence and nonviolence goes beyond the dichotomy of teleological and deontological ethics.

The Rule of Law

King, Suu Kyi and Wink all strive to emphasize the rule of law. By law, I do not refer to the idea of law in a biblical sense, but law in the sense of a system of rules practiced in a country or society. They all believe that there are laws that must be followed, and so are all, unlike Henry D. Thoreau, non-anarchists. For them, there are unjust laws as well as just laws. King asserts that only those who defy unjust laws and are willing to accept the penalty by staying in jail until that law is altered, truly expressed the highest respect for the

---

58. Kyi and Clements, *Voice of Hope*, 154.
59. Davis, "Contemporary Deontology," 206.
60. Davis, 206.

law.[61] Likewise, Suu Kyi perceives that law has been, so far, an instrument of state oppression since the military coup in 1962. Therefore, she indicates that just law can do two things: it can create a society where people's basic needs are met, and it can also prevent a country from corruption. For Wink, Jesus willingly accepted the unjust sentence imposed upon him, thereby exposing it as a legalized murder. Like Jesus, we too should refuse to obey an unjust law by experiencing the legal punishment, thereby affirming our willingness to suffering on behalf of a higher or just law. Simply put, we must be lawful in our illegality.[62]

In talking about just and unjust laws, King philosophically frames his idea on the medieval theologian Thomas Aquinas's natural law. According to Aquinas, law is a dictate of practical reason issued by a sovereign who governs a complete community. This governance is called an eternal law. Humans, as intelligent creatures, can join in and make this eternal law their own, thereby making it natural law.[63] Hence, King states that unjust law or the law that discriminates between the blacks and the whites on the basis of skin colour is not rooted in eternal and natural law.

Suu Kyi's perspective is also similar to the idea of natural law in the sense that she is, despite her belief in Buddhism, a humanistic and political progressivist. Her conviction about democratic values and human rights proves that she is humanistic. In particular, her idea of rule of law hinges on the idea of democratic values and human rights. For her, democracy is an ideology that allows everyone, without being endangered or threatened, to stand up for their beliefs.[64] The ideas of human rights and democracy are all interdependent, but democracy encompasses the other two (human rights and rule of law). In an interview, she expressed her vision to establish a culture of democracy in Myanmar.[65] She believes that democracy is comprehensive enough to include other ideas such as human rights and rule of law.

In contrast, Wink, as a theologian understands rule of law from a Christian perspective. As largely discussed in the first chapter, Wink's view of rule of

---

61. King, *Testament of Hope*, 49.
62. Wink, *Powers That Be*, 86.
63. Gill, *Textbook of Christian Ethics*, 49.
64. Suu Kyi, *Freedom from Fear*, 198.
65. Lowe, "Interview with Nobel Peace Prize Winner."

law is founded on his exposition of the *Powers*, for which he owes a huge debt to his predecessors such as Hendrik Berkhof, Howard Yoder, and so on. In prefacing Berkhof's *Christ and Powers*,[66] Yoder introduces Berkhof as a pioneer in interpreting the Powers languages through modern eyes.[67] Berkhof reread the Powers language in a modern context and regarded it as human traditions and religious and ethical rules.[68] His structural reading of the Powers impacted others. For example, Yoder, in his book *The Politics of Jesus*, reads the Powers as structures.[69] Wink follows the structural reading of his predecessors and sees the Powers as the divine creation. In regard to rule of law, Wink believes that human society cannot survive without law because God established laws for us.

To conclude, King, Suu Kyi and Wink all have a high regard for the rule of law. When King and Suu Kyi were arrested during their struggles, they accepted the punishment. In doing so, they exposed the system of unjust law. Through a Winkian perspective, what made King and Suu Kyi unique is their willingness to suffer under the "misrule of law"[70] or unjust law. They both defied the unjust laws of the systems, but accepted their unjust punishment in the name of a higher law that they wished to implant. Wink believes that our willingness to endure suffering on behalf of a higher law will expose the unjust law. In a nutshell, they both submitted to the principle of law in order to transform unjust laws into just ones.

Fear, Fearlessness and Nonviolence: Who is Nonviolence For?

Who is nonviolence for? What would be an essential prerequisite for nonviolent activists? Every reader of King and Suu Kyi notices their fearless resistance against the domination system in their respective countries. However, they were not born with courage; they struggled to overcome their fear. For example, King's "kitchen experience" and Suu Kyi's fear of darkness during

---

66. Berkhof, *Christ and the Powers*. The book was originally published in Dutch in 1953.
67. Berkhof, 5–7.
68. Berkhof, 38.
69. Yoder, *Politics of Jesus*, 143.
70. Suu Kyi, in her book *Letters from Burma*, used the phrase "misrule of law." There she described the lives of dissidents in Burma, "everyone committed to taking an active part in the endeavour to return the country to democracy has to be prepared to go to prison at any time," Suu Kyi, *Letters from Burma*, 167.

her childhood best illustrate that they have learned to be fearless. As a result of their experiences of fear, they know that fear could overwhelm and paralyze a person. Therefore, King discusses the crippling downside of fear and highlights how it should be mastered. Likewise, Suu Kyi wrote an essay on, "Freedom from Fear."[71]

Wink also notes that the path of nonviolence is costly because nonviolence is not a way of avoiding personal sacrifice. In Wink's view, there are three approaches to conflict: flight (passivity), fight (violence), and nonviolence.[72] Put differently, these three approaches may be described as three stages. The first stage may be characterized by fear and cowardice; the second by violence, aggression, being warlike and hostile; and the third by militant nonviolence and nonaggression. Wink argues that a person who is in the flight position cannot easily move to active nonviolence because that person needs to be energized by the anger against injustice. Only then can the person be taught and trained to renounce violence and begin to follow the path of nonviolence.

Through looking at the recent history of nonviolent struggles, Wink has observed that people have resorted to nonviolence not because they believed in it, but because their opponents held a monopoly over weapons. Nonviolence was not a choice, but their only option. However, they felt confident in the nonviolent method when they saw its astonishing effectiveness and transformative power. Therefore, Wink believes that active nonviolence is not for the perfect, but for frightened, fed up, and even violent people who are trying to change. It is practical and applicable to anyone of any age.[73]

From this Winkian perspective, King passed through the second stage, the "fight" position and then he came to nonviolent resistance. But Suu Kyi is quite different from King, because seemingly she did not undergo such a

---

71. Suu Kyi, *Freedom from Fear*, 180–185. To my surprise, Suu Kyi's exposition of fear is somewhat similar to Robert Holmes' understanding. Holmes argues that fear is always of loss of some sort, whether personal, social or political, "Understanding Evil from the Perspective of Nonviolence," in *The Ethics of Nonviolence: Essays by Robert L. Holmes*, 210. This essay was originally published in the *Acorn: Journal of the Gandhi-King Society*, vol. 19, No. 1, (Winter-Spring 2010), 5–13. Looking at the time of publication, Suu Kyi's "freedom from fear" came prior to Holmes because Holmes' "understanding evil from the perspective of nonviolence" was published in 2010, whereas Suu Kyi's was published first in 1991.

72. Wink, *Engaging the Powers*, 187.

73. Wink, *Powers That Be*, 118.

transition. Under the care of her mother and her upbringing in India and the West, she seems to have trained herself to become nonviolent.

Nonviolence: A Fight Against Evil, Not the Evildoer

Nonviolence is, for both King and Suu Kyi, not an attack to humiliate opponents, but against what their opponents have done. For nonviolent activists, it is important to distinguish what a person does and what that person is, because nonviolence is not a win/lose game, but a win/win approach to conflict. In the myth of redemptive violence, people tend to demonize those who do evil. For example, when a particular tyrant rules a particular state ruthlessly, inhumanely, and heartlessly, people tend to demonize that tyrant. Of course, this is true in Myanmar. The majority of Christians in Myanmar, under the rules of the cold-blooded despots Ne Win and Than Shwe, have sometimes seen those leaders as demonic. For King and Suu Kyi, depersonalizing evil in that way is important because the ultimate aim of nonviolence is to win friendship or reconciliation.

In biblical terms, what King was fighting against was principalities and powers. For King, nonviolence was directed against the evil behind the people who did it, not the people themselves. Suu Kyi also often encouraged her people to focus on deeds rather than on the person who committed evil deeds. For this separation between evil and the evildoer, Suu Kyi, as noted earlier, gave the example of Gautama Buddha and Angulimala, a mass murderer, the one who even tried to kill Buddha. Based on that story, Suu Kyi contends that the Buddha was able to separate the person from the deed. In terms of this depersonalizing evil, Wink also argues from the idea of the Powers, which are the outer and inner manifestations of an institution. Those Powers are good, bad, and redeemable – all at once, according to Wink. From this understanding, Wink asserts that we are freed from the temptation to demonize those who do evil.

As discussed in the chapter on Martin Luther King Jr, it is hard to separate entirely the evildoer from the evil they commit. Reinhold Niebuhr insists, "It is impossible to completely dissociate an evil system from the personal moral responsibilities of the individual who maintains it."[74] Hans Walton also

---

74. Niebuhr, *Moral Man and Immoral Society*, 249.

questions the concept of depersonalizing evil: "How much of a person can be separated from his actions? And who, if not that person, is to be held responsible for those actions?"[75] For the victimized who lost their lives, properties, and suffered physically, emotionally and excruciatingly under the victimizer, the unavoidable question is: where is justice? In such a context, what kind of justice would be relevant and appropriate to be exercised?

For the utilitarian, what is just is what produces the best outcome. Ethically utilitarianism focuses on the result. Whether a certain action is right or wrong depends on whether it promotes the general welfare of a community or country.[76] On utilitarian grounds, perpetrators might justify that what they did was for the sake of the well-being of the majority. In contrast, Aristotelian justice seeks to relate two ideas: the questions of fairness and rights, and of honour and virtue. Justice, for Aristotle, meant giving persons what they deserve. For example, suppose we are distributing flutes. Who should get the best ones? For Aristotle, it should be the best flute players. It would be unjust to discriminate on any other basis, such as wealth, physical beauty, or chance.[77] In other words, it is justice according to one's merit (or demerit). If we do a good deed, we will, in turn, receive good. But if we commit an evil, we would receive evil. This resembles Buddhist's ethics: act good, receive good; act evil, receive evil. In short, the Aristotelian justice seems to be retributive.

For many Christian ethicists, a biblical view of justice is basically restorative, not retributive. Justice is meant to restore, not to repay: restoration of both parties, victims and offenders. However, even with restorative justice, restitution is likely to involve an element of punishment. Likewise, punishment ought to involve an element of restitution.[78] Chris Marshall indicates that punishment in the biblical narrative is a means to an end, not an end itself; therefore, punishment serves as a mechanism for helping to promote such restoration.[79] In the case of the Truth and Reconciliation Council (TRC) in South Africa, scholars have observed some problems in performing restorative justice. For instance, there was a lack of accountability for perpetrators.

---

75. Walton Jr, *Political Philosophy*, 80.
76. Lebacqz, *Six Theories of Justice*, 17.
77. Sandel, *Justice*, 187.
78. Grenz and Smith, *Pocket Dictionary of Ethics*, 104.
79. Marshall, *Little Book of Biblical Justice*, 45.

The TRC also admits that restorative justice was undermined by the lack of the responsibility of perpetrators and because they did not take "responsibility for some form of restitution."[80] Depersonalizing evil is, in this regard, allowing perpetrators to take full advantage of forgiveness and reconciliation to cover up the evils they have committed.[81]

Nonetheless, King, Suu Kyi, and Wink, when depersonalizing evil, assert that there is no such justice that disregards punishment. King stressed the importance of the active rule of law, as he said,

> Morality cannot be legislated, but behaviour can be regulated. Judicial decrees may not change the heart, but they can restrain the heartless. The law cannot make an employer love an employee, but it can prevent him from refusing to hire me because of the colour of my skin . . . Let us not be misled by those who argue that segregation cannot be ended by the force of law.[82]

In the same way, both Wink and Suu Kyi also emphatically talk about the importance of the rule of law. If the rule of law were firmly established, justice would be done. For example, if a person steals, murders, or does something against the established law, that person would be disciplined according to the law. In this sense, depersonalization of evil is, for King, Suu Kyi, and Wink, not perverting the justice system. So the counter-question should be: what would happen if we intermix individuals and their deeds in a nonviolent struggle? Obviously, the evildoers would be personified as demonic. There would be two divisions: we (the nonviolent activists) are good, and they (the opponents) are evil. Thus, everything would go well if they were defeated. Nonviolent resistance would be no different from the use of violence. Finally, the aim of nonviolence would also be a disguised form of revenge. In short, separating a person from what they do should be seen in the light of other

---

80. Hamber, *Transforming Societies*, 132–133.

81. The same thing happens in Myanmar, too. Generals who ruled the country ruthlessly state that the public should not look back and dig deep into what the generals did in the past to find the crimes they perpetrated. The majority of the generals are averting their faces from what they did. The next chapter will discuss this in more detail.

82. King, *Strength to Love*, 34.

principles like the rule of law, the Beloved Community, democratization, and the realization of the DFO.

Nonviolence as Spiritual Revolution

Suu Kyi is committed to a revolution of the spirit, whereas Wink is emphatic about the spirituality of institutions, nations, and the Christian church. What they have in common is, of course, rendering the spiritual dimension into socio-political activism. Unlike them, King does not employ the words "spirit" or "spirituality" in defining his idea of nonviolence. What do Suu Kyi and Wink mean by spiritual or spirituality when they talk about it? How do they differ from each other? How can they enhance each other? How should King's nonviolence be comprehended through the eyes of Suu Kyi and Wink?

First and foremost, the spirit or spirituality Suu Kyi and Wink are articulating is not an unseen realm where actual spirit-beings interfere in human affairs or mysterious experiences. Both Suu Kyi and Wink, as products of modern western education, apparently pay no attention to the actual existence of spirit-beings. What they do instead is have a great regard for the interiority of a person or institution, which they call spirituality. In other words, Suu Kyi looks at the interiority of a person, whereas Wink focuses on that of an individual as well as an institution. By spiritual revolution, Suu Kyi refers to de-internalization of the values of the old system in order to re-internalize the democratic values. She believes that the way to transformation is through self-exertion. The important thing, in her view, is to internalize for oneself the values of human rights and democracy, which are in opposition to the dictatorial ideologies. For instance, the Dalai Lama perceives the difficulty of bringing about peace through the internal transformation of an individual. But he affirms that it is the only way. Peace must be, for him, first developed within an individual; love, compassion and altruism are the fundamental basis for peace.[83] Hence, Suu Kyi's revolution of the spirit can be summed up as facing the truth in oneself and changing it by self-effort.

In reviewing the idea of Suu Kyi's revolution of the spirit, an activist from Myanmar, Min Zin, contends that the dissidents from Myanmar tend to make a "we-they" distinction; as a result, there seems to be no continuity

---

83. Dalai Lama, "Foreword," in *Peace is Every Step*, vii.

between the previous regime and themselves. The we-they distinction here refers to the military being seen as a villain, whereas the dissidents regard themselves as the saviours of the country. In fact, there is no such distinction, argues Min Zin. He points out that the government was not, in fact, a foreign body, but they were among the dissidents because the people of Myanmar have been moulded by a closed society under their rule for many decades.[84] Unfortunately, a number of dissidents are unaware of those influences. So Min Zin states, "When we look at the mirror of military dictatorship carefully, we can find out some parts of our face."[85] As a result of the military dictatorship, democratic values and practices could be seen even among those dissidents, despite their fighting for democracy. In short, the influence of the military rule upon all the public – whether dissidents or not and whether they are conscious of it or not – is so immense that it is questionable whether a person could withstand such an overpowering presence.

Suu Kyi's revolution of the spirit through Min Zin's exposition is akin to the idea of Wink's domination system. The power of the DS is so deceptive that even many social and political activists are swayed to believe in redemptive violence. Therefore, Wink insists that what has to be done is to step out of that world, where violence is always the ultimate solution, into another world, where nonviolence is understood as the only transformative method. He also views nonviolent resistance as a double movement of psychic energy. For Wink, we identify our enemies as evil, and so unconsciously project our own evil onto our enemies. But what we neglect is that our enemies also evoke the evil within us. This is the two-way traffic of projection and introjection. With nonviolence, we are challenged to face this inner darkness inside us. As such, Suu Kyi and Wink are both convinced that nonviolence is not an easy way of life.

Unlike Suu Kyi and Wink, King concentrates on the inner strength of a person in expounding the notion of nonviolence, instead of using terms such as spirit or spiritual. For him, nonviolence is not passive and submissive, but active. In other words, nonviolent resistance might be bodily passive, yet it is spiritually active. So he regards nonviolent resistance as the way of the strong

---

84. See Zin, "Spiritual Revolution."
85. Zin, "Spiritual Revolution."

person, not the method of a coward. In the Montgomery Bus Boycott, King encouraged the protesters, "If another person is being molested, do not arise to go to his defence, but pray for the oppressor and use moral and spiritual force to carry on the struggle for justice."[86] In saying that, King was aware that there were a number of blacks who used nonviolence as a tactic, not as a principle. So this spiritual activism is important not only for advocates of principled nonviolence, but also for those of pragmatic nonviolence. So for King, nonviolent resistance is also a kind of spiritual activism because it requires a great deal of inner strength.

Wink and Suu Kyi understand that nonviolence is truly revolutionary because it disallows the we-they distinction – the discontinuity between the enemies and us. In contrast, the logic of nonviolence for King seems to be this: enemies are evil and wrong; we (the nonviolent activists) are good and right; therefore, we are called to make them good and right. But Wink and Suu Kyi discern another dimension that is missing in King's notion of nonviolence. That is what Wink calls "self-righteousness." Wink and Suu Kyi support nonviolent resistance as a spiritual discipline because it deters the we-they syndrome – we are good, but our enemies are bad. The logic of nonviolence, for Suu Kyi and Wink, is that everyone (our enemies and ourselves) is imperfect; nonviolence is good and right; therefore, only through nonviolence can everyone (our enemies and ourselves) exert themselves to be good and right, because nonviolence has transformative power for us as well as for our enemies.

Wink furthers our understanding of spirituality from a personal to an impersonal circle. As discussed, nonviolence is a personal spiritual discipline, yet spirituality for Wink does not end there because the Powers against which nonviolent activists resist also have, despite the impersonality of their nature, an interiority or spirituality. Wink suggests that every collective entity that has continuity through time has an angel. By angel, Wink does not mean an otherworldly celestial personal being. Angel here means the actual spirituality of a nation or institution as a single entity. The angel would then exist in, with, and under the material expressions of the nation's life as its interiority.[87]

---

86. King, *Stride toward Freedom*, 158.
87. Wink, *Unmasking the Powers*, 70.

From this Winkian perspective, King and Suu Kyi, in their nonviolent struggles, opposed the interiority or spirituality of the systems in their respective nations by exercising their spiritual discipline. In that sense, King's spiritual revolution was the revolution of the racist spirituality of America, whereas Suu Kyi's revolution was that of the despotic spirituality of Myanmar. Segregation was deeply rooted and thereby becoming a spirituality of the States. Similarly, the dictatorial mentality was so strongly instituted that it became the spirituality of the nation, Myanmar. With this Winkian eye, the struggles of King and Suu Kyi can be understood profoundly in the sense that nonviolent resistance is more than socio-political activism. Rather, it is a revolution that can transform human society and individuals.

Nonviolence and Suffering

Wink, King and Suu Kyi all acknowledge the inevitability of suffering, sacrifices, and pain in the nonviolent struggle. For King, unearned suffering is redemptive. Originally, he adapted this idea from Mohandas Gandhi, but later he conceptualized it in the Christian term, "cross-bearing." Cross-bearing is, for him, redemptive because it is the power of God in social and individual salvation. In Christian teaching, cross-bearing is a very important subject.[88] For Dietrich Bonhoeffer, it is not the sort of suffering that is inseparable from mortal life, but the suffering that is an essential part of the specifically Christian life.[89] Bonhoeffer was profoundly convinced of how it is costly to follow Christ in the context of a totalitarian regime, because he himself lived in the time of Adolf Hitler. In one of his books, Bonhoeffer states that, "the 'must' of suffering applies to his disciples no less than to himself . . ., so the disciple is a disciple only in so far as he shares his Lord's suffering and rejection and crucifixion."[90] Bonhoeffer's understanding of suffering is not limited merely to the atonement theory; he applies Jesus's death to the domain of the Christian life.

---

88. Matt 16:24–27.
89. Bonhoeffer, *Cost of Discipleship*, 88.
90. Bonhoeffer, 97.

In the studies of Christ's crucifixion, much attention is paid to his death as atonement.[91] In any atonement theory, what must be considered is that the cross not only demonstrates God's justice and love, but also directs our conduct in relation to others, including our enemies.[92] Darrin W. Snyder Belousek examines the mission of the church in the light of the cross. For him, Jesus died for us "to set us free from sin and reconcile us to God, so that we might willingly enter our role as obedient servants of God's purpose."[93] The mystic Saint John of the Cross, in meditation on Jesus's crucifixion, mentions that, "true spirituality seeks for bitterness rather than sweetness in God, inclines to suffering more than consolation."[94] King's view of cross-bearing, though learned from Gandhi, is a genuinely Christian way of comprehending the cross.

Similarly, Suu Kyi, as a political activist, believes that she has been working for something worthwhile – democracy, for which she knows that sacrifices are inescapable. Using a Buddhist term, Suu Kyi articulates that sacrifice and *mettā* go hand in hand. Thus it is the sort of sacrifice of a mother sacrificing herself out of her *mettā* for her child.[95] To describe the suffering incurred by nonviolent resistance, King used the phrase "unearned suffering," whereas Suu Kyi employs the word "sacrifice." No matter which word – suffering or sacrifice – what makes them similar is that suffering is inescapable to nonviolent activists.

---

91. There are a number of atonement theories, according to which Jesus's death is read in salvific terms. A theory, known as Moral Example, regards Jesus's death as the perfect example to follow.

92. Stott, *Cross of Christ*, 295.

93. Snyder Belousek, *Atone, Justice and Peace*, 613.

94. Burrows, *Ascent to Love*, 80.

95. Kyi and Clements, *Voice of Hope*, 40. In the later life, Suu Kyi began to be strange. In the speech given at Tokyo University in 2013, she states, "I would like to talk about the word 'sacrifice.' People talk a lot about the word sacrifice. I find it personally rather embarrassing when people talk about the sacrifices I have made. Because I don't think I have made any sacrifices," https://www.youtube.com/watch?v=311BI-5PPyo&t=911s. Peter Popham comments on that, "Suu Kyi has often faced the charge of being hard-hearted. If true it could be forgiven, considering the great stakes for which she has played and is still playing. But wrapped up in this Tokyo meditation of hers on sacrifice and free will one detects something worse – a ravenous egotism that perhaps the years of isolation only made worse," see Popham, *Lady and the Generals*, 227.

In Wink's understanding, nonviolence is not passive, as some misunderstand it to be; rather, it is active. To be specific, it is not a way of avoiding personal sacrifice. However, Wink differs from King concerning redemptive suffering. For King, suffering is the transformative power of God. In contrast, Wink looks at sacrifice and suffering from the point of view of Jesus's death and crucifixion. For Wink, what made Jesus unique was not his suffering, persecution, or death. Rather, Jesus's uniqueness lay in his total rejection of complicity in violence. What is more, his arraignment, trial, crucifixion and death also unmasked the scapegoating mechanism. With this view, Wink considers that the deaths of other people like King, Gandhi, and Oscar Romero also reflect the same truth that was revealed in Jesus. Instead of arguing if suffering is redemptive or not, suffering and sacrifices for nonviolent struggles primarily, for Wink, unmask the DS.[96] This view of suffering specifies what nonviolent resistance truly resists. That is, nonviolent resistance resists the Powers that worked visibly and invisibly behind all institutions, organizations, and nations. But King's view of redemptive suffering and Suu Kyi's idea of sacrificing out of *mettā* should not be discarded in preference of the idea of unmasking the system by absorbing violence and suffering. Wink's view of suffering in the nonviolent struggle is structurally focused because it primarily seeks to unmask the unseen powers. Thus, Wink's view reminds us never to succumb to violence in nonviolent resistance, because if we do, no distinction between violence and nonviolence can be made.

On the contrary, redemptive suffering, for King, and the courage to sacrifice out of *mettā*, for Suu Kyi, are psychologically concerned. King argued that we could transform suffering into a creative force if we respond to it without bitterness.[97] It is true that suffering or sacrifice, if responded to with bitterness, can make someone aggressive, resentful, and vengeful, and that surely leads to violence. But, if taken as a virtue or creative force, suffering can transform one's self. Of course, suffering is not a justification to prove whether a person is right. In the form of a question, for what reason do we suffer? The logic of suffering is: I am suffering, therefore what I am doing is right. Instead, do what is right and be prepared to suffer or sacrifice. If we

---

96. Wink, *Powers That Be*, 86–87.
97. King, *Testament of Hope*, 47.

juxtapose King, Suu Kyi and Wink, unearned suffering or sacrifice can, if taken as a virtue, do two things: transform our ego and unmask the real powers behind institutions, organizations, and nations. In nonviolent struggles, we have seen the inevitability of suffering and sacrifices; thus, being prepared to deal with them is always necessary for all nonviolent activists.

Nonviolence and Hope

Is there any connection between nonviolence and hope? Irrespective of whether they are pragmatic or principled, all activists, when they take a nonviolent path, have a desired end in mind. That is, they all begin with the hope that the resistance they take part in will be brought to fruition. Nonviolent resistance is always achievement-based, having hopes and expectations. If hope is an essential ingredient in the nonviolent struggle, what is its source?

Both King and Suu Kyi have the similar conviction that justice eventually prevails. For King, it was this belief in justice and a God who works with humans to create a humane society. That belief led King to stand firm in the civil rights movement until his assassination. Suu Kyi, as a Buddhist, also believes in the human potentiality to do good, so she often said, "saints are sinners who go on trying."[98] These beliefs truly infused both King and Suu Kyi with hope. Thus, they both were able to persist in their struggles against the dominating systems.

In Wink's eyes, there is an absolute and unshakable confidence that the domination system has an end. If there is a time of the reign of right, a chance of justice being done, and a time for the DS to be ended, when will that time come? For Suu Kyi, it all depends on how much effort we put into it, irrespective of hurdles. As a Buddhist, she believes in self-effort, so she characterizes herself as a trier, one who never gives up trying to be a better person. She always discourages the passive onlookers, who just sit there and hope that things will happen. But King, as a personalist, believed that faith in God entails human participation in God's activity. For him, it is not possible to solve the race problem simply through human endeavours, but only by participating with God. Human beings cannot do it alone and God will not

---

98. Kyi and Clements, *Voice of Hope*, 121.

do it alone either. What is needed is our cooperation with God, so that we will be able to build a better world.

In Wink's understanding, the DS is already broken and the God's domination-free order has already been inaugurated in our world through Jesus Christ's death and resurrection. The DFO or the reign of God is not merely in the future, it is also in the present. What we can all do is not try to save the world, but to act as if the world can be transformed. True, the presence of the DS might be still overwhelming in our current situation, yet Christ's victory has already been realized. This victory is what sustains faith; this faith is what enables victory. From the Winkian perspective, the belief that "the universe is on the side of justice" is, to an extreme degree, forward-looking and so is Suu Kyi's conviction that "in the end, right will prevail."[99] For both King and Suu Kyi, their hope is principally concerned with the future and seemingly has no connection with the present. In contrast, Wink's hope is not merely forward-looking, but also something that can be experienced in the present reign of God – the DFO is not too far distant from the historic grounds. The Winkian understanding offers us more concrete hope for the DFO than King and Suu Kyi do.

6.4 What If . . . or Self-Defence?

There are some unavoidable questions for every nonviolent activist such as, what if you are attacked by robbers? What if someone intrudes into your house and strikes your wife and children? Should we steal to feed our children? King did not ask the what if questions, but that of self-defence. Brutalities, maltreatments, and discriminations were encountered daily by blacks in the time of King. Thus, it was not a matter of choice but that of how to respond to such discrimination. In a nutshell, what if questions are for King fundamentally tentative and indeterminate; that is, someone might face such attacks or not. For blacks, various forms of discrimination and attacks on the basis of racial difference were day-to-day experiences. King, from the time he was fully committed to nonviolence as a philosophy for life, tried to stick to the principles of nonviolence in whatever circumstance. Suu Kyi, as a present politician, does not concern herself with what if questions like many ethicists

---

99. Kyi and Clements, 171.

do. Obviously, aggressive political maltreatment had been daily intruding on her and other dissidents during the previous military regime. What she and others, in turn, could do was decide how to respond to it, whether through flight, fight or nonviolent resistance. Under the suppression of aggressive injustice, many opposition parties were disestablished, and many political dissidents lost heart. Some have still persisted in their struggles. Suu Kyi and the NLD, of course, have persevered in their nonviolent struggle for the cause of democracy. In short, what if questions are not convincing and practical enough for King and Suu Kyi; thus, they are speculative for both of them. Once they have chosen nonviolent resistance, they live it out according to its principles.

But Wink, as a theorist and an activist, attempts to deal with the what if dilemma. For Wink, these questions imply that there is misunderstanding behind them. That is, the myth of redemptive violence is so entrenched that we are inured to it; therefore it seems to be almost impossible for us to think of any way except the use of violence. Another important fact is that neither violence nor nonviolence guarantees success. Nonviolence might fail where violence would fail; nonviolence might work where violence would work. However, violence might fail where nonviolence would work. Despite highlighting nonviolence over violence, Wink is aware of some special contexts in which violence is unavoidable. For example, consider an oppressive regime that has constrained all the opportunities for justice, and the people are left in despair. In such circumstances, Wink suggests that violence is a kind of apocalyptic judgment.[100] However, this does not mean that violence in that situation is justifiable because choosing either lesser or greater evil is still evil. In that case, Christians should not try to judge those who take up violence out of desperation. In saying that, Wink sees the world as being imperfect and sometimes circumstances are complex. Nevertheless, violence, for Christians, should not be an option in any situation.

Furthermore, Wink highlights the importance of nurturing a nonviolent lifestyle corporately as well as individually. He perceives how our society desperately needs people like Leo Tolstoy, Mohandas Gandhi, King and Suu Kyi. Neither King nor Suu Kyi were born and bred in a culture of nonviolence.

---

100. Wink, *Powers That Be*, 158.

Nonviolence has to be nurtured, enhanced, and cultivated, says Wink. At the same time, it should not be overlooked that the world in which we live is imperfect; thus, we should not expect that nonviolence will always succeed in any circumstance. Suu Kyi knows that there are some situations where there is no option for nonviolence. But King seemed to not allow any room for violence. Nonviolence, for him, is by no means a choice. That means that if nonviolence is temporarily discarded, it would be non-existent. What King and Suu Kyi have in common is that they both have nurtured their lives to be nonviolent in every way. King always urged and challenged his people to discard violence and stick to nonviolence. Likewise, Suu Kyi also encourages her people to be nonviolent even though she grants recognition to those who fought with arms for freedom. Wink so illuminates the importance of cultivating the culture of nonviolence so that people like King and Suu Kyi might rise up in the next generation.

6.5 Nonviolence and the Church

On his return from South Africa to India in 1915, Gandhi founded the *ashram* or monastery, which was later called *Satyagraha Ashram*, in Ahmedabad, India, with a purpose to lead a simple life of prayer, study, manual work and helping the local people.[101] *Ashram* was home to Mohandas Gandhi from 1917 until 1930 and served as one of the main centres of the Indian freedom struggle. It was also home to the ideology that set India free.[102] In the civil rights movement, the church played a vital role. For King, the church was "a second home."[103] The church was the primary source from which he gained spiritual, emotional and social strength to persevere in the struggle. Suu Kyi also recognizes the great force of the church in political or social movements across the globe. However, Buddhists are, unlike Christians, not organized around their monasteries.[104]

King, despite having a high regard for the church as a second home, did not articulate the role of the church when he discussed nonviolence. But

---

101. Rawding, *Gandhi*, 29.
102. Gandhi Ashram, "History."
103. Carson, *Autobiography of Martin Luther King*, 6.
104. Kyi and Clements, *Voice of Hope*, 152.

Wink has a clear understanding of the role of the church in nonviolence. The church, for him, is called to nonviolence to express its fidelity to Jesus Christ who taught and practiced nonviolence. This call to nonviolence is a matter of discipleship because nonviolence is God's way of dealing with evil in the world. So when the church is called to nonviolence, the call is not for pragmatic reasons, but ontological, because nonviolence reflects the very nature of God.

But Wink's ecclesiology is inclusive, and he makes no distinction between the church and other social groups. That is, the church has no special role to play in society, but is just one of the social groups that struggle to humanize the Powers – nothing more, nothing less. The church, for him, is not the only group which God has assigned to liberate us from the deception of the Powers. The church is, like other institutions in society, fallen and idolatrous.[105] However, Wink insists that the church must affirm nonviolence without reservation, because nonviolence is the way to the DFO. In short, Wink views the church, like other institutions, as an organized social group to disempower the Powers so that they may be liberated from the derailment of divine purpose. Nonviolence is forceful and powerful when it is collectively and corporately employed. In this sense, the church would become a social power to liberate the Powers when it holds steadfastly to nonviolence.

6.6 Summary of the Chapter

This chapter brings the ethical and political ideals of King and Suu Kyi into dialogue with a Winkian perspective of the Powers. In this dialogue, I have examined their views of nonviolence in three areas: leadership, religion and the ethical principles of nonviolence. The reason I have done so is that nonviolence, if it is to be regarded as more than a means to an end, must encompass many aspects of life, such as leadership, religion and ethical implications. Nonviolence must have significant implications for leadership. Therefore, in the next chapter, I will argue how the philosophy of nonviolence can create a culture of leadership, which is not based on power to control, but on power to nurture. Next, it is extremely clear that religion profoundly guided and shaped the lives and works of King and Suu Kyi. We cannot appropriately

---

105. Walter Wink, *Powers That Be*, 29.

study King's ethic of nonviolence without any understanding of Christianity. Likewise, we cannot study Suu Kyi's idea of nonviolence unless we have some comprehension of Buddhism. Hence the dialogue between King and Suu Kyi via the Winkian perspective will also be, in a later chapter, a guide to express the integral relationship between Christianity and Buddhism in the context of Myanmar.

Finally, this chapter also discussed the principles of nonviolence adopted by King and Suu Kyi in the light of Wink's *Powers*. I have examined a number of areas of correspondence between King, Suu Kyi and Wink in their views of nonviolence despite religious differences. This chapter demonstrates that Wink's view of the Powers is comprehensive enough to see the world as the DS and nonviolence as the only justifiable means to achieve another order, which is the DFO. True, King and Suu Kyi also each have their ultimate desired ends, which are similar to Wink's DFO. What makes Wink distinct is his view of the DS, the DFO, and the means of transformation from the former to the latter. In a nutshell, Wink's view is, as a whole, a comprehensive view that illuminates and sharpens the ideas of King and Suu Kyi. In the next chapter, I will examine how power, violence and religion in the politics of Myanmar have been practiced in history, and how they are interconnected in engaging the politics of Myanmar with King, Suu Kyi, and Wink. This examination will be, in one way or another, a critical assessment of the political culture of Myanmar from a Christian perspective by an integrated lens of Wink, King and Suu Kyi. This will provide the data for chapter 8 or the conclusion of the thesis to draw some political and theological implications for Christians in Myanmar.

CHAPTER 7

Engaging with the Politics of Myanmar through Wink, King and Suu Kyi

This research explores the political context of Myanmar through a dialogue between Martin Luther King Jr, Aung San Suu Kyi, and Walter Wink. In the last chapter, I discussed King, Suu Kyi and Wink in regard to the issues of violence, nonviolence, leadership, religion, and ethics. It shows that a leader who practices nonviolence, pragmatic or principled, can hardly become a tyrant or authoritarian, since the power in the notion of nonviolence is exercised to nurture and support, not to control or kill. Religion is paradoxical, in that it can be emancipatory or enslaving depending on our interpretation and the way we practice it. Nonviolence, whether it is pragmatic or principled, is morally centred on love or *mettā*, because it seeks not a win-lose, but win-win solution.

Now the study has come to its final part, which is to locate the dialogue between King, Suu Kyi and Wink in the political context of Myanmar. The discussion will be directed at areas such as leadership, religion, politics, ethics, and reconciliation. As today's Myanmar is, politically speaking, a rapidly changing nation in Asia, the study needs to be brought up to date with the recent political development of the country. Thus, I will also discuss the future of Myanmar in the last part of this chapter: how the elected National League for Democracy (NLD) has been struggling with the challenges and difficulties in cultivating a culture of democracy during the five years of their rule.

7.1 Violence, Power-Struggles, and Buddhism: A Historical Review

The nation of Myanmar is made up of a diverse range of communities that have continued to influence the distinctive nature of politics.[1] In order to discuss this complex political landscape, and particularly the interconnections between power, religion, and violence, a description of key aspects of the history that produced the contemporary politics of Myanmar is required, covering precolonial (monarchical), colonial, and post-independence Myanmar. From this, further reflections connecting Aung San Suu Kyi, Martin Luther King Jr and Walter Wink to the political environment of Myanmar will be made. Regarding Wink's idea of the domination system, this examination will lead the thesis to validate or invalidate the presence of the DS in the political tradition of Myanmar.

7.1.1 Monarchical Period

Kings of Myanmar are infamous for their violence and cruelty against their rivals. The use of violence in seizing and retaining power was a common factor among the monarchs of Myanmar throughout the precolonial period. To illustrate the point, the founder of the first empire, Anawrahta (1044–1097), became king by slaying his older brother. As a consequence, he had sleepless nights for six months until Sakra (the ruler of the Universe in the Buddhist cosmology) came to him in a dream and said,

---

1. Andrew Selth has surveyed modern Burma studies and noted another group of scholars, the Western Academics, by presumptuously considering a democracy as the best form of government, are denying the Burmese their own indigenous cultural norms, see Selth, "Modern Burma Studies," 425. In particular, Aung-Thwin, "Parochial Universalism," 483–505; Taylor, "Burma's Ambiguous Breakthrough," 62–72. Maitrii Aung-Thwin also argues the importance of reading Myanmar. He suggests that the importance is not how we write about Myanmar, but how we read and interpret it. For example, Maitrii looks at the "reader-response" theory that focuses on the processes of interpreting, the strategies employed, and the contexts that produce the interpretations rather than the differences in the interpretations themselves, see Aung-Thwin, "Introduction," 187–188. I use Myanmar and Burma interchangeably without any preference for either one. So, I will use either word depending on the sources I cite or in reference to the time that the regime changed the name. But, in describing the adjective form, I will tend to use Burmese instead of Myanmar.

> O King, if thou wouldst mitigate thine evil deed in sinning against thine elder brother, build many pagodas, *gu*, monasteries, and rest houses, and share the merit with thine elder brother. Devise thou many wells, ponds, dams and ditches, fields, and canals, and share the merit with thine elder brother.[2]

Anawrahta fulfilled the dream to atone for his evil deed. From then on, the belief that meritorious acts can compensate for evil deeds was birthed. Many kings after Anawrahta followed that tradition. Tabinshweti (1531–1550), who massacred in extending his kingdom, atoned for his cruelty by placing new spires on Mon pagodas and making a costly offering at the Shwe Dagon Pagoda.[3] Anawrahta was also a zealous Buddhist, who led a thorough reform of religion in the country and promoted Theravada Buddhism during his rule. His enthusiasm for Buddhism led him to declare war on the Mons (the Talaings) because he wanted the Buddhist Scriptures, the Tripitaka from them.[4] He spent most of his life collecting Buddha's holy relics. At the same time, Anawrahta never tolerated any potential challengers to his throne. Thus, the late scholar of Myanmar, Mya Maung, observed that in Anawrahta, the two requisite qualities of an ideal ruler, the sacred priestly person and the mighty warrior, were fused together to form a role model for his successors. The story of Anawrahta seems to have left the legacy of purging and destroying many potential challengers to the throne or "the next king-to-be," *min-lawns*, under the advice of Brahmin astrologers, *ponnars*, and soothsayers – a practice revived and most vehemently followed by the military dictatorship of Ne Win during his reign.[5] As the builder of the first Burmese empire, the legacy he left had a tremendous impact on later generations, even up until the postcolonial rulers, the first Prime Ministers Nu, Ne Win, and Than Shwe.[6]

What is more, violence for the sake of unifying the country was also a characteristic of the monarchs of Myanmar. Anawrahta consolidated various

---

2. Tin and Luce, *Glass Palace Chronicle*, 65.
3. Hall, *Burma*, 7.
4. Stuart, *Burma Through the Centuries*, 29.
5. Maung, *Burma Road to Poverty*, 21.
6. The impact of Burmese monarchs on modern Burmese politicians will be discussed more in the following as needed.

tribes into a single nation. To maintain the consolidation, he was ruthless and stern to all his subjects, for he believed that harsh measures were effective means to build a new nation.[7] Likewise, Alaung-mintaya's unification of Myanmar (the founder of the third Myanmar empire, 1752–1760) was cemented with the blood of his victims.[8] Furthermore, the kings of Myanmar never tolerated any form of rivals. Lucian W. Pye writes, "The last Burmese king, on coming to the throne in 1878, sought to eliminate all possible contenders by executing his eighty half-brothers and sisters – since royal blood could not be shed, he had his relatives tied up in sacks and trampled by white elephants."[9] Seizing power and retaining it through various forms of violence was a distinct feature of politics in Myanmar during the monarchical period. The belief that all the evils a king committed for the sake of gaining and maintaining power can be compensated for makes the politics of Myanmar distinct. Therefore, monarchs in Myanmar are perhaps notorious for their ruthless and cruel kingships. Historian Than Tun succinctly remarks that there are two distinct features of Burmese kingship: these are the right to rule first through conquest and second through descent. Of these two features, the former is the most important, and thus there were frequent rebellions from royal cousins, massacres of the king's men, and blood purges whenever the throne was in danger.[10]

Besides, the idea of the Burmese kingship was in some measure tailored to the Buddhist doctrine of *karma*. To a Buddhist from Myanmar, all the current conditions – good or bad, high or low, glory or disgrace – are not the consequences of what a person has done now, but what that person did previously in life. If a king is powerful enough that no one can dethrone him, it means that his *karma* is superior to and greater than all other opponents. Otherwise, if a rebel can overthrow a king, it means that the king's *karma* was insufficient to maintain the throne.[11] Put another way, the power

---

7. Maung Htin Aung, *History of Burma*, 37.
8. Jesse, *Story of Burma*, 16.
9. Pye, *Politics, Personality, and National Building*, 67.
10. Tun, *Modern History of Myanmar*, 91.
11. Lieberman, *Burmese Administrative Cycles*, 75. In fact, the doctrine of *karma* was politicized from the early period of Pagan. Taylor, *State in Myanmar*, 60; Aung-Thwin and Aung-Thwin, *History of Myanmar*, 85; Spiro, *Buddhism and Society*, 442–443.

struggle in the politics of Myanmar is a *karma* struggle between a king and his rivals. This notion of *karma* significantly underpins the traditional view in Myanmar that, "He who kills a king must be a king." Finally, the way monarchs of Myanmar exercised power was absolute. The king was not subject to any law – religious, legal, social, or otherwise. He was the supreme ruler, and his word was law. No constitutional boundary was there to check and limit the autocracy of the king. The king was the most powerful person in the state and being the lord of land and water; he was also the lord of life and death as the land and water were the sources of all life. There was also no organized form of government in the Burmese kingship. The king and his favourites exercised power and authority as they wished. This resulted in sycophancy, bribery and corruption.[12]

However, some patriotic authors from Myanmar argue that the kings were not despotic. They were not exempt from the operation of the civil law. These authors have tried to validate their argument by quoting Buddhist teaching on the ten moral precepts (or ten duties) of a king and other kingly rules.[13] Maung Maung Gyi counters this, saying, "If it were true, Burmese kings would be the most perfect in this world."[14] John Cady also points out that there were, of course, some occasions when monks urged the deposition of unworthy monarchs, led revolts, aided royal personages to escape, and one even acted as regent. But the Myanmar court chronicles show that the king brooked no clerical challenge to his authority over the state.[15] It was only in theory that the king was expected to observe the rules of kingship; in reality, the king was accountable to no power or authority.[16] Than Tun remarks, "the only limitation to a king's powers was his voluntary respect for Buddhist rule and precepts to rule with kindness. Otherwise, he was the lord and master of

---

12. Tun, "History of Buddhism in Burma," 39. See also Tun, *Modern History of Myanmar*, 89–90.

13. These duties are known as *dasavidha rajadhamma* in Pali. Asoka (304–232 BCE) was known as the king who practiced those ten *rajadhamma*. He ruled India for forty-one years. He was a great warrior general and won many battlers. After he embraced Buddha's teachings, Asoka endeavoured to establish a just kingdom. Thus, he was known as "Dhammasoka," meaning "pious Asoka." See "Buddhism by Numbers."

14. Gyi, *Burmese Political Values*, 21.

15. Cady, "Religion and Politics," 151.

16. Silverstein, "Evolution and Salience," 14.

the life."[17] In brief, the autocracy of the king during the monarchical period was absolute. Therefore nothing, not even Buddhism, was able to inhibit his power unless he wanted it to be so.

While his critique of monarchs in Myanmar is sometimes very sharp, Lucian Pye was moderate in commenting on the psyche of Myanmar politics. For him, the politics is paradoxical in nature: on the one hand, it is characterized by gentleness, religiosity, and a commitment to the qualities of virtue; on the other hand, it is also typified by violence, malicious scheming, and devious thinking. Therefore, he concludes, "any study which concentrates on one to the exclusion of the other will give a distorted picture of the total range of Burmese politics."[18] Similarly, the late Mya Maung scrutinized the twin mystic qualities of a Myanmar king: a just and benevolent ruler with a Buddha-like personality belonging to the nonviolent agricultural caste and also a conqueror of all enemies belonging to the Shatriyan caste of warriors.[19] If so, to whom did the kings of Myanmar show gentleness, benevolence and religiosity? And to whom did they become violent, devious and malicious? Looking back on some characteristics of kings in Myanmar, they were aggressive, devious and malicious to all the potential challengers or rivals to their thrones, whereas they showed kindness, gentleness and benevolent treatment merely to the unquestioning, obedient, sycophants and opportunists. The kings gave huge favour and opportunities to those who obeyed unquestioningly, so long as they did not pose any kind of threat to their power. So far, we can conclude that the practice of power during the monarchical era was the power to control and destroy; violence was massively employed to retain power; and the role of religion in politics was to legitimate the rule of kings. Therefore, the characteristics of the DS were deeply prevailing during the monarchical age. We will see if those characteristics of political culture continued in the colonial period.

---

17. Tun, *Modern History of Myanmar*, 91.
18. Pye, *Spirit of Burmese Politics*, 15–16.
19. Maung, *Burma Road to Poverty*, 18.

7.1.2 Colonial Period

Violence in the name of peace and order continued to prevail throughout the colonial era. Right after Britain annexed the whole nation of Myanmar in 1885, numerous resistances broke out across the country. The fighting took place for five years (1885–1890). The Burmans, who considered themselves conquerors, now repeatedly encountered failures under British attacks.[20] Those fighting years were, according to the British government, called the "Pacification of Burma."[21] As a result, the guerrillas of Myanmar and many villagers were massacred.[22] The British army had in great measure pacified the whole nation in 1890. However, rebellions continued sporadically throughout the entire colonial period.[23] According to Mary Callahan, the Burmese learned the power of the British-Indian army, against which they could not win. This greatly influenced the development of future military and civil institutions in Myanmar.[24] Htin Aung also observes that the people of Myanmar began to accept the fact that the military might of the British was superior to theirs.[25] In short, the British army power made a long-lasting impression on the people of Myanmar, in such a manner that they believed that there was no way to defeat the British, except by creating an army mightier than that of the British.

Moreover, there were some nationalist movements during the colonial era. Initially, the movements were mainly concerned about Buddhism and the decline of civilization in Myanmar. Later, the nationalist movements became engaged in politics. The majority of Buddhist monks were also actively involved in the movements. For example, U Ottama (1897–1939) and U Wisara (1888–1929), were the leading monks. Ottama was, according to Michael

---

20. Burmans here refers to the majority ethnic group, which is dominant in all aspects of the country Burma.

21. Aung, *Stricken Peacock*, 95.

22. Sir Charles Crosthwaite was a chief commissioner for the whole of Burma and served until 1890. He was known as a ruthless administrator among Burmans and he introduced carefully measures to frighten the villagers into submission. He published a book, *Pacification of Burma* in 1912, which was originally his own records of pacifying Burma.

23. Holliday, *Burma Redux*, 32.

24. Callahan, *Making Enemies*, 25.

25. Aung, *History of Burma*, 267–268.

Mendelson, more ardent and aggressive than other nationalist monks.[26] But Wisara went on hunger strike in prison and died after 166 days.[27]

The most political nationalist movement that emerged in the 1930s was the "Dobama Asiayone" (We Burmans Association) or the "Thakin Party."[28] Suu Kyi's father, Aung San, was a leading figure. The leaders of the Association searched for better means to struggle against the British. They heard about Gandhi's nonviolent resistance in India. However, the leaders of the Association, including Aung San, felt that submissive obedience to the use of force and weapons by the enemy was against the character of the people of Myanmar and their history and traditions. According to Angelene Naw, a biographer of Aung San, the younger generation of Thakin leaders adopted a more aggressive method in working towards the independence of Myanmar. In short, the colonial period has left one lasting imprint in the mind of the people of Myanmar and that is the significance of military might in politics.

What is more, another long-lasting legacy that the colonial period left is corruption – the way the colonial state handled it. The corruption during the colonial state was pervasive. In a recent study on the corruption during the colonial Myanmar, Jonathan Saha discovers that at that time "corrupt acts were not aberration from norms of state practice, as high-ranking British officials attempted to depict them."[29] Saha demonstrates a contrast between precolonial and colonial Myanmar through doing a number of case studies on the archives from the colonial period. He observes that local notables in the time of monarchy used bribery to enhance their personal power and build their local followings, thereby challenging to the authority of the ruling powers.

However, the subordinate officials of the colonial state did not commit acts of misconduct in order to increase their patronage manpower, raise an army, and attempt to overthrow the state; instead, they used their power to

---

26. Mendelson, *Sangha and State in Burma*, 205.

27. Donald M. Seekins describes how Wisara went on hunger strike for 166 days, see Seekins, *Historical Dictionary*, 474. But the history textbook in my high school says that it was 120 days. Thus the number of days is uncertain and confusing.

28. Thakin means lord or master. What promoted the young patriots to adopt the word was not love for the word itself but aversion formed when an Englishman or, worse still, an Indian used it in place of Mister, see Yi, *Dobama Movement in Burma*, 3.

29. Saha, *Law, Disorder*, 129.

gain their possessions. Therefore, the corruption and acts of misconducts during the colonial state did not weaken the state; rather, the state was even enacted as a powerful and intrusive entity.[30] Saha's research finding implies that power was overvalued at the expense of moral standards. Nothings seems more valuable than power. It does not matter whatever sacrifice has to be made so long as power is concerned. Maintaining power to the point of being corrupt and violent was at the heart of politics in the time of British Myanmar. Thus, war in the name of peace and corruption for the sake of power are two characteristics that ran deeply in the politics of Myanmar in the time of colonization. This demonstrates that certain characteristics of the DS were still prevalent in politics during the British colonization.

7.1.3 Postcolonial Period

The postcolonial era can be divided into two periods: 1948–1962 (the years of experimenting with democracy) and 1962–2010 (military dictatorship). The years of experimenting with democracy were, in fact, rife with tensions between communism, socialism and capitalism, and between the Burman ethnic majority and various ethnic minorities. Communist and ethnic minority insurgencies were widespread across the country. What is more, the post-war Myanmar in 1948 was already war-torn. Whole infrastructures were devastated, crime rates were skyrocketing, and the economy was declining. Those cries were so intense that the new government of Nu was unable to cope with them. Nu's government was thus sarcastically labelled as the "Rangoon (Yangon) government" because its rule stretched merely within Rangoon.[31] The government's power was not able to extend to other parts of the country.

More than that, the power struggle within the cabinets of parliament was so fierce that Nu mourned in the speech given on 25 May 1948, that,

---

30. Saha, 129. Instead of viewing corruption as a sign of failure in state formation, Saha proposes that it should be studied as a set of deeply embedded modern state practices of long precedent, rather than as recent symptoms of postcolonial weakness. For him, the role corruption has played in the making of the modern state is significant. Through pervasive administrative disorder the colonial state was enacted, and corruption continues to be constitutive of the modern state in contemporary Myanmar (Saha, 132).

31. Callahan, *Making Enemies*, 116.

> I unfortunately found that from the day the AFPFL (Anti-Fascist People's Freedom League) accepted office, some of its members turned away from the path of rectitude ... [one] reason for the deterioration of the AFPFL members lies in the competition for power and influence. "Shall I sink if he wins power? Will he sink if I win power?" these questions are asked and one begins to fear and distrust the others. On account of these suspicions some wish to make sure by seizing power. Others exercising power experience the sweets of office and their desire for power is intensified.[32]

During Nu's government, the most basic religious reform happened. That is, the government established Buddhism as the state religion, which inspired the non-Buddhist minorities to organize to oppose the government. The secessionist movement among ethnic minorities and factionalism within the governing party jeopardized the unity and stability of the nation. Though the first government post-independence attempted to establish democratic politics, it failed because of political ideologies, the division between the Bama majority and ethnic minorities, and enforcing Buddhism as the state religion. As a consequence, General Ne Win overthrew Nu's government on 2 March 1962, and turned the country into a socialist republic, which he called, The Burmese Way to Socialism.

Myanmar reverted to the traditional political system of authoritarian rule when Ne Win ended the parliamentary system. As a consequence, the spirit of the traditional politics was revived; the use of arms and violence for the sake of peace and retaining power was brought back; and all sorts of corruption were tolerated as long as they were not a threat to the state.[33] Ne Win ruled the country for twenty-six years. In 1988, another military regime, known as Than Shwe's government, succeeded him. To sum up, Myanmar has been in a state of unrest and unsteadiness since gaining independence. Ideological uproar between communists and democrats, discord between the Burmese majority and ethnic minorities, and power struggles among politicians were

---

32. Gyi, *Burmese Political Values*, 112.
33. I will discuss Ne Win's rule more in the later part of this chapter.

so rampant that no former politicians were able to tackle the problems. When the military ruled the country, Myanmar reverted to the traditional political system of authoritarian rule. Thant Myint-U succinctly summarizes the situation of post-war Myanmar:

> The gun has never been taken away from Burmese politics. There has not been a succession of wars; rather the same war, the same rhetoric, and sometimes even the same old rifles have staggered on and on, with only minor changes to the cast and plot and a few new special effects.[34]

7.2 Supernaturalism, Politics and Buddhism

What makes the politics of Myanmar unique is the linkage between Buddhism, supernaturalism and politics. It is not only violence for the sake of power, but also religion and animistic practices that play a crucial role in politics. Put differently, the elements of the DS run deep in the political soil of Myanmar by means of religion, animistic myths, and superstitions. As this research seeks to explore the use of power and violence in the political context of Myanmar, it needs to examine what supernaturalism has to say about politics. Buddhism in Myanmar was always mixed with *nat* (spirit) worship, astrology and alchemy even before King Anawrahta of Pagan made Buddhism the state religion.[35] In folklore of Myanmar, there are two kinds of *nat*: first, impersonal and local *nats*; and the second, thirty-seven personal and national *nats*. The former type is known as *nats* of the banyan tree, the hill, the lake, and the guardian *nat* of the village. But the latter came into being who were distinct personages with their own life histories.[36]

There are two different features to learn in looking at the nexus between politics and supernaturalist ideas of Myanmar. First, the stories of the

---

34. Myint-U, *River of Lost Footsteps*, 258.
35. Aung, *Folk Elements*, 1–5. Shwe Yeo (the pseudonym of Sir J. George Scott, a British civil servant who lived in Burma for more than thirty years) argued that *nat* worship has, in fact, nothing to do with Buddhism. Many Theravada Buddhists denounced it as heretical and antagonistic to the teachings of the lord Buddha, Yeo, *Burman*, 232.
36. Aung, *Folk Elements*, 2.

thirty-seven personal and national *nats* (how they became *nats*) demonstrate the Burmese political attitude towards power. To illustrate the point, one well-known story in the thirty-seven *nats* is that of Min Mahagiri. In his human existence, he was known as a blacksmith, Tin De, and he had a sister. They lived in the time of King Thinlikyaung. According to oral tradition, Tin De's physical strength was so immense that the whole city quaked and trembled when he struck his hammer against the anvil. When King Thinlikyaung heard of this, he was afraid that Tin De would usurp his throne one day. So, he ordered his ministers to arrest Tin De. But Tin De ran away deep into the jungle. Intending to outwit Tin De, the king took his sister to be queen. After some time, the king persuaded the queen to bring her brother to him. Tin De's sister believed the king and summoned Tin De to appear before the king. When Tin De came in, he was seized, tied to a *saga* tree (the Indian "Champa" tree) and burned alive there. The queen (Tin De's sister), upon seeing her brother being burned, rushed into the fire and died with him. They both became *nats*. Similarly, another two of the thirty-seven *nats* (Mingyi and Minlay) were also condemned to death by King Anawrahta when he no longer trusted them. A French anthropologist Bénédicte Brac de la Perrière remarks that the stories of how the thirty-seven *nats* originated "underscores a confrontation between monarchical authority and local powers."[37] Indeed, this shows that the fear of losing power had always been a concern for kings. This mentality has continued to permeate the lives of two military rulers, Ne Win and Than Shwe.[38]

Second, in Myanmar, politics, astrology, numerology, and *nat* worship are more than superstitious beliefs; they are powerful instruments to grip, prolong and continually increase one's power. One writer from Myanmar affirms that, "superstition runs deep in Burmese culture, and at times of difficulty people commonly rely on supernatural powers by consulting with

---

37. Bénédicte Brac de la Perrière, "The Taungpyon Festival: Locality and Nation-Confronting in the Cult of the 37 Lords," translated by Annabelle Dolidon, in Skidmore, *Burma at the Turn*, 68. "Taungpyon" is the name of the village which is ten kilometres distance from the northern part of Mandalay, the last Burmese royal city. Once a year, people from different parts of Myanmar gather together there and hold the festival to honour the spirits of deceased heroes or *nats* who belong to the Burmese pantheon of the thirty-seven *nats*.

38. I will discuss how Ne Win and Than Shwe were masterful in retaining power by any means in the later part of this chapter.

soothsayers and astrologers who explain how to ward off harmful influences, remedy problems, and assure a peaceful life."[39] The first Prime Minister, Nu, used to consult a *ponna* (astrologer) whenever he had important decisions to make. Likewise, Ne Win also used to ask for advice from an astrologer to protract his rule. Mya Maung, as a sharp critique of Ne Win and his regime, also points out that "all of these incidents (numerological and astrological) simply confirm . . . that Burma has been a traditional society with few changes in belief and behaviour for generations and that the reign of terror under Ne Win and his military commanders for nearly thirty years has reinforced the traditional belief system and barriers to modernisation."[40]

In the case of Than Shwe, his wife Kyaing Kyaing firmly believed in *nats* (spirits), astrology and *yadaya* (a ritual designed to ward off ill fortune). Because of her influence, Than Shwe had, reportedly, seven personal astrologers focusing on specific areas: the future of the country, his rivals within the regime, and dealing with Aung San Suu Kyi. In short, both Ne Win and Than Shwe manipulated numerology, astrology and *yadaya* in retaining their power. It is widely believed in Myanmar that they both had some skilled and powerful astrologers who were able to prevent their downfall and reinforce their personal power by doing *yadaya che* (the performance of individual acts as prescribed by astrologers to circumvent misfortune or dangers). Exploring supernaturalism and superstitious rituals in Myanmar helps us to see their attitude towards power and how it could be maintained through the manipulation of astrology. The folklores and the practice of astrology expose the certain elements of the DS that have been so dominant in the political context of Myanmar. Perhaps, some unbelievers in such supernatural superstitions might not pay considerable attention to such practices; but, numerology, astrology, sorcery, and animistic practices have been such a powerful means to usurp and sustain the power among politicians, in order for them to keep the domination system operating in the country. For Wink, the belief and practice of Burmans in astrology and *nat*-worship might be absurd, however he would consider them as a power to enforce the DS.

---

39. Wakeman and Tin, *No Time for Dreams*, 10–11.
40. Maung, *Burma Road to Poverty*, 226.

7.3 Ethnic Diversity and Religion

In chapter 3, we discussed that Walter Wink largely talked about reconciliation. For him, the final aim of nonviolence is not to defeat the opponents, but to establish reconciliation between the oppressed and oppressors. Likewise, Martin Luther King's final aim was not to defeat the white man, but to win his friendship and understanding. His desire was neither segregation nor desegregation, but integration. Like King and Wink, Suu Kyi also seeks to bring about a reconciliation with the military. Put simply, friendship and reconciliation is the ultimate aim of nonviolent resistance. In the context of Myanmar, the reconciliation to be sought is not just between the military and the opposition political parties like the NLD, but also between the Burman or Burmese-dominated military and other ethnic minorities.[41] Therefore, we need to do a brief examination of the ethnic diversities of the country Myanmar and the age-old conflict between the Burman majority and other ethnic minorities. Exploring the ethnic and religious differences will underline the importance of reconciliation.

As a country where a diverse mix of ethnic groups reside, Myanmar has not experienced a national sense of unity. There is no record of such national unity, even in precolonial Myanmar.[42] Many Myanmar observers believe that the country's long-standing minority problems must first be dealt with to establish a cohesive national and political identity.[43] To trace the history of the precolonial period, it seems that the ethnic diversity was not a central issue. Ashley South points out that ethnic, political, social and religious identities were not so fixed and unipolar in precolonial Myanmar, as they became during the colonial period.[44] Christina Fink also observes that mainland Southeast Asian kingdoms were, in the precolonial period, poly-ethnic, and rulers were constantly trying to bring in more people, regardless of ethnicity.[45] What mattered at that time was whether one was a Buddhist and a member

---

41. Here I interchangeably use the word Burmans or Burmese to describe a majority ethnic group.
42. Renard, "Minorities in Burmese History," 256.
43. Smith, "Burma's Ethnic Minorities," 98.
44. South, *Ethnic Politics in Burma*, 4.
45. Fink, "Introduction," xvii.

of an alliance with the ruling dynasty.[46] So how has the conflict between Burmans or Burmese and other ethnic minorities come into existence?

First, the British introduced a division to Myanmar to aid administration by dividing the whole nation into two areas: Burma proper (or Ministerial Burma) where the majority of the Burmese lived and the Frontier Areas where non-Burmese ethnic people resided.[47] While the British's rule was direct in the former area, they indirectly ruled the Frontier Areas through local ethnic chieftains. John Furnivall says that British rule did nothing to foster national unity: their "divide and rule" policy encouraged racial antagonism and subverted the internal balance of power, rendering it unstable.[48]

Second, the superiority mentality of the Burmese has been a dominant attitude since the monarchical period. They take pride in their race and religion and see themselves as superior to all other races, including white people. According to *The Glass Palace Chronicle of the Kings of Burma*,[49] the Burmese consider themselves as descendants of the Buddha's family. *The Glass Palace* says that their racial name was *Brahma*, which is, according to Buddhist belief, the first inhabitant of the earth. The word *Brahma* has taken many forms in past centuries, such as *Mrâmâ, Bamâ, Myanma*; but always had the same meaning.[50] For such people with a superiority mentality, British annexation of the country brought immense humiliation to them. What made the situation worse was the British's administrative policy of divide and rule. That policy led ethnic minorities, especially Karens to be much freer than Burmans. Although the British Army pacified the whole country; they failed

---

46. Gravers, *Nationalism as Political Paranoia*, 19.

47. This was known and taught in the textbooks of Burmese history in government schools as "divide and rule," that birthed the divisive spirit between Burmans and other ethnic minorities.

48. Cited from Silverstein, *Burmese Politics*, 35.

49. Tin and Luce, *Glass Palace Chronicle*.

50. Phayre, *History of Burma*, 2. This was originally published in 1883. When the ex-military regime changed the name of the country from Burma to Myanmar, they justified it by saying that the term Burma sounded colonial in tone, and the new name "Myanmar" was more inclusive to other non-Burmese ethnic peoples. However, the etymology of the world "Myanmar" is more exclusive than Burma. Martin Smith also points out that the word "Myanmar," for ethnic minority leaders, was simply the historic ethnic Burman name, Smith, *Burma: Insurgency*, 21.

to win the Burmese support, for Burmans saw them as partial measures that favoured the minorities.

Another factor that has fuelled the divisive spirit between Burmese and non-Burmese people is religion. During the nineteenth century, a significant number of Karen people were converted to Christianity. So they began to co-operate with the British people. Many Christian Karens helped crush an uprising in Lower Burma, and scores of them joined the British army and military police. They became instrumental in hunting down the Burman-led rebels that were fighting against the British.[51] Karen Christians saw the Burmans as idolatrous, and fought for the British against anti-British Burmans. They believed that their struggle would contribute to the triumph of Christianity, and to the security and well-being of the Karen nation as well.[52] In turn, Burmans also took revenge on the Karens on several occasions. For example, when the Burmese Independence Army (BIA), mainly composed of ethnic Burmans, fought against the British, the bloodshed began in the western Irrawaddy delta where many Karens lived.[53] From the time of post-independence, Burmans have begun to take a dominant position in all aspects of the country again. Buddhism, in favour of the majority Buddhists, has become the state religion under the governance of the first Prime Minister Nu. Nu's government also ignored the promise given at the historic Panglong Agreement. According to the Agreement, each ethnic group was promised the right to exercise authority in their respective areas and preserve their own languages and cultures. As a result, the ethnic minorities' distrust in Burmans has grown sterner, and some ethnic insurgencies have occurred.

When Ne Win staged a coup in March 1962, his government aggravated the racial prejudice between the Burmans and other minority groups. Key positions in government were filled by Burmese Buddhists. Promotion in government offices was largely restricted to Burmese Buddhists only. Ne Win heightened Burmanization more than Nu did.[54] To promote the Burmans'

---

51. Myint-U, *River of Lost Footsteps*, 23.
52. Cady, *History of Modern Burma*, 139.
53. Myint-U, *River of Lost Footsteps*, 231.
54. There are some reasons why Burmese support "Burmanization." The Burmese were known as warriors, who attacked and conquered neighbouring countries such as Manipur and Thailand. Their historical past gives the Burmese a distinctive national pride. This pride

chauvinistic nationalism, the Historical Research Commission at Rangoon (Yangon) University was launched under the supervision of Ne Win's wife, Ni Ni Myint. The Commission propagated the idea of Burman superiority, that it was the Burmans who had ruled and dominated all the ethnic peoples since the inception of Burmese history. Martin Smith asserts that the Commission was, in fact, to whitewash Ne Win and his army as the current embodiment of all national aspirations.[55] Burmanization reached its peak during Than Shwe's era, who ruled the land from 1992 to 2010. He promoted the slogan, "Amyo, Batha, Thathana," meaning "one race, one language, one religion." In calling his race "Maha Burman," which means "great noble or master race," Than Shwe reinvigorated Burmanization. Non-Buddhists and non-Burmans were harshly discriminated against during his rule. In short, Burmese politics is a power struggle (*ana lu pwe*). Seizing and retaining power by any means is the traditional pattern of Burmese politics. In that power struggle, Burmese supernaturalism (astrology, *yadaya*, and numerology) also plays a significant role. Violence in the name of unity and order is also another key factor in Burmese politics. What has stoked up the power struggle is the Burmans' superiority complex towards ethnic minority groups. The ethnic minorities' response to the politics of Burmanization was revolt, a heightened sense of separate and distinct identity, and a desire for political separation.[56] How could such a racial barrier be possibly bridged? Myanmar has had a historic moment when ethnic unity was once made, though it was not perfect, known as the Panglong Agreement.

Under the leadership of General Aung San, the father of Suu Kyi, the Panglong Agreement was reached and signed by Kachin, Chin, and Shan on 12 February 1947 – a year before independence. Since then, Myanmar celebrates 12 February as Union Day. Other ethnic groups – Karen, Mon, and Kaya attended there as observers. Now under the leadership of Suu Kyi, the twenty-first century Panglong was held on 31 August 2016 the first time, and the second time on 24 May 2017. However, consensus on the federal

---

led them to feel superior to other races, including the white westerners. Though historically questionable, Burmese think they are, as described, descendants of Buddha's clan and the first inhabitants of the world, Lwin, "Contextualization of the Gospel," 12–13.

55. Smith, *Burma: Insurgency*, 36.
56. Silverstein, *Burma: Military Rule*, 198.

system, which is one of the key issues to be solved, is still a long way from being reached. The way of transforming the DS, where revenge and violence reigns, to the DFO (God's domination-free order), where the division between the oppressed and oppressors is reconciled, is not easy. The country which has been shaped by the characteristics of the DS has just begun the journey of reconciliation.

7.4 A Quest for the Spirit of Burmese Politics

I have briefly surveyed the political landscape of Myanmar from the monarchical period to the present republic. In doing so, I have aimed to discover the reasons for the long-standing tradition of authoritarian rule in the country. Now I will examine the spirit of politics in Myanmar, with the aim of understanding its distinct nature. What do I mean here by the word "spirit"? On the surface, this word seems to be irrelevant in discussing politics. As a matter of fact, it is not so. Wink also observes a growing recognition of the spiritual dimension of corporate entities even among secular thinkers, like Terrence Deal and Allan Kennedy, who have written a text for business entitled *Corporate Cultures: the Rights and Rituals of Corporate Life*.[57] Max Weber's classic work, *The Protestant Ethic and the Spirit of Capitalism*, discusses how the religion of Christianity, particularly Calvinism, has birthed the spirit of capitalism. Weber also admits that the word "spirit" in discussing the sociology of religion seems pretentious.[58] However, it best describes his argument for the articulation of capitalism. Once the capitalist spirit emerged, it became deep-seated in the culture where it was born. Similarly, Manfred Kets de Vries analyzes totalitarianism and authoritarianism from the psychoanalytic viewpoint, and suggests how such despotic leaders should be prevented in the article, "The Spirit of Despotism: Understanding the Tyrant Within."[59] Kets de Vries explores the process of how a despotic leader

---

57. Wink, "Redeeming the Entire Universe," 175.

58. Weber, *Protestant Ethic*, 13. Weber found that there was no such a thing as secular or sacred work because all work, for the Protestant Christians, is sacred. God wants all Christians to work hard. For a person living according to that work ethic, it is easy to accumulate money. But Calvinism does not allow Christians to use money luxuriously or wastefully; instead they are to give to the poor. Thus, the Protestant ethic was the driving force that led to the industrialization and development of capitalism.

59. Kets de Vries, "Spirit of Despotism."

emerges and enhances his authority through various means, such as ideology, mind control, scapegoating, and creating the illusion of solidarity. Thus, the spiritual dimension in discussing politics, economics, and cultures is no longer such a pretentious discussion. Myanmar, which has suffered excruciatingly in various ways under the military rule for virtually five decades, is steeped in blood and violence. Something is fatally flawed. This flaw is seen in this study as a spiritual aspect or what Wink calls the spirit of an institution or system. Looking at the flaw as the spirit of politics in Myanmar, the following discussion will lead to the discussion of nonviolent engagement by King and Suu Kyi.

7.4.1 Understanding Politics in Myanmar

Before analyzing the spiritual side of the politics of Myanmar, I would like to begin with an etymological exploration of the word politics in Myanmar. In Burmese, politics is called *nain ngan ye*, literally meaning "affairs of the state, country or nation."[60] The idea of the state is a complex subject, and arguably the most central concept in the study of politics. Scholars define it in different ways, depending on political ideologies. The state is not synonymous with government, but essentially means "the whole fixed political system, the set-up of authoritative and legitimately power roles by which we are finally controlled, ordered, and organised."[61] In the Western concept, politics is regarded as the theory and practice of governing a country or a state. But politics originally meant what is happening between citizens in the polis, the Greek city-state. To be specific, it is "the polis, or civil community, ordering its life together on the basis of the public good."[62] In the context of Myanmar, politics and state are, to a certain degree, synonymous; though they are not entirely overlapped.

Politics or "affairs of the country/state" was, in the monarchical period, only considered a concern of the government or King; it had nothing to do with the public. Let those in the governing body alone be busy with such affairs! Those who had no part to play in it only wanted to shun these affairs.

---

60. Since state, country, and nation are loosely defined in Myanmar, I will interchangeably use these words as appropriate.

61. Robertson, *Routledge Dictionary of Politics*, 457.

62. Wogaman, *Christian Perspectives on Politics*, 13.

As described, the idea of politics or state is interestingly backed up by the Buddhist concept of *karma* (what a person did previously in life). Kings, and all those in politics became who they were because of their *karma*; and so did the public. So, the doctrine of *karma* was the dividing line between those in politics and those not. What is more, there is a remarkable traditional view of politics in Myanmar. That is, the government is regarded as one of the five common enemies.[63] How could such a view originate? Before the British occupation, the monarchical period of rule was one of fear and violence;[64] there was no constitutional law to limit the autocracy of kings, and there was no organized form of government.[65] To govern people meant to rule them by terror, that is, "to impress on the minds of the people the most reverential awe of the king's sovereign."[66] Under such autocratic rulers, engaging in politics seems unappealing.

The first political leader who attempted to dignify the idea of politics was General Aung San. Aung San remained resolutely opposed to the deeply held historical view of politics. He believed that politics is neither a dirty game nor the business of politicians alone. A person's life – where he lives, what he eats, and what he does – is, for him, always connected with politics. He insists that politics is no longer simply the business of politicians; it is for ordinary people. It permeates a person's everyday life.[67] That view was indeed revolutionary and eye-opening because it was explicitly against the prevailing idea of politics at that time. Sadly, Aung San was assassinated; and even worse, the democratic parliamentary system was also overturned.

7.4.2 General Ne Win as a Resuscitator of the Spirit of the Traditional Myanmar Politics

In trying to understand Myanmar politics, a Burma expert Robert H. Taylor considers the state not merely as a human institution, but something that has

---

63. Five common enemies are: fire that can burn properties; water in the form of floods; wind in the form of storms; theft; and kings or rulers.
64. Gyi, *Burmese Political Values*, 27.
65. Tun, *Modern History of Myanmar*, 89–90.
66. Gyi, *Burmese Political Values*, 28–29.
67. Silverstein, *Political Legacy of Aung San*, 95.

a life and spirit of its own.[68] To affirm this, Taylor quotes Benedict Anderson's idea of the state. Anderson views the state as an institution of the same species as the church, the university, and the modern corporation. Like them, it ingests and excretes personnel in a continuous, steady process, often over extended periods of time.[69] With this view in mind, Taylor examines the contemporary state of Myanmar, starting from the nature of the early modern precolonial state to the present; thereby exposing the continuities between the precolonial and contemporary periods. In his analysis, Taylor contends that the precolonial state in Myanmar was largely autonomous. The experimentation with a democratic system after 1948 fundamentally contradicted the political culture of Myanmar, so that it could not penetrate society, and therefore failed. For him, the state in Myanmar is the ultimate arbiter of societal conflicts. Hence Taylor attempts to justify the military coup and rule.[70] He believes that Ne Win's coup of 2 March 1962 is a reassertion of the state. In other words, it was Ne Win who resuscitated or reasserted the traditional pattern of Myanmar politics, which was obstructed and stymied by the British rule and the establishment of their political system in the country.[71]

Another scholar who also shared this view is Michael Aung-Thwin, who was born in Burma, and a son of a Karen woman and a Burman man. Both Taylor and Aung-Thwin are predominantly known as apologists for the two military juntas. Aung-Thwin's assessment of the regime is much more optimistic than Taylor's. Like Taylor, Aung-Thwin remarks that the so-called democracy after 1948 was a pseudo-political system because it was structurally or conceptually foreign to the political culture of Myanmar. Aung-Thwin thought that Ne Win, who suspiciously deemed Western style democracy and Marxism as inappropriate for Mynmar politics, attempted to be neutral; hence, he adopted the policy of neutrality in international relations and pursued self-reliance and self-sufficiency. According to Michael Aung-Thwin, Ne Win strived to accomplish those policies through the resurrection of and preservation of certain economic, political, and emotional/intellectual

---

68. Taylor, *State in Myanmar*, 4.
69. Anderson, "Old State, New Society," 478.
70. Taylor, *State in Myanmar*, 11–12.
71. Taylor, ch. 5.

relationships found in precolonial Burmese society.⁷² Aung-Thwin, like Taylor, concludes that Ne Win's rule was a recovery of what was lost in history, thus resuscitating and re-establishing the real political spirit of Myanmar.

The late Mya Maung's *The Burma Road to Poverty* passionately argues that Ne Win's endeavour was nothing but a retrograde step.⁷³ In reviewing that book, David Steinberg remarks that whether Myanmar was a modern socialist or capitalist state, or a reversion to traditional Myanmar political values in the period of the kingdoms under the rules of Ne Win and Than Shwe, was always a matter of issue with analysts.⁷⁴ In the following I contend that whether Ne Win endeavoured to revert the nation to the past on purpose is hard to prove, but what he did and how he ruled the country indicates a strong continuity of political values and attitudes from the monarchical period.

There are vast differences between the Burmese writers who had lived and suffered under Ne Win's government and some Western scholars like John Badgley and Jon A. Wiant. Regarding political ideology, Ne Win, after the coup, formulated the "Burmese Way to Socialism." According to John Badgley and Jon A. Wiant, Ne Win's Burmese Socialist Programme Party was a single-party government clothed in Marxian phraseology but dominated by the army elite bent on building society and culture from indigenous sources.⁷⁵ In their analysis of Ne Win's "Burmese Way to Socialism," Badgley and Wiant argue that Ne Win and his government had had a crystal-clear vision for the future of Burma. According to a Burman journalist for the Mirror newspaper, U Thaung, the paper "Burmese Way to Socialism" was indeed written within two weeks by a single man, U Chit Hlain, who was once a leader of a Burmese Communist Organization, the Red Flag. U Thaung remarks that Ne Win had had no idea what political ideology he should use to lead the nation at the beginning of his rule. He was merely a power-hungry man, so he mounted the coup.⁷⁶

---

72. Michael Aung-Thwin, "1948 and Burma's Myth of Independence," in Silverstein, *Independent Burma*, 26.
    73. Maung, *Burma Road to Poverty*, 298.
    74. Steinberg, "Review of *The Burma Road to Poverty*," 890.
    75. Badgley and Wiant, "Ne Win-BSPP Style," 61.
    76. U Thaung, *Bo Ne Win Zatlan Shuut Thamya*, 206. In Myanmar, U Thaung was known as Kyae Mone (Mirror) U Thaung or Aung Ba La. He was a famous journalist who founded the

Whatever the difference between domestic and international writers, it is undeniable that Ne Win's government was a complicated mixture of traditional Burmese political values and modern political ideology. According to Wiant, Ne Win sought to place his rule centrally within Myanmar history, and his symbolic appeals were to a legacy of the military administrator kings and more recently of Aung San, portrayed as the contemporary embodiment of the great Burmese unifiers.[77] In this sense, Ne Win is the resuscitator of the spirit of Myanmar politics that had been practiced in the monarchical period.

What are the *sui generis* characteristics of the spirit of Burmese politics? Maung Maung Gyi draws up a list of these characteristics as follows:

> First, the tendency to view the government as evil; second, reliance on the government for everything to be done; third, viewing the government as omnipotent, omnipresent, and omnicompetent; fourth, the highly personalised outlook in human relationships within the administrative infrastructure together with pleasing the superior ethics; last, failure to appreciate the rule of law.[78]

For Gyi, these characteristics are, in varying degrees, still alive and strong. Ne Win revived those characteristics. Thus, Ne Win was metaphorically a monarch figure in terms of the way he exercised power. For example, rule of law and rule of person are inseparable in the minds of people in Myanmar. Since the monarchical period, personal and institutional loyalty was to the individual monarch, and the locus of power resided in the king. This form of power is so dominant that institutions are of secondary importance to a king. No one in the modern era has exemplified that factor more than Ne Win.[79] Ne Win never tolerated anyone, even among his associates, who competed with him for influence and popularity. That kind of competition was considered a threat to him. So, Ne Win purged many of his close associates so that no one might rise against him. Therefore, though his government might be coated

---

Mirror Daily Newspaper. In 1964, he was jailed, and his newspaper was confiscated by dictator Ne Win. He died on 3 April 2008 in Fort Lauderdale, Florida, USA.

77. Wiant, "Tradition in the Service," 60.
78. Gyi, *Burmese Political Values*, 154–175.
79. Steinberg, *Burma*, 50.

with modern political ideology such as socialism, Ne Win did resurrect the spirit of Myanmar politics, thereby restoring the traditional culture that had been practiced since the monarchical period.

Moreover, Ne Win's resurrection of the political spirit is exhaustive. The features of the political culture in the precolonial period are, "the sacrosanctity and the central position of kingship, absolutism and the undifferentiated functions of kingship."[80] However, the political ideas of parliamentary democracy in the post-independence era had significantly impacted upon Myanmar politics in the postcolonial period. Upon taking power in 1962, Ne Win had set out to destroy that political system root and branch because he wanted a retrogression to traditional Myanmar politics. At last, he regenerated the precolonial political system and re-designed Myanmar with the modern political flavour of the month. Simply put, Ne Win revived the spirit of the DS in Myanmar, which was impeded by the first government of the post-independence Burma; but now it came to life and began to overwhelm the political culture of Myanmar. Once it was entrenched, it would last long until nonviolence is enforced.

What is more, Ne Win consigned his legacy to his successors, and, until now, that legacy has been heavily entrenched in Myanmar politics. Put it into the context of this research, the spirit and life of politics, which was historically handed down, was entrenched by Ne Win's successor Than Shwe. Than Shwe is the one who has institutionally and culturally empowered and heightened the spirit of Myanmar politics. In fact, Than Shwe is much more energetic and enthusiastic in keeping that spirit revitalized in politics. Regarding personality type, Ne Win was outgoing, sociable, and extroverted in relating to other people; whereas Than Shwe is introverted, a man of few words, cold, aloof and distant in interpersonal relationships. Benedict Rogers's depiction of Than Shwe's personality is vivid:

> Like Mugabe, Than Shwe faces an organised democratic opposition that has domestic and international legitimacy – one which he loathes. Like Kim Jong-il, he is reclusive, uncharismatic, and controlling. And like Saddam Hussein, Than Shwe

---

80. Gyi, *Burmese Political Values*, 14.

is intolerant of anyone within his own regime who he feels may challenge him.[81]

On one hand, both Ne Win and Than Shwe have some similar characteristics, such as having unquestioning subordinates around them, and dictatorial characteristics in decision-making and their leadership style. On the other hand, there are some differences between Than Shwe's regime and what Ne Win did before it. Robert H. Taylor lists these differences in his work, *General Ne Win: A Political Biography*, as a ceasefire agreement instead of political and military integration; diminishing the cult of Aung San; the rapid adoption of Western modes of dress; the absolute control of the army; doubling military expenditure, and so on.[82] Despite those differences, they shared similarities in how they ruled the country and the system they wanted to implant. Both were seen as despots in the eyes of local and international communities. To the surprise of all, Than Shwe was truly greater than Ne Win in exercising power. According to one of the grandsons of Ne Win, Than Shwe was hand-picked by his grandfather to become Vice Chief of Staff (Army) in 1985. But the tragedy is that his handpicked man, Than Shwe, became his worst enemy who placed him under house arrest until his death. Aung Zaw calls it the doubly disastrous legacy of Ne Win.[83]

There are three long-lasting imprints that Than Shwe left on Myanmar politics; these would, though not indelible, last for years to come. First, it was the changing of the Myanmar flag just seventeen days ahead of the general election on 7 November 2010. According to Mikael Gravers, that flag is likely the result of an astrological consultation. For some political dissidents, the flag is the symbol of the military dominance over all the people of Myanmar.[84] Taking a look at the flag, it shows no diversity, which is why many ethnic leaders wonder whether it represents all the ethnic people groups in Burma. A relatively big star in the centre of the flag symbolizes the dominance of military power.

---

81. Rogers, *Than Shwe*, 156.
82. Taylor, *General Ne Win*, 554–555.
83. Zaw, "Doubly Disastrous Legacy."
84. Kaspar, "In Burma."

The second is the relocation of the capital from Yangon to Naypyidaw, which is located in the centre of the country. To trace Burmese history, most Burmese monarchs moved their capital into the inland region of the dry zone for military consolidation when an enemy had overrun the old capital. In addition to this, a high number of kings relocated their capital to manifest power and charisma, and to follow the royal tradition that the most powerful ruler should leave the old capital and build a new one. Dulyapak Preecharushh remarks that there are perhaps other reasons for Than Shwe to relocate the capital; nonetheless, the relocation has characteristics similar to those of the monarchical period.[85] Richard Cockett, in his latest work, sees "all the military regime's attempts as recreating the Burma kingdom of old and reimagining Burma as if much of the country's recent history never happened."[86] Hence, Than Shwe was much more determined and devoted than Ne Win to increase and intensify the spirit of Burmese politics that had been practiced from the time of monarchy.

The third imprint that Than Shwe left is the 2008 Constitution, which was drafted by the handpicked constituent assembly. According to David Williams, the Constitution has problems which are too deep and reinforce historical tendencies.[87] By historical trends, Williams refers to the military regime's dominance over the nation from the time of 1962. He lists the root flaws of the Constitution in different ways. Power was concentrated in the military, generally to men, or a single strongman ruler. In addition, the government does not pay much attention to individual rights and the ethnic minorities' demands.[88] Williams concludes that the 2008 Constitution is at best a murky smear of light on the horizon. Thus, it could soon be extinguished by a military coup or civilian retrenchment, aided by international complacency and indifference.[89] Simply stated, the 2008 Constitution places restraints on the elected government, for the president has no control over the military.

Having seen what Ne Win and Than Shwe did and how they ruled the country, we have concluded that there are obvious continuities between the ways

---

85. Preecharushh, *Naypyidaw*, 132–135.
86. Cockett, *Blood, Dreams and Gold*, 64.
87. Williams, "What's So Bad," 118.
88. Williams, 118–119.
89. Williams, 138.

of monarchical rule and those of Ne Win and Than Shwe. Perhaps Ne Win might not follow the path of monarchs in ruling the nation with the intention of reverting to the past. But Than Shwe, looking at the way of his rule, might have every intention of making a retrogressive change to traditional political attitude and values. In the new capital (Nay Pyi Taw) that he established, we can see the ten metre high statues of Burma's three warrior kings (Anawratha, Bayinnaung, and Alaungpaya), standing high over the main parade ground. To sum up, Ne Win rebirthed the spirit of traditional Myanmar politics. What Than Shwe did, in turn, was to invigorate and bolster the spirit that Ne Win resurrected. Additionally, Than Shwe has structurally intensified the Myanmar political spirit through the symbol of the country's flag, the relocation of the capital, and the power of the Constitution so that no one or no alternative system can oppose it. Therefore, the politics that Ne Win and Than Shwe created is simply a renovation of precolonial politics with modern terms and tones. From Wink's perspective, the political legacy that Ne Win and Than Shwe left was that of the DS. Since the DS is deeply entrenched in the land of Myanmar, can it be possible to transform it into the DFO where democratic values prevail? Will the DS that they generated last always? Can it be superseded by another alternative? Of course, nothing in this world is permanent; everything we humans create is always changeable. Now we will see how Suu Kyi has come to engage with Burmese politics, where the DS is rooted, with a view to transforming the DS into the DFO where democratic values reign.

7.4.3 Suu Kyi as an Agent for Political Transformation

If Ne Win and Than Shwe were seen as resuscitator and energizer of the traditional Myanmar political spirit, respectively, Suu Kyi would be an agent for transforming that spirit, or the DS, into the DFO. In the time of the previous regime, Suu Kyi was accused of implanting the incongruous ideas and values of Western democracy in Myanmar. What she, in turn, tries to do is to validate the compatibility of democratic values and Buddha's teachings: how politics, morality, *mettā*, and other Buddhist teachings correspond to one another. What, specifically, has Suu Kyi attempted to change or transform in Myanmar politics?

First, Suu Kyi has primarily encouraged the Myanmar people to see and understand the inseparability of politics or "affairs of state or country" (*nain gan yae*) and their daily lives. According to the regime of that time, the real problem that the country had been facing was not solely political, but also economic. The regime cunningly diverted the public attention to economic issues instead of politics. But Suu Kyi knew the real motive behind the regime's subtle advice. And so she said,

> If you are concentrated on just making money in this country, you have to indulge in a lot of things that are . . . not quite strict. There is a lot of bribery and corruption going on. You do lose the morality if you are told to concentrate only on making money.[90]

Suu Kyi is so convinced that democracy is not just about a change of government, but a change in their everyday lives. Here her political understanding is very similar to that of her father, Aung San, who also saw the inseparable nature of politics and daily living. This view of politics radically challenges the traditional understanding, according to which politics is merely the business of the state or the rulers.

Besides, Suu Kyi's conviction of the integral link between politics, morality and religion is also radical enough to confront traditional Myanmar politics. In Myanmar history, morality is not completely separated from politics. Even the previous military regime, which gunned down a number of Buddhist monk protesters in 2007, proudly called themselves devoted Buddhists. During their rule, ex-Senior General Than Shwe and his fellow generals all used to go and pay homage to the monks in any place they visited. As Buddhists, they believed that making merits (such as offering some useful materials to Buddhist monks, ornamenting pagodas with gold and other precious stuffs, and building pagodas) is itself part of morality.[91] Monarchs and emperors, throughout Buddhist Asia, saw the patronage of monks and monasteries as both a moral duty and an advantage.[92] As aforementioned, whatever evil is done in the name of or for the sake of power can be compensated for or atoned by making the aforementioned merits. To recall the

---

90. Cited from Pederson, *Burma Spring*, 275.

91. Merit-making is a common and key practice among Burmese Buddhists. That is, a person can earn and accumulate merits for this life or the next, by doing the things such as donating materials to monks, building pagodas, and so on.

92. Reynolds, "Power," 221.

king Anawrahta, he was religiously a zealous Buddhist, so he waged war on the Mons (previously called the Talaings) to obtain a Buddha image and the Buddhist scriptures. So, John Stuart remarks, "in spite of all his zeal for religion [Buddhism], he [Anawrahta] had caught nothing of its inner meaning or of the spirit of its founder."[93] For the previous regimes, doing such rituals seemed to be considered as morality. Morality, for them, is self-oriented because it focuses on what a person does and can gain. Therefore, it has nothing to do with others.

On the contrary, Suu Kyi's approach to morality and politics is a socially engaged form of Buddhism, according to which *mettā* (loving-kindness) is at the heart of all relations.[94] Instead of religious rites and rituals, what matters most to her is to abide by Buddhist principles in worldly dealings. For her, Buddhist morality is essentially the five precepts: abstaining from the destruction of life, theft, adultery, falsehood and indulgence in intoxicants. Her argument is that when the ruler fails to keep these precepts, what ensues is always disastrous. In her words, "the root of a nation's misfortunes has to be sought in the moral failings of the government."[95] In a nutshell, Suu Kyi's view of morality is other-oriented because it is not merely a private or individual business. With this view in mind, Suu Kyi challenges the traditional values of Myanmar politics. Indeed, the challenge is radically subversive, which is why it annoyed and angered the former regime. Wink also argues that we are dead insofar as we have been socialized into patterns of injustice. Wink reconsiders the notion of dying to ourselves as dying to the Powers, thereby rebirth is not just a private, inward event, but dying to whatever in our social surroundings has shaped us inauthentically. In other words, we must die to the DS in order to live authentically.[96]

To juxtapose King and Suu Kyi, King spent a great deal of time striving to see an alternative way to solve the social evil at that time through an

---

93. Stuart, *Burma Through the Centuries*, 29. The second edition of this book was published in 1910 by the publisher Kegan Paul in London.

94. Sallie B. King, in her book on *Socially Engaged Buddhism*, includes Suu Kyi as a socially engaged Buddhist, and refers to her interpretation of human rights and Buddhism, King, *Socially Engaged Buddhism*, 139.

95. Suu Kyi, *Freedom from Fear*, 171.

96. Wink, *Engaging the Powers*, 157–158.

in-depth study of various philosophers and thinkers. Through reading those philosophers and integrating their thoughts skilfully, King interpreted the Bible differently from those who used it to support the segregation. In particular, reading Gandhi opened his eyes to understand the ethics of Jesus in his Sermon on the Mount, turning the other cheek, and loving enemies as the method for social reform. Prior to reading Gandhi, King took for granted that Jesus's ethics were only effective in individual relationships.[97] Therefore, Wink, King and Suu Kyi all have their own hermeneutical lens to interpret the contexts in which they are.

In terms of religion and politics, Buddhism is principally regarded as a powerful tool to legitimize a kingship, government, and regime throughout the history of Myanmar – beginning from Anawrahta to the President Thein Sein. The previous government made every effort to justify their rule through the means of Buddhism. Similarly, Suu Kyi also saw Buddhism as a means of opposition against the then regime. Her appraisal of the regime was not based on other religious texts or sources, but on the same religious teaching of Buddhism. Just as the regime used Buddhism to defend and support their rule, so did Suu Kyi in critiquing them, and her attempts to unmask their pseudo-Buddhism through the Buddha's teachings. Thus, Buddhism for the regime was a tool for the legitimacy of their rule, whereas for Suu Kyi, it is an instrument to correct the quality of the rule. Pointedly stated, both Suu Kyi and the regime forcefully employed Buddhism, but the way they did this was different: while one was for self-justification, the other was for self-correction.

More importantly, Suu Kyi's interpretation of democratic values, such as human rights, freedom, and through the lens of Buddhism and its traditions, revolutionizes the prevailing Burmese view of politics. To be precise, Suu Kyi investigates two ideas on politics in the history of Buddhism – *Mahasammata* and the Ten Duties of Kings[98] – in order to demonstrate the correspondence between Buddhism and democratic government. *Mahasammata* was a devout Buddhist monarch who followed the general pattern of Indic kingship in Southeast Asia. True, he was a king who had absolute power on his own, but he was chosen by popular consent and required to govern in accordance

---

97. King, *Stride toward Freedom*, 84–86.
98. See Suu Kyi, "In Quest for Democracy," in *Freedom from Fear*, 167–179.

with just laws. Therefore, Suu Kyi asserts that the concept of government elective and *sub lege* are not alien to traditional Myanmar thought.[99] Further, Suu Kyi through invoking the Ten Duties of Kings, insists that the idea of democratic government is not entirely strange to people in Myanmar. Even some of the traditional values serve to justify and to explain the widespread expectation of democratic government.[100] In one way or another, Suu Kyi points out that the regime's attempt to legitimize their rule on the basis of Buddhism and its tradition is just one-sided. She shows that there are other positive characteristics which align with democratic values and principles. Suu Kyi has exposed these features, thereby substantiating the compatibility of democratic government in the context of Myanmar.

Besides this, the path of nonviolence that Suu Kyi and her party, the NLD, have taken in resisting against the regime is a radical catalyst to transform the spirit of Myanmar politics because the tradition of changing the political situation through the force of arms has been a dominant feature since the monarchical era as observed before. Against such a political culture of violence, Suu Kyi and the NLD have resolutely committed to following the path of nonviolence, so as to resist the regime. In taking the nonviolent path, Suu Kyi's hope is to transform the traditional spirit that has permeated the politics of Myanmar. For Suu Kyi and the NLD, achieving democracy through the use of violence would permeate the tradition of changing the system in that way. Only through nonviolence will a genuine democratization be realized. Suu Kyi argues that if democracy were achieved through violence, the result would be the continual development of more effective methods of violence than those of the opposition, in order to pursue power. Being aware of the vicious cycle of violence, Suu Kyi regards nonviolence as more than a political tactic but a spiritual belief.[101] Like Wink and King, Suu Kyi is aware that once violence is rooted in culture, we become addicted. That means it is not easy to discard the myth of redemptive violence in such a culture because it prevents us from looking at another alternative. Wink, therefore, sees violence as the spirit of the DS and nonviolence as that of the DFO. King also avers that the choice

---

99. Suu Kyi, *Freedom from Fear*, 170.
100. Suu Kyi, 172.
101. Kyi and Clements, *Voice of Hope*, 154.

we have is not violence or nonviolence, but nonviolence or nonexistence. Therefore, considering violence and nonviolence as merely tactics to achieve a desired outcome is a shallow idea, for it trivializes the real nature of each.[102]

Most importantly, Suu Kyi's call for revolution of the spirit best depicts the epitome of her political involvement. Myanmar politics throughout history had been merely power struggles between oppositions and even between those within the same political units. Pursuing power by whatever means available matters most to many politicians. Knowing the fundamental flaw of Myanmar politics, Suu Kyi notes that what the country needs is more than a political revolution or changing one political system with another; it is a "revolution of the spirit."[103] The majority of the population, except those who experienced economic gains through cooperating with the junta, suffered under the overpowering force of unjust regulations in their everyday living for almost five decades. The mindset of the people is conditioned to believe that having power is most important. In such a context, Suu Kyi has strongly sensed that what the country needs is not just a political or a social movement. It is not enough to call for freedom, democracy, and human rights; it is not sufficient to aim at changing institutional policies and improving material conditions. There are forces behind the system which demonstrated the iniquities of the old order. To transform that old order, Suu Kyi calls for a revolution of the spirit, born of an intellectual conviction concerning the need for change, with the determination to make sacrifices in the name of enduring truths, to resist the corrupting influences of desire, ill will, ignorance, and fear.[104]

---

102. Now Suu Kyi became the State Counsellor, or a de facto leader of the country, in 2016. She has been scathingly criticized by the international community, especially the Muslim community and some western countries for the way she is dealing with the Rakhine-Rohingya conflict. On 25 August 2017, the military operation launched in response to an attack by Rohingya insurgents. As a result, more than 600,000 Rohingya refugees fled to the neighbouring Bangladesh. This military crackdown was labelled "ethnic cleansing" by the UN. She gave a speech on that particular issue at the end of September 2017, but it did not satisfy the international community. Therefore, Suu Kyi has been blamed for her reticence about the brutal crackdown of the military. So the question is, "Has she shifted her belief in nonviolence to pragmatic violence?" This question will be discussed in detail in the conclusion of the thesis.

103. Suu Kyi, *Freedom from Fear*, 183.

104. Suu Kyi, 183.

In other words, the spiritual revolution that she talks about is not just changing material things, but transforming political and spiritual values. In this sense, Suu Kyi's spiritual revolution bears a striking resemblance to Wink's view of the DFO, according to which nonviolence is the only mode to transform the DS into the DFO. Suu Kyi and her team also knew that the end they had been pursuing was a peaceful nation; therefore, the means to attain it could not be violence. If the people of Myanmar want to change from one political system to another, the new system should not just be a system of rules, but should be something that represents their moral and spiritual values as well. Thus, those involved in the democracy movement in Myanmar are called not just for a change from the regime, but also for the revolution of the soul of politics. This spiritual revolution requires courage because fear, which the military regime has implanted in the minds of the people of Myanmar for so long, can only be mastered by courage.

Now, what has become evident is the contradictory views and practices of politics between the then regime and Suu Kyi. Both the regime and Suu Kyi have deployed traditional values and Buddhism to justify their conflicting views of politics. What makes them different is that the former follows the pattern of the traditional Myanmar politics, while the latter sees it from the angle of socially engaged Buddhism. Thus, the regimes of Ne Win and Than Shwe focused on preserving the historic political traditions. Ne Win's BSPP (Burmese Socialist Programme Party) coated the traditional politics with the modern political ideologies, whereas Than Shwe's SLORC/SPDC retold the history of the military (Tatmadaw) by tracing the prominent monarchs (Anawrahta, Bayinnaung, and Alaungpaya) in the precolonial era, in order to legitimize their rule.

In contrast, Suu Kyi reads the Myanmar political situations through the lens of socially engaged Buddhism. In doing so, she has dug deep into the Buddhist history of Myanmar to show that human rights and democracy are not alien to the Myanmar context. This is how Suu Kyi has made every effort to transform the political spirit that Ne Win renewed and Than Shwe entrenched, into the modern democratic norms and values, supported by socially engaged Buddhism. It is a revolution of the spirit. Thus, this discussion about Ne Win, Than Shwe and Suu Kyi sheds light on the fatally flawed nature of the traditional Myanmar politics. Ne Win and Than Shwe resurrected the spirit of Myanmar politics in the precolonial period but Suu Kyi has put every effort into transforming it into the culture of democracy through nonviolence. Looking at the way two military regimes and Suu Kyi practiced politics through Wink's eyes, Ne Win made every endeavour to resurrect the spirit of the DS that had been practiced during the monarchical period, whether he did it on purpose or not. Than Shwe, as his successor, put in more effort to invigorate and deeply infuse the idea of the DS in the political culture of Myanmar. But Suu Kyi, knowing the political culture of Myanmar, has strived with all her might to transform the DS into the DFO through nonviolent, spiritual revolution.

7.4.4 The Failure of the Four Eights Protest

Can we now say that nonviolent resistance against the military dictatorship in Myanmar has been successful? Maria Stephan and Erica Chenoweth not only did an empirical research from the nonviolent campaigns in contemporary history, but also a comparative case study on East Timor (1988–1999), the Philippines (1986), and Myanmar (1988–1990).[105] In the conclusion of case study, they discovered that there are several reasons why Myanmar failed while East Timor and the Philippines succeeded. In East Timor and the Philippines, repression against nonviolent resistance backfired to produce mass mobilization, which in turn heightened the political costs of regime repression. Further security forces shifted their loyalty to the nonviolent resistance campaign. In addition to that, the international community came down heavily against the regimes.[106] However, in Myanmar, nonviolent campaigns failed because it could not raise the costs of regime repression to the degree that the regime control was threatened. Further, overreliance on single personalities, the inability to reconcile across competing factions, and a lack of consistent information about human rights abuses left the nonviolent opposition campaign in disarray. Likewise, violent campaigns in Myanmar also failed because they were unable to mobilize the masses.[107] In addition to that,

---

105. Chenoweth and Stephan, "Why Civil Resistance Works," 37–41. This case study does not include the 2007 Saffron Revolution, mainly led by Buddhist monks. It is focused only on the Four Eights protest.

106. Chenoweth and Stephan, 41.

107. Chenoweth and Stephan, 39.

the international sanction did not produce the desired results; mobilization was selective and leader dependent.[108]

To comparatively analyze the Four Eights Protest and King's Selma march, which resulted in the franchise to African Americans, we can conclude that the reasons why the former failed and the latter succeeded were the domestic factors – first, over-relying on a single personality and the inability to reconcile across competing factions.[109] The whole population looked to a single personality, Suu Kyi, thus the movement was paralyzed when she was put under house arrest. For the latter, although it was true that King was the most outstanding personality during the civil rights movement, there were also other contemporaries like Malcolm X.

In the case of Myanmar, there was no one who might compare favourably with Suu Kyi. The second factor was indeed much more serious than the first. During the Four Eights movement, there were a number of competing factions that desired to lead the movement in their own ways. In contrast, through leading the Selma march, the whole population of African Americans had learned after many years of intimidation that their salvation was only in united action. When one stood up, he was run out of town; if a thousand stood up together, the situation was bound to be drastically overhauled.[110] Those two decisive factors play such a crucial role in determining success or failure.

However, we can also see the Four Eights protest, which lasted two years (1988–1990), in such a manner that instead of viewing it from a pragmatic outlook (either win or lose), it still had a great impact and has become a milestone for the political history of Myanmar. The protest united a number of university students who have not given up and have kept fighting against the dictatorship, and some have still been working as activists and politicians in the present day. Thus, the Four Eights protest was not a total failure in the sense that it has generated a strong abhorrence of the despotism in the population of the nation.

Moreover, what needs to be observed along with the success of the Four Eights protest is the political and cultural history of the country. Why did

---

108. Chenoweth and Stephan, 41–42.
109. See chapter 4 where I analyzed the marches King led.
110. Carson, *Autobiography of Martin Luther King*, 272.

military dictatorship last so long? Even now, it can hardly be said that military rule is over. We can say that Myanmar is partly on the path to democracy, and at the same time, the army is still in control of politics. That is, the army still has the power to hamstring the present government. In studying politics in Myanmar, it is insufficient to assess it without examining the political and cultural values, attitude, and history. It would not be adequate to gauge the success and failure of nonviolent resistance by having a comparative analysis between Myanmar and other Southeast Asian countries. Thus, there are other reasons why the Four Eights protest failed to overthrow the military government. As this research examines, Myanmar political values, which have dominated politics for nearly a century, are still predominant even in this modern era. So Myanmar desperately needs a genuine transformation from the old political values of the DS to the democratic values of the DFO. The question to ask is, should we follow the path of Ne Win and Than Shwe, or of Suu Kyi? To put it another way, should the people of Myanmar still stick to the old political values of the DS? Or should they make every endeavour to transform the DS into the DFO?

7.4.5 Traditionalism or Transformation?

Since gaining independence, the country of Myanmar has encountered the question of where it should be heading. Specifically, should Myanmar be traditionalistic or transformative concerning its future? By traditionalism, I mean the belief that regards traditions as more important than any other idea. In contrast, transformation refers to a process of changing something inside out from one thing into another. In other words, should the country continue to dwell in the glorious days of premodern political values in a monarchical era, or strive for change, or metamorphosis? This is the existential question for all of Myanmar to respond.

There are two scholars whose views are fundamentally similar and poles apart from other scholars because of the cultural relativism and historical determinism in their interpretations of the politics of Myanmar. Hence, they both are viewed as advocates of traditionalism, who contend that the values of democracy and human rights or of the DFO are incompatible with those of Myanmar culture. They are Robert H. Taylor and Michael Aung-Thwin. In fact, they both are academicians trained in the area of the history of Southeast

Asia. I have briefly interacted with them in the earlier discussion. I will now clarify their analysis of Myanmar politics in more detail. Taylor is a veteran specialist in Myanmar politics, whereas Aung-Thwin is a Burmese historian, a professor of Asian Studies and chairman of the Asian Studies Program at the University of Hawaii. Both were trained to be historians, particularly regarding the history of Southeast Asia.

As historians, both Taylor and Aung-Thwin examine Ne Win's military coup in 1962 and the army rule in the light of Myanmar history. Chao-Tzang Yawnghwe observes that, for both of them, the military rule is seen "as restoring to the Burmese polity certain positive traditional values and symbolism, i.e., as an experiment, as it were, in a form of Burmese-Buddhist socialism designed to bring about some modernising changes while minimising its ill-effect."[111] In many of his writings, Taylor has strongly stressed the importance of the nation's history for all readers in understanding the current political situations of Myanmar. So, he asserts that all the attempts for political change – whether democratic or authoritarian – are likely to result in failure unless the history of Myanmar, and how it came to be in its current condition, is not carefully studied.[112] By emphasizing the country's cultural distinctions, his writings on Myanmar have praised the military rule. His work, *The State in Myanmar*, is, according to David Scott Mathieson, almost an ode to autocratic expedience.[113] Taylor believes that the Myanmar people welcomed the 1962 coup, and so they approved the authoritarian rule. For him, the Myanmar state after the postcolonial period has two major weaknesses: parliamentary democracy itself and federalism, which were easily manipulated by politicians representing landlords, capitalists, and others seeking power and wealth for personal rather than public ends.[114] Therefore, Taylor concludes that abolishing them (parliamentary democracy and federalism) was necessary for the state to reaffirm itself over other institutions in civil society.[115] In that book, Taylor also expresses his opinion on Suu Kyi. For him, Suu Kyi is an inexperienced politician without a good knowledge

---

111. Yawnghwe, "Ne Win's Tatmadaw Dictatorship," 28.
112. Taylor, "Pathways to the Present," 1.
113. Mathieson, "Myanmar Meanderings."
114. Taylor, *State in Myanmar*, 294.
115. Taylor, 294.

of the political history; she has simply become popular because of her father, Aung San. In particular, he criticized her for her confrontational approach to generals.[116]

Likewise, Aung-Thwin sees the era from the time of British annexation (1885) to the end of parliamentary democracy or Ne Win's coup (1962) as "meaningless order"[117] – order that was largely irrelevant to the Myanmar socio-political values and norms. With this view in mind, he interprets the 1962 military coup as an effort to restore "meaningful order"[118] to a psychologically disoriented society, and resurrect a (Burmese) cultural identity.[119] He insists that the 1948 independence from Britain, for the majority of people, was largely a meaningless event; and for most it made little difference to the primary concerns of their daily lives.[120] In general, Taylor and Aung-Thwin have something in common in the way they interpret the political situations in Myanmar. Not only do they both justify the military rule from a historical perspective, they also see it as culturally the most relevant. Taylor sees the contemporary political tension between the forces of militarism and the forces of democracy as a clash between the values of traditional indigenous communalism versus the values of modern and Western individualism.[121] In his view, the military focused on the maintenance of tradition, while Suu Kyi and the NLD favour a concept of individual electoral rights and obligation. He is, therefore, sceptical about the democratization of Burma in the future.

Aung-Thwin is much more supportive than Taylor in regard to assessing the military rule in Myanmar. In the article, "Parochial Universalism, Democracy *Jihad* and the Orientalist Image of Burma: The New Evangelism," he laid himself wide open to the criticism of those who regard him as an apologist of the regime. By parochial universalism, Aung-Thwin refers to taking the ideals of democracy and human rights as universal doctrines.[122] For him, Myanmar has its own cultural and political characteristics, which

---

116. Taylor, 412.
117. Aung-Thwin, "British 'Pacification,'" 245–261.
118. Aung-Thwin.
119. Aung-Thwin, 247.
120. Aung-Thwin, "1948 and Burma's Myth," 23.
121. Taylor, "Political Values and Political Conflict," 33.
122. Aung-Thwin, "Parochial Universalism," 484.

are different from the westernized American values. In such a culturally diverse world, no values – American or other European western values – have a monopoly on others. He insists,

> I think it is because the arrogance that usually goes along with power requires more than just having it; it must also be validated by the powerless. Much like the white slave owner whose actual power over the black slave was simply not enough, he also needed to have the slave *admit* that the unequal relationship was the "correct" order of things; Burma – small, poor, weak and (to the U.S) insignificant (like Cuba) – by not kowtowing to the most powerful nation on earth, has, in effect, refused to acknowledge that desired link between power and virtue that is so important to the American self-image.[123]

There are some critical points in the views of Taylor and of Aung-Thwin in interpreting politics in Myanmar. First, they both are mainly trained as historians, not as political scientists. As historians, they have significantly contributed many writings to Asian histories, especially Burmese; they both unequivocally encourage us to read carefully the history of Myanmar, in order to understand the military rule that had persistently dominated for more than five decades. However, their interpretation of politics in Myanmar through historical eyes is unwarranted. They, as historians, are seemingly too focused on historical factors – how the past has produced the present. In an interview, Aung-Thwin insists that the current political situations in Myanmar are simply the products of the past – the past is in the present.[124] Put simply, both Taylor and Aung-Thwin appear to be heavily influenced by historical determinism. In historical determinism, all human acts are determined exclusively by their antecedents; suggesting that given the same circumstances, people always behave in the same way.[125] As historians, what Taylor and Aung-Thwin are trying to do is to show that all the political movements of

---

123. Aung-Thwin, 505.
124. Aung-Thwin, "Michael Aung-Thwin for a Look at Modern Burma."
125. "Historical Determinism," *Catholic Dictionary* https://www.catholicculture.org/culture/library- /dictionary/index.cfm?id=33934.

the country Myanmar are perfectly regular and that, like all other movements, they are solely determined by their antecedents.

Though Taylor and Aung-Thwin may be regarded as the regime's apologists, the former is somewhat moderate compared to the latter. In an interview, Taylor states that he is not the regime's apologist; his argument is that the responses made by the international community – such as Western sanctions, repeated condemnations, and so on – created more problems and made the regime more reluctant for change. As a historian, he is convinced that it is not that easy to overcome years of history in the blink of an eye.[126] Despite this statement, Taylor's writings basically underline the importance of the country's history in dealing with the politics. The irony is that his works on Myanmar, by implication, happen to support the military regime whether he wants to admit it or not. D. S. Mathieson, in his review of *The State in Myanmar*, points out that Taylor barely acknowledges the fact that the military rule caused widespread repression for two decades. In his recent work *General Ne Win: A Political Biography*, he examines the dictator Ne Win in a positive way. He acknowledges that many lives were lost, and opportunities for development and enrichment were destroyed during the Ne Win era. Nonetheless, he looks at the positive side of Ne Win's rule, arguing that Ne Win created a nation that had the resilience to withstand more than twenty years of post-Cold War economic sanctions.[127] On the other hand, he seems to ignore how Ne Win's government impoverished the country in numerous ways – economically, educationally, morally, and so on; and how the current and coming generations are still affected by it. To justify his perspective, Taylor quotes George M. Fraser:

> You cannot, you must not, judge the past by the present; you must try to see it in its own terms and values, if you are to have some inkling of it. You may not like what you see, but do not on that account fall into the error to trying to adjust it to suit your own vision of what it ought to have been.[128]

---

126. Farrelly, "Interview with Professor Robert Taylor."
127. Taylor, *General Ne Win*, 5.
128. Taylor, 5. See also MacDonald Fraser, *Quartered Safe Out Here*, 125.

Of course, to objectively examine someone (in this case Ne Win) in the past, it is of supreme importance to understand the historical context of his time. But it does not mean that all the things Ne Win did for the sake of gaining power should be sidestepped merely on the basis of the historical context of that time. Put differently, it is a lopsided view to justify and favour the past at the cost of the future. It seems that Taylor, in his biography of Ne Win, is trying to justify all the evils Ne Win committed. In short, Taylor's biography of Ne Win is, in fact, an attempt to optimistically explore what Ne Win had achieved; thereby suggesting that Ne Win was not such an evil dictator people think he was. The way in which Ne Win and Than Shwe ruled the country was apparently despotic; and to be precise, gaining power through the use of arms and violence reflects the practice of power in the DS, and it is radically poles apart from the practice of power in the DFO.

Even worse, Aung-Thwin's articulation of the military rule as rebuilding the authentic Myanmar is much stronger than Taylor's work. His article "Parochial Universalism" is, in one way or another, a support of the military rule from the perspective of cultural relativism. There, he looks at the two conflicting cultural values between the United States of America and Myanmar. According to him, America's political culture fundamentally values democratic principles, while the culture of Myanmar accentuates a traditional hierarchical system. But in Aung-Thwin's understanding, what the US has been doing is universalizing the ideals of democracy and human rights and forcing them to be implanted in the soil of Myanmar, which has its own political values.

In the article, Aung-Thwin presents the two overpowering approaches in Myanmar studies – whether one supports Suu Kyi's political values or those of the military rule. It is, for him, not an either/or choice. He suggests that there should be more than two approaches in studies of Myanmar. According to him, the approach he has undertaken is neither one, whereby he received an unsigned death threat during the height of anti-Burma government sentiment.[129] In "Parochial Universalism" Aung-Thwin, by way of illustration,

---

129. The letter said, "Dear Ko Aung-Thwin, Even though you are a teacher of history, partial to the military government, and wrote and talked of the economic success of the military government, one day, on the victorious day of the students' revolution, you are going to repay the blood-debt of the students. [this can also be translated as "you will repay in blood."]

quotes from a Hindu myth, the *Ramayana*, in order to comparatively describe the military rule and America's universalisztion of democratic values and human rights.[130] He represents the military rule as Vali, a monkey king, and America as Rama, the perfect human and a deity Vishnu incarnate. In the myth, Rama shoots Vali in the back because Vali took the wife of his brother who just died. In the monkey's culture, taking care of one's brother's wife after his death was common and expected. But Rama tells Vali that there are higher ideals which, whether human or monkey, are to be followed. According to Aung-Thwin, Rama (representing the US) is universalizing his human values to which all, whether human or monkey, should aspire to. Vali (representing Myanmar) is eventually convinced and acknowledges his inferior way of thinking. He deserves to die at the hands of such an honourable man, Rama.[131]

Aung-Thwin, through this myth, argues that like Rama, the United States should not shoot Myanmar in the back. On the surface, this example appears to be illuminating. However, in thinking deeply about this comparison, it degrades Myanmar as inferior while it eulogizes the US as superior. Myanmar, needless to say, is much weaker and smaller in global relations than the US. However, it does not mean that the United States has a higher morality than Myanmar. If Aung-Thwin is a cultural relativist, he should look for another suitable example to back up his argument. His treatment of equating Myanmar to the monkey king Vali, while viewing the US as the deity Vishnu incarnate does not do justice enough to the politically complicated situation of Myanmar.

Moreover, what Aung-Thwin seems to neglect is the other side of the same coin. That is, the world in which we live is becoming a single village, which scholars call globalization. Despite researchers' diverse definitions of the term

---

You have also betrayed your mother's Karen race. All of this is going to be recorded in the students' historical document. Victory to the Students' revolution," Aung-Thwin, "Parochial Universalism," 495. Truly, it was such an unwise and audacious reaction against Aung-Thwin's cultural relativistic approach, for which Burmese pro-democratic groups owe him an apology.

130. The *Ramayana* (Sanskrit: "Rama's Journey") is one of the two great epic poems of India, the other being the *Mahabharata* ("Great Epic of the Bharata Dynasty"). The *Ramayana* was composed in Sanskrit, probably not before 300 BCE, by the poet Valmiki, and in its present form consists of some 24,000 couplets divided into seven books, *Britannica Academic, s.v.* "Ramayana" http://academic.eb.com/EBchecked/topic/490529- /Ramayana.

131. Aung-Thwin, "Parochial Universalism," 483.

"globalization," what they have in common is connection, interpenetration, or interdependence. For example, Manfred B. Steger defines globalization as "a multidimensional set of social processes that create, multiply, stretch, and intensify worldwide social interdependencies and exchanges while at the same time fostering in people a growing awareness of deepening connections between the local and the distant."[132] Globalization, in short, touches both internally and externally every aspect of humankind and society; it touches politics as well as economics, and culture as well as academics. For Aung-Thwin, universalizing human rights is a form of Pax Americana. What is more, he criticizes that even awarding the Nobel Peace Prize to Suu Kyi has political intent; therefore, it is a form of the secular canonization. This criticism shows that Aung-Thwin, in favour of cultural relativism, goes too far. As a result, he also forgets the historical existence of the Universal Declaration of Human Rights.[133] Evidently, the declaration is not the American invention but it has come into existence through the cooperative endeavour of many nations. Historically, it is very strange to deem human rights as Pax Americana. The country Myanmar itself signed the bill of the declaration. To take a look at the declaration from the perspective of globalization, human rights are:

> a set of universal claims to safeguard human dignity from illegitimate coercion ... These norms are codified in a widely endorsed set of international undertakings: the "International Bill of Human Rights;" phenomenon-specific treaties on war crimes, genocide, and torture; and protections for vulnerable groups such as the UN Convention on the Rights of the Child and the Convention on the Elimination of Discrimination against Women.[134]

---

132. Steger, *Globalization*, 13.

133. The Declaration did not just happen to come instantly, but it took time to come into reality. Being drafted by the Commission of Human Rights, which consisted of eighteen members from various nationalities (Asia, Middle East, North and South Americas, and so on) and adopted by the General Assembly by a vote of forty-eight, Myanmar was one of the countries that voted in favour of the Declaration.

134. "Introduction," in Brysk *Globalization and Human Rights*, 3.

Obviously, Aung-Thwin's lopsided argument here suggests a wanton disregard for globalization because he seems to be trapped in the web of cultural relativism and historical determinism. A. G. Hopkins, unlike the Aung-Thwin, invites historians to engage in the debate on globalization: "In a globalised world, ideas flow across boundaries even more smoothly than capital; therefore historians now have an opportunity to cross disciplinary frontiers by engaging this debate."[135] In saying so, I do not mean that all the things that globalization brings about are to be uncritically accepted. The important thing is that it is not wise in this contemporary world to stick to one's culture and isolate oneself from others in the name of cultural relativism.

Further, the historical condition of Myanmar overwhelms the interpretation of Taylor and Aung-Thwin so much so that they fail to see politics in Myanmar from any other perspective. Academically, politics is a different discipline that attempts to study the politics of humankind scientifically. In the study of dictators and dictatorship, Matasha Ezrow and Erica Frantz observe several causes of tyranny. They are the reduced level of institutionalization, economic conditions, and the role of ethnicity.[136] Culture is just one of the reasons for tyranny. In this regard, the interpretations of Taylor and Aung-Thwin are too subjectively in favour of the cultural history of Myanmar.

Now we have viewed the considerable overlaps between the politics in the monarchical era and the postcolonial Myanmar politics. Attaining and retaining power, peace, unity through violence, and the purge of any potential challengers is deep-seated in the political practice of those in Myanmar. It is a reigning culture of Myanmar politics from the monarchical period to the present. Or apparently it is the characteristics of the domination system, where the idea of power through violence is at the centre. The military regime as cultural conservatives discouraged and scorned the idea of democracy, human rights and freedom by saying that these are alien to the cultural and political nature of Myanmar. Aung-Thwin and Taylor, from the cultural relativist approach, support that Ne Win and Than Shwe did their best in making a regressive change. Unfortunately, what Taylor and Aung-Thwin might not

---

135. Hopkins, "History of Globalization," 36.
136. Ezrow and Frantz, *Dictators and Dictatorships*, 28–32.

be conscious of is that their argument for the traditional political nature of Myanmar is supportive of two successive military regimes of the nation.

What can King, Suu Kyi and Wink provide for such a political culture? Evidently, they are not traditionalists who resist changing culture. They are all forward-looking: for King, it was the dream; for Suu Kyi, a culture of democracy; and for Wink, the domination-free order. Each has a vivid dream for their future. In spite of being future-oriented, they did not forget the past, but learned from it without dwelling on it. Likewise, they did their best in their present time in order to realize the future they desired.

Thus, human beings are not merely products of the past, but they are also creative and forward-looking beings. It is absolutely fair to say that what happened in the past has a significant impact on the present. But, we are also naturally endowed with creativity for the future. What Taylor and Aung-Thwin fail to pay enough attention to is the question of the future. For them, the past continues to be the present reality, which is why we are facing its consequences. Logically we were, therefore we are. They neglect to ask the question: so what can we do in the present for the sake of the future? More simply: if the past is in the present, how can we deal with the present for the good of the future? We are reaping now what we sowed in the past. Simply stated, we ought to plant the good seeds now for the interests of the future.

Therefore, traditionalism, represented by the military, Taylor and Aung-Thwin, concentrates merely on the past and the present. Put simply, traditionalists dwell on the past and they keep the past in the present. The past determines everything at all times – the past, the present, and the future. In contrast, the transformational approach is different from cultural conservatives and radicals; the former esteems the cultural heritage and preserves it, whereas the latter focuses on changing cultural values more radically. Thus, what Myanmar needs is neither cultural conservatives nor radicals, but the transformational approach, which examines the past with great care, dwells on the present, and strives towards the future with a purpose. If the people of Myanmar have a desire to enhance the characteristics of the DFO, they have no option except transforming the values of the DS, because peace, justice and reconciliation can never be found within the DS. King, Suu Kyi, and Wink are advocates of transformation, who learn from the past and endeavour in the present to achieve the desired future. They look at the past and stay in the present with the future in mind. For Wink, it is the people who embody the characteristics of the DFO through whom a genuine transformation of the DS will be launched. King also had a dream which strengthened him to endure any form of suffering with the hope of the future. For Suu Kyi, her task is cultivating the culture of democracy in the land where tyrannic culture reigned.

7.5 Summary of the Chapter

In this chapter, I have explored the idea that gaining and retaining power by any means is the spirit of traditional politics in Myanmar. In the power struggle, Buddhism becomes a means to legitimize the power usurped by violence and the traditional rituals (astrology, numerology, and *yadaya*) are the backups for maintaining power. These political distinctives reflect the nature of the domination system. Therefore, the conclusion to be drawn is that Myanmar political culture has been a part of the DS since the monarchical period.

Under such a culture of the DS, Myanmar is faced with questions: where should the country be directed? Would the country go back to the traditional politics of the nation? Or continue metamorphosing it in the light of democratic principles and human rights? Two successive military despots, Ne Win and Than Shwe, have resuscitated the spirit of Myanmar politics that had been practiced since the precolonial period. In contrast, Suu Kyi has attempted to lead the country into somewhere higher than it has been. This is, for her, a spiritual leadership. In this sense, the journey towards the revolution of the spirit must still be ongoing. Only through such a revolution would the country that existed beneath the spirit of military despotism for many decades be able to be transformed. Furthermore, in the process of this spiritual leadership or metamorphosis, Myanmar needs to recognize the inseparability of the means and end, and rule of law. In the next, and concluding chapter, I will draw some political implications for Christians in Myanmar with the aim of showing how Christians should engage in the political system of Myanmar.

CHAPTER 8

Conclusion: Political Implications for Christians in Myanmar

Walter Wink views the world as the domination system (the DS) where violence lies at the centre. There is also an alternative order that Wink calls God's domination-free order (the DFO), which can only be realized through nonviolence. This view is theoretically comprehensive, but it necessitates a detailed order of praxis. In order to be theoretically robust and practically relevant, the study has taken two practitioners of nonviolence, Martin Luther King and Aung San Suu Kyi, and has engaged them in a dialogue with the theology of Wink. From this discussion, what political implications can be drawn for Christians in Myanmar – Christians who see politics as an un-Christian thing, and who live in the country where despotic leaders reigned for nearly half a century? From chapters 2 to 6, we have seen a critical interaction between Wink, King, and Suu Kyi. In the last chapter, we examined the political culture of Myanmar through the integral lens of Wink, King, and Suu Kyi. As this study is located in the field of practical theology, this chapter will draw practical political implications for Christians in Myanmar with a view to challenging how they should engage in the political context of Myanmar.

8.1 Implications of Nonviolence for Christians in Myanmar

What implications can we draw from the study of Wink, King, and Suu Kyi for Christians in Myanmar – the implications expected to be the sources for Christians in Myanmar to engage with the political culture, which mirrors the features of what Wink calls, the domination system? The implications are categorized into three divisions: theological, ethical, and socio-political.

8.1.1 Theological Implications

The first theological implication to draw from this study is that Wink's view of the DS and the DFO is a new paradigm for Christians in Myanmar who were born and bred into such an authoritarian context. Wink reminds Christians that, whatever their socio-cultural locations, they do not belong to the system of this world. There is the alternative that Jesus calls the kingdom of God but Wink renames it the domination-free order. Unless Christians in Myanmar grasp such a sharp distinction between the two contrasting systems, they would be trapped under the delusion of the DS or worldly system. Seeing a distinction between the DS and the DFO helps Christians not only to identify with the values of the DS, but to embody those of the DFO. On the other hand, making a distinction between the DS and the DFO does not necessarily mean that Christians are supposed to isolate themselves from the surrounding society. In fact, Christians are called to live out the values of the kingdom of God with the aim of not separating themselves from the world but transforming the world or the DS into the DFO.

King and Suu Kyi, despite the fact that they do not view the world as Wink does, have clear mental pictures that envision, navigate, and empower them. King called it the dream of America, whereas Suu Kyi names it the culture of democracy. Their visions enable them not to identify with the values and ways of the system that they are overcoming. Instead, they live with the values of the system that they seek to bring in. Therefore Christians as a minority group in Myanmar should be aware of the values and standards of the DS, lest they be inadvertently engulfed by those.

Most importantly, seeing the distinction between the DS and the DFO makes all the difference to Christians in Myanmar. First, it will change the way in which power is exercised. The way in which Christians in Myanmar exercise power will no longer be abusive but supportive, not controlling but nurturing, not overbearing but meek. Therefore, Suu Kyi asserts that the present need for Myanmar is a spiritual leadership. In a lecture at Singapore Management University, she introduced a new idea of Spiritual Quotient (SQ). SQ is, for her, different from Emotional Quotient (EQ) and Intelligence

Quotient (IQ). By SQ, she refers to reaching out somewhere we have never been before. The leader Myanmar needs is someone who can lead the country to somewhere higher and better than we have been. Where we have been in the past is under military and authoritarian leadership. Such a spiritual leader will lead the nation to a new place, where democratic values are experienced.[1] She believes that only through such a spiritual leadership can the mindset of the military or domineering leadership be transformed. For Suu Kyi, the mindset of such a spiritual leadership is, "the determination to serve, not to lead, and it is the resolve and the commitment to serve that decides who is the real *spiritual* leader, and not the desire to be a leader."[2] Spiritual leadership, simply put, is a servant leadership. In authoritarian leadership, to lead is to control; but in spiritual leadership, to lead is to support.

In the DFO, Christians are called to serve, not to seek power. What matters for Christians is no longer gaining power but serving wherever they are. Since it is not the power to control, the people in the DFO always have a role to play because the world in which they live is always in desperate need of service. Unlike the politicians who cannot do a single thing unless they are elected, those in the DFO are always of service to the people who want to be served. This changes the way in which all politicians practice their politics. This kind of service would overturn the spirit of authoritarian leadership and bring about an authentic revolution of the leadership culture in Myanmar.

Next, seeing a distinction between the DS and DFO also deepens the way Christians in Myanmar practice Christianity. Religion in the DS is a powerful instrument to validate the system; but in the DFO, it is a tool for self-correction. In Wink's perspective, religion has two dimensions: outer and inner. For Wink and King, God is more concerned with our inner attitude than observing the outward rituals. Similarly, Suu Kyi believes that the essence of Buddhism is not the observance of Buddhist rituals, but having a right intention and attitude. When this central or inner teaching is overlooked for the sake of the outer or peripherals, the essence of religion becomes perverted. The repercussion of replacing the central teaching of religion with the

---

1. Suu Kyi, "SMU Ho Rih Hwa."
2. Suu Kyi.

peripherals has suffocated the spirit of religion. Eventually, religion becomes an instrument of oppression and a legitimacy for terror and violence.

Buddhism is dominant in every aspect of Burmese culture. Being Buddhist defines social and cultural identity as well as personal identity. Unfortunately, many people become so-called Buddhists just for the sake of identifying social and cultural standing. This means Buddhism becomes, for those people, a cultural identity rather than a way of life. When the essence of Buddhism, which is practicing *mettā* in every area of life, is replaced with a racial identity, the religion becomes overbearing and exclusive to others.

As a matter of fact, both Christianity and Buddhism encourage us not to take everything for granted but to be self-critical. Self-examination is hugely emphasized in both religions. But the problem is that our ego or self is a product of the web of socialization. Thus Wink stresses that it is imperative to die not only to our ego but also to the Powers. That means we are to notice the power of socialization – how our culture and society has significantly impacted on us, whether we are conscious of it or not. We are not to be trapped by the outer forms of religion and forgetful of the spirit. If we do so, the consequence will always be calamitous. Focusing on the external forms of religion at the cost of its interiority always adds fuel to the flames of the domination system. When that happened Christianity became a tool to vindicate segregationism and Buddhism, an instrument to legitimate the despotic regime.

Therefore King, using the prophetic traditions in the Old Testament, exposed how white Christians' use of the Bible in reinforcing segregation contradicts the real biblical teaching. Likewise Suu Kyi's socially engaged Buddhism has shed light on the inseparable relationship between politics and morality. Therefore Buddhism and Christianity, if their essential teachings are carefully practiced, can emancipate us individually and collectively from corruption, prejudice, and injustice. In this sense, Christians in Myanmar should search for a deep sense of meaning behind every outward form of Christianity, thereby performing their faith with deep conviction.

However one important thing to note is that the distinction between the DS and the DFO does not create the we/they or us/them syndrome. Instead understanding that the unsurmountable impact of the web of socialization is upon both Christians and non-Christians breaks down the we/they or us/

them syndrome. The real problem is not just our enemies or opponents, but also us because we both are products of the same socialization. As discussed in chapter 6, Min Zin reflects Suu Kyi's idea of revolution of the spirit, that there is continuity between the previous military regime and the dissidents. The regime was not a foreign body, therefore, when we look at the mirror of military dictatorship carefully, we can find some parts of our face.[3] This will also shed the prejudice that the problem is them, not us, thereby leading us to genuine humility. And this humility will be a source out of which Christians can learn to work together with those who are different.

The third theological implication from this study of Wink, King and Suu Kyi is the knowledge of the integral relationship between spiritual and political, personal and social. Wink is convinced of the paradoxical nature of the personal and social: the irreducibility of the personal to the social and the irreducibility of the social to the personal. For him, God's will is not just the transformation of people but also of society.[4] Similarly, King also learned the integral relationship between the personal and the social, at first from his father, and later from the father of social gospel, Walter Rauschenbusch. The gospel, for King, deals with the whole man, not only his soul, but his body; not only spiritual well-being, but material well-being.[5]

Likewise Suu Kyi separated herself from previous politicians, who dichotomized politics and Buddhism. Instead politics, for her, is integrally related to Buddha's teaching of *mettā* (loving-kindness) and *thissa* (truth). She believes that it is appropriate to talk about *mettā* and *thissa* in the political context because politics is about people.[6] Wink, King, and Suu Kyi all shed light on the integral nature of politics and the religion they practice. An overemphasis on the personal at the cost of the social, and on the spiritual at the risk of the political, is apparently lopsided. This radically challenges the mindset of Myanmar Christians who regard politics as non-spiritual. As mentioned in chapter 1, Christians in Myanmar – especially Pentecostal Christians – are unconcerned

---

3. See chapter 6, pp. 245–247.
4. Wink, *Engaging the Powers*, 73–85.
5. King, *Stride toward Freedom*, 78.
6. Suu Kyi, *Letters from Burma*.

about politics.[7] In the country where military despots ruled for a nearly half century, Christians with such an attitude and outlook should no longer remain themselves aloof from the political affairs of the nation; instead they desperately need to be transformed into a consciousness-raising community.

Finally, King, Suu Kyi and Wink are all fully conscious that what they are fighting is not an individual person but the system. In a nutshell, all of them see evil which is resided not only in an individual person but also within society. Put simply, it is systemic evil or sin – an evil or sin that is entrenched in the system of a nation or institution. We are not to blame a particular person for this systemic sin. The people in a society, institution, or nation are all responsible for that systemic evil. This is a great challenge to Christians in Myanmar who regard sin merely as individual such as stealing, cheating, smoking, adultery, fornication, killing, and so on. In contrast, King, Suu Kyi and Wink see that evil that they are fighting against is more than what we personally did. This leads them to distinguish what a person is from what they do; so they encouraged their supporters to hate what people did, not the people themselves. Therefore, Christians in Myanmar are called to seek to fight against systemic sin as well as the individual.

8.1.2 Ethical Implications

The first ethical implication for Christians in Myanmar is the integral nature of means and end. If the desired end is peace, the path to it can never be through violence because they contradict each other. Wink and King have a firm conviction regarding the inseparable nature of means and end. But Suu Kyi, as a politician, is too compromising because she would allow a short burst of violence if it could prevent worse things happening in the long run. Previously, she took the nonviolent path in resisting the military regime, so she was known as an icon of human rights. Since she has become a politician, she has started to change some of the principles she adhered to before. For

---

7. Some months ago, I met a prominent Pentecostal leader. We had a talk about my dissertation. He knew the title of my research. He said, "Hay your thesis is about nonviolence and politics, right?" I replied, "yes." And I continued to explain more to him about my thesis. Then he concluded, "brother, be aware that your thesis would be merely about political things." What he meant by that implies that politics is an entirely different thing that has nothing to do with Christianity.

Conclusion: Political Implications for Christians in Myanmar

example, her silence in the time of warring between Kachin and the Burmese army, and her response to the conflict in the Rakhine state disappoint the international community. During the time of resisting Ne Win and Than Shwe's regimes, Suu Kyi was prompt in making responses to what the regimes did in terms of breaking human rights. Now she seems to be too conscious of commenting on the military in either a negative or positive way. But it is understandable that Suu Kyi is faced with the hardliner's military officers from the time she becomes a politician. It is inevitable for her to negotiate and compromise with them.

In this book, we have seen that there are two ethical consequences for the political context of Myanmar presented in the interaction between King, Suu Kyi, and Wink. First, nonviolence is the only means to end the tradition of violence in politics because of the vicious circle of violence. Political change throughout the history of Myanmar has always been brought about through violence. The history of politics in Myanmar affirms this reality. Arms were always a means to achieve peace, order, and power. In other words, it is the culture of "might is right" or redemptive violence. So the tradition of violence has been prolonged in the political struggles of Myanmar. King and Wink are ethically deontologists, seeing the inseparable nature of means and end in regard to building a culture of peace and order. The debate between teleological or utilitarian and deontological ethics is ongoing. But in the case of violence and nonviolence, it is hard to put it into the category of teleological-deontological debate. Using violence as a means to build peace and order as an end is self-contradictory because the means itself opposes the end. Violence itself is inherently malevolent toward others; whereas nonviolence is intrinsically benevolent.

Despite Suu Kyi's compromising position in her political dealings, the integral nature of means and end is one of the principles of nonviolence that Christians in Myanmar should bear in mind. This principle challenges the Christians in the military and who join the insurgencies to fight against the military. For Christians, Jesus's death on the cross indeed proves that if the end is peace, the way to it cannot be through violence or arms. Jesus Christ paid his life on the cross so that the enmity between God and humanity may be ended and peace be made. Thus the integral nature of means and end is Christ's way and so it should be the way of Christians.

Second, seeing the person as separate from what he or she does is a very crucial ethical principle for Christians in Myanmar to learn. Wink, King and Suu Kyi all stress the importance of this principle in such a way that in nonviolent resistance, what we are to fight against is not the persons who do evil things, but the evils that they do. Theologically speaking, it is also the way in which God redeemed humankind. That is, God loves sinners but hates sin; therefore he paid the wage for sin on the cross in order to save sinners.[8] Unless we separate a person from their deed, we will end up fighting people, not the evil or system.

Third, nonviolent resistance for Wink, King and Suu Kyi is not a win/lose solution, but win/win. To put it another way, the aim of nonviolence is not revenge but friendship, reconciliation, or ending enmity. This is also very vital to Christians in Myanmar, most of whom are from ethnic minority groups such as Chin, Kachin and Karen, racially discriminated against from the time of Ne Win's coup in 1962. Burmans' racial discrimination caused a grievance and hatred among minority groups. As a consequence the Christians from these ethnic minorities have a strong dislike and distrust for the ethnic majority, the Burmans. That nonviolent resistance is not to defeat enemies, but to win friendship, radically challenges Christians in Myanmar to see their hatred and grievance inside.

Further this implication can also be applied to the whole nation of Myanmar in its journey to national reconciliation. Myanmar, as a country of diverse ethnic and religious groups, has been struggling with racial divisions since the colonial period. At present, the conflicts that are going on are not just between the military and the opposition political parties but also between majority Burmans and ethnic minorities. The most long-lasting tension is between the Buddhist majority and non-Buddhist minorities. On 3 November 2012, Thein Sein's government launched the Myanmar Peace Centre (MPC) with the vision of playing a key role in the development of a

---

8. That God loves the sinners but hates the sin does not necessarily affirm the teaching of universalism that says that everyone will be saved at the end because God will not let them be tormented eternally in hell. The point here is to put an emphasis on the "way" in which God saved sinners through Jesus Christ. This is theologically a controversial issue that the thesis does not focus on. So, I mention that the emphasis is not to support the universalism, but the way in which God saved sinners.

Conclusion: Political Implications for Christians in Myanmar 313

peaceful nation inclusive of Myanmar's ethnic diversity.[9] However, the centre was criticized for its incapability to cope with the violent conflict in the Rakhine state and the fighting between the military and the ethnic armed groups in the Kachin and Shan states. According to Bertil Lintner, the centre is incapable of promoting the peace, thus becoming an organization which is being paid for doing nothing.[10]

However, a glimmer of hope dawned for Myanmar in November 2015 when the NLD won a landslide victory in the general election. The government, when power was transferred to them in March 2016, said that Suu Kyi would lead the country's peacebuilding.[11] With the name of the twenty-first century Panglong, the first conference was held on 31 August 2016 under the leadership of Suu Kyi. Suu Kyi did her best in bringing many key players to the table including the rebel armies that did not sign a ceasefire drafted by the previous government. However, the conference ended with a long way ahead. An attendant reported, "We were able to present our proposals at this conference, but nothing important happened."[12] The second Panglong conference resumed on 29 May 2017, and ended much better than the first. A Chinese reporter Song Qingrun describes, "Notably, some important consensuses are federal democracy, equal rights of all ethnic groups, decentralisation of power to autonomous areas."[13] The present government, with a deep conviction, is committed to establishing a national reconciliation, therefore they resolved to run the twenty-first century Panglong conference until the conflict is resolved. However, the Panglong conference could not go further than expected because the fighting between the military and many ethnic insurgences in Kachin, Shan, and Karen states go on.

Truly the road to reconciliation in Myanmar cannot be reached overnight, it will take time. The conflicts between the then military regime and opposition parties, between the Burman majority and non-Burman minority, and between Buddhists and non-Buddhists are not recent, but age-old issues.

---

9. "Myanmar Peace Center (MPC)."
10. Yan Naing, "Peace Brokers Lack a Mandate."
11. Irrawaddy, "Suu Kyi and Government Peace Negotiator."
12. Myanmar Peace Summit Ends with Long Road Ahead," https://www.daily-sun.com/amp/post/164405.
13. Song Qingrun, "Second Panglong Conference."

Wink argues that the discrete steps towards reconciliation or peacebuilding have to be created depending on the cultural context. Hence, these steps might vary from case to case depending on contexts.[14] There is no one way approach to reach reconciliation in Myanmar. Despite the variety of these measures, there are certain elements without which the journey towards true reconciliation would be impossible. They are truth telling, forgiveness, and apology.

According to the two models of reconciliation, the IR (Interpersonal or Individual Reconciliation) and the NUR (National Unity and Reconciliation), King, Suu Kyi and Wink all may be categorized into the former because forgiveness for them plays a crucial role in the process of reconciliation. However, they do not all neglect the structural aspect of reconciliation in favour of the personal focus. It is not a choice of either the IR or the NUR. In Myanmar, a number of people had been victimized under the despotic regime in various ways. The hatred toward the military men is so seriously entrenched that reconciliation without forgiveness would not heal the wounds of the nation. At the same time, the people of Myanmar also suffered structural injustice under the military rule. Therefore, reconciliation without structural change and without giving proper attention to truth telling, forgiveness, and apology would be unable to establish the culture of democracy, human rights, and rule of law. In this context, what Myanmar needs is not merely personal, but also structural aspects in processing reconciliation.

Overall, the ethics of nonviolence is neither dogmatic nor legalistic. Wink is very precise in this regard, the church is called to nonviolence not in order to preserve its purity, but to express its fidelity – fidelity to its master Jesus Christ.[15] Since nonviolence is not a matter of legalism but of discipleship, Christians are not called to impose nonviolence on others, and if they do, it will negate the essence of nonviolence. The very reason why Christians follow the way of nonviolence is not because it works, but because it reflects the very nature of God.[16] For Christians, nonviolence is not an option because they follow the path of nonviolence out of their love for God, not out of the sense of obligation. Thus the basis of ethical choice is love, not law. Transferring

---

14. Wink, *When the Powers Fall*, 21.
15. Wink, *Engaging the Powers*, 217.
16. Wink, 217.

from the DS into the DFO is a process since we live in the same world where these two orders are in conflict. If nonviolence is a matter of discipleship, then discipleship is a process – the process of transferring from the DS into the DFO.

8.1.3 Socio-political Implication

King, Suu Kyi, and Wink all believe that nonviolent struggle never disparages the rule of law. Historically the idea of the rule of law was first introduced in Myanmar by the British colonial administration. However the Burmese society is person-centred. That is, what a person of high social status says is stronger than what is written in the law. Therefore the idea of rule of law is strange and alien to Myanmar culture. People in Myanmar have had difficulty in understanding the concept of the rule of law since the postcolonial era. For instance a political leader in the post-independence era saw the rule of law as disintegrating social life in Myanmar because it was an outlandish idea to tradition.[17] The people of Myanmar believe that humans are not made for a law but a law is made for humans. On the other hand, the idea of the rule of law is, by implication, that no one is above the law. Everyone, whether the ruler or the ruled, is subject to the law. In such a context, how can the culture of the rule of law be cultivated? Doing so will be countercultural between the cultures of person-centred and rule-centred. In other words, it will be an encounter between "law for humans" and "no one is above the law." The former sees humans as being at the core of everything while the latter looks at all humans on an equal level. Neither is entirely wrong. At the same time, they are not also against each other. So the question that arises in the process of democratization in Myanmar is how can we meaningfully engage these two cultures?

To take a closer look at the encounter, in Myanmar the traditional concept of law and the rule of law do not contradict each other but they unveil the paradoxical nature of law. On the one hand, law should be made for humankind in order for us to live in peace but on the other hand, everyone – including the ruler or the governor – should be subjected to the same law; all citizens should be considered equal before the law. In fact, they do not contradict each other. When it says that law is made for humans, it should

---

17. Maung, *Law and Custom in Burma*, 25–26.

not mean that a particular group or person is in control of the law. Instead, it says law is made for humans so that human society may exist in order and peace. Likewise when it mentions that no one is above the law it does not mean that we all are, like robots, supposed to live under lifeless regulations and rules. Rather, it means that we humans have a tendency to commit evil or stupid acts, therefore we need rules.

Thus, we need something that might prevent us from committing evil or perverting justice. In this sense, law for humans does not contradict the idea of rule of law; but instead they complement and mutually correct each other so that the former may not be stressed over the latter and vice versa. The point here is not to debate which one (law for humans or rule of law) is more important than the other but how they should be engaged. In the process of democratization in Myanmar, this engagement would play a vital role.

8.2 How Should Christians in Myanmar Begin to Engage with Politics?

In discussions of violence and nonviolence, many studies focus on the tactical or strategic and moral aspects. However, Walter Wink argues that nonviolence is not merely a socio-political tactic to achieve the desired end, a moral or religious code to gauge somebody's moral eminence or religious standing. It has a spiritual character. In the same way, violence is not merely a means to change a government or system. It also has, like nonviolence, a spiritual dimension. In this study, the word "spiritual" or "spirit" refers not to an otherworldly realm or extrasensory perception, but to the internality or innerness of an institution. In the previous chapter, we have seen that the political culture of Myanmar throughout its history mirrors the spirit of the DS, which is redemptive violence – massive use of violence for gaining power and making changes. How can the spirit of the DS in Myanmar be transformed?

First and foremost, the misconception of politics as non-spiritual or un-Christian among Christians in Myanmar has to be exposed. Distinguishing Christianity from politics is unwarranted because what matters is not whether Christianity is apolitical. In fact, Christianity itself is an alternative political order because it stands for the kingdom of God or the DFO, and at the same time, it contrasts sharply with the DS. This provides a theological framework for Christians in Myanmar to scrutinize the political context of Myanmar. This examination will be a lens to lead to a paradigm shift in the way Christians in Myanmar see politics and Christianity.

As examined in chapter 6, religion – Christianity or Buddhism – can be a means either to liberate the oppressed or to oppress people. This gives Christians in Myanmar advanced warning that the way they practice Christian faith does matter. So how should they practice Christianity in such a manner that it would bring about a genuine liberation for people? As noted, what makes a distinction between those who use religion for justifying their power and those who regard religion as self-correction is that the former lays huge emphasis on the observance of rituals and regulations of their religion, whereas the latter looks at the teachings of the religion to examine themselves for correcting their lives. Therefore Christians in Myanmar are called to ask themselves, why do we do what we do? They are not to practice outward aspects of their faith, e.g. going to church, reading the Bible and spending time in prayer for the sake of religiosity. Instead practicing Christian faith should be a heartfelt response to the God who first loves us.

Of course, there are always a number of people who just happen to be Christians or Buddhists simply because of their parents and the race to which they belong. For example, there is a saying in Myanmar that, "to be a Burman is to be a Buddhist." In other words, nationality and religion are intertwined. This mentality leads many people to simply become Buddhists not because they personally are convinced, but because of their parental and racial background. The same thing also happens with Christianity. According to the two contrasting systems (the DS vs the DFO), everyone is born and bred into the DS; no one has happened to be in the DFO by birth. Transferring from the DS into the DFO is the second event that happens later, when they receive the gospel of Jesus Christ.[18] Therefore the church should be the place in which people come to know the gospel and receive it, thereby transferring from the DS into the DFO.

As mentioned, Christians in Myanmar are not just religiously a minority group but majority of them are from ethnic minorities. As a consequence

---

18. I think that this kind of second event would restrict the entry into the DFO and Wink might disagree with me. But I would say this as a gospel-centred Christian. This might be also where we disagree each other.

Christians in Myanmar have double discrimination. That is, they are discriminated on the bases of both religion and ethnicity. This discrimination has socio-political repercussion, resulting in many Christians in Myanmar weakening a sense of responsibility for the affairs of the nation. Therefore Wink's perspective of the DS and the DFO can help Christians in Myanmar to see that they are not to be trapped in that bondage of the DS but to overcome it. When it is overcome, they can seek a way to work with Buddhists or other non-Christian religions for the betterment of the nation.

How should Christians in Myanmar start to engage in the politics that have been overwhelmed by the power of the DS? For Christians who have been under the socio-cultural context of authoritarian rule, there is no doubt at all that they must be more or less irresistibly influenced by the system. Where can they learn the alternative standards and values of the DFO? There is no place for Christians in Myanmar to learn those of the DFO except a church where they gather together for worship and fellowship. This is where Wink's argument is feeble because he considers the church as nothing but one among other social organizations. Perhaps the people of Myanmar, for Wink, could learn to be part of the DFO through the practice of Buddhist dhamma. As this research seeks to encourage Christian influence on society, I want to put an emphasis on the important role of the church in society. So it does not mean that Buddhists can never be part of the DFO by practicing Buddha's teaching of dhamma.

In contrast to Wink, I argue that here comes the vital role of the local church in nurturing new standards and values of the DFO in Christians in Myanmar. In sociological terms, the church should be the social location where Christians would be newly socialized. Stephen Charles Mott rightly argues for this:

> If we are to reject significant aspects of the cultural context, we must be able to react against the approval of the very community that previously has been crucial to us. This calls for a higher form of community, which can "out-vote" the influence of the former community. A new process of socialization is needed.[19]

---

19. Mott, *Biblical Ethics*, 134.

Conclusion: Political Implications for Christians in Myanmar

Since the day of birth Christians in Myanmar have been socialized into the realm of the DS. What they are accustomed to are its standards, values and criteria. Therefore when we decide to follow Christ and his ways, we are called to a new process of socialization. This new socialization can never be realized aside from the church or community where Christians, irrespective of cultural and racial differences, learn the new standards, values and beliefs of the kingdom of God or the DFO. Today what Christians in Myanmar desperately need is the community that embodies the standards and values of the DFO and the community where Christians can be newly socialized. Like for King, the church one belongs to should be like a second home for Christians in Myanmar. Therefore local churches in Myanmar should not be constrained by observing rituals, denominations and doctrines; they should preach, teach and witness the whole gospel holistically to their neighbourhoods in such a way that people will join in the process of new socialization.

Most of all, the church should be a place where Christians not only learn Jesus's teaching of nonviolence, but also where Christians see what nonviolent lifestyle looks like. As violence and the abuse of power has been prevailing in all areas of life in Myanmar, local churches in Myanmar are called to open their eyes to see its pervasiveness and cultivate the culture of nonviolence or create a new social reality so that a new socialization may take place among the congregation. Here the culture of nonviolence or a new social reality does not refer to the approach of pragmatic nonviolence but that of principled nonviolence. Throughout the thesis, it has been emphasized that nonviolence is far more than a tactic or method to respond a certain social evil; rather it is a spirit which someone might not see it but have a sense of its penetrating presence. When Christians in Myanmar begin to realize this call to nonviolent lifestyle, the hope for a genuine transformation in the nation will be dawned.

In the process of cultivating nonviolent lifestyle, what the church has to be aware of is that nonviolence is not merely a character which an individual person should cultivate in life but a soul that the Christian community is called to foster. In other words, Christians as the followers of Christ are, both individually and communally, called to practice and nurture the life of nonviolence in order that the church may bear witness to its master in such a violent world. Invigorating the spirit of nonviolence individually and corporately within the church will reflect the glory of its master, Jesus Christ.

In spite of putting an emphasis on the crucial role of local churches in Myanmar, this research does not exclude the role of non-Christian communities such as Buddhist, Hindu and Muslim in working for the advancement of the nation. Of course, Christian churches are not perfect community; they are communities of sinners, saved by the grace of God – sinners who are saved not by their own merit but by God's grace. Since they are saved by God's grace alone, there can never be moral superiority between Christians and non-Christian people irrespective of their religious identities. This opens the door for both of them to work together for the good of their country. As discussed in chapter 6, the logic of nonviolence is that nobody (us and our enemies) is perfect. Nonviolence has transformative power; therefore, only through nonviolence, will the division between them and us be broken. Nonviolence, in this sense, humbles Christians not to see others as different but to welcome them so that they can cooperate with them for the sake of the country.

Despite the importance of partnership with non-Christian communities in cultivating a culture of democracy, Christians should have a commitment to peace and nonviolence – an unswerving commitment that is not based on effectiveness or result, but on wholehearted obedience to God. To quote Yoder, "Christians commit themselves to nonviolence and peace not to show that they are wonderful people, not to ensure that their love guarantees success, not to indicate that they have better political or economic system. Instead Christians are called to love their enemies because God does so and commands his followers to do so."[20]

This might be somewhat unpromising or even bleak for the Christians in Myanmar, at a time when people are preoccupied with result or desired end. A time where if a certain method or approach does not result in the desired end, they just discard it. But Christians do not follow the path of nonviolence because it is effective, but because it is "God's method of overcoming evil with good."[21] Only through such a radical commitment will Christians in Myanmar, together with those from other faiths, be individually and collectively able to truly revolutionize the dominant values of the political culture of Myanmar.

---

20. Yoder, *He Came Preaching Peace*, 20.
21. Yoder, 19.

Bibliography

Abernathy, Ralph D. *And the Walls Came Tumbling Down*. New York: HarperPerennial, 1989.

Aljazeera. "Myanmar Police Crack Down on Students Protesters." *Aljazeera*, Asia Pacific, 10 March 2015. http://www.aljazeera.com/-news/2015/03/myanmar-police-crack-student-protesters-150310123609713.html.

Allan, Davina. "Secularization." In *Key Ideas in Human Thought*, edited by Keith McLeish, 668. New York: Crown Publishing, 1993.

Anderson, Benedict R. O. G. "Old State, New Society: Indonesia's New Order in Comparative Historical Perspective." *Journal of Asian Studies* 62, no. 3 (1983): 477–496.

Ansbro, John J. *Martin Luther King, Jr: Nonviolent Strategies and Tactics for Social Change*. Maryknoll, NY: Orbis Books, 1994.

Aquinas, Thomas. *The Summa Theologica of Saint Thomas Aquinas, Volume II*. Translated by Fathers of the English Dominican Province, revised by Daniel J. Sullivan. Chicago, IL: Encyclopaedia Britannica, 1952.

Arendt, Hannah. "On Violence." In *Crises of the Republic: Lying in Politics, Civil Disobedience, On Violence, Thoughts on Politics and Revolution*, 103–184. New York, NY: Harcourt Brace, 1972.

Arnold, Clinton E. *Ephesians, Power and Magic: The Concept of Power in Ephesians in Light of Its Historical Setting*. Grand Rapids, MI: Baker Books, 1992.

———. *Powers of Darkness: Principalities and Powers in Paul's Letters*. Downers Grove, IL: InterVarsity Press, 1992.

Arrow, Ruaridh. "Gene Sharp: Author of the Nonviolent Revolution Rulebook." *BBC News*, 21 February 2011. http://www.bbc.co.uk/news/world-middle-east-12522848.

Attridge, Harold W. "*Cracking the Gnostic Code: The Powers in Gnosticism* by Walter Wink." *Journal of Religion* 75, no. 2 (1995): 267–268.

Augustine, Saint. "Letter CLXXIX." Christian Classics Ethereal Library (website). https://www.ccel.org/ccel/schaff/npnf101.vii.1.CLXXXIX.html?highlight.

Aulén, Gustaf. *Christus Victor: An Historical Study of the Three Main Types of the Idea of the Atonement*. Translated by A. G. Hebert. London: SPCK, 1983.

Aung, Maung Htin. *Folk Elements in Burmese Buddhism*. Rangoon: Religious Affairs Department Press, 1959.

———. *A History of Burma*. New York, NY: Columbia University Press, 1967.

———. *The Stricken Peacock: Anglo-Burmese Relations 1752–1948*. The Hague: Martinus Nijhoff, 1965.

Aung-Thwin, Maitrii. "Introduction: Communities of Interpretation and the Construction of Modern Myanmar." *Journal of Southeast Asian Studies* 39, no. 2 (June 2008): 187–192.

Aung-Thwin, Michael. "The British 'Pacification' of Burma: Order without Meaning." *Journal of Southeast Asian Studies*, 16. no. 2 (1985): 245–261.

———. "1948 and Burma's Myth of Independence." In *Independent Burma at Forty years: Six Assessments*, edited by Josef Silverstein, 19–34. Ithaca, NY: Cornell University Press, 1989.

———. "Michael Aung-Thwin for a look at Modern Burma: The Past is in the Present." Video on Vimeo. Accessed 10 June 2015. https://vimeo.com/35333912.

———. *Pagan: The Origins of Modern Burma*. Honolulu: University of Hawaii Press, 1985.

———. "Parochial Universalism, Democracy Jihad and the Orientalist Image of Burma: The New Evangelism." *Pacific Affairs*, 74, no. 4 (2001): 483–505.

Aung-Thwin, Michael, and Maitrii Aung-Thwin. *A History of Myanmar Since Ancient Times: Traditions and Transformations*. London: Reaktion Books, 2012.

Badgley, John, and Jon A. Wiant. "The Ne Win-BSPP Style of Bama-Lo: A Strange Revolution." In *The Future of Burma in Perspective: A Symposium*, edited by Josef Silverstein, 43–64. Athens, OH: Ohio University, 1974.

Barak, Gregg. *Violence and Nonviolence: Pathways to Understanding*. Thousand Oaks, CA: SAGE, 2003.

Barth, Markus. *The Broken Wall: A Study of the Epistle to the Ephesians*. London: Collins, 1960.

BBC News. "Burma Leader Than Shwe 'Not Presidential Nominee.'" *BBC News*, Asia-Pacific, 1 February 2011. http://www.bbc.com/news/world-asia-pacific-12332274.

———. "EU Chief Barroso Offers New Development Aid to Burma." *BBC News*, Asia, 3 November 2012. http://www.bbc.co.uk/news/world-asia-20189448.

———. "Myanmar Riot Police Beat Student Protesters with Batons." *BBC News*, Asia, 10 March 2015. http://www.bbc.com/news/world-asia-31812028.

Beasley-Murray, George R. *Jesus and the Kingdom of God*. Grand Rapids, MI: Eerdmans, 1986.

———. *John*. Word Biblical Commentary 36. Nashville, TN: Thomas Nelson, 1999.

Bekker, Corné J. "The Values of Incarnation Leadership." Leadership Talks audio series. Accessed 10 May 2015. http://www.regent.edu/acad/global/leadershiptalks/archive/dec_06_bekker.htm.

Bell, Rob. *Love Wins: A Book about Heaven, Hell, and the Fate of Every Person Who Ever Lived*. New York, NY: HarperCollins, 2011.

Bengtsson, Jan Olof. *The Worldview of Personalism: Origins and Early Development*. Oxford: Oxford University Press, 2006.

Bengtsson, Jesper. *Aung San Suu Kyi: A Biography*. Translated by Margaret Myers. Dulles, Virginia: Potomac Books, 2012.

Bennett, John C. "Reinhold Niebuhr's Contribution to Christian Social Ethics." In *Reinhold Niebuhr: A Prophetic Voice in Our Time*, edited by Harold R Landon, 45–57. Greenwich, CT: Seabury, 1962.

———. "Reinhold Niebuhr's Social Ethics." In *Reinhold Niebuhr: His Religious, Social and Political Thought*, edited by Charles W. Kegley and Robert W. Bretall, 99–141. New York, NY: Macmillan, 1956.

Bennett, Lerone. *What Manner of Man: A Biography of Martin Luther King Jr.* Chicago: Johnson Publishing, 1964.

Berger, Peter L. *The Sacred Canopy: Elements of a Sociological Theory of Religion*. Garden City, NY: Anchor Books, 1969.

Berkhof, Hendrik. *Christ and the Powers*. Translated by John H. Yoder. Scottdale, PA: Herald Press, 1962.

Bernard Hill, Johnny. *The Theology of Martin Luther King, Jr. and Desmond Mpilo Tutu*. New York: Palgrave Macmillan, 2007.

Bevans, Stephen. *Models of Contextual Theology*. Revised and expanded. Maryknoll, NY: Orbis, 2002 (1992).

Bingham, June. *Courage to Change: An Introduction to the Life and Thought of Reinhold Niebuhr*. New York, NY: Charles Scribner, 1972.

Bloesch, Donald G. *The Church: Sacraments, Worship, Ministry, Mission*. Downers Grove, IL: InterVarsity Press, 2002.

Bloom, Stephen. "The 'Rule of Law' in Burma." *The Irrawaddy*, Opinion, 1 February 2012. http://www2.irrawaddy.org/article.php?art_id=22960.

Bonhoeffer, Dietrich. *The Cost of Discipleship*. New York: Touchstone, 1995.

Borer, Tristan Anne. "Truth Telling As a Peace-Building Activity." In *Telling the Truths: Truth Telling and Peace Building in Post-Conflict Societies*, edited by Tristan Anne Borer, 1–58. Notre Dame, IN: University of Notre Dame Press, 2006.

Borg, Marcus J. *Conflict, Holiness, and Politics in the Teachings of Jesus*. London: Continuum, 1998.

Britannica Academic. "Ramayana." *Britannica Academic*. Accessed 20 August 2015. http://academic.eb.com/-EBchecked/topic/490529/Ramayana.

Bruce, Steve, and Steven Yearley. *The Sage Dictionary of Sociology*. London: Sage, 2006.

Brueggemann, Walter. *The Prophetic Imagination*. 2nd edition. Minneapolis, MN: Fortress, 2001.

Brysk, Alison, ed. *Globalization and Human Rights*. Berkeley, CA: University of California Press, 2002.

"Buddhism by Numbers." *Buddha Space* (blog), 9 July 2012. http://buddhaspace.blogspot.com/2012/07/buddhism-by-numbers-10-duties-of-king.html.

Budziszewski, J. *Evangelicals in the Public Square: Four Formative Voices on Political Thought and Action*. Grand Rapids, MI: Baker, 2006.

Bultmann, Rudolph. *New Testament and Mythology and Other Basic Writings*. Translated by Schubert M. Ogden. Philadelphia, PA: Fortress, 1984.

Burrow, Rufus. *Extremist for Love: Martin Luther King Jr., Man of Ideas and Nonviolent Social Action*. Minneapolis, MN: Fortress, 2014.

Burrowes, Robert J. *The Strategy of Nonviolent Defence: A Gandhian Approach*. Albany, NY: State University of New York Press, 1996.

Burrows, Ruth. *Ascent to Love: The Spiritual Teachings of St. John of the Cross*. London: Darton, Longman and Todd, 1987.

Cady, John F. *A History of Modern Burma*. Ithaca, NY: Cornell University Press, 1965.

———. Religion and Politics in Modern Burma." *The Far Eastern Quarterly* 12, no. 2 (February 1953): 149–162.

Cahalan, Kathleen A., and Gordon S. Mikoski, eds. "Introduction." In *Opening the Field of Practical Theology: An Introduction*, edited by Kathleen Cahalan and Gordon Mikoski, 1–10. Lanham, MD: Rowman & Littlefield, 2014.

———. *Opening the Field of Practical Theology: An Introduction*. Lanham, MD: Rowman & Littlefield, 2014.

Caird, George Bradford. *Principalities and Powers: A Study in Pauline Theology*. Oxford: Clarendon, 1956.

Callahan, Mary P. *Making Enemies: War and State Building in Burma*. Ithaca, NY: Cornell University Press, 2003.

Cameron, Helen, Deborah Bhatti, Cathrine Duce, James Sweeny, and Clare Watkins. *Talking about God in Practice: Theological Action Research and Practical Research*. London: SCM, 2010.

Campbell, Charlie. "EU Sanctions End When Reform 'Irreversible.'" *The Irrawaddy*, 19 July 2012. http://www.irrawaddy.org/-sanctions/eu-sanctions-end-when-reform-irreversible.html.

Carey, Peter, ed. *Burma: The Challenge of Change in a Divided Society*. London: MacMillan, 1997.

Carr, Wesley. *Angels and Principalities: The Background, Meaning and Development of the Pauline Phrase, Hai Archai Kai Hai Exousiai*. Cambridge: Cambridge University Press, 1981.

Carson, Donald Arthur. *Exegetical Fallacies*. 2nd edition. Grand Rapids, MI: Baker, 1996.

———. *The Gospel According to John*. The Pillar New Testament Commentary. Grand Rapids, MI: InterVarsity Press, 1991.

Carson, Clayborne, ed. *The Autobiography of Martin Luther King Jr*. New York, NY: Grand Central Publishing, 1998.

Carson, Clayborne, Ralph Luker, and Penny A. Russell, eds. *The Papers of Martin Luther King, Jr: Called to Serve, January 1929-June 1951*. Volume 1. Berkley, CA: University of California Press, 1992.

———. *Papers of Martin Luther King, Jr.: Threshold of A New Decade, January 1959-December 1960*. Volume 5. Berkley, CA: University of California Press, 2005.

Cartledge, Mark J. *Practical Theology: Charismatic and Empirical Perspectives*. Carlisle, Cumbria: Paternoster, 2003.

Catholic Dictionary. "Historical Determinism." *Catholic Culture.org (website)*. https://www.catholicculture.org/culture/library/dictionary/index.cfm?id=33934

CBS News. "Suu Kyi: Burma Army Could Block Reforms." *CBS News*, 5 January 2012. http://www.cbsnews.com/news/suu-kyi-burma-army-could-block-reforms/.

Chakrabarty, Bidyut, and Clayborne Carson. *Confluence of Thought: Mohandas Karamchand Gandhi and Martin Luther King, Jr*. Oxford: Oxford University Press, 2013.

Chalke, Steve, and Alan Mann. *The Lost Message of Jesus*. Grand Rapids, MI: Zondervan, 2003.

Chappell, David. *A Stone of Hope: Prophetic Religion and the Death of Jim Crow*. Chapel Hill, NC: University of North Carolina Press, 2004.

Chapman, Mark. "The Kingdom of God and Ethics: From Ritschl to Liberation Theology." In *The Kingdom of God and Human Society*, edited by Robin S. Barbour, 140–163. Edinburgh: T&T Clark, 1993.

Charles, J. Daryl. *Between Pacifism and Jihad: Just War and Christian Tradition*. Downers Grove, IL: InterVarsity Press, 2005.

Chatterjee, Deen K. *Encyclopedia of Global Justice*. New York: Spinger, 2011.

Cheesman, Nick. *Opposing the Rule of Law: How Myanmar's Courts Make Law and Order*. Cambridge: Cambridge University Press, 2015.

Chenoweh, Erica, and Maria J. Stephan. *Why Civil Resistance Works: The Strategic Logic of Nonviolent Conflict*. New York: Columbia University Press, 2011.

———. "Why Civil Resistance Works: The Strategic Logic of Nonviolent Conflict." *International Security* 33, no. 1 (2008): 7–44.

Childress, James F. "Reinhold Niebuhr's Critique of Pacifism." *The Review of Politics* 36, no. 4 (September 1999): 467–491.

Cicovacki, Predrag, ed. *The Ethics of Nonviolence: Essays by Robert L. Holmes*. New York, NY: Bloomsbury, 2013.

Clements, Alan. *Instinct for Freedom: A Maverick's Guide to Spiritual Revolution*. Novato, CA: New World Library, 2002.

Clements, Alan, and Leslie Kean. *Burma's Revolution of the Spirit: The Struggle for Democratic Freedom and Dignity*. Bangkok: White Orchid Press, 1995.

Cobb, Jr, John B., and David Ray Griffin. *The Process Theology: An Introductory Exposition*. Philadelphia, PA: Westminster, 1976.

Cockett, Richard. *Blood, Dreams and Gold: The Changing Face of Burma*. New Haven, CT: Yale University Press, 2015.

Coleman, Landon M. "Principalities and Powers: A Historical and Biblical Study with Strategic Application in North American Churches." PhD dissertation, Southern Baptist Theological Seminary, 2010.

Cone, James H. *Martin & Malcolm & America: A Dream or a Nightmare?*. Maryknoll, NY: Orbis, 1991.

———. "Martin and Malcom on Nonviolence and Violence." *Phylon* 49, no. 3/4 (2001): 173–183.

Cook-Huffman, Celia. "Christianity and Nonviolent Resistance." In *The Wiley-Blackwell Companion to Religion and Social Justice*, edited by Michael D. Palmer and Stanley M. Burgess, 607–619. Malden, MA: Blackwell, 2012.

Crouch, Melissa and Tim Lindsey, ed. *Law, Society and Transition in Myanmar*. Oxford: Hart, 2014.

Dalai Lama. "Foreword." In *Peace is Every Step: The Path of Mindfulness in Everyday Life,* by Thich Nhat Hanh, vi–ix. London: Bantam Books, 1992.

Dalton, Dennis. *Mahatma Gandhi: Nonviolent Power in Action*. New York, NY: Columbia University Press, 1993.

Daniels, T. Scott. "Passing the Peace: Worship that Shapes Nonsubstitutionary Convictions." In *Atonement and Violence: A Theological Conversation*, edited by John Sanders, 125–150. Nashville, TN: Abingdon, 2006.

Davis, Nancy. "Contemporary Deontology." In *A Companion to Ethics*, edited by Peter Singer, 205–218. Oxford: Blackwell, 1991.

Dixon, James M. "*The Sacred Canopy: Elements of a Sociological Theory of Religion*, by Peter L. Berger." *Sociological Analysis* 29, no. 1 (1968): 40–42.

Duthel, Heinz. *Aung San Suu Kyi: Leading the Burmese Democracy Movement*. Lexington, KY: CreateSpace Independent Publishing Platform, 2011.

Ebbighausen, Rodion. "Aung San Suu Kyi's Sacrifice for Politics." *DW*, 9 November 2012. http://www.dw.de/aung-san-suu-kyis-sacrifice-for-politics/a-16369029.

Ellingsen, Mark. *Reclaiming Our Roots: An Inclusive Introduction to Church History*. Harrisburg, Pennsylvania: Trinity Press International, 1999.

Ellul, Jacques. *The Humiliation of the Word*. Grand Rapids, MI: Eerdmans, 1985.

———. *Violence: Reflections from a Christian Perspective*. New York, NY: The Seabury Press, 1969.

Elwell, Walter A. *Evangelical Dictionary of Theology*. 2nd edition. Grand Rapids, MI: Baker, 2001.

Emerson, Michael O. and Christian Smith. *Divided by Faith: Evangelical Religion and the Problem of Race in America*. New York, NY: Oxford University Press, 2000.

Epp, Eldon Jay. "Mediating Approaches to the Kingdom: Werner George Kummel and George Eldon Ladd." In *The Kingdom of God in 20th-Century Interpretation*, edited by Weldell Willis, 35–52. Peabody, MA: Hendrickson, 1987.

Erickson, Millard J. *Truth or Consequences: The Promise & Perils of Postmodernism*. Downers Grove, IL: InterVarsity Press, 2001.

Ertis-Kojima, Veronica. "The Significance of Dietrich Bonhoeffer Today." MA thesis, Wilfrid Laurier University, 1981.

Evans, C. Stephen. *Pocket Dictionary of Apologetics and Philosophy of Religion*. Downers Grove, IL: InterVarsity Press, 2002.

Ewusie Moses, Robert. *Practices of Powers: Revisiting the Principalities and Powers in the Pauline Letters*. Minneapolis, MN: Fortress, 2014.

Ezrow, Natasha, and Erica Frantz. *Dictators and Dictatorships: Understanding Authoritarian Regimes and Their Leaders*. New York: Continuum, 2011.

Facing History and Ourselves. *Eyes on the Prize: America's Civil Rights Movement (1954–1985), A Study Guide to the Television Series*. Colorado Springs, CO: Blackside Publicaation, 2006. Available as a PDF online at, http://wgbhprojects.s3.amazonaws.com/EYES%20ON%20THE%20PRIZE/Study%20Guide/EyesOnThePrize-StudyGuide_202.pdf

Fairclough, Adam. "Was Martin Luther King a Marxist?" In *History Workshop* 15, no. 1 (1983): 117–125.

Farrelly, Nicholas. "Interview with Professor Michael Aung-Thwin." *New Mandala (blog)*, 28 November 2007. https://www.newmandala.org/interview-with-professor-michael-aung-thwin/.

———. "Interview with Professor Robert Taylor." *New Mandala (blog)*, 7 November 2007. https://www.newmandala.org/interview-with-professor-robert-taylor/.

Faubion, James D, ed. *Power*. Essential Works of Foucault 3. Translated by Robert Hurley. New York, NY: New Press, 2000.

Fink, Christina. "Introduction." In *Burma and the Karens,* by San C. Po, ix–xlv. Bangkok: White Lotus Press, 2001.

Flintoff, John-Paul. "Gene Sharp: the Machiavelli of Nonviolence." *NewStatesman*, Politics, 3 January 2013. http://www.newstatesman.com/politics/your-democracy/2013/01/gene-sharp-machiavelli-non-violence.

Foucault, Michael. *Power/Knowledge: Selected Interviews and Other Writings, 1972–1977*. Edited by Colin Gordon. New York: Pantheon, 1980.

Friesen, Duane K. "The Convergence of Pacifism and Just War." In *War and Christian Ethics*, edited by Arthur F. Holmes, 365–375. 2nd edition. Grand Rapids, MI: Baker Academic, 2005.

Gandhi Ashram. "History." *Gandhi Ashram*, About. http://www.gandhiashramsabarmati.org/en/about-gandhi-ashram-menu/history-menu.html.

Gandhi, Mohandas K. *An Autobiography: The Story of My Experiments with Truth*. Boston, MA: Beacon Press, 1993.

———. "My Faith in Nonviolence." In *The Power of Nonviolence: Writings by Advocates of Peace*, edited by Howard Zinn, 45–46. Boston, MA: Beacon Press, 2002.

———. *Selected Writings of Mahatma Gandhi*. Selected and introduced by Ronald Duncan. London: Faber and Faber Limited, 1951.

Garrett, Duane A. *Angels and the New Spirituality*. Nashville, TN: Broadman & Holman, 1995.

Garrow, David J. *Bearing the Cross: Martin Luther King Jr., and the Southern Christian Leadership Conference*. New York, NY: Quill, 1999.

Gecker, Jocelyn. "Suu Kyi's Silence on Rohingya Draws Rare Criticism." *The Irrawaddy*, 16 August 2012. https://www.irrawaddy.com/news/burma/suu-kyis-silence-on-rohingya-draws-rare-criticism.html.

Geok, Ang Chin. *Aung San Suu Kyi: Towards a New Freedom*. London: Prentice Hall, 1998.

Gides, David M. "Dietrich Bonhoeffer's Theology of the World as a Key to Understanding His Political Involvement." PhD diss, Fordham University, 2004.

Gill, Robin. *A Textbook of Christian Ethics*. 3rd edition. New York, NY: T&T Clark, 2006.

Gingerich, Ray. "The Economics and Politics of Violence: Toward a Theology for Transforming the Powers." In *Transforming the Powers: Peace, Justice and the Domination System*, edited by Ray Gingerich and Ted Grimsrud, 113–128. Minneapolis, MN: Fortress, 2006.

Gingerich, Ray, and Ted Grimsrud, eds. *Transforming the Powers: Peace, Justice and the Domination System*. Minneapolis, MN: Fortress, 2006.

Girard, René. *The Girard Reader*. Edited by James G. Williams. New York, NY: Crossroad, 1996.

———. *The Scapegoat*. Translated by Yvonne Freccero. Baltimore, MD: Johns Hopkins University Press, 1986.

———. *Violence and the Sacred*. Baltimore, MD: Johns Hopkins University Press, 1977.

Goddard, Andrew. *Living the Word, Resisting the World: The Life and Thought of Jacques Ellul*. Carlisle; Waynesboro, GA: Paternoster, 2002.

Gravers, Michael. *Nationalism as Political Paranoia in Burma: An Essay on the Historical Practice of Power*. Richmond: Curzon, 1999.

Green, Joel B., and Mark D. Baker. *Recovering the Scandal of the Cross: Atonement in New Testament and Contemporary Contexts*. Cumbria: Paternoster, 2000.

Grenz, Stanley J. and Jay T. Smith. *Pocket Dictionary of Ethics*. Downers Grove, IL: InterVarsity Press, 2003.

Grimsrud, Ted. "Introduction: Engaging Walter Wink." In *Transforming the Powers: Peace, Justice and the Domination System*, edited by Ray Gingerich and Ted Grimsrud, 1–16. Minneapolis, MN: Fortress, 2006.

———. "A Tribute to Walter Wink." *Peace Theology*, 12 May 2012. https://peacetheology.net/2012/05/12/a-tribute-to-walter-wink/.

———. "A Pacifist Critique of the Modern Worldview." In *Transforming the Powers: Peace, Justice and the Domination System*, edited by Ray Gingerich and Ted Grimsrud, 53–65. Minneapolis, MN: Fortress, 2006.

Gyi, Maung Maung. *Burmese Political Values: The Socio-Political Roots of Authoritarianism*. New York, NY: Praeger, 1983.

Hall, D. G. E. *Burma*. 2nd edition. London: Hutchinson's University Library, 1998.

Hamber, Brandon. *Transforming Societies After Political Violence*. New York: Springer, 2009.

Harriden, Jessica. *The Authority and Influence: Women and Power in Burmese History*. Copenhagen: Nordic Institute Asian Studies, 2012.

Hasday, Judy L. *Aung San Suu Kyi: Activist for Democracy in Myanmar*. New York, NY: Chelsea House, 2007.

Hauerwas, Stanley. *Christian Existence Today: Essays on Church, World, and Living in Between*. Grand Rapids, MI: Brazos, 1988.

———. *In Good Company: The Church as Polis*. Notre Dame, IN: University of Notre Dame Press, 1995.

———. *The Hauerwas Reader*. Edited by John Berkman and Michael Cartwright. London: Duke University Press, 2001.

———. *The Peaceable Kingdom: A Primer in Christian Ethics*. Notre Dame, IN: University of Notre Dame Press, 1986.

——— *The Peaceable Kingdom: A Primer in Christian Ethics*. 2nd edition. London; SCM, 2003.

———. *Resident Aliens: Life in the Christian Colony*. Nashville, TN: Abingdon, 1989.

Hauerwas, Stanley, and William H. Willimon. *Resident Aliens: Life in the Christian Colony*. Nashville, TN: Abingdon, 1989.

Hegel, G. W. F. *The Philosophy of History*. Translated by J. Sibree. Kitchener, Ontario: Batoche Books, 2001.

Heitink, Gerben. *Practical Theology: History, Theory and Action Domains*. Translated by Reinder Bruinsma. Grand Rapids, MI: Eerdmans, 1999.

Hitchens, Christopher. *God Is Not Great: How Religion Poisons Everything*. London: Atlantic, 2007.

Hlaing, Kyaw Yin, Robert H. Taylor, and Tin Maung Maung Than, eds. *Beyond Politics to Societal Imperatives*. Singapore: Institute of Southeast Asian Studies, 2005.

Holliday, Ian. *Burma Redux: Global Justice and the Quest for Political Reform in Myanmar*. New York: Columbia University Press, 2011.

Holmes, Arthur F. "Response to Willard Swartley and Alan Kreider." In *Pacifism and War: 8 Prominent Christians Debate Today's Issue*, edited by Oliver R. Barclay, 61–67. Leicester: InterVarsity Press, 1984.

Holt, Steve. "Confronting the Powers: An Interview with Walter Wink and June Keener Wink." *Sojourners Magazine* 39, no. 11 (December 2010): 31–33.

Hopkins, Antony Gerald, ed. *Globalization in World History*. London: Pimlico, 2002.

———. "History of Glovalization – and the Globalization of History?" In *Globalization in World History*, edited by A. G. Hopkins, 11–45. London: Pimlico, 2002.

Hordern, William. *A Layman's Guide to Protestant Theology*. New York: Macmillan, 1955.

Horrocks, Chris, and Zoran Jevtic. *Introducing Foucault*. Cambridge: Icon Books, 2000.

Horsley, Richard A. *Jesus and the Spiral of Violence: Jewish Resistance in Roman Palestine*. San Francisco, CA: Harper & Row, 1987.

———. "Response to Walter Wink, 'Neither Passivity nor violence: Jesus' Third Way.'" In *The Love of Enemy and Nonretaliation in the New Testament*, edited by Willard M. Swartley. 126–132. Louisville, KY: Westminster, 1992.

Horton, Michael. "N. T. Wright Reconsiders the Meaning of Jesus' Death." *The Gospel Coalition US*, 10 October 2016. https://www.thegospelcoalition.org/reviews/the-day-the-revolution-began/.

Houtmann, Gustaff. *Mental Culture in Burmese Crisis Politics: Aung San Suu Kyi and the National League for Democracy*. Tokyo University of Foreign Studies Monograph Series No. 33. Tokyo: Institute for the Study of Language and Cultures of Asia and Africa, 1999.

Htoo, U Aung. "The Depayin Massacre: A Crime Against Humanity and Its Effect on National Reconciliation." Asian Human Rights Commission. http://www.humanrights.asia/resources/journals-magazines/article2/0206/the-depayin-massacre-a-crime-against-humanity-and-its-effect-on-national-reconciliation.

Humphreys, Christmas. *A Popular Dictionary of Buddhism*. London: Curzon, 1997.

Hunter, Andrew. "Aung San Suu Kyi's Quest for Democracy Raises Questions." *The Sydney Morning Herald* (online), 11 November 2013. http://www.smh.com.au/comment/aung-san-suu-kyis-quest-for-democracy-raises-questions-20131110-2x9so.html.

Huskinson, Lucy. *The SPCK Introduction to Nietzsche*. London: SPCK, 2009.

Hyde, J. Keith. *Concept of Power in Kierkegaard and Nietzsche*. Surrey: Ashgate, 2010.

Hyde, Maggie, and Michael McGuinness. *Jung for Beginners*. Cambridge: Icon, 1992.

The Irrawaddy. "Analysis: Using the Term 'Rohingya.'" *The Irrawaddy*, 21 September 2017. https://www.irrawaddy.com/news/burma/analysis-using-term-rohingya.html.

———. "Suu Kyi and Government Peace Negotiator Aung Min Meet in Naypyidaw." *The Irrawaddy*, 9 December 2015. http://www.irrawaddy.com/burma/102541.html.

Jeffery, Steve, Mike Ovey, and Andrew Sach. *Pierced for Our Transgressions: Rediscovering the Glory of Penal Substitution*. Nottingham: Inter-Varsity Press, 2007.

Jesse, F. Tennyson. *The Story of Burma*. London: Macmillan & Co, 1946.

Johnson, James Turner. "Aquinas and Luther on War and Peace: Sovereign Authority and the Use of Armed Force." *Journal of Religious Ethics* 31, no.1 (2003): 3–20.

Johnson, Nicole L. "Practising Discipleship: Lived Theologies of Nonviolence in Conversation with the Doctrine and Teachings of the United Methodist Church." PhD diss., Boston University School of Theology, 2007.

Johnston, Britton W. "René Girard's Mimetic Theology as the Basis for a Fundamental Practical Theology." PhD diss., Fuller Theological Seminary, 2015.

Jones, Nicolas A., Stephan Parmentier, and Elmar G. M. Weitekamp. "Dealing with International Crimes in Post-War Bosnia: A Look Through the Lens of the Affected Population." *European Journal of Criminology* 9, no. 5 (1999): 553–564.

Jordt, Ingrid. "Breaking Bad in Burma." *Religion in the News*, 19 December 2014. http://religioninthenews.org/2014/12/19/breaking-bad-in-burma/.

Kabiro wa Gatumu, Albert. *The Pauline Concept of Supernatural Powers: A Reading from the African Worldview*. Milton Keynes: Paternoster, 2008.

Kaspar, Andrew D. "In Burma, a Vexing Vexillology." *The Irrawaddy*, Politics, 21 October 2013. http://www.irrawaddy.org/multimedia-burma/burma-vexing-vexillology.html.

Kaufmann, Walter, trans and ed. *Basic Writings of Nietzche*. New York: The Modern Library, 2000.

Kegley, Charles W., and Robert W. Bretall. *Reinhold Niebuhr: His Religious, Social and Political Thought*. New York, NY: Macmillan, 1956.

Kets de Vries, Manfred. "The Spirit of Despotism: Understanding the Tyrant Within." *Human Relations* 59, no. 2 (2006): 195–220.

———. *Lessons on Leadership by Terror: Fidning Shaka Zulu in the Attic*. Cheltenham: Edward Elgar, 2004.

King Jr, Martin Luther. *The Papers of Martin Luther King, Jr. Volume I: Called to Serve, January 1929–June 1951*. Edited by Clayborne Carson, Ralph E. Luker, Penny A. Russell, and Louis R. Harlan. Berkeley, CA: University of California Press, 1992.

———. *The Papers of Martin Luther King Jr. Vol. II: Rediscovering Precious Values, July 1951–November 1955*. Edited by Clayborne Carson, Stewart Burns, Susan Carson, Peter Holloran, and Dana L. H. Powell. Berkeley, CA: University of California Press, 1994.

———. *The Papers of Martin Luther King, Jr. Volume III: Birth of a New Age, December 1955-December 1956*. Edited by Clayborne Carson, Stewart Burns, Susan Carson, Peter Holloran, and Dana L. H. Powell. Berkeley, CA: University of California Press, 1997.

———. *The Papers of Martin Luther King Jr. Volume V: Threshold of A New Decade, January 1959–December 1960*. Edited by Clayborne Carson, Stewart Burns, Susan Carson, Peter Holloran, and Dana L. H. Powell. Berkeley, CA: University of California Press, 1992.

———. *The Papers of Martin Luther King, Jr. Volume VI: Advocate of the Social Gospel, September 1948-March 1963*. Edited by Clayborne Carson, Susan

Carson, Susan Englander, Troy Jackson, and Gerald L. Smith. Berkeley, CA: University of California Press, 2007.

———. *The Papers of Martin Luther King, Jr. Volume VII: To Save the Soul of America, January 1961-August 1962*. Edited by Clayborne Carson and Tenisha Armstrong. Berkeley, CA: University of California Press, 2014.

———. *Strength to Love*. Glasgow: Collins Sons, 1977.

———. *Stride toward Freedom: the Montgomery Story*. Boston, MA: Beacon Press, 2010.

———. *A Testament of Hope*. Edited by James Melvin Washington. New York, NY: HarperCollins, 1986.

———. *Where Do We Go from Here: Chaos or Community?* Boston, MA: Beacon Press, 2010.

———. *Why We Can't Wait*. New York, NY: Harper & Row, 1963.

King, Sallie B. *Socially Engaged Buddhism*. Honolulu: University of Hawaii Press, 2009.

King, Winston Lee. *Buddhism and Christianity: Some Bridges of Understanding*. London: George Allen and Unwin, 1963.

Koller, Charles W. "Emphases in Preaching." In *Baker's Dictionary of Practical Theology*, edited by Ralph G. Turnbull, 21. Grand Rapids, MI: Baker Books, 1967.

Krupa, Stephen Thomas. "Dorothy Day and the Spirituality of Nonviolence." PhD diss., Graduate Theological Union, 1998.

Kyi, Aung San Suu, and Alan Clements. *The Voice of Hope*. 2nd edition. New York: Seven Stories, 2008.

Labanow, Cory E. *Evangelicalism and the Emerging Church: A Congregational Study of a Vineyard Church*. Surrey: Ashgate, 2009.

Lebacqz, Karen. *Six Theories of Justice: Perspectives from Philosophical and Theological Ethics*. Minneapolis, MN: Augsburg, 1986.

Lee, Ronan. "A Politician, Not an Icon: Aung San Suu Kyi's Silence on Myanmar's Muslim Rohingya." *Islam and Christian-Muslim Relations* 25, no. 3 (June 2014): 321–333.

Lehman, F. K. ed. *Military Rule in Burma Since 1962*. Singapore: Maruzen Asia, 1981.

Lemert, Charles. *Why Niebuhr Matters*. New Haven, CT: Yale University Press, 2011.

Lenski, R. C. H. *The Interpretation of St. John's Gospel*. Minneapolis, MN: Augsburg, 1961.

Lieberman, Victor B. *Burmese Administrative Cycles: Anarchy and Conquest, C. 1580–1760*. Princeton, NJ: Princeton University Press, 1984.

Liechty, Daniel. "Principalities and Powers: A Social-Scientific Perspective." *Transforming the Powers: Peace, Justice and the Domination System*, edited by Ray Gingerich and Ted Grimsrud, 39–52. Minneapolis, MN: Fortress, 2006.

Limnatis, Nectarios G. *The Dimensions of Hegel's Dialectic*. New York, NY: Continuum, 2010.

Lintner, Bertil. *Aung San Suu Kyi and Burma's Struggle for Democracy*. Chiang Mai: Silkworm Books, 2011.

———. *Outrage: Burma's Struggle for Democracy*. 2nd edition. Bangkok: White Lotus, 1990.

Lochman, Jan Milič. *Encountering Marx: Bonds and Barriers Between Christians and Marxists*. Philadelphia, PA: Fortress, 1977.

Lopez Jr, Donald S, ed. *Critical Terms for the Study of Buddhism*. Chicago, IL: University of Chicago Press, 2005.

Lovin, Robin W. *Christian Realism and the New Realities*. Cambridge: Cambridge University Press, 2008.

———. *Reinhold Niebuhr and Christian Realism*. Cambridge: Cambridge University Press, 1995.

Lowe, Rebecca. "Interview with Nobel Peace Prize Winner Aung San Suu Kyi – Transcript." *International Bar Association*, 4 December 2014. Accessed 1 February 2016. https://www.ibanet.org/Article/NewDetail.aspx?ArticleUid=E53612E3-C8DB-4362-986B-64538CC9E243.

Luther, Martin. *Martin Luther's Basic Theological Writings*. 2nd edition. Edited by Timothy F. Lull. Minneapolis, MN: Fortress, 2005.

———. *Luther's Works: The Christian in Society, III*. Volume 46. Edited by Robert C. Shultz. Philadelphia, PA: Fortress, 1967.

Luz, Ulrich, and Axel Michaels. *Encountering Jesus & Buddha: Their Lives and Teachings*. Minneapolis, MN: Fortress, 2006.

Lwin, Tint. "Contextualization of the Gospel: An Effective Strategy for the Evangelization of the Theravada Buddhists in Myanmar." PhD dissertation, Southern Baptist Theological Seminary, 1997.

Lynch, Chloe. "How Convincing is Walter Wink's Interpretation of Paul's Language of the Powers?" *Evangelical Quarterly* 83, no. 3 (July 2011): 251–266.

MacDonald Fraser, George. *Quartered Safe Out Here: A Recollection of the War in Burma*. London: Harper Collins, 2000.

Mackay, Mairi. "Gene Sharp: A Dictator's Worst Nightmare." *CNN World*, 25 June 2012. http://edition.cnn.com/2012/06/23/world/gene-sharp-revolutionary.

Marshall, Chris. *The Little Book of Biblical Justice: A Fresh Approach to the Bible's Teachings on Justice*. Intercourse, PA: Good Books, 2005.

Mattox, John Mark. *Saint Augustine and the Theory of Just War*. London: Continuum, 2006.

Maung, Maung, ed. *Aung San of Burma*. The Hague: Martinus Nijhoff, 1962.

———. *Law and Custom in Burma and the Burmese Family*. The Hague: Martinus Nijhoff, 1963.

———. *The 1998 Uprising in Burma*. New Haven, CT: Yale University Press, 1999.

Maung, Mya. *The Burma Road to Poverty*. New Yok, NY: Praeger, 1991.

Majmudar, Uma. *Gandhi's Pilgrimage of Faith: From Darkness to Light*. Albany, NY: State University of New York, 2005.

Mathieson, David Scott. "Myanmar Meanderings." *The Irrawaddy* Magazine 17, no. 5, August 2009. http://www2.irrawaddy.org/article.php?art_id=16444&page=1.

Matsumoto, David, ed. *Cambridge Dictionary of Psychology*. New York: Cambridge University Press, 2009.

Mawdsley, James. *The Heart Must Break: The Fight for Democracy and Truth in Burma*. London: Arrow, 2002.

McAfee Brown, Robert, ed. *The Essential Reinhold Niebuhr*. New Haven, CT: Yale University Press, 1986.

McAlpine, Thomas H. *Facing the Powers*. Eugene, OR: Wipf & Stock, 2003.

McCarthy, Stephen. "The Buddhist Political Rhetoric of Aung San Suu Kyi." *Contemporary Buddhism* 5, no. 2 (2004): 67–81.

McClendon, James William. *Systematic Theology: Ethics*. Nashville, TN: Abingdon, 1986.

McLaughlin, Timothy. "Suu Kyi's State Counsellor Bill Passes Vote Despite Military Protest." *Reuters*, 5 April 2016. http://uk.reuters.com/article/uk-myanmar-politics-idUKKCN0X218E.

Meilaender, Gilbert, and William Werpehowski. *The Oxford Handbook of Theological Ethics*. Oxford: Oxford University Press, 2005.

Mendelson, Edward Michael. *Sangha and State in Burma: A Study of Monastic Sectarianism and Leadership*. Ithaca, NY: Cornell University Press, 1975.

Meyssan, Thierry. "The Albert Einstein Institution: Nonviolence According to the CIA." *Voltaire Network*, 4 January 2005. https://www.voltairenet.org/article30032.html.

Miller, Ed. L., and Stanley J. Grenz, ed. *Fortress Introduction to Contemporary Theologies*. Minneapolis, MN: Fortress, 1998.

Miller-McLemore, Bonnie J. *The Wiley-Blackwell Companion to Practical Theology*. Chichester: Wiley-Blackwell, 2012.

Myint-U, Thant. *River of Lost Footsteps*. London: Faber & Faber, 2008.

Morris, Aldon D. *The Origins of the Civil Rights Movement: Black Communities Organizing for Change*. New York, NY: The Free Press, 1984.

Mott, Stephen Charles. *Biblical Ethics and Social Change*. Oxford: Oxford University Press, 1982.

Mouw, Richard J. *Politics and the Biblical Drama*. Grand Rapids, MI: Eerdmans, 1976.

Murphy, Nancey. "Social Science, Ethics, and the Powers." In *Transforming the Powers: Peace, Justice and the Domination System*, edited by Ray Gingerich and Ted Grimsrud, 29–38. Minneapolis, MN: Fortress, 2006.

———. "Traditions, Practices and the Powers." In *Transforming the Powers: Peace, Justice and the Domination System*, edited by Ray Gingerich and Ted Grimsrud, 84–95. Minneapolis, MN: Fortress, 2006.

"Myanmar Peace Centre (MPC)." http://www.myanmarpeace.org/about/vision_mission.

Myers, David. *Social Psychology*. 10th edition. New York, NY: McGraw-Hill, 2010.

Naw, Angelene. *Aung San and the Struggle for Burmese Independence*. Chiang Mai: Silkworm Books, 2001.

Newbigin, Lesslie. *Foolishness to the Greeks: The Gospel and Western Culture*. WCC Mission Series 6. Geneva: World Council of Churches, 1986.

———. *The Gospel in a Pluralist Society*. London: SPCK, 1989.

———. *The Household of God: Lectures on the Nature of the Church*. New York, NY: Friendship Press, 1954.

New Perimeter, Perseus Strategies, and Jacob Blaustein Institute for the Advancement of Human Rights. *Myanmar Rule of Law Assessment: March 2013*. Available online, http://www.burmalibrary.org/docs15/Myanmar-Rule-of-Law-Assessment-3-5-13.pdf.

Newton Poling, James. *Rethinking Faith: A Constructive Practical Theology*. Minneapolis, MN: Fortress, 2011.

Niebuhr, Reinhold. *Christianity and Power Politics*. New York: Scribner, 1952.

———. *Moral Man and Immoral Society: A Study in Ethics and Politics*. New York, NY: Charles Scribner's Sons, 1960.

———. *The Nature and Destiny of Man, Volume 1: Human Nature*. Louisville, KY: Westminster, 1996.

———. "Why the Christian Church Is not Pacifist." In *War and Christian Ethics: Classic and Contemporary Readings on the Morality of War*, edited by Arthur F. Holmes, 301–370. 2nd edition. Grand Rapids, MI: Baker Academic, 2005.

Nietzsche, Friedrich. *The Will to Power*. Translated by Walter Kafumann and R. J. Hollingdale. Edited by Walter Kaufmann. New York: Vintage, 1967.

Nojeim, Michael J. *Gandhi and King: The Power of Nonviolent Resistance*. London; Westport, CT: Praeger, 2004.

Noll, Stephen F. *Angels of Light, Powers of Darkness: Thinking Biblically about Angels, Satan & Principalities*. Downer Grove, IL: InterVaristy Press, 1998.

———. "Thinking about Angels." In *The Unseen World: Christian Reflections on Angels, Demons and the Heavenly Realm*, edited by Anthony N. S. Lane, 1–27. Grand Rapids, MI: Baker Books, 1996.

Oates, Stephen B. *Let the Trumpet Sound: A Life of Martin Luther King Jr*. New York, NY: Harper & Row, 1994.

O'Brien, Barbara. "The Buddha's Raft Parable." *Learn Religions*, updated 9 March 2019. https://www.learnreligions.com/the-buddhas-raft-parable-450054.

O'Brien, Kelli S. "Book Review: The Human Being: Jesus and the Enigma of the Son of Man." *Interpretation* 57, no. 4 (2003): 454–455.

O'Brien, Peter Thomas. *The Letter to the Ephesians*. Pillar New Testament Commentary. Grand Rapids, MI: Eerdmans, 1999.

———. "Principalities and Powers: Opponents of the Church." In *Biblical Interpretation and the Church: The Problems of Contextualization*, edited by D. A. Carson, 110–150. Nashville, TN: Thomas Nelson, 1985.

Orwell, George. *Burmese Days*. London: Penguin, 2010.

Osborn, Lawrence. "Angels: Barth and Beyond." In *The Unseen World: Christian Reflections on Angels, Demons and the Heavenly Realm*, edited by Anthony N. S. Lane, 29–48. Grand Rapids, MI: Baker Books, 1996.

Otten, Herman, ed. *Bonhoeffer and King: Their Life and Theology Documented in Christian News 1963–2010*. New Haven, MO: Lutheran News, 2011. Kindle edition.

Packer, J. I., and Mark Dever. *In My Place Condemned He Stood: Celebrating the Glory of Atonement*. Wheaton, IL: Crossway Books, 2007.

Pal, Amitabh. "Gene Sharp Interview." *The Progressive*, 28 February 2007. https://progressive.org/magazine/gene-sharp-interview-2007-pal/.

Pandit, Moti Lal. *Did Marx Kill God?: Man and History in Marxism and Christianity*. New Delhi: ISPCK, 1981.

Pederson, Rena. *The Burma Spring: Aung San Suu Kyi and the New Struggle for the Soul of a Nation*. New York, NY: Pegasus Books, 2015.

Phayre, Arthur P. *History of Burma: From the Earliest Time to the End of the First War with British India*. London: Routledge, 2002.

Phillips, Donald T. *Martin Luther King, Jr., On Leadership: Inspiration & Wisdom for Challenging Time*. New York, NY: Warner Books, 1998.

Pitts, Jamie. *Principalities and Powers: Revising John Howard Yoder's Sociological Theology*. Eugene, OR: Pickwick, 2013.

Pope, Stephen. "Reason and Natural Law." In *The Oxford Handbook of Theological Ethics*, edited by Gilbert Meilaender and William Werpehowski, 148–160. Oxford: Oxford University Press, 2005.

Popham, Peter. *The Lady and the Generals: Aung San Suu Kyi and Burma's Struggle for Freedom*. London: Rider Books, 2016.

———. *The Lady and the Peacock: The Life of Aung San Suu Kyi of Burma*. London: Rider, 2011.

———. "Why Does Aung San Suu Kyi Not Speak Up?" *The Daily Beast*, 1 July 2013, updated 11 July 2017. https://www.thedailybeast.com/burmese-muslims-are-being-murdered-in-vicious-attacks-why-does-aung-san-suu-kyi-not-speak-up-by-peter-popham?ref=author.

Prasse-Freeman, Elliott. "Conceptions of Justice and the Rule of Law." In *Myanmar: The Dynamics of an Evolving Polity*, edited by David I. Steinberg, 89–114. Boulder, CO: Lynne Rienner, 2015.

Preecharushh, Dulyapak. *Naypyidaw: The New Capital of Burma*. Bangkok: White Lotus Press, 2009.

Pye, Lucian W. *Politics, Personality, and Nation Building: Burma's Search for Identity*. New Haven, CT: Yale University Press, 1962.

———. *The Spirit of Burmese Politics: A Preliminary Survey of a Politics of Fear and Charisma*. Cambridge, MA: Center for International Studies, 1959.

Pye, Lucian W., and Mary W. Pye. *Asian Power and Politics: The Cultural Dimensions of Authority*. Cambridge, MA: Harvard University Press, 1985.

Quek, Tracy. "Myanmar Reforms Irreversible, Thein Sein Tells UN." *The Straits Time*, 28 September 2012. http://www.asianewsnet.net/news-36889.html.

Rabinow, Paul, ed. *The Foucault Reader*. New York, NY: Vintage, 2010.

Rasmussen, Larry, ed. *Reinhold Niebuhr: Theologian of Public Life*. London: Collins, 1989.

Rauschenbusch, Walter. *Christianity and Social Crisis*. New York, NY: HarperCollins, 2009.

———. "The Kingdom of God." In *An Eerdmans Reader in Contemporary Political Theology*, edited by William T. Cavanaugh, Jeffrey W. Bailey, and Craig Hovey, 165–173. Grand Rapids, MI: Eerdmans, 2012.

———. *The Social Principles of Jesus*. New York, NY: Association Press, 1917.

Rawding, F. W. *Gandhi*. Cambridge Introduction to the History of Mankind. Cambridge: Cambridge University Press, 1980.

Reed, Charles. *Just War? Changing Society and the Churches*. London: SPCK, 2004.

Reid, Daniel Graham. "The Christus Victor Motif in Paul's Theology." PhD dissertation, Fuller Theological Seminary, 1982.

Renard, Ronald D. "Minorities in Burmese History." *Sojourn: Journal of Social Issues in Southeast Asia* 2, no. 2 (August 1987): 255–271.

Reynolds, Craig J. "Power." In *Critical Terms for the Study of Buddhism*, edited by Donald S. Lopez Jr, 211–228. Chicago, IL: University of Chicago Press, 2005.

Richards, Glyn. *The Philosophy of Gandhi: A Study of his Basic Ideas*. London: Curzon, 1991.

Robertson, David. *The Routledge Dictionary of Politics*. 3rd edition. London: Routledge, 2004.
Robertson, Edwin H. *The Shame and the Sacrifice: The Life and Preaching of Dietrich Bonhoeffer*. London: Hodder & Stoughton, 1989.
Rogers, Benedict. *Than Shwe: Unmasking Burma's Tyrant*. Chiang Mai: Silkworm Books, 2010.
Rotberg, Robert I., ed. *Burma: Prospect for a Democratic Future*. Cambridge, MA: The World Peace Foundation, 1998.
Rupp, E. Gordon. *Principalities and Powers: Studies in Christian Conflict in History*. London: Epworth, 1952.
Safieh, Afif. *The Peace Process: From Breakthrough to Breakdown*. London: Saqi, 2010.
Saha, Jonathan. *Law, Disorder and the Colonial State: Corruption in Burma c. 1900*. Basingstoke: Palgrave Macmillan, 2013.
San, Aung. *The Political Legacy of Aung San*. Edited by Josef Silverstein. Ithaca, NY: Cornell University Press, 1972.
Sandel, Michael J. *Justice: What's the Right Thing to Do?* New York, NY: Farrar, Straus and Giroux, 2009.
Sangermano, Vincentius. *The Burmese Empire: A Hundred Years Ago*. Westminster: A. Constable and Company, 1893.
Sardar, Ziauddin. "Kept in Power by Male Fantasy." *New Statesman* 127, 7 August 1998, 23–35.
Satterwhite, James. "Christian Peace Maker Teams as an Alternative to Redemptive Violence." *Peace and Change* 31, no. 2 (April 2006): 222–243.
Scheper-Hughes, Nancy. *Death without Weeping: The Violence of Everyday Life in Brazil*. Berkeley, CA: University of California Press, 1992.
Southern Christian Leadership Conference. "SCLC History." *SCLC*. https://nationalsclc.org/about/history/.
Scott King, Coretta. *My Life with Martin Luther King, Jr*. New York, NY: Holt, Rinehart & Winston, 1969.
Seay, George Russell Jr. "Theologian of Synthesis: The Dialectical Method of Martin Luther King Jr. as Revealed in his Critical Thinking on Theology, History, and Ethics." PhD diss., Graduate School of Vanderbilt University, 2008.
Seekins, Donald M. *Historical Dictionary of Burma (Myanmar)*. Lanham, MD: Scarecrow, 2006.
Selth, Andrew. "Modern Burma Studies: A Survey of the Field." *Modern Asian Studies* 44, no. 2 (2010): 401–440.
Sharp, Gene. *The Politics of Nonviolent Action: The Dynamics of Nonviolent Action, Part III*. Manchester, NH: Porter Sargent Publisher, 1973.

———. *The Role of Power in Nonviolent Struggle*. Cambridge, MA: Albert Einstein Institution, 1990.

———. *Social Power and Political Freedom*. Boston, MA: Porter Sargent, 1980.

Sider, Ronald J. "A Call for Evangelical Nonviolence." *Religion Online*. Accessed 27 June 2013. http://www.religion-online.org/article/a-call-for-evangelical-nonviolence/.

Silverstein, Josef. *Burma: Military Rule and the Politics of Stagnation*. Ithaca, NY: Cornell University Press, 1977.

———. *Burmese Politics: The Dilemma of National Unity*. New Brunswick, NJ: Rutgers University Press, 1980.

———. "The Evolution and Salience of Burma's National Political Culture." In *Burma: Prospect for a Democratic Future*, edited by Robert I. Rotberg, 11–32. Cambridge, MA: World Peace Foundation, 1998.

———, ed. *The Future of Burma in Perspective: A Symposium*. Athens, OH: Ohio University Press, 1974.

———. "The Idea of Freedom in Burma and the Political Thought of Daw Aung San Suu Kyi." *Pacific Affairs* 69, no. 2 (1996): 211–228.

———, ed. *Independent Burma at Forty Years: Six Assessments*. Ithaca, NY: Cornell University Press, 1989.

———, ed. *The Political Legacy of Aung San*. Ithaca, NY: Cornell University Press, 1972.

Singer, Peter, ed. *A Companion to Ethics*. Oxford: Blackwell, 1991.

———. *Marx*. Oxford: Oxford University Press, 1980.

Singh, Aakash and Rimina Mohapatra, eds. *Reading Hegel: The Introductions*. Melbourne: Re.Press, 2008.

Skidmore, Monique, ed. *Burma at the Turn of the Twenty-First Century*. Honolulu, HI: University of Hawaii Press, 2005.

Slack, Kenneth. *Martin Luther King*. London: SCM Press, 1970.

Smith, Donald Eugene. *Religion and Politics in Burma*. Princeton, NJ: Princeton University Press, 1965.

Smith, Martin. "Burma's Ethnic Minorities: A Central or Peripheral Problem in the Regional Context?" In *Burma: The Challenge of Change in a Divided Society*, edited by Peter Carey, 97–129. London: MacMillan, 1997.

———. *Burma: Insurgency and the Politics of Ethnicity*. London: Zed Books, 1991.

Synder Belousek, Darrin W. *Atone, Justice and Peace: The Message of the Cross and the Mission of the Church*. Grand Rapids, MI: Eerdmans, 2012.

Song Qingrun. "Second Panglong Conference Sees Significant Breakthroughs." *Mizzima*, 1 June 2017, http://www.mizzima.com/news-opinion/second-panglong-conference-sees-significant-breakthroughs.

South, Ashley. *Ethnic Politics in Burma: States of Conflict*. London: Routledge, 2009.

Spence, Alan. "A Unified Theory of the Atonement." *International Journal of Systematic Theology* 6, no. 4 (October 2004): 404–420.

Spiro, Melford E. *Buddhism and Society: A Great Tradition and Its Burmese Vicissitudes*. 2nd expanded edition. Berkley, CA: University of California Press, 1982.

Spohn, William C. "Scripture." In *The Oxford Handbook of Theological Ethics*, edited by Gilbert Meilaender and William Werpehowski, 93–111. Oxford: Oxford University Press, 2005.

Stassen, Glen Harold. "The Fourteen Triads of the Sermon on the Mount (Matthew 5:21–7:12)." *Journal of Biblical Literature* 122, no. 2 (2003): 267–308.

———. "Jesus' Way of Transforming Initiatives and Just Peacemaking Theory." In *Transforming the Powers: Peace, Justice and the Domination System*, edited by Ray Gingerich and Ted Grimsrud, 129–142. Minneapolis, MN: Fortress, 2006.

———. *Just Peacemaking: Transforming Initiatives for Justice and Peace*. Louisville, KY: Westminster John Knox, 1992.

———. "The Kind of Justice Jesus Cares About." In *Transforming the Powers: Peace, Justice and the Domination System*, edited by Ray Gingerich and Ted Grimsrud, 157–176. Minneapolis, MN: Fortress, 2006.

Stassen, Glen H., and David P. Gushee. *Kingdom Ethics: Following Jesus in Contemporary Context*. Downers Grove, IL: InterVarsity Press, 2014.

Stassen, Glen H., and Michael L. Westmoreland-White. "Defining Violence and Nonviolence." In *Teaching Peace: Nonviolence and the Liberal Arts*, edited by J. Denny Weaver and Gerald Biesecker-Mast, 17–38. New York: Rowman & Littlefield, 2003.

Steger, Manfred B. *Globalization: A Very Short Introduction*. Oxford: Oxford University Press, 2003.

Steinberg, David I. *Burma: The State of Myanmar*. Washington, DC: Georgetown University Press, 2002.

———, ed. *Myanmar: The Dynamics of an Evolving Polity*. Boulder, CO: Lynne Rienner, 2015.

———. "Review of *The Burma Road to Poverty*, Mya Maung." *Economic Development and Cultural Change* 42, no. 4 (July 1994): 888–893.

Stevenson-Moessner, Jeanne. *Prelude to Practical Theology: Variations on Theory and Practice*. Nashville, TN: Abingdon, 2008.

Stott, John R. W. *The Cross of Christ*. Leicester: InterVarsity Press, 1989.

———. *The Message of Ephesians: God's New Society*. Downers Grove, IL: InterVarsity Press, 1986.

Stringfellow, William. *An Ethics for Christians & Other Aliens in a Strange Land*. Eugene, OR: Wipf & Stock, 2004.

———. *Free in Obedience*. New York, NY: Seabury, 1964.

———. *A Private and Public Faith*. Eugene, OR: Wipf & Stock, 1999.

Stuart, John. *Burma Through the Centuries*. London: K Paul, Trench, Trubner & Co., 1910.

Suhrud, Tridip. "Gandhi's Key Writings: In Search of Unity." In *The Cambridge Companion to Gandhi*, edited by Judith M. Brown and Anthony Parel, 71–91. Cambridge: Cambridge University Press, 2011.

Suu Kyi, Aung San. "The Benefits of Meditation and Sacrifice." Taken from the *Bangkok Post*, September 1996. Posted to *BuddahSasana*. http://www.budsas.org/ebud/ebmed001.htm.

———. *Freedom from Fear and Other Writings*. London: Penguin Books, 1995.

———. *Letters from Burma*. London: Penguin Books, 2010.

———. "Securing Freedom 2011: Dissent." The Reith Lectures. Radio 4 Recording. 16 July 2011. https://www.bbc.co.uk/programmes/b0126d70.

———. "Securing Freedom 2011: Liberty." The Reith Lecutres. Radio 4 Recording. 28 June 2011. http://downloads.bbc.co.uk/rmhttp/radio4/transcripts/2011_reith1.pdf.

———. "SMU Ho Rih Hwa Lecture: Daw Aung San Suu Kyi." Singapore Management University. 22 September 2013. YouTube video, https://www.youtube.com/watch?v=T670NhXXtoI.

———. "Tokyo University Daw Aung San Su Kyi's Lecture (Tun Wai Tokyo)." Kotun Wai. 17 April 2013. YouTube video, https://www.youtube.com/watch?v=311BI-5PPyo&t=1406s.

Sweet, Leonard, ed. *The Church in Emerging Culture: Five Perspectives*. Grand Rapids, MI: Zondervan, 2003.

Swinton, John, and Harriet Mowat. *Practical Theology and Qualitative Research*. London: SCM Press, 2006.

Taylor, Robert H. "Burma's Ambiguous Breakthrough." *Journal of Democracy* 1, no. 4 (1990): 62–72.

———. *General Ne Win: A Political Biography*. Singapore: Institute of Southeast Asian Studies, 2015.

———. "Pathways to Present." In *Beyond Politics to Societal Imperatives*, edited by Kyaw Yin Hlaing, Robert H. Taylor, and Tin Maung Maung Than, 1–29. Singapore: Institute of Southeast Asian Studies, 2005.

———. "Political Values and Political Conflict in Burm." In *Burma: Prospects for a Democratic Future*, edited by Robert I. Rotberg, 33–47. Cambridge, MA: The World Peace Foundation, 1998.

———. *The State in Myanmar*. Singapore: National University of Singapore Press, 2009.

Thawnghmung, Ardeth Maung. "Contending Approaches to the Communal Violence in Rakhine State." In *Burma/Myanmar: Where Now?*, edited by Mikael Gravers and Flemming Ytzen, 323–339. Copenhagen: NIAS Press, 2014.

Theopedia. "Christus Victor." *Theopedia: An Encyclopaedia of Biblical Christianity (website)*. http://www.theopedia.com/Christus_Victor.

Thoreau, Henry David. "Civil Disobedience." In *The Power of Nonviolence: Writings by Advocates of Peace*, edited by Howard Zinn, 15–36. Boston, MA: Beacon Press, 2002.

Thornton, Edward E. "Book Review: Naming the Powers: The Language of Power in the New Testament." *Review & Expositor* 83, no. 1 (1986): 120–121.

Tidball, Derek. "Penal Substitution: A Pastoral Apologetic." In *The Atonement Debate: Papers from the London Symposium on the Theology of Atonement*, edited by Derek Tidball, David Hilborn and Justin Thacker, 345–360. Grand Rapids, MI: Zondervan, 2008.

Tin, Pe Maung and G. H. Luce, trans. *The Glass Palace Chronicle of the Kings of Myanmar*. Yangon: Unity Publishing House, 2008.

Todd, Anne M. *Mohandas Gandhi*. Philadelphia, PA: Chelsea House, 2004.

Todd, Julie Marie. "Evaluating Violence and (Non)Violence: A Critical, Practical Theology of Social Change." PhD diss., University of Denver, 2012.

Tombs, David. "Lived Religion and the Intolerance of the Cross." In *Lived Religion and the Politics of (In)tolerance*, edited by R. Ruard Ganzevoort and Srdjan Sermac, 63–83. Cham, Switzerland: Palgrave Macmillan, 2017.

Tun, Saw. "The Military Mind-Set." *Irrawaddy*, 13 March 2009, https://www2.irrawaddy.com/opinion_story.php?art_id=15290.

Tun, Than. "History of Buddhism in Burma: A.D. 1000-1300." PhD diss., University of London, 1956.

———. *A Modern History of Myanmar – 1752-1948*. Yangon: Loka Ahlinn, 2010.

Turner, Philip. "Tradition in the Church." In *The Oxford Handbook of Theological Ethics*, edited by Gilbert Meilaender and William Werpehowski, 130–147. Oxford: Oxford University Press, 2005

Tutu, Desmond. *No Future without Forgiveness*. London: Rider, 2000.

Uchiyama, Kosho. "What Is a Bodhisattva?" *Tricycle* (online). 2016. https://tricycle.org/magazine/what-bodhisattva/.

Vanhoozer, Kevin J. "The Atonement in Postmodernity: Guilt, Goats, and Gifts." In *The Glory of the Atonement: Biblical, Historical, and Practical Perspectives*, edited by Charles E. Hill and Frank A. James III, 367–401. Downers Grove, IL: InterVarstiy Press, 2004.

Van Rheenen, Gailyn. "Modern and Postmodern Syncretism in Theology and Missions." In *The Holy Spirit and Missions Dynamics*, edited by C. Douglas McConnell, 164–189. Pasadena, CA: William Carey Library, 1997.

Veling, Terry A. *Practical Theology: "On Earth as It Is in Heaven."* Maryknoll, NY: Orbis, 2005.

Volf, Miroslav. *Exclusion and Embrace: A Theological Exploration of Identity, Otherness, and Reconciliation*. Nashville, TN: Abingdon, 1996.

———. "Exclusion and Embrace: Theological Reflections in the Wake of Ethnic Cleansing." In *A Spacious Heart: Essays on Identify and Belonging*, by Judith M. Gundry Volf and Miroslav Volf, 33–60. Harisburg, PA: Trinty Press, 1997.

———. "Forgiveness, Reconciliation, and Justice: A Christian Contribution to a More Peaceful Social Environments." *Millennium: Journal of International Studies* 29, 3 (December 2000): 861–877.

———. *Free of Charge: Giving and Forgiving in a Culture Stripped of Grace*. Grand Rapids, MI: Zondervan, 2006.

———. "The Social Meaning of Reconciliation." *Occasional Papers on Religion in Eastern Europe* 18, no. 3 (1998): 1–12. Available online, http://citeseerx.ist.psu.edu/viewdoc/download?doi=10.1.1.884.6389&rep=rep1&type=pdf.

Wagner, C. P. "Third Wave." In *The New International Dictionary of Pentecostal and Charismatic Movements*. Revised and expanded. Edited by Stanley M. Burgess, 1141. Grand Rapids, MI: Zondervan, 2002.

Wai Moe. "The Struggle for Peace in Northern Myanmar." In *Burma/Myanmar: Where Now?*, edited by Mikael Gravers and Flemming Ytzen, 262–278. Copenhagen: NIAS Press, 2014.

Wakeman, Carolyn, and San San Tin. *No Time for Dreams: Living in Burma Under Military Rule*. Lanham, MD: Rowman & Littlefield, 2009.

Walsh, Eamonn. "Aung San Suu Kyi: 'I Have Personal Regrets.'" *BBC News*, 23 September 2012. http://www.bbc.com/news/magazine-19667956.

Walton, Jr, Hanes. *The Political Theology of Martin Luther King, Jr*. Westport: Greenwood Press, 1971.

Walton, Matthew. "Buddhism, Politics, and Political Change." In *Myanmar: The Dynamics of an Evolving Polity*, edited by David I. Steinberg, 115–134. Boulder, CO: Lynne Rienner, 2015.

Washington Davis, George. "God and History." *Crozer Quarterly* 20, no. 1 (January 1943): 18–36.

Watley, William Donnel. "Against Principalities: An Examination of Martin Luther King Jr.'s Nonviolent Ethic." PhD diss, Columbia University, 1980.

Weaver, John Denny, and Gerald Biesecker-Mast, eds. *Teaching Peace: Nonviolence and the Liberal Arts*. Lanham, MD: Rowman & Littlefield, 2003.

Webber, Robert E. *The Younger Evangelicals: Facing the Challenges of the New World*. Grand Rapids, MI: Baker Books, 2002.

Weber, Max. *The Protestant Ethic and the Spirit of Capitalism*. Translated by Talcott Parsons. London: Routledge, 2001.

———. *The Theory of Social and Economic Organization*. Translated by A. M. Henderson and Talcott Parsons. Glencoe, IL: Free Press, 1947.

Weiner, Robert G., ed. *Captain America and the Struggle of the Superhero*. Jefferson, NC: McFarland, 2009.

Werntz, Myles. "Ontology, Ecclesiology, Nonviolence: The Witness Against War in the Theologies of John Howard Yoder, Dorothy Day, and William Stringfellow." PhD diss., Baylor University, 2011.

Werpehowski, William. "Reinhold Niebuhr." In *The Modern Theologians*, edited by David F. Ford, 204–212. Oxford: Blackwell, 2005.

Whitehead, Alfred North. *Religion in the Making*. New York: Meridian Books, 1971.

Wiant, Jon A. "Tradition in the Service of Revolution: The Political Symbolism of *Taw-Hlan-Ye-Khit*." In *Military Rule in Burma Since 1962*, edited by F. K. Lehman, 59–76. Singapore: Maruzen Asia, 1981.

Williams, David C. "What's So Bad about Burma's 2008 Constitution?: A Guide for the Perplexed." In *Law, Society and Transition in Myanmar*, edited by Melissa Crouch and Tim Lindsey, 117–139. Oxford: Hart, 2014.

Wink, Walter. *The Bible in Human Transformation: Toward a New Paradigm for Biblical Study*. Philadelphia, PA: Fortress, 1973.

———. *Cracking the Gnostic Code: The Powers in Gnosticism*. Atlanta, GA: Scholars Press, 1993.

———. *Engaging the Powers: Discernment and Resistance in a World of Domination*. Minneapolis, MN: Augsburg, 1992.

———. *Jesus and Nonviolence: A Third Way*. Minneapolis, MN: Fortress, 2003.

———. *Just Jesus: My Struggle to Become Human*. New York, NY: Image, 2014.

———. *Naming the Powers: The Language of Power in the New Testament*. Philadelphia, PA: Fortress, 1984.

———. "Neither Passivity nor Violence (Mt. 5:38–42)." In *The Love of Enemy and Non-Retaliation in the New Testament*, edited by Willard M. Swartley, 102–125. Louisville, KY: Westminster John Knox, 1992.

———. *The Powers That Be: Theology for a New Millennium*. New York, NY: Doubleday, 1998.

———. "Redeeming the Entire Universe: The Spirit of Institutions." In *Compassionate Eschatology: The Future as Friend*, edited by Ted Grimsrud and Michael Hardin, 171–176. Eugene, OR: Cascade, 2011.

———. *Transforming Bible Study: A Leader's Guide*. London: Mowbray, 1990.

———. *Unmasking the Powers: The Invisible Forces that Determine Human Existence*. Philadelphia, PA: Fortress, 1989.

———. *Violence and Nonviolence in South Africa: Jesus' Third Way*. Philadelphia, PA: New Society, 1987.

———. *When the Powers Fall: Reconciliation in the Healing of Nations*. Minneapolis, MN: Fortress, 1998.

Wintle, Brain, and Ken Gnanakan. *Ephesians*. Singapore: Asia Theological Association, 2006.

Wintle, Justin. *Perfect Hostage: A Life of Aung San Suu Kyi, Burma's Prisoner of Conscience*. London: Arrow, 2007.

Wogaman, J. Philip. *Christian Perspectives on Politics*. Louisville, KY: Westminster John Knox, 2000.

Wright, N. T. *The Day the Revolution Began: Reconsidering the Meaning of Jesus' Crucifixion*. San Francisco, CA: HarperOne, 2016.

———. *How God Became King: The Forgotten Story of the Gospel*. New York, NY: HarperOne, 2012.

———. "N. T. Wright | The Cross (10/11/1207)." Wheaton College. 12 October 2017. YouTube video, https://www.youtube.com/watch?v=GGJ7M1CDhBU.

———. "Tom Wright The Atonement Debate." StJohnsTimeline. 24 September 2009. YouTube video, https://www.youtube.com/watch?v=IA8CY5iC_ww.

Wylie Kellermann, Bill, ed. *A Keeper of the Word: Selected Writings of William Stringfellow*. Grand Rapids, MI: Eerdmans, 1994.

———. "Not Vice Versa. Reading the Powers Biblically: Stringfellow, Hermeneutics, and the Principalities." *Anglican Theological Review* 81, no. 4 (1999): 665–880.

———. "Struggling to Become Human." *Sojourner* Magazine, August 2014. Available online, https://sojo.net/magazine/august-2014/struggling-become-human.

Yancey, Philip. "Confessions of a Racist." *Christianity Today* (online), 1 January 200. http://www.christianitytoday.com/ct/2000/januaryweb-only/12.0b.html?start=2.

———. *Soul Survivor: How Thirteen Unlikely Mentors Helped My Faith Survive the Church*. Manila: OMF Literature, 2006.

Yan Naing, Saw. "Peace Brokers Lack a Mandate: Burma Expert." *The Irrawaddy*, 18 March 2014. http://www.irrawaddy.com/burma/peace-brokers-lack-mandate-burma-expert.html.

Yawnghwe, Chao-Tzang. "Ne Win's Tatmadaw Dictatorship." MA Thesis, University of British Columbia, 1990.

Yi, Khin. *The Dobama Movement in Burma, 1930–1938*. Ithaca, NY: Cornell University Press, 1988.

Yoe, Shwe [pseud.]. *The Burman: His Life and Notions*. New York: W. W. Norton & Company, 1963.

Yoder, John H. *Christian Attitudes to War, Peace and Revolution*. Edited by Theodore J. Koontz and Andy Alexis-Baker. Grand Rapids, MI: Brazos Press, 2009.

———. *For the Nations: Essays Public and Evangelical*. Grand Rapids, MI: Eerdmans, 1997.

———. *He Came Preaching Peace*. Scottdale, PA: Herald Press, 1985.

———. *Nevertheless: Varieties of Religious Pacifism*. Scottdale, PA: Herald Press, 1976.

———. *The Original Revolution: Essays on Christian Pacifism*. Scottdale, PA: Herald Press, 1971.

———. *The Politics of Jesus*. Grand Rapids, MI: Eerdmans, 1994.

———. *The Priestly Kingdom: Social Ethics as Gospel*. Notre Dame, IN: Notre Dame University Press, 1985.

———. *War of the Lamb: The Ethics of Nonviolence and Peacemaking*. Grand Rapids, MI: Brazos, 2009.

———. *What Would You Do?* Scottdale, PN: Herald Press, 1995.

Young, Frances. "Tom Wright, *The Day the Revolution Began: Rethinking the Meaning of Jesus' Crucifixion*." *Theology* 120, no. 5 (2017): 381–382.

Urofsky, Melvin I. "Jim Crow Law: United States (1877–1954)." *Encyclopaedia Britannica*. http://www.britannica.com/event/Jim-Crow-law.

U Thaung, Mirror. *Bo Ne Win Zatlan Shuut Thamya*. Yangon: Aphyu Yaung Sarpae, 2014.

Zaw, Aung. "The Doubly Disastrous Legacy of Ne Win." *The Irrawaddy*, 28 February 2014. http://www.irrawaddy.org/commentary/doubly-disastrous-legacy-ne-win.html.

———. *The Face of Resistance: Aung San Suu Kyi and Burma's Fight for Freedom*. Chiang Mai: Mekong, 2013. Kindle edition.

Zin, Min. "Spiritual Revolution." *The Irrawaddy, magazine* 7, no. 2 (February 1999), 1–3. http://www2.irrawaddy.org/article.php?art_id=1064&page=3.

Zöllner, Hans-Bernd. *The Beast and the Beauty: The History of the Conflict Between the Military and Aung San Suu Kyi in Myanmar, 1988–2011*. Berlin: Regiospectra, 2012.

Langham Literature, with its publishing work, is a ministry of Langham Partnership.

Langham Partnership is a global fellowship working in pursuit of the vision God entrusted to its founder John Stott –

> *to facilitate the growth of the church in maturity and Christ-likeness through raising the standards of biblical preaching and teaching.*

Our vision is to see churches in the Majority World equipped for mission and growing to maturity in Christ through the ministry of pastors and leaders who believe, teach and live by the Word of God.

Our mission is to strengthen the ministry of the Word of God through:
- nurturing national movements for biblical preaching
- fostering the creation and distribution of evangelical literature
- enhancing evangelical theological education

especially in countries where churches are under-resourced.

Our ministry

Langham Preaching partners with national leaders to nurture indigenous biblical preaching movements for pastors and lay preachers all around the world. With the support of a team of trainers from many countries, a multi-level programme of seminars provides practical training, and is followed by a programme for training local facilitators. Local preachers' groups and national and regional networks ensure continuity and ongoing development, seeking to build vigorous movements committed to Bible exposition.

Langham Literature provides majority world preachers, scholars and seminary libraries with evangelical books and electronic resources through publishing and distribution, grants and discounts. The programme also fosters the creation of indigenous evangelical books in many languages, through writer's grants, strengthening local evangelical publishing houses, and investment in major regional literature projects, such as one volume Bible commentaries like the *Africa Bible Commentary* and the *South Asia Bible Commentary*.

Langham Scholars provides financial support for evangelical doctoral students from the majority world so that, when they return home, they may train pastors and other Christian leaders with sound, biblical and theological teaching. This programme equips those who equip others. Langham Scholars also works in partnership with majority world seminaries in strengthening evangelical theological education. A growing number of Langham Scholars study in high quality doctoral programmes in the majority world itself. As well as teaching the next generation of pastors, graduated Langham Scholars exercise significant influence through their writing and leadership.

To learn more about Langham Partnership and the work we do visit **langham.org**

www.ingramcontent.com/pod-product-compliance
Lightning Source LLC
Chambersburg PA
CBHW052011290426
44112CB00014B/2203